The China Management Handbook

The China Management Handbook

A Comprehensive Question and Answer Guide to the World's Most Important Emerging Market

Engelbert Boos

Christine Boos

Frank Sieren

Foreword by Chris Patten

Important disclaimer
The material in this book is of the nature of general comment only.
It is not offered as advice on any particular matter and should not be
taken as such. The contributing authors expressly disclaim all liability
to any person in respect of the consequences of anything done or
omitted to be done wholly or partly in reliance upon the whole or any
parts of the contents of this book. No reader should act or refrain from
acting on the basis of any matter contained in it without taking
specific professional advice on the particular facts and circumstances
in issue.

First published 2003 by
PALGRAVE MACMILLAN
Houndmills, Basingstoke, Hampshire RG21 6XS and
175 Fifth Avenue, New York, N. Y. 10010
Companies and representatives throughout the world

ISBN 1–4039–0024–8

This book is printed on paper suitable for recycling and made from
fully managed and sustained forest sources.

A catalogue record for this book is available from the British Library.

Library of Congress Cataloging-in-Publication Data
Boos, Engelbert, 1960–
    The China management handbook: a comprehensive question & answer guide to
the world's most important emerging market / by Engelbert Boos, Christine Boos,
Frank Sieren.
        p. cm.
    Includes bibliographical references and index.
    ISBN 1–4039–0024–8
    1. Management—China—Miscellanea. I. Boos, Christine, 1962– II. Sieren, Frank,
1967– III. Title
HD70.C5 B66 2002
658'.00951—dc21   2002072347

10   9   8   7   6   5   4   3   2   1
12   11   10   09   08   07   06   05   04   03

Printed and bound in Great Britain by
Antony Rowe Ltd, Chippenham and Eastbourne

For Julia

Contents

List of Illustrations

List of Tables

Preface

China, the promised as well as the feared land of the world economy, doesn't give itself away easily. It took us longer than expected to understand much about the basics of the China market. Like everybody else, we made quite a few mistakes during our time in China, as well as learning a lot. We hope this book at least helps you avoid making the mistakes we did.

With 384 pages, our book can hardly claim to encompass all business aspects of this 1.3 billion people country. Some problems can only be outlined, others are reduced to their core aspects. We therefore try to provide you with tools to enable you to find your own way around China. Some of these tools might make the decisive difference even for Old China Hands with profound knowledge and experience.

We do not expect you to read our book straight through from beginning to end, but rather use it as a reference book. Divided into concise question and answer chapters, you can easily look up the appropriate section when confronted with a certain problem. Questions and answers are summarised at the beginning and end of each chapter, and one plane ride to China should be enough to grasp the basics.

Those readers who want an overview in order to make fundamental decisions and need to know the implications of China's economic framework for everyday business will find the most important basic questions and aspects in the first and second chapters.

Our goal is fairly simple: we want you to spare your nerves, save money and be successful in the China market.

We hope to get feedback to our e-mail address **Managementhandbook@ china.com**. We will gratefully accept suggestions, but will also accept criticisms. Please don't hesitate to contact us for further advice.

We want to thank our publishers at Palgrave Macmillan, namely Stephen Rutt and Caitlin Cornish, and our editor, Keith Povey, who were helpful and patient with us throughout the publishing process, despite the problems of distance between England and China.

Our particular thanks go to Chris Paterson, who has for years shared our fascination with China, for his crucial support of our book. Michael Grabner, an impressively experienced businessman who quickly learned to move in the China market, has helped to give this book its structure with his intelligent and unerring questions. Stefan Baron, a long-time China expert, has long been a knowledgable as well as humorous discussion partner. Clemens Riedl has found China to be an appropriate playing field for his vitality and analytical power. Anke Redl always keeps a clear and clever head in critical situations. And of course we are grateful to all our Chinese friends in various ministries, institutions and companies who are working hard to integrate China into the global economy and have therefore provided us with invaluable insights.

Without Bernhard Bartsch's intensive collaboration and profound China expertise, this book would still not be finished.

CHRISTINE BOOS
ENGELBERT BOOS
FRANK SIEREN

Acknowledgements

Much of the material that we assembled for *The China Management Handbook* has been based on exclusive one-on-one interviews with China managers, consultants and other specialists. We would like to personally thank all our interview partners, proofreaders, information providers and all other persons that supported us writing this book, for their enthusiastic involvement and assistance, which we deeply appreciated.

Andreasen, Andrew, Managing Director, Asia Information Associates Ltd, Beijing
Arntz, Willi G., Managing Partner in charge for GIN Asia, Arthur Andersen, Düsseldorf
Barth, Dr, Ruediger, Chairman, Aventis China Investment, Beijing
Berweger, Rolf, former Head of Corporate and Institutional Banking, Standard & Chartered, Beijing
Berthold, Peter, Managing Director, Deutsche Asiatische Beteiligungsgesellschaft (DBA) Ltd and Chairman, Sino Investment Management Services Limited, Hong Kong
Boeckle, Dr Hardy, former Counsellor, Economic Department, German Embassy, Beijing
Büchsenschütz, Alexander, Senior Consultant, KPMG, Frankfurt
Chia, Hui Tian, Senior Manager, PriceWaterhouseCoopers, Beijing
Chow, Patrick, General Manager, Beijing Better Life Automobile Import Export Co. Ltd, Beijing
Claussen, Christian, former Senior Manager Market Research, Volkswagen Group, Beijing
Dai, Henry, Manager, Winterthur Insurance (Asia), Shanghai
Dehoux, Genevieve, China Manager, Asia Invest Secretariat, Brussels
Etgen, Dr, Bjoern, Partner, BBLP Law Firm, Beijing
Giannakaros, Vangelis, Director China, The Economist Conferences, Beijing
Girsewald, Alexander von, former Director, DEG Investment, Beijing
Goujon, Eric, Partner, Price WaterhouseCoopers, Beijing
Grimm, Dr, Klaus, Delegate and Chief Representative, Delegation of German Industry and Commerce, Shanghai
Groenegres, Martina, Manager Group Coordination and eCommerce, Lufthansa German Airlines, Beijing
Heltmann, Pit, Counsellor, Head of the Trade Promotion Office, German Embassy, Beijing
Heraeus, Dr, Juergen, Chairman, Heraeus Holding GmbH, Hanau

Jessen, Dr, Franz, Counsellor of the European Delegation, Beijing
Kaemmerer, Dr, Peter, Executive Vice President Overseas, LBBW, New York
Kauw, Dr, Volker, Managing Director, Peiniger International, Shanghai
King, Adrian, Media Com/Grey Advertising, Hong Kong
Klingspor, Nina, Vice-President Business and Risk Controlling, Allianz AG, Munich
Kracht, Jürgen, Managing Director, Fiducia Consultants, Hong Kong
Kreuzberger, Peter, PhD, OECD, Paris
Kühl, Christiane and Martin, Correspondents, *German Financial Times*, Beijing
Laschan, Dr, Ernst, former Commercial Counsellor, Austrian Embassy, Beijing
Lauber, Jürg, former Head of the Economic and Commercial Section, Embassy
   of Switzerland, Beijing
Lauffs, Dr, Andreas, Partner, Baker & McKenzie, Hong Kong
Lee, Addy, Managing Director Industrial Practice, Korn\Ferry, Hong Kong
Legner, Peter, General Manager, Schenck AG, Shanghai
Mak, Grace Y.P., Regional Director Asia-Pacific, E.J. Krause, International Exhib-
   ition Management, Beijing
Marson, Allan K., Attorney, Baker & McKenzie, CA
Müller, Prof. Dr, Bernd, University of the Armed Forces, Munich
Murray, Hermann, former General Manager, Krupp, Beijing
Nieter, Ulrike, former Partner, Heidrick & Struggles, Hong Kong
Pack, Prof., Heinrich, Member of Executive Board, Demag Cranes & Compon-
   ents, Wetter
Redl, Anke, Managing Director, cmm-Intelligence, Beijing
Reisach, Dr, Ulrike, Economics and Corporate Relations Office, Siemens AG,
   Munich
Schmidt, Peter, General Manager, Dresdner Kleinwort Benson, Beijing
Schneider, Helmut, Regional Manager Asia, Messer Group, Beijing
Schütz, Michaela, LogistiX, Beijing
Seidlitz, Peter, former Asia correspondent of *Handelsblatt*, Beijing
Seitz, Dr, Konard, former German Embassador to China, Beijing
Stucken, Dr Bernd-Uwe, Chief Representative and Partner, Haarmann, Hem-
   melrath & Partner, Shanghai
Tang Haisong, CEO, Etang, Shanghai
Tauber, Dr, Theresia, Intercultural Training Manager Asia, Siemens AG, Munich
Ueberschaer, Dr, Christian, former German Ambassador to China, Beijing
Weber-Liu, Kosima, Director of the Directory of German Companies in China,
   Beijing
Wei, Lisa, Buying Director, Mind Share/JWT, Beijing
Weinmüller, Alf, General Manager, Porsche China, Beijing
Yu, Arthur, Managing Director, J. Walter Thompson, Beijing
Zhang, Max, Manager, Sedgwick Insurance & Risk Management, Shanghai
Zhang Wei, Researcher, Beijing

List of Abbreviations

ACC	Anti Counterfeiting Coalition
ADB	Asian Development Bank
AIESEC	Association International des Etudiants en Sciences Commerciales et Economiques
APA	Advanced Pricing Agreements
ASC	Accounting Society of China
ASME	Technical Inspection Standard (USA)
B2B	Business to Business
B2C	Business to Consumer
BAIC	Beijing Municipal Administration for Industry and Commerce
BMRB	British Marketing Research Bureau
BMS	Business Management Service
BT	Business Tax
CCCPC	Central Committee of the Communist Party of China
CCIB	Product label
CCOIC	China Chamber of International Commerce
CCPIT	China Council for the Promotion of International Trade
CCTV	China National Television
CE	Label for electrical products
CEIBS	China European International Business School
CICPA	Chinese Institute of Certified Public Accountants
CIEC	China International Economic Consultants
CIIC	China International Investment Corporation
CIRC	China Insurance Regulation Committee
CITIC	China International Trade and Investment Corporation
CKD	Completely Knocked Down
CMMS	China Media Marketing Servises
COS	Cost of Sales
CPBS	Central Broadcasting System
CPIC	China Pacific Insurance Company
CPPCC	Chinese People's Political Consultative Conference
CSRC	China Securities Regulatory Commission
CV	Curriculum Vitae
CVSC	China Central Viewers Service and Consulting Centre
DIN	German Industrial Standard
ECIP	European Commodity Investment Partners
EDI	Electronic Data Exchange

EHA	Employment Housing Account
EPA	Employment Personel Account
FDI	Foreign Direct Investment
FEIT	Foreign Enterprise Income Tax
FESCO	Foreign Enterprise Service Corporation
FIE	Foreign Invested Enterprise
FIFO	First In First Out
FTZ	Free Trade Zone
GAAP	Generally Accepted Accounting Practices
GDP	General Domestic Product
GfK	Association for Consumer Research (Germany)
GIP	General Inland Product
GM	General Manager
GPS	Global Procurement Services
GS	Electrical and mechanical safety label
GTZ	Association for Technical Co-operation (Germany)
HGB	German Accounting Standards
HR	Human Resources
ID	Identity
IPO	Initial Public Offering
ISO	International Standardisation Organisation
IT	Information Technologies
IWF	International Monetary Fund
JV	Joint Venture
L/C	Letter of Credit
LIFO	Last In First Out
MBA	Master of Business Administration
MBO	Management by Objectives
MOF	Ministry of Finance
MOFTEC	Ministry of Foreign Trade and Economic Co-operation
NBS	National Bureau of Statistics
NPC	National People's Congress
OECD	Organisation of Economic Co-operation and Development
OEM	Own Equipment Manufacturer
P&L	Profit and Loss
PAIC	Pingan Insurance Company
PBOC	People's Bank of China
PICC	People's Insurance Company of China
PRC	People's Republic of China
PYAMS	Previous Years Averaged Monthly Salary
QS	Quality Standard
R&D	Research and Development

RMB	Renminbi (Chinese Currency)
SAFE	State Administration for Foreign Exchange
SAIC	State Administration for Industry and Commerce
SAIECI	State Administration of Import and Export Commodity Inspection
SKD	Single Knocked Down
SOE	State Owned Enterprises
SRC	State Regulation Council (Auditing)
STA	State Tax Administration
SWOT	Strengths Weaknesses Opportunities Threats (Analysis)
TQM	Total Quality Management
TRIPS	Trade Related Intellectual Rights
TÜV	Technical Inspection Association (Germany)
VAT	Value Added Tax
WFOE	Wholly Foreign Owned Enterprise
WTO	World Trade Organisation

Foreword

Everyday the headlines warn us about the awesome social, economic and environmental problems confronting China. But however much I read the papers, I still find it difficult to change my view: I am bullish on China.

To be a bear on China's prospects is, after all, to be gloomy about the outlook for mankind. China represents between a fifth and a quarter of humanity, with more than its share of creative and hardworking men and women. It is one of the biggest markets in the world; its consumers are as essential to international corporations as is China's cheap, yet well-educated, workforce. All this makes China a major player in the world economy, and its influence is set to grow rapidly. Should this worry us? Certainly not.

If China the country doesn't overcome the challenges that it faces, the future for all of us will be pretty bleak. So it's not China's success that should worry us, but rather what happens if China fails.

Any visitor to China is overwhelmed by the contradictions inherent in its helter-skelter progress. During a journey in any direction, but particularly from the rich coastal provinces into the hinterland, you cover in the space of a few hundred miles every stage of economic development – from high-tech industrialisation to primitive subsistence agriculture.

Travelling from Shanghai through Jiangsu province during Easter 2002, I was amazed by the pace of economic change. Yet even in China's richest province there were pockets of severe underdevelopment and backwaters of tradition – reminders of how difficult it must be to govern a country so extreme in its diversity.

Naturally, any visitor is impressed by the changes in China's physical landscape. The transformation of Shanghai since my last visit 13 years ago was astonishing. A former Governor of Britain's crown colony Hong Kong, I was amazed at how fast Shanghai has started to follow suit. But the changes that most excited me were more personal.

First, there is the pragmatic approach and the open mindedness of young entrepreneurs determined to bring their companies up to international standard. I also admire their optimism and the ability to put set-backs behind them. Furthermore, I was impressed by the candour with which people talked about their own experiences during China's darkest days of revolution, tumult and economic collapse. There were the 500 or so young students at Fudan University listening to and apparently understanding a no-holds-barred speech in English, and throwing questions at me about social stability, Tibet, Taiwan and other subjects that are important for the prosperity of a country and might previously have been thought taboo.

Now please don't misunderstand me. Is this now a country that takes its cue from Adam Smith and Alexis de Tocqueville? Hardly.

There is still nothing like a comprehensive rule of law. Managers and ordinary citizens who come into contact with the legal system can experience extreme arbitrariness. Corruption, mainly amongst party cadres who still hold key positions, not only frustrates foreign investors, but also endangers social stability and a sustained growth of the country. The Chinese people are less and less willing to live with these crimes, forcing the reformers to crack down heavily on corruption. China is far from having the freedom of reporting on business issues which is a precondition for modern prosperous markets. There are still terrible human-rights abuses. Capital punishment is meted out with mindless frequency. The treatment of the Falun Gong betrays the nervousness of a regime that remembers too well the dramas of the last Chinese dynasty.

I will grant China's sceptics these points. But even when you've thrown into the balance the country's haemorrhaging banks, loss-making rust-belt state industries and creaking social services, you still haven't, in my judgement, won the argument for the pessimists. Why? Because China crackles with energy. The young people I met and spoke to can no longer be sequestered from the rest of the world. The implications of economic development and modern communications, including the Internet, for the political system seem to me ineluctable. And the more China gets integrated with the international economy, the higher the price for disrespecting common standards.

Many historians doubt that China can manage the required economic and political change peacefully. They point to the bloody history of the last century as a harbinger of things to come. And their doubts are reinforced by the modern problems that crowd in on China's leaders. But I do not believe that we have no choice but to watch nervously as events unfold. We should make clear that we regard China's success as good for all of us, and encourage China to take its full place and responsibility in global institutions.

Only with China as a member does the 'World' in World Trade Organisation sound appropriate. However, after accession of China to WTO, many Western business people and companies are frustrated because they are still waiting eagerly to take advantage of all the promised opportunities. We will monitor closely whether China is correctly implementing her WTO commitments.

Western companies that invest in China have considerable influence in integrating China with the global economy. Western managers bring with them established social and economic rules; when they work with Chinese colleagues in joint ventures, they show them an alternative to the life and habits they knew before. It is an important side-effect of their investment that they further establish China as a member of the world community.

This book supports managers in this effort. It helps managers not only to make money and be successful, but it also helps integrate China and the West by pointing out social and economic differences and pragmatic ways to overcome them together in everyday business. Without brushing anything under the carpet, the authors show the weaknesses of the current system – which is the best way to confront pessimists. This supports China's reformers, who are steadily working to become the country's mainstream. It is difficult to believe that many of the new generation who are climbing the ladder of power really believe that China will not keep integrating into the world economy at a very high speed.

The goal of the western world should be obvious. We want to bring China more fully into the world trading system and to support the economic and social reforms which are under way. We want to see the sustainable development of China into a prosperous and stable country. I am positive that this will be achieved.

Challenged once for being an optimist, Winston Churchill replied that there didn't seem much to be said for spending one's life in the opposite camp. A pretty good way for a manager to approach China, too, it seems to me.

CHRIS PATTEN
External Relations Commissioner, European Union
Last British Governor to Hong Kong

1

What Should a China Manager Know about China's Economy, Politics and Society?

Frank Sieren

1.1. Is China's economy more reliable or only bigger than other economies?

One of the most important preconditions for successful business in China is a reliable evaluation of the political, economic and social situation of this complex country. Managers need a number of parameters that allow them to get a relatively clear picture without too much research. They have to foresee coming developments at an early stage, allowing them to change their strategy and inform their head office before it has to find out itself. Furthermore, these parameters help to support a long-term market entry strategy. The last two economic crises (Asian crisis, global recession) have proved the parameters China's stability is built on.

The Asian financial crisis in 1997 and the world recession in 2001 heavily upset Asian people's dreams of a pacific century. Not only Japan, but also the four little tigers, South Korea, Taiwan, Singapore and Thailand still have serious economic problems that can only be solved by an upswing of the global economy. Of all Asian countries, the only one that could live up to its economic promises until now is communist China. Western companies reward the right mix of stability and growth in this big market with high investment. In most other countries foreign direct investment (FDI) has been sinking significantly. However, China's contracted FDI grew 10.4 per cent to 69.2 billion US dollars (6 per cent of GDP) in 2001. In times of crisis it has become even more obvious how much the international business community trusts China. Today, China is second only to the US as the world's biggest receiver of FDI and gets 80 per cent of FDI that flows into Asia. By comparison, India only receives 10 percent. China's WTO membership, officially starting on 11 December 2001, has given China euphoria an extra boost.

China's transformation economy can only be understood if one keeps in mind that constant policy changes are inevitable to keep the country stable.

1

For example, the Chinese government might sometimes offer preferential treatment to foreign companies in a particular business sector in order to attract more FDI, only to scrap these bonuses if it gets the impression that foreign businesses are getting too strong and threaten to push out local industry. While frustrating to foreign businesses this policy might in the long run turn out to be a well-advised one, because, other than the Russian economic shock therapy of the early nineties, it stabilises the country. Maintaining social and economic stability being the government's most daunting task, there are three main areas of conflict that have to be kept in balance: firstly, the overstaffed, unprofitable and poorly run state owned enterprises (SOEs) have to be made competitive with the emerging and rapidly growing private sector. Secondly, two thirds of Chinese people live in the mostly poor countryside with its uncompetitive agriculture; many try to make their way to the cities to seek better jobs and income perspectives. Thirdly, China's growth currently mainly benefits the boom cities on the east coast, while the vast inland and western regions lag far behind and their poor inhabitants find it hard to benefit from the country's development.

The most important questions
- How long can China keep up its strong growth?
- How stable is China?
- Is China playing games with western companies' dreams of a giant market with 1.3 billion consumers?
- Which parameters allow an evaluation of the country's internal strengths?
- What role does WTO membership play?

Even after the 2001 global recession, during which risk evaluation became extremely rigid, it very much looks like the trust in the Middle Kingdom's stability is still justified. The assessment, that China is not only a big market, but also a strong and seminal one, is based on the following requirements:

- Stable growth, low inflation/deflation rate; supported by useful, moderate government spending;
- Conservative, protective fiscal, monetary policy;
- Down-to-earth reform management, which puts stability as first priority;
- Balanced mix of high tech and low cost;
- Patient people willing to carry the burden of reforms;
- WTO membership forcing China to apply international business standards.

Naturally, the factors are very interdependent. If in case of an inflation the government stopped controlling it, the people would lose confidence in their Chinese money, withdraw their savings from the banks and spend them on durable goods. Demand would rise faster than the necessary supplies could follow, further driving up inflation and pushing the black market for local currency. Consequently, people's real earnings would drop dramatically until they'd finally lose patience with the government. This is what happened in Argentina in the first half of 2002, and the government had to close the banks. Therefore it's useful to take a closer look at the factors that stabilise China's economy.

High, stable growth

Emerging from a very low level of economic development China's high growth is no luxury, but a basic necessity to guarantee the country's stability. In the short-run, it serves the stability of the labour market. Every year, about 10 million workers lose their jobs in SOEs and seek new employment. Every year, China has to create 14 million jobs to provide for them and the young people who enter the job market. Analysts see the root of the countrywide protest movement of 1989 in the low growth rate and high inflation of the late 1980s. This served as a warning to politicians, who in the early 1990s subsequently moved to a policy that accelerated growth at any rate. The overheated economy again led to galloping inflation. Therefore, the main goal of People's Bank of China president and later Premier Zhu Rongji's economic policies in the mid-1990s was a soft landing for China's boom. Since then, the official growth rate was between 7.1 and 8.8 per cent and inflation was later.

Since the Asian financial crisis in 1997, the government has had to make sure that growth is not slowing down too much. In times of falling exports, which are one of the main engines for China's growth, state planners used infrastructure projects to keep the economy busy. Mainly used as a means of fiscal policy, government domestic spending rose 80 per cent between 1998 and 2001. This sounds alarming at first, but is actually quite reasonable. There are two reasons: first, if compared to other countries, China's government spending is still quite acceptable. Only 20–30 per cent of tax income is used to pay interest for mostly long-performing loans, a rate comparable to that of Germany. In 2000 infrastructure development made up for about 1.5 per cent of GDP growth. Second, these projects are not merely employment projects; they are mostly reasonable investments that will make the country more competitive in future and also benefit international corporations. After all, in contrast to Japan, China still needs a lot of infrastructure if it wants to meet the needs of a modern economy. Many of today's problems are burdens from Mao Zedong's regime. He promoted the self-reliance of all regions, leaving the country with a miserable infrastructure. Connecting underdeveloped, poor western China with the booming coastal area is especially important if the whole country is to prosper. However, China's authorities sometimes have odd priorities, even in the coastal areas: Beijing's *hutongs*, the traditional courtyard houses, have been provided with broad-band Internet access, but are still waiting for private toilets and running water.

One of the biggest projects, the highly controversial Three Gorges Dam, is hoped to produce an annual 18,000 megawatts of power as well as controlling the devastating floods that regularly hit the Yangtse River. The dam, to be completed sometime in the second decade of the twenty-first century, will cost an estimated 90 billion US dollars; 1.3 million people have to be resettled.

Another power supply project that is currently under construction is a 2,500-kilometre gas pipeline. The 20 billion US dollar project will connect Xinjiang, which is rich in oil, gas and other natural resources, with Shanghai and the adjoining boom-area on the east coast. A 1,200-kilometre channel is going to provide China's dry northeast with water from the subtropical south.

A nationwide highway network is also very important. The basic skeleton, soon to be finished, is a system of two north-south and two east-west highways; smaller roads will then connect to every corner of the country. At the beginning of the decade, the total length of highways was 16,000 kilometres. By 2010 China hopes to have a network of 12 main highways. And China's construction projects follow a long-term strategy: the new highways are in no way inferior to the ones in developed countries. With regard to railways, a German state-of-the-art magnetic levitation (maglev) train, Transrapid, is under construction in Shanghai. Starting in 2003, the train will connect Pudong, Shanghai's Manhattan, with the new airport 37 kilometres away. Should the first-ever commercial maglev connection stand the test, this system is likely to be used for a 1,200-kilometre high-speed connection between Shanghai and Beijing.

China is like a huge high potential company that has to invest in all fields of core business in order to become more successful. Today, the country with 20 per cent of the world's population produces only about 3 per cent of the world's general inland product (GIP). In comparison, the US produces 30 per cent of global GIP with only 4.5 per cent of the world's population.

But Table 1 shows that global trends seem to be working for China. China is the only country with long-term rising nominal GDP.

Table 1   Nominal GDP increase in US dollars (per cent)

	1980–90	*1990–2000*	*2000–2010 (estimation)*
China	28	178	200
Tigers	265	95	60
US	108	70	55
Japan	185	56	20

Source: Morgan Stanley Research.

Over the coming decades, the Chinese government will still be able to rely on infrastructure spending without running into dangerous overspending, especially if it can stimulate private consumption at the same time.

Conservative fiscal and monetary policy

The Chinese government handles its money reserves carefully, always ensuring it has enough in reserve to be independent from others. Foreign reserves exceed 210 billion US dollars (2001). According to Moody's Investors Service, this is four times more than China needs to cover 12 months of imports. On Moody's rating list, China reaches a good A3. At 30 per cent of GDP, national debt is still relatively moderate.

For the time being, the Chinese leadership has also made sure that big international finance players cannot put China under pressure.

- Trading on international stock markets cannot influence China's interests because access to local markets is still mostly restricted for foreigners (see question 1.8).
- The Renminbi (RMB), China's currency, is not freely convertible; just like the Hong Kong dollar, it is tied to the US dollar by a peg. As the government chooses a realistic exchange rate, there is no significant black market.
- China does not take high-risk short-term credits ('hot cash'–borrowing huge amounts at high interest rates) from international capital markets. Therefore China, although its banks are technically bankrupt, does not risk bankruptcy in times of crisis, when most foreign creditors suddenly call in their loans and debtors cannot pay back. Thailand chose this risky strategy in the 1990s and triggered the Asian financial crisis in 1997.

Down-to-earth reform management

Not a democratic mandate from the voters but robust economic success determines the Chinese government's legitimacy. Beijing's communist leaders are well aware that they have the best chances of staying in power if China succeeds in becoming a competitive player in the global economy. Therefore, the more successful cadres in the leadership leave behind ideological limitations and mostly base their decisions on down-to-earth economic considerations, which put stability as the first priority. In this respect, China does not reject the help of acclaimed international consultants. The economic reform policy, triggered in the early 1980s by paramount leader Deng Xiaoping and revived in the early 1990s by the party's reformer wing around Premier Zhu Rongji and President Jiang Zemin, has become the broad party line. If the reform process is occasionally slowed down, it is mainly because the government has to protect weak state owned enterprises to guarantee social stability.

But even then, the losers of the reform process, such as party hardliners headed by former premier Li Peng, are unable to stop it (see question 1.2).

Balanced mix of high tech and low cost

China has a unique position in the economic world because it is attractive for both low cost as well as high tech production. Therefore, China is not dependent on one sector only. In comparison, countries such as Indonesia or Bangladesh rely mainly on low cost products, while Taiwan, South Korea and Japan are almost fully dependent on the IT sector and have a population that is no longer willing to work for low salaries.

There are no signs that China is likely to grow out of or give up its dual approach in the near future. China is increasingly able to produce sophisticated IT products, and China's west provides an inexhaustible pool of cheap labour. The only drawback is the high cost of transportation to the east coast.

During the Asian crisis, China insisted on the peg of the Renminbi to the US dollar, making the country a more expensive production base than other Asian economies. The Asian Crisis has shown how stable China's position is. Lasting only a little more than one year, the crisis was too short for western companies to move to other cheap labour countries. Considering that it takes quite some time to teach factory staff to produce output of reliable, consistent quality.

Also, China has rising numbers of well-educated young people, making it attractive for foreign companies to not only move their production sites to China, but also their research and development centres. Especially in research-intensive sectors like biotechnology or life sciences, China is emerging as a very competitive player.

Patient society

Currently there are no signs of a general country wide opposition to the central government. It seems like the government and its people have reached some kind of 'society agreement': as long as the Beijing leadership sets the country on the track to prosperity, the people will not directly interfere with the central government. On the side of the people, this is surely more an act of toleration than acceptance. Still, the people show a certain willingness to carry the heavy burdens of the reforms. After all, the hard times of the Cultural Revolution (1966–76) are still fresh in the memory of those who are now in their mid-30s. Even the poor peasants have experienced a slow rise in living standards.

Although there are frequent demonstrations in China, they still mainly attack regional problems and usually end when the dispute is solved locally. This balance, however, is unstable. It would be a very alarming sign if demonstrations increased and started attacking the system as a whole (see question 1.11).

WTO membership

WTO membership not only makes it easier for foreign enterprises to enter the Chinese market. This will boost the reform development of the Middle Kingdom in two possible ways.

Firstly, the reform wing of the government gets more leverage to speed up the restructuring of state owned enterprises. The message is simple: companies have to become competitive by international standards or face the consequences of being shut down. This pressure has already led to impressive modernisation in sectors such as banking, airlines, telecommunications and extractive industry.

Secondly, foreign corporations that invest in China call for international standards. They not only demand open markets, but also a reliable legal system, less corruption, greater transparency of Chinese enterprises and, last but not least, well-educated, experienced Chinese employees. This will put pressure on politicians and the public sector to speed up reforms, as long as stability is not in danger.

Nevertheless, the current strength of the Chinese economy should not lead western investors to drop their guard and underestimate the fact that the country's most complicated transition period since the death of Mao Zedong in 1976 is still ahead. For the last 20 years, China's economy was based on turnover. The only goal was growth at any rate, which led to corruption (see chapter 1.6) and businesses run by poorly educated but very charismatic leaders that resembled the so called 'robber barons' (Rockefeller, Vanderbilt) of the United States at the turn of the nineteenth to the twentieth century.

Now, the economy has to produce sustainable growth. That includes a functioning social system, efficient banks and a reliable legal system. The fairly closed financial sector, which is protecting China's economy now, becomes a growing disadvantage as the economy gets more sophisticated: the lack of transparency raises doubts about the stability behind the walls. Using these parameters the only thing one can be sure of now is that external pressure (Asian crises, global recession) has so far not been high enough to fundamentally destabilise China. But apart from that, we have to rely on estimates.

At least there is no doubt about the general direction: the government will have to give up its tight grip and strive to strike the right balance between *laissez faire* and control. This will definitely lead to less control. Should the government lose this balance, foreign enterprises will feel a painful slow-down of the boom. Nobody knows how deep China could fall again, but experiences of the past allow us to be cautiously hopeful. Even the last big crisis, the bloody crackdown of student protests on Beijing's Tiananmen Square in 1989, threw the country's economy off track for little more than a year.

Summary/Recommendations

On the basis of the above-mentioned six parameters, China's economy currently seems to be stable and prospering on the turning point from a turnover economy to a sustainable economy. By keeping these six factors in mind, it should be possible to make relatively reliable evaluations and forecasts about the country's development. However, if one or two parameters take a major turn for the worse, it is advisable to be careful and reconsider the long-term strategy.

Further sources

Guo, R. (1999) *How the Chinese Economy Works: A Multiregional Overview* (Studies on the Chinese Economy), UK, Palgrave Macmillan.

Schell, O. and Shambaugh, D. (1999) *The China Reader: The Reform Era*, Vintage Books.

Zweig, D. (2002) *Internationalizing China: Domestic Interests and Global Linkages* (Cornell Studies in Political Economy), Cornell University Press.

1.2. How stable are the Communist Party and the government?

In everyday business, one often has to deal with Communist Party cadres. They draw up the nation's economic policies and decide which sectors will get how much government support and how fast China opens its doors for international investors. Every company, including western-Chinese joint ventures, has its own party committee, and the party secretary wields considerable influence. Even though the party's influence seems to be slowly fading, it is and will remain a major factor for China's economic success.

The most important questions

- What are the Communist Party's power instruments?
- What are the party's main weaknesses?
- What are the party's strengths?
- Is the party flexible enough?
- What forces the party to act according to modern economic developments?

During the 1990s, China was Asia's pillar of stability, not only economically, but also politically. While the region's big players (Japan, Indonesia, Philippines etc.) were paralysed by interior turbulences and power struggles, China has been able to take a stable course for over a decade. The main reason for this is the strong position of the Communist Party. It defends its unrivalled power using the following instruments:

- top-down decision-making;
- occupation of all leading positions;

- control over career opportunities;
- control over media;
- ban on political competition;
- ban on separation of powers.

All influential government positions and decision-making processes are in the hands of the party, making it impossible to distinguish where affairs of the party end and affairs of the state begin. For example, all provinces and cities have a head of government and a party secretary, with the latter being the more powerful body.

The most influential positions, currently all held by Jiang Zemin, are the following: Party Secretary General, State President and Head of the Central Military Commission. The innermost power circle is the standing committee of party's politburo, formed by the country's seven most high-ranking politicians.

Formally the highest state organ is the approximately 3,000-strong National People's Congress (NPC), which comes together in Beijing's Great Hall of the People every spring. It is at these meetings the premier in a comprehensive political declamation, carefully drafted by all government sectors, announces the new guidelines for the government's work, including economic policies. The following discussion is of great importance to the leaders, giving them an overview over their parlamentarians' opinions and worries throughout the country. Sometimes delegates will even show their discontent. In one case in 1992, one-third voted against the construction of the Three Gorges Dam. Having its annual meeting at the same time is the Chinese People's Political Consultative Conference (CPPCC), a body made up of representatives from all fields of society, which acts in an advisory capacity, and includes businessmen like Jing Shuping, Chairman of Minsheng Bank, China's only privately owned bank listed on the local stock market, and Henry Fok Ying-Tung, one of the richest and, politically, most influential businessmen in Hong Kong.

However, the main legislative work of the NPC is done by its 150-strong standing committee, which meets every two months. Parallel, the Central Committee of the Communist Party of China (CCCPC) meets to discuss state and party affairs and make the necessary decisions. Although the party does its best to speak with only one voice, behind the Scenes there are several factions struggling for influence.

There has been much speculation about a coming collapse of China's Communist Party. Most analysts that predict an imminent end to communist rule point out that the party's weaknesses are becoming more and more of a hindrance for the development of the country. The following are the main weaknesses mentioned:

- avoidance of political competition;
- phase-out model: ideology and the cult of leadership do not work any more;

- complex economy cannot be centrally planned;
- too big (60 million members);
- cannot be controlled (corruption);
- clinging to power is more important than economic reasoning;
- too much emphasis on uncertain leadership personalities.

Until now, much to the surprise of many China watchers, a collapse has not happened, and there are strong arguments that suggest that there will be few changes in the near future. On the one hand, government and party try their best to go with changing times and adapt to the market economy. On the other hand, there is no general opposition or underground movement that could challenge the party's position. The question is why?

The main reason is that the party has a number of structural strengths that are quite helpful for the modernisation of the huge country:

- ability to make long-term plans for modernisation;
- successful balancing of different currents within the party;
- ability to implement and balance reforms nationwide.

Still, the strongest advantage of the Chinese Communist Party is definitely its pragmatic flexibility in the economic field, necessary to cope with huge national and international interests and pressure.

Flexibility

Compared to other communist systems, China's Communist Party has shown a great amount of economic flexibility over the last 20 years. Taking a very pragmatic approach, the party has managed to fend off massive pressure from two directions.

One is the people's desire for higher living standards but also for personal freedom and the pursuit of happiness. The other is the competition of the global economy. This at least makes the government aware of the huge problems that urgently have to be solved, as Premier Zhu Rongji's speech to the National Peoples' Congress in spring 2002 shows:

> *However, we are clearly aware that there are still many problems demanding prompt solution in our economic and social life.*
>
> *The principal problems are as follows: farmers' incomes are growing slowly; incomes for farmers in some major grain producing areas and disaster-afflicted areas are decreasing; in some places, wage areas are now a serious problem; some enterprises are still having difficulties in production and the life of some workers remains hard; and employment pressures are increasing. Industrial structure remains irrational and deep-seated problems in our economic system have not been solved.*

Problems of the ecological environment are outstanding.

Local Protectionism remains a problem despite repeated orders to ban it, and the order of the market economy is yet to be fully rectified.

In some localities and government departments and among some leading cadres, formalism and bureaucracy are rife, deception, extravagance and waste are serious problems, and some forms of corruption are relatively conspicuous.

There are cases of work units misappropriating budgetary funds or special funds in disregard of the relevant rules and regulations. Failure to abide by the law in handling affairs and laxity in law enforcement are common occurrences. Grave worksite accidents frequently occur. Public security order is poor in some places. Some of these problems have remained unsolved for many years, and there are also some that are caused by shortcomings and errors in our work. We must attach great importance to these problems and take effective measures to solve them.

When it comes to major decisions, pragmatism usually wins over ideology. However, this does not necessarily mean that these decisions are what foreign investors hope for. For example, even though China has entered the WTO, the banking sector will only open up to foreign competition very slowly. This is not caused by the ignorance of communist ideology, but by the simple fact that China's state banks still need time to overcome weaknesses and deficiencies and prepare for foreign competition. The Government's first priority is always to maintain social and economic stability.

National pressure

Apparently, China's communists thoroughly analysed the fall of Eastern Europe's communist systems. They came to the conclusion that there is only one thing that can save them from being swept away by uprisings and rebelling masses: economic prosperity. They reckon that as long as Chinese people are mainly concerned with raising their own salary and consumer power and as long as the majority can afford more today than it could yesterday, nobody will challenge the central government. In that respect the people controls the party.

The party, however, has all the instruments it needs to influence the people. Whoever wants to be successful in his career has to act in harmony with the party because it controls all state run business up to the top positions. In a way this even applies for private entrepreneurs. Without close ties to local cadres, no enterprise will be able to establish a successful business. Lawmaking, judging, law enforcement and administration are all controlled by one organisation – the party's politburo (see chart below). Therefore, rules can be enforced easily and propagated through the media. This has advantages and disadvantages. The politburo can reach decisions, for example on long-term development plans, quickly and efficiently. Also, only a few groups are involved in the decision-making process. There is little competition when it comes to fighting over the best ideas, but this power monopoly leads to a huge problem with corruption.

Within the party, different directions struggle for power. During recent years, party secretary general and state president Jiang Zemin succeeded in balancing the fighting fractions. The losers were those cadres whose know-how or connections were not strong enough to compete in the new market economy environment. They therefore try to slow down the reforms. What is obvious is that development cannot be turned back: ideology and the cult of leadership might still work to control peasants, but the educated city dwellers will not fall for it. Party leaders increasingly have to develop pragmatic project manager qualities.

Global pressure

The party's economic policy not only depends on its own people, but also on the international community. It has learned from mistakes it made in the 1960s and 70s. Efforts to build up a new, independent third way economic system have been abandoned; the party now follows the mainstream of global developments. Under pressure to survive in the global economy, China has to implement international business standards. In this respect, WTO membership is a very important step in the right direction.

Promising foreigners a huge market of 1.3 billion consumers bought time for the party because international companies, not wanting to miss out, were willing to set up businesses under unstable conditions. However, this will not be enough to make China competitive in the long run. International support,

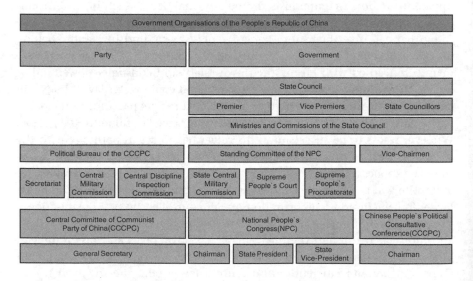

Chart 1   Government organisations of the People's Republic of China

acceptance and stability depend on consequent, reliable and fast implementation of international standards. Should party managers wield too much power, this might be harmful to the party's long-term control. Government and Party can only maintain their credibility with its own people and the international community if they succeed in checking corruption in their own ranks (see question 1.5). The government tries its best, but for outsiders it is hard to judge if the efforts are successful. The economic sector is particularly difficult, because central planning of all details of the economy has become virtually impossible. The most important task for government party in the coming years is letting the economy have its fling without losing control. The conflict lies between clinging to power and giving in to economic necessities. As long as leaders do not try to ignore national and international pressure and move ahead with reforms, party and government may hope to remain stable for quite a while.

Summary/Recommendations

The party's stability depends on its success in coping with the above-mentioned weaknesses. For the time being, there seems to be no alternative, as no other organisation is as well structured as the party.

In recent years, the reform-oriented government has had a lot of support from its own people and also from abroad. Even if China officially remains communist, in reality it has long launched pragmatic economic reforms towards market economy and international standards. Opposition movements that knocked over the socialist systems in Eastern Europe do not yet exist; mass protests only occur locally. The country's stable growth supports the trust of the international community in the government's stability.

Still, the system is too dependant on leadership qualities and personalities. For the time being, the leadership seems to fully back the reforms, being aware that internal quarrels could be harmful.

Further sources

Salisbury, H.E. (1993) *The New Emperors: China in the Era of Mao and Deng*, Avin Books.
Shambaugh, D.L. (ed.) (2000) *Is China Unstable: Assessing the Factors* (Studies on Contemporary China) M.E. Sharpe.

1.3. When making business, what is important to know about China's history?

The Middle Kingdom had its time of greatest prosperity between the third century BC and the seventh century AD. During that time, China came up with groundbreaking inventions such as the plough, paper, pasta and porcelain. But these times, when China was a world power, have long passed.

By the fifteenth century, development of this empire stagnated when conservative officials barred the great discoverer Zheng He from seafaring and increasingly isolated China from the outside world. Since then, inventions and discoveries that drove global development have come from Europe, North America (a little later) and, in the second half of the twentieth century, from Japan as well. China lagged behind, becoming for several hundred years a second-rate, if not third-rate country. The emperors tried to live off the shine and glamour of older times and keep the huge middle Kingdom together. Opposed to progress and reform, the imperial court rejected all impulses for change necessary to cope with the requirements of a modern world. By the beginning of the twentieth century, the empire fell apart under international pressure and different forces, mainly provincial warlords, struggled for power. Japan, trying to dominate Southeast Asia, benefited from internal chaos and ongoing fights between the nationalist forces of the *Guomindang* and the Chinese Communist Party, occupying a big part of the country in the late 1930 and early 1940s.

The new leader (1934–49)

It was under these chaotic conditions that Mao Zedong, a charismatic revolutionary and strategist, came to power. Trying to escape nationalist *Guomindang* troops, he led China's communists through a 10,000-kilometre hike later known as the Long March (1934–5) to Yan'an in northwestern China. After the Japanese lost World War II, the United States forced communists and the *Guomindang* to form a coalition, which didn't last long and led to continued civil war. In 1949, the communists succeeded in forcing the *Guomindang* off the mainland to Taiwan. Most of China's successful entrepreneurs fled with them or made their way to the British colony of Hong Kong; some of them even disassembled whole production lines and carried them off. On 1 October 1949, Mao Zedong, the leader of the Communist Party, proclaimed the People's Republic of China, triggering a few years of euphoria. An economic boom fuelled this optimism. In these promising times, many people willingly followed the party leadership. Unfortunately, it soon turned out that Mao, an outstanding political strategist, was less skillful and knowledgeable when it came to economic reforms.

The most important questions

- Which are the main phases that influenced the People's Republic?
- What were the goals of the different leaders?
- How did they implement their goals?
- How successful were they?
- How did these developments affect the Chinese people?
- Which historical experiences and events can still be felt today in everyday business?

China's dark ages didn't end with Mao's rise to power and proclamation of the People's Republic. Centuries of lethargy in imperial times and chaos during the republican transition period were now followed by a time of unbalanced, precipitate reforms.

Short-lived hopes (1949–56)

Mao was not hesitant; he knew he had to move swiftly to restructure China. And his analysis of the situation was correct: after centuries of immobility under the emperors, China had fallen far behind the west. In order to become competitive, China had to make enormous efforts to catch up. But Mao's conclusion tragically had a small, but momentous error. Mao was convinced that a well-organised mass movement that selflessly laboured for the good of the community would be much better at building up the country than a system of competition that offered material incentives and social promotion to the individual. His strategy was the setting up of collectives in the countryside, nationalising privately-owned property and decentralising the economy. He wanted to win over workers and peasants by offering them lifetime employment and social security, the so-called 'iron rice bowl' including housing, medical care, schooling, pensions, in return for low wages. Unfortunately, this system did not have a very motivating effect. Shanghai, the booming coastal metropolis of the early twentieth century should have taught him better. Unfortunately, he was charismatic enough to press ahead with any idea he had. Without any sign of comprehension, Mao forced China's economy to follow this course for over 20 years, further ruining the country. He was obsessed with having found a revolutionary shortcut to economic modernity. Tragically for millions, this bypass never worked out.

'Let a hundred flowers blossom...' (1956–7)

Mao, born into a family of farmers, always sympathised with peasants and workers, but had ambivalent feelings towards intellectuals including engineers, managers, doctors and lawyers. While at the same time feeling inferior to them, he had to rely on their co-operation in order to succeed. They constituted up to 14 per cent of his 20 million plus party comrades. About the same number of party members had a working-class background, while the majority was made up of farmers.

In 1956 he ventured to improve the intellectuals' situation and asked them for helpful criticism and new ideas. The criticism soon turned against him. The results were devastating for Mao. He called off the campaign after only five weeks and turned it into a witch-hunt against all his critics. Between 300,000 and 700,000 intellectuals were detained or sent to the countryside to be 're-educated' by the farmers. For decades, this sent out a warning to the leadership elite of the country that Mao's ideas were not negotiable.

The 'Great Leap Forward' (1958–60)

After unsuccessfully lobbying the intellectuals, Mao was afraid that the peasants and workers would lose their enthusiasm and motivation. In order to stop the country he had 'liberated' (as the official Chinese vocabulary puts it) breaking apart again, Mao tried to keep the people busy with new mass campaigns. The 'Great Leap Forward' was a massive effort to push the borders of growth and catch up with the West within a few years. Unrealistic as it was, the campaign ruined most that was left of the country's economy. Instead of counting on automation and division of labour, millions had to use the most primitive of tools or even their own hands to till the land and build bridges, streets or channels. Everybody was supposed to do everything. Villagers were forced to produce their own steel in tiny little steel mills, live off their own agricultural products and build their own roads. The results were disastrous. The newly set up industry broke down. Western scholars estimate that between 20 and 30 million people starved to death because of famines partly caused by this economic insanity.

At the same time, Mao, still fully convinced of the success of his campaigns, broke with the Soviet Union that had until then been like China's older brother. Choosing to do things his way, he expelled 1,300 Soviet experts. They took with them the blueprints for 600 major projects, thus causing immense damage. This move finally isolated China from the rest of the world after the West had already installed a strict embargo against China after the Korean War (1951–3)

Not until 1960 did Mao gave in and call off the campaign in order to avoid losing all political influence. Struggles within the Communist Party had reduced the great helmsman to the leader of a minority fraction. Economic specialists took over, amongst them Deng Xiaoping who would become China's paramount leader from the late 1970s till to his death in 1997.

The Cultural Revolution (1966–76)

Mao, weakened by his failure, tried to regain absolute power with all his might. Having lost all influence with intellectuals, peasants and workers, he now set his hopes on the young generation. He developed a marketing campaign for himself: in order to show off his still youthful strength and revive his charisma, he went for a historic swim in the strong currents of Yangtse River in 1966. The photographs, spread by mass media, had the desired effect. Mao proclaimed an unlimited school-free period making himself the admired leader of a 110 million-strong youth movement that formed the Red Guards. With the support of the military, still Mao's stronghold in the party, the students once again unhinged the country. Their goal was to eliminate the four old things: old ideology, old thinking, old culture and old habits. In reality, it was the country's culture and its economic know-how that was swept away.

During the 'Great Proletarian Cultural Revolution', many middle–aged people were sent to the country side or to factories for 're-education by the proletarian masses'. This, it was hoped, would lead to an economic boom. Instead, anarchic chaos spread across the country. Zhu Rongji, the later premier and top economic reformer of the 1990s, spent years herding pigs and doing other odd jobs, as did most members of the elite. Even Deng Xiaoping, who served his country by working in a tractor plant. His son, trying to escape from Red Guards, jumped out of a window and was paralysed for life. Mao himself, ageing quickly, spent these years speeding around the country in his luxury train and celebrating the heyday of his personality cult.

With all experienced experts being sidelined, another collapse of the country was inevitable and came in the early 1970s. Mao, trying to ignore the chaos, turned towards foreign policy. In 1972 he established diplomatic ties with the United States; in February of that year, US President Richard Nixon visited China.

Still, it was not until Mao's death in 1976 that the country could be brought back under control and the cleaning up of the 'Ten Dark Years' began. The state of the country after the Cultural Revolution was disastrous. China had basically suffered an economic standstill; the living standard of most people had remarkably decreased. However, the Chinese still hold Mao in high esteem today. He is credited with liberating, unifying and holding together the country. But most of all, it was Mao who gave the Chinese a new feeling of national pride. Even today, Mao's picture dangles off the mirror in many Chinese cars.

Social market economy with Chinese characteristics (1978–88)

After a short power struggle and an interregnum, Deng Xiaoping eventually became Mao's successor and put the country on a new track. Although the great helmsman had left behind economic chaos, between 40 and 90 million unemployed workers and a GDP that was a sixth of Taiwan's (which only has a population of 20 million), Deng was wise enough to carry on Mao's personality cult to keep the country together.

Politically and economically, Deng Xiaoping had a completely different approach. Starting in 1979 the pragmatic communist radically modernised the economy by turning towards the western mainstream of development. Deng followed a double strategy: on the one hand he kept the central planning system, on the other hand he introduced market economy mechanisms. Thus prices were controlled and free at the same time, even for the same kind of product. His major changes were:

- Small private business was allowed. The industrial sector was opened for new market players.
- He sent students to study abroad, even though he knew not all of them would come back.
- He established special economic development zones near the former Portuguese colony of Macao (Zhuhai), Hong Kong (Shenzhen) and Taiwan

(Xiamen). Foreign experts were invited to come to China to co-ordinate the new start.

- In order to collect foreign investment, special finance institutions were founded, such as China International Trade and Investment Corporation (CITIC), which is still a powerful bank today.
- State-owned companies were given more leverage. If they produced more than the required quotas, they could sell the overproduction – even on the global markets.
- Peasants were given their own fields and were free to decide what to do with at least part of their harvest.

This 'social market economy with Chinese characteristics' could soon show off remarkable success. By 1983, China's trade surplus had grown from virtually nothing to 5.2 billion US dollars. Direct foreign investment rose to 910 million US dollars. Between 1978 and 1985, the percentage of people living in poverty dropped from 30 to 10 percent. 'Don't be afraid of prosperity!' was the message party secretary general Hu Yaobang spread on his tours through the provinces. After a couple of months of scepticism about the seriousness of the movement, the Chinese people were happy to follow, and ironically replaced Mao's 'four must-haves' (bicycle, radio, watch and sewing machine) with the 'three high things': high income, high education and high body build.

The Tiananmen crackdown (1989–91)

The euphoria and cry for more personal independence resounding in this saying were soon to become a huge problem for Deng. Having been voted *Time* magazine's 'Man of the Year 1986', Deng saw his boom running out of control: everybody wanted to make a quick buck instead of relying on long-term investment; some products were over produced and others not produced at all. Corruption surged in this chaos economy. In the late 1980s, GDP growth slumped to less than 6 per cent. And even those who didn't produce anything demanded more freedom, including students. Deng had underestimated the complexity of this transition economy and its liberating effects on the people.

In the mid-1980s, more and more students and other people staged joint demonstrations, publicly airing their discontent. In 1989, after weeks of mass protests on Beijing's Tiananmen Square, Deng finally decided to send in the army, leading to the so-called Tiananmen massacre on 4 June. This, along with Deng's harsh rhetoric calling the student protesters 'social scum', cost not only him, but also China the trust it had just started to regain in the world. Foreign companies pulled out of the Chinese market and western foreign investment totally went down. Ageing Deng lost power to the conservative forces within the party. Whoever could afford it went abroad to study, mostly to the US. Many students never came back, leading to a brain drain that China still suffers from today. Even those who had retained same socialist ideals gave them up after the crackdown, joining the big group of pragmatists who would pursue freedom in their own business ventures.

The trip to the south (1992)

Ironically, the same man who had ordered the crackdown on the movement for more social and economic freedom fought against his successors, that he had elevated to their positions, for more economic openness three years later. Conservatives in government and party were lacking strategies and Deng himself was unable to regain power in Beijing's leadership circles.

In this hopeless situation, 88-year-old Deng made a clever move: in January and February 1992, he travelled to China's southern provinces and criticised State President Jiang Zemin and Premier Li Peng in front of economically minded cadres for being to slow in opening the country to foreign economic influence, ideas and investment. International trends and progress should no longer be ignored, Deng demanded: 'That includes progressive working and management methods developed by other countries, including capitalist ones.' For weeks, the Beijing leaders tried to hush up the trip, but after it became obvious that substantial parts of the population and military supported Deng, the central government had to give up its resistance.

The wise old strategist was able to rally the people behind him for the last time by giving a public voice to their dreams of a better life. Deng was able to live up to his promise by triggering an unprecedented boom. He forced President Jiang Zemin in the right direction of market-oriented reforms. Deng appeared for the last time in public in 1994 and died in 1997.

The golden 1990s (1992–9)

While the Chinese were busy earning money, the collective memory in the West would not forget the Mao times of 'little blue ants' and the tanks on Tiananmen Square. Even today, China's rise to a major political and economic world power is being much underestimated. China's economic statistics underline this impression. In 1978, China was listed as the number 32 of international trade. Now, more than 20 years later, China has reached rank nine. Since 1993, China has been second only to the United States in receiving direct foreign investment. After Japan, China has saved up the largest amount for foreign exchange reserves – more than 200 billion US dollars. This gives Chinese economy planners a lot of leverage, as does the 40 per cent saving rate of Chinese people.

When Premier Zhu Rongji came to power in 1996, he successfully fought inflation (as he had as a central bank governor) and opened the country towards more international know-how and advice. Many global players started investing and set up huge joint ventures on China's mainland, and FDI surged.

In 1997 China regained control over the British crown colony of Hong Kong. The party decided to keep it as one of the freest market economies in the world.

Beijing is only partly to blame for the big problems Hong Kong faces in the first decade of this century. On the one hand it is simply losing its position as the gate to China, as foreign companies not longer depend on Hong Kong's help as much as they used to. On the other hand, the communist leaders want to show the world that they don't need British colonial help to build up a modern city by trying to make Shanghai the new gate to China.

Also in 1997, the government decided to further boost the reform of state owned enterprises (SOEs). SOEs had to become profitable instead of only fulfilling plans.

During the Asian crisis (1997–9), which started just after the Hong Kong handover, the government had to protect its economy against unexpected outside pressure. It refused to devaluate the Chinese currency and eventually emerged from the crisis with a strengthened position.

In October 1998, the government closed down the Guangdong International Trust and Investment Corp (GITIC) investment arm of Guangdong Province, that had accumulated 5.4 billion US dollars in liabilities many of them to foreign banks. These had, until then, expected the central government to stand up for liabilities even of provincial finance institutions, although the central government had repeatedly denied this. The closing down of GITIC came as a rude awakening to many foreign banks. The biggest bankruptcy in Chinese history shows that Beijing will not bail out just any provincial institution. Instead, they will have to learn to play by the rules. In late 1999, after 15 years of negations, China achieved a breakthrough in the negotiations with the US and the European Union to join the World Trade Organisation (WTO).

The rough new century (since 2000)

The start of the century was marked by a big success: the first big public offering of a Chinese company on the New York stock exchange, Petro China (fourth largest petrochemical enterprise in the world) raised 3.9 billion US dollars for 10 per cent of the shares. However, it has to be added that the buyers where mostly foreign competitors who believed that this was a good way to get access to the Chinese market.

The euphoria did not last long. In autumn 2000 the worldwide boom was over and the government had to protect its country against stormy weather. At the same time, under the pressure of its coming WTO membership, it had to further accelerate reforms of state owned enterprises, build up a stable social system and fight corruption (see question 1.5).

The most important event of national pride since the establishment of the People's Republic in 1949 occurred in July 2001, when Beijing won the right to stage the Olympic games in 2008. A spontaneous all-night party swept the country for the first time, with people using Mao's famous 1949 quote: 'China has stood up.'

How does Chinese history influence everyday business?
How it can be useful to a China manager?

These questions are often posed by expats who only spend a limited time in China and don't want to read huge numbers of books. The answer is obvious: Chinese habits that seem strange to a foreigner relate to the individual, but also the cultural background. Behavioural patterns have their roots in collective experiences as well as in traditions passed on by older generations. People usually try to learn from mistakes and make these experiences available to others. Knowledge about China's collective background makes it easier to successfully deal with Chinese counterparts and be on friendly terms with them.

That there are many differing attitudes and changing ratios lies in the nature of a large country with a huge population. Nevertheless the economic development of a country is reflected in its common behaviour and the performance of its people. Some characteristics and habits that western managers are often confronted with are explained below.

Having suffered under Mao's obsession with mass movements and collectives, Chinese today tend to be quite selfish and individualistic. After 30 years of campaigns, this is not surprising, especially since those were usually short lived and quickly replaced by other movements that called for the exact opposite.

What Chinese care most about is the pursuit of their *personal material wealth*. For the system as a whole, this leads to the problem that people care less and less for their relatives who are not yet protected by a social system. Eventually today's people seek to be spiritually and economically *self-sufficient*. For companies this implies that, in contrast to Japan, for example, it is hard to build up a corporate identity and make young people fully committed to their employer. Job-hopping is quite common. Although some people keep looking for salvation in movements like the pseudo-Buddhist religion Fa Lun Gong, most have developed immunity towards dictatorial prophets.

Mao's social experiments have taught the Chinese that too much individuality can be dangerous. Playing with the band was the most important principle. *Creativity means trouble*, fighting openly for the best idea has no tradition in China and is not taught in schools. Mao's harsh reactions to the 'Let a hundred flowers blossom...' movement as well as Deng's Tiananmen crackdown made it clear that free brainstorming could lead to punishment.

Egoism is one of the strongest engines of the economic boom. Having lived through difficult times, today's Chinese are *pragmatic* and willing to make compromises. Although they are *tough negotiators* and start out with high expectations, they usually *prefer a small solution to no solution*. Big solutions were not available in the troubled past; slipping through narrow gaps was the usual way to reach one's goal.

When it comes to business, they mostly *think in the short term*. Setting up a stable company step by step that will promise solid, long-term profits sounds far less attractive to them than making a quick buck. Collective experience has taught them that policies can change suddenly and opportunities be wasted forever.

Because it is hard to win the support of Chinese people for new social experiments, they tend to be quite *open towards successful western developments* and products. Whatever seems to work or is successful in the West will quickly earn the trust of Chinese people. That does not keep them from sometimes showing *exaggerated national pride*. For centuries, they had nothing to be proud of. The lethargy of the old emperors, the colonial influence, including the Japanese invasion and Mao's vain efforts to modernise the country have deeply hurt Chinese national feelings. But for the past 20 years, things have been looking up. A feeling of 'now its our turn' sometimes leads to ultra-elation. This occasionally goes along with a lack of self-criticism and arrogance towards other countries, which the government often uses for its own purposes. Still, nationalism is also a growth engine. The Chinese are desperate to impress their competitors such as the US, Japan, Europe or India. This makes them *very impatient*.

However, the Chinese have shown impressive *patience regarding painful reforms*, such as mass lay-offs in state owned enterprises, because they still believe that it will eventually make the country strong (see question 1.11). Those born by the middle of the 1960s still remember the deprivations of the Cultural Revolution and know that painful reforms are inevitable. But they also know that standing up and talking politics can be dangerous. In companies, this behaviour can eventually lead to severe grievances, with problems swelling for a long time before breaking out with great force.

That institutions and their rules are not functioning or unreliable is a key experience of all people living in the People's Republic of China. Therefore, it will probably take a long time before the Chinese people accept the rule of law and stop showing a deep *mistrust for institutions* (see question 1.5). The Chinese proper to provide for themselves or seek help from relatives and friends rather than relying on support from state or company institutions.

This short excursion into Chinese habits, which could be easily prolonged, shows that the Chinese and their history are much less mysterious than one might expect.

Summary

- By the fifteenth century, the development of the huge kingdom stagnated.
- At the beginning of the twentieth century, the empire fell apart and was crippled by several wars until the new leader, Mao Zedong, took over and established the People's Republic of China (1949).

- After a short period of economic prosperity (1950–56), it soon turned out that Mao was an unskilful and incapable economic reformer, pressing ahead with idealistic, compelled reforms.
- Calling for 'a hundred flowers to blossom', Mao asked the country's elite for advice, but violently hit out against them when their criticism turned out to be too harsh (1956–7).
- During the 'Great Leap Forward' (1958–60), Mao ruined the economy even more by dividing the country into many small, self-sufficient units, the so-called People's Communes.
- In the 'Great Proletarian Cultural Revolution' (late 1965–76), Mao swept away what was left of economic know-how by sending the middle-aged to the countryside for re-education and giving all power to the young people's Red Guards.
- After Mao's death in 1976, Deng Xaioping took over and opened the country to 'social market economy with Chinese characteristics' (1976–88).
- In 1989 the economy was about to collapse after wildly booming years; Deng violently cracked down against mass demonstrations by students on Beijing's Tiananmen Square.
- Deng, sidelined by the party's conservative wing, regained power in 1992. With his 'trip to the south' he successfully fought for further economic liberalisation.
- In the golden 1990s (1992–9), the government of President Jiang and Premier Zhu prevented the booming economy from over heating and then successfully protected the country against the Asian financial crisis (1997–8).
- At the beginning of this decade, China has to fend off the global recession. Having joined the WTO in 2001, the country is under pressure to accelerate its internal reforms; the biggest steps are still ahead.

Further sources

Hutchings, G. (2001) *Modern China: A Guide to a Century of Change*, Harvard University Press.
Pomeranz, K. (2001) *The Great Divergence: China, Europe, and the Making of the Modern World Economy*, Princeton, Princeton University Press.
Spence, J.D. (2001) *The Search for Modern China*, W.W. Norton & Company.

1.4. Why do the Chinese negotiate the way they do?

Negotiating with the Chinese is widely feared by western managers: big delegations, people that are hard to tell apart for the western eye, expressionless faces, beating about the bush, demanding the impossible and results agreed upon in the evening being questioned again the next morning.

Still, these extreme cases have become as rare as Chinese bikers wearing Mao suits. After 20 years of political opening, the way the Chinese – in particular the ones living on the developed east coast – negotiate, has become much more transparent and factual.

However, this does not mean that centuries-old strategies passed on from generation to generation have suddenly vanished under western influence. In order to adapt one needs to know why the Chinese behave the way they do.

The most important questions

- What cultural traditions do Chinese negotiators follow?
- What institutional weaknesses influence the Chinese?
- How does this show in negotiations?
- What are powerful tools to achieve one's goals?
- What are the chances for western managers?

Chinese people's approach to negotiations is different from westerners' for two reasons. One lies in their rich cultural heritage: Chinese managers are under the influence of China's centuries-old impressive tradition of strategic thinking. The acquirements of this tradition, however, are complemented by a social shortfall that is just as important: they negotiate differently because they cannot rely on functioning institutions such as a legal system.

Cultural tradition

The cultural differences can well be illustrated by the board games that are most popular in the respective cultures. While westerners play chess, East Asians play 'Go', a game that is said to have been invented in the third millennium BC by the legendary Chinese emperor Yao.

While chess' aim is to incapacitate the enemy and ending the game with 'checkmate' (*shah mata* – the king is dead), Go aims at winning as much territory on the board as possible, encircling the opponent. At the end of a good game of chess, the board will be almost empty, while two good Go players will have filled almost all of the board's 361 reticule points with black and white stones. Put simply, one could say that chess is a game of destruction, while Go is a game of construction.

These different games call for different strategies. The chess player pursues an outright attack on the very heart of his opponents' power – the king. The Go strategist will choose an indirect approach to encircle his enemy. Thus, the Asian game promotes integration, the western game confrontation.

The games and their strategies became popular mostly because they are closely related to the different kinds of war fought in Europe and China. China was always a large country and therefore mainly concerned with protecting its empire from interior uprisings and from central and northern Asian nomads like Tschingis Khan. In contrast, Europe's smaller nations' wars were mainly of expansionist nature, as were those of the young United States.

A Chinese philosopher and war strategist held in high esteem by managers is Sunzi, who in 350 BC, after 1,500 years of Chinese history, summed up Chinese strategic thinking:

> *The art of manoeuvring is difficult. The task is to make a detour into a direct way and a disadvantage into an advantage. For this reason, use the indirect way and detract your enemy by giving him some bait. If he reacts to that, follow him and get there before him (Sunzi Bingfa, Chapter VII).*

The prevalent western strategy has been laid down by his colleague Carl Gott-fried von Clausewitz (1780–1831), a German general also well known by management strategists who probably knew Sunzi's theories: 'The best strategy is to always be quite strong. At first generally, and soon in the decisive spot.' (For Clausewitz, this, 'spot' is very physical: 'Just like the centre of gravity is where most mass is found, and just like a strike against a load's centre of gravity is the most efficient, and like the strongest strike is inflicted in the centre of gravity, it is also in war' (Carl Von Clausewitz, 1990, Vom Kriege, Augsburg, p. 531.)

The different strategies can also be observed in martial arts. The western boxer tries to serve a well-directed blow to the weakest spot he is allowed to aim at, that is the chin or the temples, in order to knock his opponent out. Most Asian martial arts, such as Chinese Gongfu, try to make use of the opponent's strength and turn it against him, unbalancing him in order to disable him.

Dysfunctional institutions

Probably more important than Chinese tactical traditions are the country's often incompetent, unreliable institutions, which force managers to use negotiations to emphasise points that are different from a westerner's concern.

From the very beginning of reform economy, Chinese managers have experienced that they cannot rely on state institutions to guarantee the establishment and implementation of certain rules (see chapter 1.6). Even today, China's businesses have to survive without a functioning legal system. Therefore connections and networks are much more important than in the West (where they are nevertheless known to be very important too). To solve a problem, good contacts to the partner's network can be used to get advice or to put on pressure. A written contract plays a much less important role than good personal relationships. Insisting on a contract in case of conflict is not a smart approach in China, where it is almost impossible to agree on a verbatim implementation of an agreement. Instead of discussing the meaning of an old paragraph that is not appropriate to solve a new problem, Chinese have a more pragmatic approach: if harmony between the business partners is disturbed, they have to find a new balance of harmony. Therefore the order should be: stable, reliable relationship first, a well-founded contract later.

The different cultural traditions and social conditions in negotiation habits can be summarised in opposite word pairs as illustrated below:

West	**China**
Direct	Indirect
Confrontation	Integration
Based on facts	Based on trust
Reassurance through contract	Reassurance through connections
Fixed, comprehensive set of rules	Flexible, complicated set of rules
Negotiations to be closed	Negotiations everlasting

Although both sides insist on the superiority of their method, neither the western nor the Chinese approach can be said to be better or more successful *per se*.

Still, the Chinese undoubtedly have a home advantage. As negotiations are usually about business deals for the Chinese market, the Chinese partners have more clout to determine the style of discussion. They often even force ignorant foreign counterparts to accept their rules by implied argument. The Chinese partner, with the support of powerful state institutions, has a huge market to offer, with western companies queuing up, begging to be let in. If one can convince the Chinese that the opposite is true, that China urgently needs your product that only you can provide, success is within sight.

An even bigger possibility for western companies to succeed lies in the fact that a lot of Chinese enterprises in the transition from state owned enterprise to market economy company sometimes have goals that are less based on economic reasoning. Under certain circumstances, political aims will be even more important than economic ones. Negotiating with that in mind can suddenly open the doors and enable both sides to find a stable, long-term win-win relationship.

However great the pressure may be, or however one might be impressed with Chinese people's negotiation skills, one should not leave one's own tradition further behind than common sense allows. The frequently discussed topic of losing face is a pertinant example regarding the fundamental approach towards Chinese managers. Whether in China or in the West, if possible the counterpart should be spared a 'loss of face'. But if someone repeatedly behaves inappropriately, embarrassing him in front of others can work wonders, especially with Chinese, who tend not to be very sensitive when amongst people they do not know well. In fact, in Chinese tradition one can only lose face in front of friends, not in front of foreigners.

Clever Chinese negotiators have therefore started using the 'losing face' myth to trap their foreign business partners. One Chinese negotiation team left a delegation of European board members flabbergasted when they got up in the middle of a banquet and left the restaurant without further explanation. The westerners racked their brains trying to find out which Chinese custom they had neglected and how they made them lose face. At the next round of talks two days later the Chinese behaved as normal, while the westerners where highly nervous and unsure of themselves. That was exactly what the Chinese had wanted to achieve. In fact, the Europeans had done nothing wrong at all – indeed, a very modern way of putting the Chinese managers at an advantage. This new Chinese negotiations strategy is to make use of the foreigner's perception of Chinese negotiation tradition.

Summary/Recommendations

- Chinese negotiation strategies are becoming more modern, but are still influenced by cultural traditions and dysfunctional institutions.
- Their cultural background teaches Chinese negotiators a more indirect approach in negations.
- Dysfunctional institutions (no rule of law) make the Chinese rely on stable, balanced networks rather then on contracts.
- Western and Chinese strategies are equally strong, but Chinese have a home advantage.
- One should serve the political needs of a Chinese business partner to realise one's own business interest and create a win-win situation.

Further sources

Blackman, C. (1998) *Negotiating China: Case Studies and Strategies*, Australia, Allen & Unwin.
Brahm, L.J. (1998) *Sun Tzu's Art of Negotiating in China*, NAGA Group.
Seligman, S.D. and Trenn, E.J. (1999) *Chinese Business Etiquette: A Guide to Protocol, Manners and Culture in the People's Republic of China*, Warner Books.

1.5. To what extent is corruption undermining the economy?

With China rapidly changing from a state owned economy to a modern market-oriented one, corruption could hardly be avoided. All companies in China were originally run and controlled by cadres and military officials. At the beginning of the reforms, they were the only people who had assets and licences, and naturally they had no intention of giving up their privileges. Therefore, many of them would only support new business if they could expect to make some personal profit, too. The officials would demand anything from bribes to shares, or keep the business inside the family. For businessmen who were faced with having to bribe officials, it was a simple and rational choice: the one who is the first to pay an influential cadre will have the best contacts and first mover advantage. Even nowadays where there are many private entrepreneurs, foreign business is still dependent on cadres when it comes to applying for permission or licences.

The most important questions

- How did corruption support China's growth?
- Why does corruption not support growth any more?
- Why is the government fighting corruption?
- How is the government fighting corruption?
- What kind of corruption are foreign managers faced with?
- How should they deal with this phenomenon?

Corruption supported China's growth

In the first 15 years of market economy reforms since the early 1980s, the government largely ignored the corruption problem. The focus was on setting up market economy operations and boosting the economy in every way possible. Economic planners reckoned that, in the short run, economic growth caused by corruption would succeed economic loss. China had no functioning tax system and the money involved would stay within the Chinese economy anyway. This strategy guaranteed prosperity for cadres and managers of state owned companies who were thus willing to support reforms. High growth fuelled by corruption was better than little, honest growth.

Corruption slows down growth

This strategy only worked for little more than a decade. Then corruption started to strangle the economic boom. Old networks that manoeuvred business around the state and market forces did immense damage to the economy. The government started to worry for the following reasons:

- Chinese money disappeared to foreign accounts and was thus lost for the Chinese economy;
- although a tax system had been set up and the companies were wealthy enough to pay, there was large-scale tax evasion;
- corruption scares away foreign investors who demand a reliable and fair business environment;
- corruption scandals involving high-ranking government officials did a lot of harm to the public image of the Communist Party.

The last two reasons in particular forced the government to react strongly.

Internal pressure

The Chinese public puts a lot of pressure on the government. According to surveys, the Chinese believe that corruption is the country's most urgent problem. Therefore, the Beijing central government feels it has to demonstrate that it is serious about fighting what President Jiang Zemin calls the 'cancer of corruption' on all levels. The leadership is well aware that in order to maintain the Communist Party's credibility it has to do more than just proclaim a general crackdown. The Chinese people demand equality of all citizens in front of the law, including cadres. With stability of the country depending on the party's credibility, security advisers tell the politburo that it would be too risky to ignore the sentiments of the people. President Jiang said with unusual openness: 'If corruption is not controlled, it will soon threaten the government.'

External pressure

With competition for foreign investment on the world market heating up (in the last years China has reaped in 40 billion US dollars per year), the government needs to provide foreigners with a stable environment that encourages them to embrace long-term projects. Looking at China World Bank President James Wolfensohn emphasised: 'An effective legal and judical system is not a luxury, but a central component of a well functioning state.' China promises that as a WTO member it will administer its laws in a 'uniform, impartial and reasonable' and transparent manner. And it will be judged by the international business community on those acknowledgements.

Government measures

For these reasons, the party and the government have started a countrywide crackdown on corruption with a particular focus on its own members and comrades.

- In the 1980s, almost all foreign luxury cars were smuggled into the country. Today, this number has dropped to under 2 percent.
- In 2000, 77-year-old Cheng Kejie, vice-chairman of the National People's Congress, was charged with corruption for embezzling 5 million US dollars and eventually executed. Only State President Jiang Zemin and National People's Congress Chairman Li Peng were senior to him, making Cheng the highest-ranking Chinese official ever to be charged and executed for corruption in the history of the People's Republic.
- Also in 2000, Li Jizhou, vice-minister of the Ministry of State Security was surprisingly charged for accepting millions in bribes. The case against Li is obviously part of a huge smuggling scandal in the coast town of Xiamen in southern China. Cars, oil, mobile phones and computers worth 10 billion US

dollars were brought into the country; at a certain point the smugglers supplied one-fifth of Chinese oil demand. Smuggling kingpin Lai Changxing managed to escape to Canada, where he is currently under house arrest fighting extradition. The most senior administration elite of the city are among the 200 officials who have been charged. The case was widely reported all over the country and several members of the smuggling ring have since been executed.

- Former Bank of China President Wang Xuebing, one of the country's top bankers and a close ally of Premier Zhu Rongji, apparently obstructed an investigation into mismanagement of his bank. The National Audit Office, suspicious of Wang but lacking evidence, managed to have him moved to another post as president of the China Construction Bank in February 2000. In January 2002, with enough evidence collected, Wang was finally dumped and charged. During his term 800 million US dollars disappeared.

Better anti-corruption institutions

As a strong tool in fighting corruption, the National Audit Office was reorganised and made into a powerful institution. It has turned out to be something like an anti-corruption ministry. Premier Zhu Rongji vested it with strong authority, allowing it to implement a security system that makes corruption much harder for managers and politicians. Up to the level of ministers or bank presidents, officials are being checked and their institutions audited as soon as they change their post or retire.

But the corruption police not only target high-profile cases. It has also been successful in the middle ranks. In 2000, more than 130,000 corrupt cadres were charged, 17 of whom were ministers. Around 20,000 illegal or even criminal companies belonging to the military or police were closed down. In smuggling cases alone, customs officers in 2000 uncovered more than 1,000 cases involving goods worth over 600 million US dollars. That year, the National Audit Office audited 55 government institutions, 18 of which turned out to have embezzled a total of 250 million US dollars, while 36 institutions had misused 300 million US dollars. The most corrupt ministry was the Ministry of Water Resources. Instead of using 72 million US dollars for flood-fighting and prevention, former minister Niu Maosheng, an ally to party headliner and former Premier Li Peng, took the funds to build a luxury hotel and office complex. The ministry was just preparing an auction to sell the hotel when the case was discovered.

Only a drop in the ocean?

It is hard to say whether all these cases brought to justice are more than just a drop in the ocean. The rankings of international corruption fighters also say little about the real extent of corruption in China: Transparency International ranks China at 58 out of 99 countries. And even National Audit Office Minister Li Jinhua admits that the most difficult problem is to change the attitude of the people: cadres 'still think that they were very clever, acted smartly and were only caught because they had bad luck. This attitude stems from their experience that public institutions were sometimes not audited for years. They were corrupt without even knowing.' Corruption increases with greater distance from the central government.

Naturally the controllers cannot be everywhere at the same time. 'We execute one to scare a hundred others,' Premier Zhu sums up the strategy. This naturally leads to drastic exaggerations: the vice-mayor of Ningbo in east China was given the death penalty for accepting bribes worth 50,000 US dollars. He was granted a delay of his execution for two years. In a similar case, the general manager of the International Trust and Investment Corporation in Hunan province was sentenced to death for accepting 25,000 US dollars over three years.

The reformers still have to shake off the suspicion of using the anti-corruption campaign for their own political purposes. The National Audit Office's corruption busters, who are under liberal Premier Zhu's direct command, have repeatedly targeted party hardliner and reform opponent Li Peng: executed congress vice-chairman Cheng Kejie, for example, was a close ally to Li. Such cases not only strengthen the reform wing, they are also good publicity. Li is not very popular amongst the Chinese, who not only regarded him as incompetent, but also accuse him of being responsible for the massacre in Tiananmen Square in 1989.

Western business and corruption

Foreign investors claim that the anti-corruption campaign has not yet taken effect and that levels of corruption have not decreased. Paying local authorities for permission and licences is common practice and part of the budget. No case of high bribes involving foreign companies and local officials has been unveiled. Particularly annoying for foreign enterprises are corrupt approval procedures.

- Manufacturers of machines are forced to work with suppliers that deliver bad-quality parts that make the whole product hard to sell.
- Successful telecom companies suddenly had their licences withdrawn because their Chinese partner was allegedly not allowed to sign the co-operation agreement.
- The whole car import business relies on licences that have to be bought on the black market.
- Pharmaceutical companies have to reveal the chemical composition of their products to Chinese authorities. A Chinese copy of the product will often hit the market before the foreign company has received its licence.

Still, corruption in China is a relatively calculable risk, at least when compared to other regions of the world. Western managers in China normally have to make their own arrangements with the phenomenon, as reporting cases to the authorities will usually lead to even bigger trouble. Ripping off foreign companies is seen as a petty crime in China. Western managers therefore have to find a way to make corruption calculable, reasonable and predictable.

How to deal with corruption?

Here are three basic rules China managers count on when having to deal with corruption:

- bribes are only paid for specific services;
- the sum must have an appropriate relation to the service;
- every 'service' is only paid for once and to one person.

Note that bribery is also common practice amongst foreign businesses in China, graft crimes committed in foreign countries can be prosecuted in many western countries. To find out which kind corruption is common in which field of business, it is advisable to confer with colleagues from the same sector and work out some basic standards. Sometimes it is possible to use the press to curb the most serious abuses. Still, it is difficult to keep control over the process.

   At least the Chinese have one advantage. They are too keen to make business to let corruption get in their way. If a manager budgets some time and money for such cases, it is a problem that one can live with, especially as the government promises that its anti-corruption campaigns will show results soon.

Summary/Recommendations

The government has finally declared war on corruption, mainly using the tool of deterrence. The policies are enforced with spectacular arrests and executions. Furthermore, it tries to implement powerful auditing institutions and control tools to curb nepotism and abuse of position. No quick results should be expected. Still, the pressure on the government is rising because the people are now less willing to tolerate the dealings of corrupt cadres.

   Foreign investors demand reliable rules. In every day business, western managers have made their arrangements with corruption, trying to make it calculable and predictable.

Further sources

Lu, X. (2000) *Cadres and Corruption: The Organizational Involution of the Chinese Communist Party* (Studies of the East Asian Institute). Stanford University Press.

Wei-Arthus, H. (2000) *A Study of Authority and Relations in Chinese Governmental Agencies and Institutional Work Units: New-Patrimonialism in Urban Work Units*, Edwin Mellen Press.

1.6. How to do business in a country with a weak rule of law?

'How can you tell an honest judge?'

'He will pay back the bribe to the losing party.'

Unfortunately, this Chinese lawyers' joke is not far from reality. Lacking an established legal system to support social life or the economy, party cadres are free to make highhanded decisions. Adapting to these conditions, western managers and lawyers can still find ways to get their rights and solve conflicts.

The most important questions

- Why does China lack a stable legal system?
- What difference will the WTO make?
- What is the Chinese perception of law?
- How should western managers change their attitude?
- Who can you team up with to get your rights?
- What alternative ways are there to protect your rights?

Lack of law enforcement

The lack of legal security and transparent, impartial and independent courts is currently the main deficiency of the Chinese social system. It is corrupt, unpredictable and incalculable; getting involved in legal conflicts is one of the main fears of Chinese people. Only ten per cent of all judges actually have legal training. Equally, the absence of a functioning legal system is the biggest concern of foreign managers in China. If delivered materials are not being paid for, if the Chinese partner thievishly copies machines, if the joint venture's money trickles away into delinquent accounts, if decisions by the joint venture's western management are not followed, taking the offenders to court usually won't help much. Although China certainly still lacks many of the laws that support social life and economy in the West, the main problem is not the laws themselves, but their implementation. Since the beginning of the decade, there have been an increasing number of cases in which foreign companies get their rights through lawsuits, but these cases are still exceptions. And even if a case is won in court, that does not necessarily imply that the losing party will accept the verdict and act accordingly. The police are not always willing to enforce a verdict.

Increasing pressure

The government has recognised this problem and is trying to solve it in order to make China internationally competitive. In his annual government speech in 2002. Premier Zhu Rongji told the country what he wants to change about the business environment:

The financial order needs to be thoroughly rectified. We need to earnestly investigate and deal with business activities that violate laws and regulations concerning banks, securities and insurance companies, and other financial institutions. We need to resolutely ban illegal financial institutions and illegal financial activities. Financial swindling, illegal fund-raising, manipulation of the securities market, insider trading, and malicious evasion and cancellation of the debts should be investigated and dealt with according to law.

During the WTO negotiations China agreed not to allow provincial governments to pass local laws that do not comply with WTO obligations. Decisions favouring particular parties or interest groups and undermining competition will be illegal. Laws have to be reasonable. Obviously, China can't adopt measures that don't comply with basic principles of fairness. Although WTO membership will increase the pressure, there is no quick solution. China's lawmakers know that they have to synchronise the legal system to keep up with the rapidly changing social reality and the pressure of globalisation.

No legal tradition

Today, Chinese lawmakers try to adapt the European and American legal system because there is no time to develop their own. The country has no legal tradition comparable to that of the West. For decades, cadres' words were law and verdict in one. An independent legal system only existed in theory. Judges were appointed without having studied law. Most of them came from the military – and still do today. While odd in westerners' eyes, Chinese people have been used to this not only since the times of Mao Zedong, but for thousands of years of imperial China.

For 'higher' political reasons, the government still keeps up this tradition. Before the Olympic Council's evaluation committee visited Beijing in early 2001 to gather information about the city's Olympic bid, the government quickly got rid of some eyesores. These included thousands of old houses considered too unrepresentative for the world to see. Residents and shop owners had to leave within days and were moved to the suburbs. Compensations paid by the city government could not buy them a comparable flat. Expecting protests from angry residents, the city warned lawyers and courts not to take on or allow any related cases. Still, more than 100 residents went to local courts. All cases were turned down.

The official position sounds cynical to western ears, but is not altogether unreasonable: a big country like China needs a different balance between individual rights and public interests to western societies. For the time being there is no balance at all; it is the government that makes all decisions.

Adaptation of the western legal system

While China's long-term goal is a system modelled on European abstract norms, the transition period is dominated by American case law.

The last thing China wants is to scare away investors, so it appeases them by granting special treatment to foreign companies who do not have to follow Chinese company law in all cases. While lawmakers try to do their homework and set up a modern legal system (working together with several western countries), law enforcement is much more difficult. It will take decades before law enforcement officers, lawyers and judges all have law school education. Whether they will ever work in an independent legal system is impossible to predict.

Problems of implementation

Chinese judges' everyday work has little to do with interpretation of the law. A western lawyer, who was invited by the Chinese government to give seminars for high-ranking judges, was amazed to find out about their working methods: when given a model case to solve, all of them came up with different verdicts. Asked about the reasons for their decisions, 'experience' was the common answer. Further questions revealed that none of the judges knew the relevant law or had bothered to consult legal texts. 'Experience' in this respect means that judges know what superiors want to hear. If no politically sensitive matters are concerned, right and wrong is often decided on instinct. Sometimes, Chinese judges tend to have a social instead of 'legal' adjudication. A foreign manager involved in a traffic accident with his company car was found innocent in a court hearing. Still he was asked to pay damages to the other party. The argument: the western company has much more money than a Chinese individual. As the amount was moderate, the manager's foreign lawyers advised him to accept the verdict.

But even before courts are approached, the different perceptions of law can be felt. A joint venture contract in China is rather a communicative tool for both sides to sketch out their ideas about the co-operation than a binding document. Therefore contracts between Chinese and western companies should be longer rather than shorter, allowing both sides to use the negotiations to get to know each other. The differences are obvious: western managers want to be prepared for all possible conflicts, while Chinese businessmen insist that it is impossible to predict the future, making it unnecessary to include all eventualities in the contract. Problems should be solved when they occur.

Not being able to rely on contracts and courts, foreign lawyers have found unconventional, creative ways to deal with conflicts. They try to turn the tables on their Chinese partners and use alternative methods to fight for their client's rights. Therefore, when choosing a law firm in China, one should check whether the company is willing and able to look beyond ordinary western legal patterns. Basically, the trick is to find influential groups that can put pressure on the other party.

Pressure through banks

Recently, the state banks have turned out to be good coalition partners. After decades of central planning, they are now forced to work in a competitive market and take more responsibility for the credits they grant. Therefore, it is in their best interests to ensure that their creditors' companies work properly. A well-worded tip-off to the right person can do wonders.

In some particularly serious cases, banks have started to impound the Chinese partner's shares, an option the Chinese law has provided for a long time and that the high court has just recently encouraged banks to make more use of. In that case, the foreign investor might get the chance to buy his Chinese partners' shares. Usually it will be the bank that negotiates the deal.

Political pressure

When trying to use political channels to take influence, the arguments one has to use have changed significantly over the last couple of years. Until recently, the state machinery took pride in the fact that a little turn on the party's disciplinary screws could solve any problem. Today foreign lawyers in the Middle Kingdom use competitiveness as a key argument. In polite letters they write to political institutions, warning them that there might be trouble in store for them if their superiors find out that the respective political body does not implement market reforms as smoothly as demanded. In other cases they threaten that the foreign company might move its operations to another city or province if the situation does not improve. With competition for foreign investment rising, this can be quite a scare for authorities. In any case, it is important to launch one's complaint on the appropriate political level.

Pressure through media

Some lawyers make use of the Chinese press. Media are much more willing to report on economics, business and corruption than on delicate political topics. However, this does not imply that Chinese journalists have the same work ethics as their western counterparts. One has to make sure that the information is used in the intended way and has the desired effect.

Ambition

The young heroes of China's market economy have a weakness that foreign lawyers like to use against them – their ambition. If they repeatedly find stumbling blocks slowing them down, they will soon be willing to negotiate.

This is much more useful than direct confrontation, which can sometimes bring immediate results, but cannot solve the basic problems of a joint venture. The general manager of a British company, for example, reacted to a long-lasting conflict by taking away his Chinese partner's company stamp, which in China is more important than a signature. The Chinese partner was blocked, but without his co-operation the joint venture was unable to go on working as a whole, too. If the situation is unresolvable, lawyers sometimes advise investors to end the co-operation and rebuild the operation from scratch, this time as a wholly owned enterprise or joint venture with a larger foreign share. This might be easier and even cheaper then treading the path of legal battle. In many cases, the Chinese side will not be able to lead the company on its own and might soon be forced to give up.

Image

Sometimes clients are surprised to see their lawyers win cases that wouldn't have a chance if the relevant laws were applied. A foreign company's lawyer complained, in legal terms, to the Bank of China that his client had been ripped off. The bank promptly replied in English, saying there was no breach of Chinese law. Two weeks later, however, the money was transferred to the client's bank account without further comment. In the hard competition of market economy, Chinese companies cannot afford a bad image any more.

Ethics

The Chinese are known to be tough negotiators. Still, ethics can be helpful where law is of no avail. The Chinese have a good feeling for right and wrong. That does not stop them from giving their partners bad deals, but at least there is something like a bad conscience that can be used to get one's rights. If you tell a Chinese entrepreneur that his actions are illegal, that will hardly bother him, as man-oeuvring around the law is seen as clever. But if you tell him that his methods are unfair and a disgrace for serious businessmen, you might be successful.

Summary/Recommendations

China, lacking a legal tradition of its own, has the long-term plan to build up a system modelled on European law. But even after the country's WTO entry, it will be a long time before judges and lawyers have received proper education and developed a modern sense of justice.

For the time being, it is important to know the peculiarities of China's legal system. At the same time, one has to form interest coalitions with influential institutions to get one's rights: Chinese banks want to know the behaviour of their debtors; regional politicians want foreign investment, and young Chinese entrepreneurs do not want to be slowed down.

Further sources

Long, C. (ed.) (2000) *Intellectual Property Rights in Emerging Markets*, The AEI Press.

Wang, Y. (2001) *Chinese Legal Reform* (European Institute of Japanese Studies, East Asian Economics and Business), Routledge.

Zimmerman, J.M. (1999) *China Law Deskbook: A Legal Guide for Foreign-Invested Enterprises*, American Bar Association.

1.7. How important is the WTO for the Chinese economy and western business?

No doubt, China's accession to the World Trade Organisation (WTO) that officially started on 11 December 2001 after 15 years of negotiations is good news for the global economy. This date stands for the international community's hope that China will, in future, follow the rules of international market economy. China has proudly celebrated the accession, seeing it as proof that the world accepts China as a strong, respected country.

The most important questions

- Can the government implement the reforms demanded by the WTO?
- How will WTO membership change China's economy?
- What are the new possibilities for foreign investors?
- What will change for the different industry sectors?

More reform pressure

For China's leaders, the WTO means more than rising exports. In that field, China was on the right track anyway: in January 1992 Korea and Taiwan together exported three times as much as China did; in 2001 China exported goods worth 266 billion US dollars (up 6.8 per cent) more than the two countries combined.

As far as the leaders are concerned, the most important reason for China to join the organisation is to get more power to press ahead with domestic reforms. Finally they have a strong tool to push state enterprises towards modernisation and restructuring, putting them under pressure by pointing at rising foreign competition. Thus, they have the possibility to speed up the reforms when social stability allows for it.

In recent years, the government could only appeal to its managers' understanding. Still, they often avoided to take the necessary steps, either because they lacked know-how, or because of insuperable resistance within the enterprise's staff. Some managers opted for a corrupt quick buck, giving away the company's assets to some close followers and then making off. With controlling and accounting still primitive, they could also get away with forged numbers, weak excuses and playing for time.

The problems that have to be solved urgently were mentioned by Premier Zhu Rongji in front of the 2002 meeting of the National Peoples' Congress (see Chapter 1.2):

> *This year we need to concentrate on increasing our international competitiveness and fulfilling the following tasks on the basis of what has been achieved.*
>
> *First, following the principles of the uniformity of law, nondiscrimination, and openness and transparency, we need to quickly improve the system of foreign-related economic laws and statutes so that they are suitable to domestic conditions and the WTO rules and able to guarantee fair and efficient law enforcement.*
>
> *Second, according to China's commitments in its entry into the WTO, we need to gradually expand the spheres of activity open to foreign businesses. In addition, we need to promptly formulate and revise market access standards for quality, sanitation, epidemic prevention, environmental protection and safety.*
>
> *Third, we need to study, master and fully exercise all the rights that China enjoys as a member of the WTO, and promote and participate in regional economic co-operation.*
>
> *Fourth, we need to study and publicize information about the WTO and its rules, and we need to provide training to public servants, especially leading cadres at and above county and division level and managerial staff in large and medium-sized enterprises by stages and in groups. We need to bring forth, through training, a contingent of people who are well acquainted with the WTO rules and international economic co-operation and trade.*

Since WTO membership the performance of foreign companies pushing into the market has easily brought to light the shortcomings of the local Chinese companies, leaving them with no more excuses. Most of the companies have no stable management structure and, at best, are held together by a charismatic leader.

Only companies that adhere to international profitability criteria will survive. Latecomers stand no chance.

Balancing act

The all-important question for the coming years is: will the government be able to uncompromisingly stay on the reform course? Surely, it cannot let local industry be forced into bankruptcy by foreign players. Mass lay-offs and social instability threaten to push the country to the brink of being governable. Whatever the contracts say, China's WTO policies will be a balancing act. The government has to put as much pressure as necessary on its local enterprises, while at the same time protecting them in order to keep the country competitive. This balancing act will be influenced by two further factors: consumer behaviour and attractiveness for international investors.

The consumers

As the sale of imported goods shows clearly, China's consumers simply hope that WTO membership will lead to falling prices. In the last quarter before the WTO entry, sales dropped sharply. Right afterwards they picked up just as strongly. Should the government not meet the expectations of its people, it risks a slow-down of consumption or even social unrest. This mainly concerns goods that are much more expensive in China than they are in the rest of the world, e.g. computers.

Still, the government is optimistic and expects a rise of 50 billion US dollars in private consumption. International trade is also likely to increase. A research institute of the State Council has estimated that imports and exports will both rise by 1.5 per cent. However, the government won't be able to ignore WTO rules and artificially protect local industries with their high product costs. The political costs would be too high if consumers refused to accept higher prices.

Foreign investors

China has fuelled foreign investors' hope that WTO membership will considerably improve investment conditions. A State Council research institute estimates that WTO membership will raise China's growth by 1 per cent. That means that by 2010, China's GDP should be 34 per cent higher than without the WTO. Foreign investment should double in the next couple of years, reaching 100 billion US dollars. These expectations are impossible to verify because nobody can know-how China would have developed without the WTO. Still, one thing is obvious: expectations are high and the Chinese government will have to work hard to avoid disappointing many foreign investors, because it depends on them to carry through its reforms.

While the Chinese government's scope is limited by these four factors (reform pressure, protection of local industry, consumer behaviour and foreign investors), governments in the US, Europe and Japan have other criteria to measure China's performance as a member of the global business community:

- scope for foreign companies will increase;
- protective taxes on imports will gradually be lowered until they reach international standard;
- rapid elimination of over 300 non-tariff barriers like quotas, licences and local content requirements;
- set-up of a legal system that will guarantee compliance with the rules;
- growing competition between foreign and Chinese companies.

Table 2 WTO influence on different business sectors

| | Market focus | |
	China	Rest of world
Value added in China low	**To China** (Companies which export to China) WTO impact: **MEDIUM**	**From China** (Companies which import form China) WTO impact: **LOW**
Value added in China high	**In China** (Companies that conduct business in China for the Chinese market) WTO impact: **HIGH**	**To China for the world** (Companies that use Chinese cheap resources for export) WTO impact: **MEDIUM**

In order to analyse the impact on the respective business sectors, it is useful to divide the companies according to their business scope. Depending on where the produce goes, WTO entry will have different strategic consequences. Companies that manufacture their products in China and have to import parts for that reason will benefit much more from WTO entry than companies that produce in China for the world market, as illustrated in Table 2.

Western managers are well advised to be careful when analysing the impact of the WTO on their respective businesses. Japan's WTO entry has shown that membership itself is not enough to bring a country under the control of international regulations. For years Japan refused to give foreign businesses the contractually agreed access to the local market. China has already made it clear that it has no intention of letting go of any decision-making power. After having reached agreements with the US in November 1994 and the European Union, China suddenly slowed down the speed of negotiations over the last details. Thus the government won time to implement further reforms.

Influence of WTO entry on specific industry sectors

Paper

Over 2,000 years ago, the Chinese invented paper. Back then it was a valuable material, available to the rich and powerful only. Today, every Chinese uses an average 25 kilos a year. Although that is only half the worldwide average, consumption is rising rapidly. By 2010, China will be the world's biggest paper consumer. Many products need high-quality paper, be it for newspapers printed for a billion readers or for China's 350 million smokers. Currently, China is unable to feed its own demand. On the one hand, China lacks technology: many factories are small and work with old machines that cause serious environmental pollution. On the other hand, China lacks natural reserves: with only 3.9 percent of China is covered with forests, wood for better-quality paper has to be imported. More than half of China's paper is produced using straw or reed. Most of the paper imports come from international paper heavyweights such as Scandinavia, Indonesia, Japan or Korea. Although the government offers favourable conditions to foreign investors, industry sources do not regard the impact of WTO as very strong.

Clothing/Shoes

Western managers in the clothing industry are sceptical: 'If the WTO forces the Chinese government to get rid of import or export quotas, it will come up with a new tax on needles to make up for it.' China has good reasons to make life difficult for foreign clothing companies. The efficiency of state owned enterprises that produce around 60 per cent of export textiles, still lags behind their western competitors. In 2001 1.2 million workers were laid off. But more and more Chinese companies have discovered that they can earn more with quality garments than with cheap, low-quality produce. The WTO will accelerate this trend: in the next five years, production is expected to double, and by 2003 growth will have reached 20 per cent.

China is the world's biggest producer of shoes, and that is not only because 1.3 billion pairs of feet walk around the country. Having produced 1.6 billion pairs in 2001, China has a world market share of 40 per cent. WTO entry means more work for China's shoemakers. As soon as prices for the expensive imported raw materials fall, production cost will also fall and increase China's competitiveness. Big international shoe companies, who currently have their shoes sewn in several different countries, eyeing China, will plan to move all production to one country.

Plastics/Chemicals

Chinese construction sites currently need 2 million tons of plastics each year. However, only 0.5 per cent of that is locally produced. Although demand for China's huge infrastructure projects grows by 25 per cent each year, local production can only come up with a growth rate of 10 per cent. Therefore, China's plastics industry heavily depends on foreign companies. More than 50 per cent of plastic products are imported, mainly from neighbouring Asian countries. Western global players such as Bayer or BASF are currently making billion US dollar investments.

China's chemical industry faces the same problem. Still, the industry is developing quickly. Foreign business insiders expect hard competition from Chinese companies. Many life science products can already be produced by Chinese enterprises; the niche for foreign companies again lies in up-market products.

China has used a clever import substitution policy to attract foreign companies, who come up with 35 per cent of the sector's investment. Although foreign-produced goods are far superior in quality, they cannot match the Chinese for price. Tax benefits for foreign companies will slowly be phased out. Foreign businessmen see the WTO as a means to make the sector more transparent. Still, the government will have ways and means to interfere.

Cars

If people in the West want to drive an Audi A6 limousine, it will cost them 50,000 US dollars. The Chinese have to come up with 100,000 US dollars for an imported Audi. If that is too much, they can settle for a locally produced A6, which comes for 70,000 US dollars and is inferior in quality.

High tariffs, quotas and a bad environment for car production give foreign car producers a hard time. Production costs are high for two reasons: western carmakers only produce relatively small numbers and they have to buy a certain percentage of parts from local suppliers at horrendous prices. Quality is below and costs above world market standards.

Despite several ambitious tries, China has not succeeded in producing its own quality cars. China has an annual production capacity of 2 million cars, but only 1 million were produced in 2002. However, 10 million potential buyers are in the queue. Therefore, China depends on foreign imports and know-how.

The WTO is forcing China to lift tariff barriers and reduce tax, which will be of benefit to foreign companies. Still, tough competition is to be expected. Several international carmakers are fighting for the market for small and family cars. It is possible that China will produce these cars itself.

Toys

China is the world's biggest producer of toys: 30,000 different kinds are available, covering a quarter of the world market and generating an export turnover of 5.1 billion US dollars a year. Currently, 97 per cent of exports are soft-toys and dolls of low quality. Because the low-price market is more or less saturated and labour cost in other Southeast Asian countries is lower than in China, the country has to start technical modernisation of its toy industry. By 2004 China hopes to have 6,000 companies, half of them foreign-owned, that have reached international standard. The WTO will be of help: tariffs will disappear and access to international markets will become easier; imports of raw materials will get cheaper and more foreign companies will be able to invest.

China will also open its doors to import of foreign toys, which are seen as much more educational. Chinese families invest 30 per cent of their income in the education of their 'little emperors', as they call their indulged single children. With China's 300 million kids, this adds up to a market potential of 6 billion US dollars. Currently, Chinese toys only make up 1 billion US dollars.

Household goods

Gone are times when a bicycle, a radio, a watch and a sewing machine were the four symbols of wealth. Rising living standards have lead to an increase in the purchase of household goods, many of which are imported. While imports of finished products are on the decline, demand for components such as compressors for refrigerators is rising, allowing China to produce high-quality products. Ten big companies, the most prominent being Haier, control the local market and are now targeting the rest of the world. Every second fan and one in five air-conditioners comes from China. Therefore, Chinese companies welcome the WTO. Although imports will rise and many old state enterprises will not be able to withstand the pressure, consumers can look forward to falling prices as components get cheaper and more investment flows into China.

Agriculture

The WTO agreements for the agricultural sector were the last to be reached, showing how strongly the accession to the world trade body is going to affect China's farming industry. Today, prices for domestic wheat, soya beans, corn and oil are 20–50 per cent above international market prices. With Chinese production costs still rising, imports can be expected to increase substantially. Tariffs, quotas, licence requirements and state trading still protect China's farmers. But all quotas will eventually be turned into tariffs that will gradually be reduced until they reach an average 14.5 per cent by 2005, down from 31.5 per cent today.

The Chinese government will try to give its 600 million farmers maximum protection because of the huge potential of social instability. Fifty million farmers live below the poverty line (income 60 US dollars per year), and not all of them will be able to shift to more profitable, labour-intensive products such as flowers, plants, fruits and vegetables. This is where China has a huge, mostly untapped, export potential.

Distribution, retail, wholesale, trading, after-sales services

Today, there are harsh restrictions on foreign investment in wholesale, retail and after-sales service. Only a small number of big cities are open to foreign distributors, but even here, business scope is limited. The application process is time consuming and unpredictable. The reason for this discrimination is obvious: China's logistical sector is highly inefficient; damage rate is high and payment unreliable. WTO regulations will force the government to liberalise the sector, putting local companies under extreme pressure. For most products, restriction on distribution services will be phased out by 2004. But although they might have superior know-how and technology, foreign enterprises will have a hard time competing with Chinese connections and networks.

Telecommunication

China is the biggest telecommunication market in the world. Currently, it has 180 million fixed lines and 140 million mobile phone users. In 2001, the industry turned over 32 billion US dollars; double digit growth is predicted for the next couple of years. These numbers cannot disguise the fact that China's telecom system is far from compliant with the WTO agreement. The four big players (China Telecom, China Mobile, China Unicom, China Netcom) are all state owned. The government tries to stimulate competition between them, but this has nothing to do with fair competition.

The WTO will play an important role in opening up the sector, which has long been seeking foreign management know-how, technology and capital. Within a few years, foreign companies can take 49 percent stakes in telecom companies. Global players are already queuing up: Siemens has teamed up with a Chinese partner to develop its own third-generation telecom standard TD-SCDMA. Corporations like Telstra, AT & T and Vodafone have formed strategic alliances with Chinese partners.

Banking and leasing

More than 500 international banks have set up offices in China. For the time being, their business scope is reduced to representation, risk management and foreign exchange services for foreign companies and other small businesses, with their assets making up only 3 percent of China's total bank assets. But they are preparing for the moment when regulations allow them to start 'real business' in Chinese currency. For this they will have to wait until 2006, and even then, foreign banks do not expect to get a market share bigger than 1.5 per cent in the near future. The reason for China's reluctance to speed up the opening of the sector is obvious: the country first wants to modernise its own state banks. These still drag along about 30–50 per cent of bad loans from the times of central planning and the speculative property project throughout the mid-and early 1990s. The state has set up asset management companies to relieve the banks from the non-performing loans. The General Audit estimates that two of the country's big four banks, the Industrial and Commercial Bank of China and the China Construction Bank have each lost 1.2 billion US dollars through illegal activities. Most of the banks are technically insolvent. But as long as they are state owned banks and the government is able to take care of the debts there is no existential harm for the whole economy.

Securities

The securities market has so far been the most heavily guarded sanctum of modern Chinese economy (see chapter 1.8). Although B-shares, traded in US dollars, are available to foreigners, China will make sure that it stays invulnerable to international speculators. Though growing quickly, the stock market is still small in size. But most important of all, neither the companies nor the trading comply with international transparency standards. Although an independent China Securities Regulatory Commission has been set up, government influence is still strong and law enforcement lax. Therefore, China seeks to first restructure its own weak system before it can allow foreign financial institutions full entry. For the time being, foreign enterprises are restricted to minority joint ventures that engage in fund management, debt restructuring, asset management and financial advising.

Insurance

Formerly, a single state owned company monopolised the whole insurance sector. In the meantime, more than 200 international insurers have set up offices in China, which has an insurance market of an estimated 15 billion US dollars, with several European and American insurers already holding licences. By 2003, all customers will be available to foreign insurers, and according to the WTO agreement, licences will be awarded solely on the basis of prudential criteria, with no quantitative limits on the number of licences issued. Being under extreme pressure to set up a working social system, the government has a special interest in life insurances and has been trying to attract the know-how and financial strength of foreign insurers. Ownership for life insurance will be permitted to 50 per cent, while reinsurance has been fully opened to 100 per cent ownership. This shows that the government follows a very aggressive strategy towards local companies: they enjoy less protection from foreign competition than banks. But insurers are still sceptical, remembering that in Japan, a long-time WTO member, they haven't reached more than 7 per cent market share.

Summary

The WTO will make it easier for foreign enterprises to enter the Chinese market. However, the speed of the opening-up depends on four factors that the Chinese government has to consider:

- useful reform pressure through a rising number of foreign enterprises;
- protection of local industry;
- healthy consumer behaviour through falling prices;
- international competitiveness for foreign investors.

Examples such as Japan and South Korea suggest that the contract will hardly be followed in every detail – generally at a disadvantage to foreign companies.

Further sources

Baker & McKenzie (2002) *Guide to China & the WTO*, HK, Asia Information Associates Limited.

Panitchpakdi, S. and Clifford, M. (2002) *China and the WTO: Changing China, Changing World Trade*, John Wiley & Sons.

1.8. What role does the stock market play in China's economic development?

Many analysts underestimate the trade volume of China's stock markets and the role it plays in the country's economy. In the 1920s and 30s, Shanghai already had the world's third largest stock exchange after New York and London. And it is well on the way to regaining that position. If you add up the market capitalisation of the partner marketplaces of Shanghai and Shenzhen, China is already the number three in Asia with a market capitalisation of 580 billion US dollars in 2001. Only Japan's Nikkei Index and Hong Kong's Hang Seng are stronger. But it has to be taken into consideration that about 30 per cent of the stocks traded in Hong Kong are Chinese and will in future probably be traded in China as well.

The most important questions

- What are the problems of China's stock market?
- How strong is the reform pressure on the government?
- How is the government cleaning up the stock market?
- Why is a modern stock market important for foreign companies?

China's stock market has a huge potential. Although at about 40 per cent China has one of the highest saving rates in the world (in 2000), only 4 per cent of Chinese citizens own shares. At the moment, the stock market has an annual growth of 12 per cent, accelerating quickly.

Present problems

But there are several good reasons why the Chinese stock market is only slowly winning the attention of investors.

- Of all listed companies 90 per cent are state owned enterprises; 62 per cent of all stocks belong to the government. Even, the English language party mouthpiece *China Daily* complains: 'The management of listed companies is bad because the state holds the majority.'
- Foreign company's stocks are still not being traded in China. Only a very small amount of shares, so-called B-shares, are available to foreigners and traded in US dollars.
- The daily B-share turnover of 20–60 million US dollars is relatively small.

- Few stocks compete for a lot of capital. In such a so-called liquidity-managed market, single stocks are not too closely analysed, because high turnover has to be achieved anyway.
- Reliable rules, such as the ban of insider trading, are still not the standard for Chinese traders. Dealers arrange prices; funds trade stocks back and forth to raise the trade volume and details of major sales are agreed on in bathhouses.
- Although some progress has been made, most companies still lack modern management.
- Transparency is insufficient. The accounting standards do not give a realistic picture of the companies. The reason: most of today's managers grew up to meet the demands of the central planning commission.

A short overview of the last rallies shows even better, what is still going wrong on the Chinese market:

Red-chip rally (1997)

The first impressive rally of Chinese stocks happened on the Hong Kong stock market. Shares of mainland Chinese companies traded in Hong Kong are called 'red-chips'. They even have their own index, the so-called Red-Chip Index. The listed companies are usually subsidiary companies of big state owned enterprises. They had their first boom in 1997, shortly before the crown colony was handed back to the People's Republic. High hopes for the companies' good political connections sent share prices soaring. Conglomerate China Enterprise's IPO, for example, was oversubscribed 1,300 times; however, the company was not a big success, showing a poor performance and proving that government relations alone do not make a successful company.

WTO rally (1999)

The mainland's stock market had its first big rally at the change of the millennium, shortly after dramatic negotiations led to agreements with the United States that finally put China on track for WTO membership. The general expectation that this would benefit the economy was enough to start the rally, which gained an extra momentum through the New York Nasdaq rally. But it was like betting on a horse you don't know just because the climate is good for fast running.

Market liberalisation rally

In February 2001, China's stock market experienced another big upturn when the government allowed Chinese citizens to buy B-shares (traded in US dollars) that were previously only available to foreigners. Thus the government successfully raised the trade volume because Chinese people rushed to invest their savings on the stock market. In March of that year, the 35 billion US dollar-strong B-share market had already by far exceeded the A-shares, although ten times as many companies are listed there. While the rest of the world was falling head on into a recession, China's boom just wouldn't stop. The Chinese, who still have few investment options, didn't worry when P/E rates of 15 to 20 suddenly rose to 50, although 90 per cent of listed companies belong to traditional industries that usually don't perform exciting growth leaps. While inexperienced investors had already spent an estimated 1 billion US dollars on the stock market, many foreign investors – mostly professionals – found it too risky. Before China opened the B-share market for locals, 30 per cent of these stocks were in the hands of foreigners. This rate has dropped to 10 per cent. Where the Chinese are ready to burn themselves, foreigners leave the casinos.

WTO rally (2001)

In May 2001, another tide of success rolled over the country, after China and the European Union had solved the final issues for China's WTO accession. About 20 local insurance companies, which had been promised months ago they would be allowed to set up China stock funds, got more space through new regulations, which further fuelled the rally. Until now, only 3.5 per cent of insurance companies' assets were invested in stocks, making up for around 1 per cent of stock market capitalisation. Social security and pension funds were also set up.

Reform pressure

What kind of pressure forces the government to quickly reform the stock market? There are three reasons:

- The government needs a booming stock market to finance China's social and economic reforms. A reliable growth in the stock market stabilises China.
- The degree of the stock market transparency and profitability will be an important indicator for foreign analysts to evaluate the development of the Chinese economy in the coming years.
- Chinese people save about 40 per cent of their income, adding up to total savings of 850 billion US dollars. The government wants to see this capital invested on the stock market.

Importance for foreign investors

The stock market will be of growing importance for foreign enterprises: share offerings will provide them with a new alternative to raise local currency capital. Currently, they can only do so through joint ventures. Stock offerings will make them less dependent on underdeveloped Chinese state banks or western banks with subsidiaries in China, who can only offer Renminbi loans with less favourable conditions. But what is even more interesting is that western enterprises will be able to buy their way into profitable state owned enterprises, or they can buy out their Chinese joint venture partners. Such Chinese companies under new western leadership will be the snips for western investors. These options, however, will only become relevant when the IPO market is liberalised.

Cleaning up

In 2001, after four years of successive losses, Shanghai Narcissus Electric Appliances had the dubious honour of being the first company to be banned from the stock market by the China Security Regulatory Commission (SRC). This was seen as a warning that showed the central government's determination to put an end to messy stock trading.

The reform pressure on entrepreneurs should not be underestimated. Those who are too slow to comply with international standards of transparency will not stand the pressure of competition. Multinationals are all ready to list their Chinese subsidiaries and will steal the show from local corporations.

Companies that are too slow in reforming themselves are the shelf-warmers of old times and the government can only sell them at bargain prices. Sooner or later, Chinese investors will see that a well-managed company might be slower developing at the beginning, but will soon be far superior to the alleged snips. The China Securities Regulatory Commission has already been restructured under the guidance of Hong Kong experts. Progressive opening of the market is hoped to get China's stock market used to international standards. Certain amounts of A-shares, which are currently reserved for local investors, will be made available to so-called 'qualified foreign investors', which are common for example on the Taiwanese or Indian stock exchanges. Foreign brokerages will soon be allowed to trade in Shanghai and Shenzhen. Both markets will be unified to form one big trading place.

Under such pressure, the China Securities Regulatory Commission has set itself the goal to push government-owned shares under 12 per cent. Some government shares will probably be used to set up a social security fund. The most important sign, however, is the government's determination to crack down on corruption. Market manipulation is often exposed in state media. Courts have started correcting the government's licensing procedures. Foreign brokerages and investment banks are all set to enter the Chinese market. In Shanghai in 2001, 30 of them were working out strategies for the time when China opens up its markets. It will take until the middle of this decade for the market to be at international level.

Summary/Recommendations

The Chinese stock market is not far away from reaching international standard and is therefore becoming more and more interesting for investors. Still, the government urgently needs a modern stock market to finance the reforms. Recently, quite a number of regulations and control organs were established to get the stock market on the right track. Foreign enterprises will then have new possibilities to buy themselves into Chinese companies or use the stock market to get local currency capital.

Further sources

Heilmann, S. and Gottwald, J. (2002) *Der chinesische Aktienmarkt*, Mitteilungen des Instituts für Asienkunde, Hamburg.
Thomas, W.A. (2001) *Western Capitalism in China: A History of the Shanghai Stock Exchange*, Ashgate.
Yao, C. (1998) *Stock Market and Futures Market in the People's Republic of China*, Oxford University Press.

1.9. How will the Internet change China?

'Chinese will be the No 1 language on the World Wide Web by 2007' is the slogan of a leading international consulting agency's worldwide advertising campaign. The ad probably overestimates the expansion of the Chinese language. At the beginning of the decade, 8.8 per cent of all Internet users spoke Chinese, compared to 57 per cent of native English speakers (2001).

But this does not mean that the potential of China's cyber-world is small. At the end of 2001, the United States had more than three times as many users as China (119 million and 33.7 million respectively). But with 46 per cent of Americans already online, US growth is slow, while China at 2.8 per cent is still at the beginning of its boom. Furthermore, the Internet's impact on social development is much stronger in China than in western countries.

The most important questions

- Why could the Internet have a stronger impact on China than on western countries?
- How does this impact show?
- What possibilities does the Internet offer for western companies?
- How does the government regulate the Internet?

Even during the 2001 global cyber slump, China's Internet usage grew by 50 per cent. Traditional infrastructure is still underdeveloped: Therefore, be it for the modernisation of state owned enterprises, cross-linking companies (B2B) or knowledge transfer, the Internet is a relatively easy way to build up new systems, skipping traditional technologies used in developed countries.

Modernisation of state owned enterprises

The Internet offers astonishing solutions for the reforms of state owned enterprises (SOE). While latest technology is only slowly being implemented in western countries because many companies are used to working with older, expensive systems like SAP, new Internet solutions are without competition in China. The catchword is EDI-Web – electronic data interchange.

EDI-Web needs nothing but a computer and Internet access to connect a company with all its suppliers, distributors and different departments. For example suppliers can handle the whole business process from order to settlement through a website instead of having to use an expensive direct line or a special software. Joint venture partners can synchronise their accounting without sitting in the same office.

At the centre of the system is a main server that all users can access via Internet. With most of China's hinterland having stable Internet connections, this poses no problem. The advantage: the software does not need laborious installation in every single company, and the computers do not break down because of misuse or lack of service. Little training is needed, with software and hardware centrally maintained; costs for every single company are low. For China's state owned enterprises this technology could mean a breakthrough because it only takes a relatively small investment to catch up with international IT standards, making them more competitive.

B2B

Chinese business to business benefits from the country's huge demand for the exchange of goods. In order to get political backing and easy market access, most B2B forums have forged alliances with influential state institutions. For example, Guangzhou-based Hong Kong Internet company Chinaproducts.com has teamed up with the powerful China Council for the Promotion of International Trade (CCPIT), and Meet.China.com has an alliance with the Ministry of Information Industry. However, the web is useful for making first contact, maintaining established business ties, and to a certain degree for finding new clients. Getting to know each other well on the web is impossible, though, as nobody will order 200,000 drilling machines without knowing the factory and its manager.

B2C

Although China's potential for the business to consumer sector is huge, there are too many problems that still have to be solved. Credit card payment is difficult. Fearing that someone else might hack into their bank account, many users refuse to reveal their card number. And after decades of inferior products of unreliable quality, Chinese customers are still not used to buying something they haven't seen and checked. Before B2C really takes off in China, consumer habits will have to change.

Learning

The Chinese are eager to acquire international know-how and are willing to invest a lot of time and money. As many regions of the country still lack facilities for advanced or professional training, the Internet is a good option. According to a 2001 survey conducted by Hong Kong-based Internet Network Information Center, 25 per cent of Chinese users claim that they mainly use the Internet for educational reasons. Already there are more than 200 online schools, including numerous business schools. Fifty per cent of users believe that online schools are the greatest opportunity the Internet has to offer. People use spare time in the office to get an extra degree or qualification, with some employers even willing to pay for it. Furthermore, the Internet is a very useful tool for acquiring traditional knowledge sources: 46 per cent of users say they want to use the web to purchase books or magazines online. At 50 per cent, only computer products get a higher rating.

Political regulations

In 1994, the Chinese leadership realised it had run into a dilemma with the fast-growing Internet: it wanted to make the best economic use of efficient mass communication systems, while at the same time not relinquishing the information monopoly. China's politicians were aware of this conflict of interests, but did not want to sacrifice one for the other. Eventually the state council passed control regulations in 1996 that it was hoped would guarantee a 'healthy development' in the information age.

- All networks and their 20,000 users had to register again.
- Choosing a wording that countries without a strong legal system like to use as an all-purpose weapon for interference, the regulations made it clear that the government would not tolerate any activities that 'endanger state security or state secrets'.

Six months later sites containing 'critical content' were blocked: US media, Chinese language information on Taiwan, China-critical news sites from Hong Kong, dissidents' sites and pornography. Never before has a state tried practising such all-round control of the Net. But such tight control was hard to keep up for any length of time. The Net grows at such a speed that, in the long

run, only random checks will be practicable. Today, almost every village has a telephone line and Internet access.

Thus, a big Internet crackdown in 2001 was of limited success. User information has to be saved for 60 days. Systematic surveillance of China's 33.7 million users and all e-mails is impossible. The government still blocks websites, but its firewalls are not able to fend off the avalanche of new pages. Internet cafés that lack an official registration are shut down but soon reopen somewhere else. Chat-rooms have become the country's main forum for occasional criticism of the government, discussing corruption cases. Popular Internet portals sometimes even publish foreign news, which is almost impossible for newspapers.

The Internet industry regards these crackdowns as warnings rather than a real constraint on personal freedom. Total control of the Internet is impossible, and powerful institutions such as China's official news agency Xinhua have an interest in liberalising information policies. They want to make money out of knowledge and information transfer, which is only possible if they can quickly and independently report on business developments.

Three factors suggest that China could be the country that will be most influenced and changed by the Internet. In many areas, China lacks traditional infrastructure, making it easier to implement modern technology; China is so big, that the Internet is probably the only way of effectively organising data transfer; and, most importantly, China not only has high demand, but the market is booming and direct foreign investment is high, allowing China to implement and develop new solutions.

Summary/Recommendations

The Internet could have a stronger impact on China's society and economy than on western countries because the country lacks traditional infrastructure. For outdated companies, EDI-web solutions are a cheap and effective way to reach modern standards. Because of a general lack of educational institutions, the Internet is used by many Chinese to get professional training. B2B is a useful way to manage established business relations. The B2C sector is troubled by underdeveloped payment methods and the Chinese habit of not buying things one has not seen.

Further sources

Baker & McKenzie (2001) *China and the Internet: Essential Legislation*, Asia Information Associates Limited. China management handbook – a practical question & answer guide.

Li, G. and Wong, E. (2001) *The Rise of Digital China: Investing in China's New Economy*, China Books and Periodicals.

Ling, N.S. and Wong, J. (2001) *China's Emerging New Economy: The Internet and E-Commerce*, World Scientific Pub. Co.

1.10. Will tensions between Taiwan and the People's Republic increase?

China has been divided since 1949. During the civil war following the end of Japanese occupation during World War II, the communists managed to drive Jiang Jieshi's (Chiang Kai-shek) republican forces off the mainland. The *Guomindang* army was accompanied by most of China's business elite. Other's fled to the British crown colony of Hong Kong. While mainland China suffered under Mao's collectivisation experiments and was economically crippled until the 1980s, medium-sized industries brought Taiwan an unprecedented boom.

Today, Taiwan's computer and semiconductor industry has made the island an important player in the global economy. With only 2 per cent of the mainland's population, it generates a GDP of 309 billion US dollars – one-third of the People's Republic's. Taiwan has foreign reserves of 80 billion US dollars, 40 per cent of what China has in its treasure trove.

Most countries followed the example of the United States, who severed their diplomatic ties with Taiwan in 1972 in favour of China with its huge market and strong political standing. Regarded as a break-away and rebel province by China, Taiwan has been fighting for its political survival and independence ever since. There are almost no direct connections between the island and the mainland.

The most important features
- Why is the possibility of a war not very high?
- Which factors keep the two partners at bay?
- Under what conditions will the situation relax?
- What role does economic development play?

The relationship between Taiwan and China is determined by two factors that point in opposite directions and are getting ever harder to harmonise. The young generation of the 23 million Taiwanese show little interest in their ancestors and relatives on the mainland. They feel independent and have a Taiwanese identity. But the economies on both sides of the Taiwan Strait are growing together and have developed a strong dependency on one another. Despite the dividing aspects it is likely that the relationship could be stable for the next couple of years. There are several reasons.

The role of the United States

The United States plays the major role in maintaining this stability. The superpower wants to underpin its influence in the region and follows a simple strategy. In the official, diplomatic arena they stand by China with its huge economic potential, but backstage they grant Taiwan military assistance.

The US and Japan have no interest in any kind of reunification between Taiwan and China, which would give China a much stronger political and economic position not only in Asia Pacific. On the other hand, the US does not support a Taiwanese declaration of independence, which would lead to regional destabilisation and a restructuring of power. When former Taiwanese president Lee Teng-hui caused strong protests from Beijing in the late 1990s by talking about a *de facto* state-to-state relationship between Taiwan and the mainland, Washington refused him the hoped for support. Obviously the US wants to avoid China having its back up against the walls. US President diplomatically Clinton and Bush Jr even supported the 'three nos': no support for Taiwan's entry into the UN; no independence; and no entry into international organisations that demand national status.

But as long as the present power constellation is stable, strategic analysts see no reason for concern that the aggressive rhetoric and ritualised provocations from both sides could lead to a war. In February 2002, exactly 30 years after Richard Nixon's historic China visit, US President George W. Bush called on both sides to deepen their dialogue.

Possible loss of face for China

The more China is integrated into the global community, the higher the political and economic price China would have to pay for a sudden military attack on Taiwan. Acceptance of China as a reliable trade partner would suffer for years and western countries would impose heavy sanctions. Unless China is threatened by internal collapse and a war against a foreign enemy is the government's last chance to stabilise the country, the risks and costs of an attack on Taiwan already seem too high.

Economic approach

Meanwhile, the Taiwan boom seems to have reached its limit. The high-tech island has become too small and too expensive, so that Taiwanese companies now move their investment to the mainland. With Taiwan having modern technology and know-how, and the mainland having a huge market and cheap labour, the two parts of China complement one another well. The exodus to the mainland has reached quite a respectable size. In 2000, Taiwanese investment in China doubled to 2.6 billion US dollars. Consequently the growth of Taiwanese enterprises, in particular the big ones, lies in China. WTO membership of both China and Taiwan will invigorate this trend. Already, 300,000 Taiwanese live in Shanghai. The heir to Formosa Plastics, the biggest Taiwanese company, runs a joint venture with a company run by the son of China's President Jiang Zemin. With the help of Taiwanese companies, China has already outrun Taiwan as the world's biggest producer of IT products and will soon overtake Japan. Then only the US is bigger.

And it is not only production that moves to China for the sake of cheap labour. Boasting many qualified scientists that work for salaries far below that of their Taiwanese or western colleagues, China has also become an attractive base for the research and development departments of Taiwan's industries. With a population of only 23 million, Taiwan has a lack of young people. Schools and universities are not well known for promoting creativity and innovation. And compared to Shanghai, Taiwan's infrastructure is quite old fashioned. In this light, political confrontation seems to be a secondary problem. The latest economic crisis has accelerated the inevitable: Taiwan and China have moved closer together. However, there are still foreign enterprises that size up their investment in Taiwan and in return are punished by the Chinese by being barred from entering the Chinese market.

Most probably there will be a gradual change over the next few years. Politically Taiwan will neither be independent nor part of the People's Republic. Economically, the two Chinas will grow together. Taiwan's economic planners are already developing concepts to deal with this new situation.

Centre for regional headquarters

With its geographical location between Shanghai, Hong Kong, Seoul, Manila and Tokyo and its high living standard, Taibei is the ideal city for multinational companies' regional headquarters. However, western managers agree that it would only be practicable to move to Taibei if there was a direct connection to the mainland. Currently, flights between Taibei and Beijing are one-day trips, stopping over in Hong Kong where one has to change plane. Taibei's tough stance (no direct links) is starting to waver. Direct ship connections could run through one of Taiwan's off-shore ports. Taiwanese travellers have repeatedly succeeded in making their way from the small island of Matzu to the Chinese port of Xiamen. Airlines are getting ready for the next step. Taiwan's China Airlines has bought a 25 per cent stake in the cargo daughter of Shanghai's China Eastern Airlines.

Centre of innovation

China and Taiwan will probably see less and less sense in economic competition. Taiwan will have to act like a company that tries to stay first class in some selected technological fields. Thus, Taiwan will not be competing with China any more, a fight the small island would have no chance of winning anyway.

Summary/Recommendations

For western companies, the troubled relationship between Taiwan and China will gradually cease to be a problem. Political tension will ease off and economic co-operation will grow. The taboo of direct connections won't hold very long. Taiwan and China will grow together and form one big economic zone. Politically, the status quo is likely to be held.

Further sources

Kemenade, W. van, and Webb, D. (Translator) (1998) *China, Hong Kong, Taiwan, Inc.*, Vintage.
McBeath, G.A. (1998) *Wealth and Freedom : Taiwan's New Political Economy*, Ashgate.
Tsai, I. (2002) *A New Era in Cross-Strait Relations? Taiwan and China in the WTO*, January, Washington, DC, The Heritage Foundation.

1.11. Is the gap between rich and poor getting wider?

In the past 20 years, China has experienced incredible growth. While per capita income was only 120 US dollars in 1980, it increased to 840 US dollars by the turn of the millennium. According to government statistics, 3 per cent of Chinese live in poverty today, down from 30 per cent in 1980. The growth has mainly been generated by Deng Xiaoping's opening policy of the early 1980. After the disasters of the Maoist era and the Cultural Revolution, his main goal was to stabilise the country politically and economically.

Pragmatic politics took over from ideological social experiments. Deng opened the country towards the western way of modernisation by gradually introducing a market economy and inviting foreign investors. The Chinese had to learn to fight for their own prosperity instead of relying on the state to provide them with everything. 'Who cares whether the cat is black or white, as long as it catches mice it's a good cat,' was Deng's credo that shocked communist hardliners. After two decades of Maoism, this sentence sounded quite sensational to Chinese ears. Critics warned of social injustice and saw Deng's policies as a betrayal of the communist ideal of equality, but Deng wouldn't listen to them. Still, he knew very well that a market economy and competition would not result in better conditions for everyone at the same time. Social injustice was inevitable, but convinced that it was the only way to revive the economy Deng, the pragmatic communist, coined the liberal phrase: 'Let some get rich first.'

The most important questions

- Is the gap between rich and poor increasing despite constant high growth?
- Why is the country still stable?
- How predictable are future social tensions?
- Which are the groups that most depend on social stability?
- What measures does the government take?
- Which role do the young urban elite play?

Less poverty

Deng's economic policies brought to an end a turbulent century and gave China two decades of social stability and economic growth. Today, China's economic situation is better than ever before. At 840 US dollars, average per capita income is still modest by international standards, but only few regions still suffer real poverty. The Human Development Index has reached 70.1 per cent and GINI currently stands at 40.30. The social situation still is mostly stable.

Wider gap

Nevertheless the gap between rich and poor is getting wider and wider. While the urban elite enjoy living standards quite similar to that of their western counterparts, many of China's 800 million peasants are still poor, even if they are now better off than they used to be. In 2000, peasants' per capita income grew by 2.1 per cent, reaching an average 270 US dollars. Ordinary city dwellers earned an average 760 US dollars, up 6.4 per cent, while Shanghai people go home with 4,200 US dollars. Tensions are obviously growing. Criticism voiced by Deng's opponents at the beginning of the opening policy is more justified today than ever before. Is China heading towards social upheavals because the gap between rich and poor is increasing?

No immediate danger

For the time being, there seems to be no immediate danger. Some China analysts have been warning for years that China is heading for serious instability, but until now everything seems to be under control. It is therefore interesting to analyse why the country has stayed relatively stable, even though the opposite has been predicted so many times.

Several reasons have to be mentioned:

- The fast growth of the coastal regions does not imply that the West has no growth at all. There are exceptions, but usually stagnation is as bad as it gets. Most people have felt some improvement over the last couple of years. For the time being, this is obviously enough to keep the people more or less quiet and peaceful.
- The Chinese are much more willing to resignedly accept their fate than modern westerners. Many people still keep telling themselves: 'I myself can't change much, anyway. Today my life is better than it used to be, and with a little bit of luck there will be some improvement in the future.'
- The success of boom-towns like Shanghai does not necessarily lead to jealousy. Just like the 2008 Olympics in Beijing, success is also seen as a symbol of national pride country-wide.
- The Chinese are very flexible. They are willing to accept a small solution rather than waiting for a big coup or other people's help.

The Chinese government has shown violence and arbitrariness towards the student movement in 1989 and the Falun Gong sect since 1999. It is prepared to do anything in order to suppress mass movements that could destabilise the country. All potential movements are suffocated at once – and everybody in the whole country knows that. Therefore, people think twice before publicly voicing their criticism and organising demonstrations.

- Those who stage mass demonstrations are modest and avoid major provocations. They protest against local problems without holding the central government or the system as a whole responsible. Alternatives to the current system do not play a prominent role in the life of average Chinese.

Summing up, the relationship between party leadership and the people can be characterised using a football related metaphor. There is only one team playing in the premiership, but the fans still support it even if it occasionally loses by scoring own goals. Fans hope the team will be more successful in future; after all there is only one team they can pin their hopes on.

Nevertheless, China seems to be more stable than other Southeast Asian countries such as Indonesia or the Philippines.

Near future

Nobody, not even the government, can know when the people's flexibility will come to an end and the current united-front breaks apart. It is also difficult to predict how the situation will change when more state owned enterprises are shut down or when Chinese peasants lose the basis of their income after WTO entry (China's agricultural products are one-third above world market prices).

Which groups does social stability mainly depend on?

The most problematic group is the floating population of more than 100 million, mainly peasants. Even though they are not very well respected, they are more successful than the state wants them to be, more multifaceted than government propaganda proclaims, and more capable than the police admit. They are not only mobile and flexible; they are clever enough to take their lives into their own hands. Having opted against badly paid fieldwork, they are a very heterogeneous lot: migrant worker statistics include students and flower girls, accountants and actors, garbage collectors and restaurant owners. By the beginning of this decade, an estimated 2.5 million of the 12 million people living in China's capital Beijing, were migrants: 80 per cent are under 40 years of age and most of them can read and write. Those who are successful will stay; more than half of them spend more than a year in Beijing, with one-third staying for more than three years. In Beijing, many of them already belong to the 'small healthy one's', as the well-off middle class is called. Although they are officially registered as living in the country, they have even opened their own schools, because migrant-worker children from outside the city are not permitted to attend the regular local schools. The losers amongst the migrant workers are those that do not manage to set up a network of relationships. Many come to the cities through agents that tell them tall tales. Some don't succeed in getting a grip anywhere and are doomed to travel from one construction site to the next.

It will become harder to belong to the winners because competition with city dwellers is increasing rapidly. A study by the European Union suggests that WTO membership will cause at least 13 million peasants to lose their jobs because their small fields will not be able to compete with big farms in Europe or the US. Some experts predict that privatisation of state owned enterprises might lead to as many as 50–60 million additional migrants heading for the big cities. Women and children staying in the villages will be left with the hard fieldwork. By 2010, 520 million Chinese, or 40 per cent of the population, are expected to live in cities. Currently, the quota stands at only 20 per cent.

City governments' strategy

The city governments try to solve the problem with three short-term strategies:

- in order to get an overview, all migrants have to register;
- migrant workers will be legalised, but they will have to apply for work permits. The goal is to make successful workers official, tax-paying city citizens;
- deterrence through crackdowns: the city governments want to spread the message that it has become very difficult to be successful in the city.

This approach has many problems, but one big advantage: China's mega-cities have so far avoided slums, which are part of many big Southeast Asian metropolises, such as Manila in the Philippines or many big cities in India. Also, Chinese cities are relatively safe.

Central government's strategy

The central government tries to develop China's west in order to make it less attractive for people to migrate to the coastal boom-cities. This includes large-scale infrastructure programmes as well as tax privileges and special economic zones. Some foreign companies that try to enter the Chinese market will only get the necessary license if they are willing to set up their production plants in the west or at least the country proper. Some big companies such as airlines attempt to relocate 'back office' work that is labour-intensive but requires no high qualifications. As long as the necessary information technology is available, this approach is quite practicable.

After having been neglected for the last 20 reform years, the development of the west is now proving to be extremely difficult. Infrastructure is underdeveloped, enterprises are outdated, social values are old fashioned and purchasing power is low. Many clever young people head for the big cities, leaving behind the less qualified, non-flexible ones.

Urban elite

The emergence of a new urban elite makes the gap between rich and poor even bigger. Having prospered only recently, they don't want to have anything to do with their poor compatriots. They earn an average monthly salary of 1,500 US dollars or more, speak English, drive their own car and invest money into education or trips to Hong Kong, Thailand and Singapore. While widely accepted in the US and Southeast Asia, they still fight the image of being mere assembly-line workers or blind followers of communist propaganda in Europe. Before, strong family ties used to guarantee that successful city dwellers would support a whole clan of relatives living in the country. But now, these traditions are breaking up. Young successful urbanites will only provide for their immediate family, while at the same time trying to preserve their personal flexibility and improve their economic situation. According to one survey at the beginning of the decade, 80 per cent of employees in Chinese enterprises and 75 per cent of employees of joint ventures dream of one day having their own company.

Summary

Although China has shown incredible growth in the last 20 years, the gap between rich and poor is getting wider. The life of the poor has improved to some extent but problems are likely to increase. The growing tensions are best seen in the plight of the migrant workers. How long the peasants will be willing to accept the growing injustice is hard to predict. However, a mix of pressure, lack of alternatives and identification with the central government have led to a resilience of the population that is higher than many analysts expected.

Further sources

Perry, E.J. and Selden, M. (2000) *Chinese Society: Change, Conflict and Resistance*, Routledge.

Solinger, D.J. (1999) *Contesting Citizenship in Urban China: Peasant Migrants, the State, and the Logic of the Market* (Studies of the East Asian Institute), University of California Press.

Tang, W. and Parish, W.L. (2000) *Chinese Urban Life Under Reform: The Changing Social Contract* (Cambridge Modern China Series), Cambridge University Press.

Whiting, S.H. (2001) *Power and Wealth in Rural China: The Political Economy of Institutional Change* (Cambridge Modern China Series), Cambridge University Press.

1.12. What are China's future problems?

China has experienced the most unique growth in world economic history. But there is no doubt that China has a long way to go before it can count as a modern, international, competitive economic power. The aftermaths of Mao's painful social experiments are still much more evident than the jolly surface of today's new China would suggest. The most important and fundamental reforms, such as privatization of state owned enterprises, a social security network, modern financial institutions and a reliable, stable legal system are still in their infancy. While the turnover of China Inc. looks promising, its structure is still alarming.

The most important questions

- How far have China's reforms come so far?
- What kind of reform pressure is on China's leadership?
- Which reforms have not yet been completed?
- Which will be China's main problems in the future?
- What is the leadership's key dilemma?
- What weakens the fundament of future reforms?
- Which are the impacts on China business?

For most of the last 20 years, China's leadership liberalised the country's economy but was hesitant to take the above-mentioned reforms and tasks head on. With foreign investment pouring into the economic low-density zones of China, the pressure for those reforms was not very high; especially since foreign investors met a leadership and a people with a good feeling for basic business. In the 1980s and 90s, Chinese and foreigners teamed up to create a huge boom that even the Tiananmen crackdown could only interrupt for little more than a year. As long as it made sure the economy didn't boil over, the leadership was on the safe side.

The Asian financial crisis in 1997 and the global recession in 2001 were the government's wake up call. Weakened by external slumps beyond its influence, it suddenly feared it would lose control over the country and again face *luan* (chaos), a nightmare which has been the leitmotiv of modern Chinese history. Since China's entry into WTO, structural weaknesses have become even more visible and the fear rising. However, this fear has its favourable side as it forces the Chinese government to increase its reform efforts. Concern for the stability of the country, declining economic power and loss of face have always been factors that spurred Chinese leaders' ambition.

More than ever before, State President Jiang Zemin and Premier Zhu Rongji feel the pressure to quickly change this turnover economy into a sustainable one. At the same time they have to avoid that growing social problems that might endanger or destroy the country's stability.

Controlling this increasingly difficult constellation will also be the main task that their successors will have to tackle. The first decade of the twenty-first century will not be a decade of boom for China but of fundamental social and economic reforms, which will make business easier. After the Olympic games have been successfully held in 2008, an event of the utmost importance for the Chinese people's and leaders' national pride, that should pass without social disturbances, these will become the most challenging tasks ahead. It is likely that these problems can be technically solved: for most modernisation tasks, western blueprints are available, such as Germany's civil code, the US Federal Bank system, Hong Kong's stock exchange or Britain's social legislation. With international support, it should be possible to adapt these to China's specific needs. The most important question is whether the government can keep social stability during the time of implementation.

Even if these hurdles are successfully overcome, China is still not on the safe side. For the first time, China will have to solve problems that are without examples or ready-made solutions in modern civilisation. Questions like the following will be have to be answered:

• Does modern China have enough work for all its people?
• What kind of economy can prevent China and the rest of the world from sailing straight into ecological disaster? Where will enough water come from? What about energy?
• How can the exploding population be handled without interfering too much with modern Chinese people's wish for individual freedom.
• How will other countries deal with a Chinese economy that is becoming very powerful?
• How could a democracy for 1.5 to 2 billion people work?

An additional problem will make the life of the Chinese government harder: where challenges become more and more comprehensive, the scope of its political action is diminishing. The possibility of making long-term plans and taking immediate action, that dictatorships in booming countries have and that some western politicians envy, will shrink further and with it the means to make corrections.

This will be unavoidable for two reasons: on the one hand, with rising economic power the Chinese people will eventually ask for more independence from government restrictions. On the other hand globalisation is progressing, further impairing the sovereignty of national states and forcing them to follow common rules. This trend will be particularly strong in a country like China, whose ups and downs are of rising importance for the world economy. It will no doubt be tough for China's leaders to accept that their young, proud, national autonomy and power will have to be shared with others even before coming to full blossom. The greater China's economic success and the bigger its affect on the world, the more the Chinese government will have to share its power. Even in the best case, China's leaders will never be able to achieve the same amount of power as their colleagues in the US. Much rather China will be one of several big industrial powers competing with one another, while goes along with the Chinese government, concept of a multiples world circle .

But this could lead to new global conflicts: The fight for natural resources and its sensible use could take the place of the fading struggle between capitalism and communism or religious fundamentalism and liberal civil societies. The Afghanistan conflict might develop into a fierce battle between China and the US for oil and gas. Even if some problems can possibly be solved through technological innovation, such as hydrogen-powered cars, the Chinese population strives to achieve western living standards and will eventually demand its share of the world's natural resources, at least according to the size of its population. However, the Chinese government, already buying big oil and gas fields as well as forests in other countries, will meet no support from foreign governments because only a cutback in western living standards could give China the space it needs. Naturally, this is hardly acceptable to the West. This new global castellation is huge interest for business people because internationally operating companies and their businesses may get caught between the two sides.

Still, these future power plays should not shift the focus from China's currently most harmful weakness: its lack of what economists call 'social capital'. A lack of responsibility of Chinese individuals towards their country's economy is visible almost anywhere, mainly in spreading corruption, which is still the country's dominating problem. China's boom is built on one great weakness that puts all successes on an unstable foundation: the rapid development overstrains the people's ability to take responsibility for their actions. China's boom is built on a gold rush mentality.

While the hardware of technical modernisation is relatively easy to update, the software of modern mindsets, the social capital, takes much longer to develop. The dilemma: people are asking for more freedom, which means less control by the government. Less institutional control needs more sense of responsibility, but this develops too slowly in comparison with the impatience of the people and the speed of the boom.

It took western countries a long time to establish the standards for a modern society and economy, with mixed success and a constant danger of falling back. Unfortunately, China does not have the same timeframe. But it is not possible to modernise an economy without having responsible market players who act reasonably even without immediate control. In the first 40 years of the history of the People's Republic, the leadership tended to underestimate this problem: Mao Zedong failed several times with his mass education campaigns which relied too much on social reliability within a totally idealistic economy. But even in the second half of the 1980s, Deng Xiaoping had to witness how a wildly sprawling economy gets out of control if everybody does what he wants. Premier Zhu Rongji and State President Jiang Zemin also had to learn the bitter lesson that not only the losers of the reforms were against them in their goal to establish a clean, sustainable economy, but also the winners, who had made a fortune through corruption.

The lack of responsibility that China's leaders have to cope with is a challenge for China's managers as well. They have to deal with this problem in their daily work. Many joint ventures in China are in trouble because certain rules, which where taken for granted by westerners, were not at all common for their Chinese partners. Establishing a functioning corporate communication is therefore one of the most important preconditions for success in a Chinese business environment. Convincing your Chinese partners of voluntarily sticking to some common rules in order to keep their own position comfortable in the long run is one of the most difficult tasks. Neither China's leadership, nor western managers should hope for quick success. As long as human beings are concerned, there is simply no shortcut to modernity.

Summary

For most modernisation tasks western blueprints are available and they are relatively easy to implement. But there are other questions which are much more difficult to solve, being without examples or ready-made solutions in modern civilization. These questions are particularly serious as they not only affect China but also the whole world. The process of China's development is hindered by one great weakness which puts all successes on an unstable foundation: as massive corruption shows, the rapid development overstrains the sense of responsibility of the people. China's future development relies on progress in these critical matters.

Further sources

Chang, G.G. (2001) *Coming Collapse of China*, London, Random House.
Studwell, J. (2002) *The China Dream: The Quest for the Last Great Untapped Market on Earth*, Publishers Group West.
Swaine, M.D. and Tellis, A.J. (2000) *Interpreting China's Grand Strategy: Past, Present and Future*, Rand Corporation.

2
What Kind of Strategic and Organisational Issues Have to be Taken into Consideration?

Engelbert Boos and Christine Boos

2.1. How do I prepare strategic planning for my investment in China?

A well-prepared strategic planning and stringent implementation accounts for at least 50 per cent of business success in China. Consequently, it is very important to spend enough time in the investigation and formulation of the feasibility study as well as the due diligence investigation of the potential investment partners. The investment must fit the global strategy of the western investor and the chosen legal framework and business platform must suit the needed scope of business including the servicing requirements for all of the business activities on a global basis. Special consideration should be given to the size and shape of the investment. The cost level and market volume must fit the profitable establishment of the business.

The most important questions for strategic planning
- Definition of the vision and strategic objectives for market entry.
- Thoroughly done feasibility study and market research (market volume, production quantities, cost level, price levels, achievable margins, realistic growing rates).
- Evaluation of suitable products (standard, tailor- or system-made products).
- Definition of the targets, size and time-frame of the investment.
- Fixing of a suitable legal frame (joined or wholly owned entity) and location for the investment.
- Selection and treatment of the best suitable investment partner (finance and market performance and intercultural behaviour).
- Optimising finance, taxation and legal framework (see chapter 9.13).
- Strategic co-ordination of local and global business activities.

Definition of the vision and strategic objectives for market entry

Before entering and investing in the Chinese market, the investor should have a clear perspective and strategy for going to China. A prerequisite of success is that the engagement in China fits the global strategic orientation. China must be a clearly defined and active part within the overall global strategy and business activities of the investor. The acceptance and full support through the headquarters' staff is also quite important. In case of major resistance, the staff has to be convinced by frequent information exchange that the China investment is important for the global growth and healthy development of the whole company. In most cases the quick success in China greatly depends on such arrangements. One of the biggest problems of western companies in China is that the senior management of the headquarters often has no idea about China. They did no homework, have overinvested, and now they expect the management to make them a fast return. As a consequence, they often suffer a big turnover in their management team, because the managers just can't achieve the results the head office wants. The set objectives often are impossible to fulfil, but the superiors won't listen to their people on the ground. US-based companies are the worst offenders when it comes to impossible demands. They insist on short-term results, and are obsessed with quarterly profits. European investors mostly are more long-term oriented. Therefore, it is the job of the management to educate the superiors in the head office.

Most investors follow one of the two strategic objectives for their China investments. Some of them want make use of lower labour cost and sell the products both to the domestic and international markets. Then, the production cost level must be competitive with other global locations. Special tax and finance optimisation policies will support the maximisation of profits. The other investors may be more interested in building up a smaller assembly, production, servicing and sales organisation for promoting their premium products. Chinese customers prefer to purchase from legally established local production and service platforms of the foreign supplier. This enables them to pay in local currency, to get quicker deliveries through local stocks and better tailor-made solutions fitting their individual needs. Consultation regarding product and system application as well as face to face meetings with major suppliers are always useful. Such platforms are also a good and cost efficient basis for the promotion of other or additional businesses from the headquarters. Only clearly defined and implemented strategic approaches make business in China finally successful.

Thoroughly done feasibility study and market research

A further critical obstacle for success of investments in China is a poorly done feasibility study and market research. Especially in the 1990, many western investors went to China thinking only of more than one billion potential customers. Potential Chinese joint venture partners and local governmental bodies also did everything to become an attractive partner for a western investor and increased the positive outlook. Therefore, the statistical and market potential had been overestimated dramatically by both investors. This put a lot of pressure on the management of the young joint company and is the reason for many disappointing board meetings in such organisations. Painful restructuring processes had to be initiated in order to cope with the problems of too-low market and sales volumes and these resulted in unsatisfactory production quantities. Consequently, the respective cost level became too high and the achievable profit margins too low. In many cases, the realistic growth rates for profitability and break-even could only be achieved by the initiation of additional products or services for the whole group of companies out of the existing workshop.

Evaluation of suitable products

The success in entering the Chinese market depends very much on the respective products and technologies under consideration. Some investors may be complacent and just transfer old production lines and outdated products and technologies to China. Then, they may be surprised that the whole market segment is shrinking and that the required production volumes are not forthcoming with the final result of losses. In fact, most qualified Chinese customers are asking for the latest technological standards of products or components. Long-term success in China requires products of world market standards in terms of technology, quality and competitive price levels. Most of the profitably run private companies apply such a philosophy. They takeover higher-qualified and experienced employees of local state run competitors and develop their skills to international standards. They prefer to buy competitively priced and tailor-made high-quality components from the premium market with the objective of becoming market leader in quality and quantity in their own sector. Therefore, good co-operation with the supplier and support in system integration and international application know-how is very important for them in any purchasing decision. The right products in combination with a well-arranged spare parts and after-sales service are a good basis for success in the long term. The success of more standardised products depends mainly on the achievable total cost and quality level for the realisation of higher production quantities and improved competitive selling. Labour-intensive and standardised mass products are particularly suitable for such criteria of success.

Targets, size and planned time-frame

Some investors go to China just because many others are doing so. Other investors calculate their production platforms on the basis of a population of more than 1 billion potential customers. In addition, both of them may expect to be able to establish the business quickly and to achieve break-even within two years of operation. In case of failure, it must be the poor performance of the appointed management of the entity. Any aspect of the above-mentioned scenario will certainly lead to failure, but it is the strategic decision-makers of the investment who are mainly responsible. The targets, size and planned time-frame of the investment must be fixed very carefully with special consideration of the products and market segments in question. In doubtful cases it is always better to start with preliminary test sales through representative offices in combination with good market research. It may also make sense to start with a smaller production platform, which is flexibly adaptable to growing customer demand. Otherwise, the management team get burned by promising to make money fast. Many experts advise starting small and growing steadily with the market, whilst not being so conservative that the demands on the business are greater than the infrastructure and business obligations can meet. An established month by month business analyses helps to show where the business is going and to keep the finger on the pulse of the market. The estimated time schedules must meet the special circumstances of starting a business platform in China, especially in case of a joint venture with complicated communication and intercultural implications.

Fixing a suitable legal frame and location for the investment

In China, different kinds of legal investment structures can be entered into, such as a joint venture, contractual venture, wholly owned venture, a representative or branch office or just a trading or servicing company. The success of the business operation depends to a huge extent on the right choice of legal structure depending on the targeted products and markets as well as on the decided short to long term strategic planning of business development. Under special circumstances it may also make sense to combine different legal structures of business operation. If an existing joint venture is not performing well, it may make more sense to switch the entity to a contractual venture or a wholly owned venture. In some special cases such as where imported products are the main focus, it may even be better just to operate a representative office or a service or trading company in a special free trade zone. The location of the venture is also very decisive for success. A good infrastructure, such as flight connections, schools, hospitals, social and cultural events etc., helps to make an employer more attractive for high-potential locals and expatriates and enables a more efficient market penetration. To gain and retain higher-qualified people and to develop the whole business more effectively is a major factor for strategic and operative success.

Selection and treatment of the best suitable investment partner

A good investment partner can help a lot, especially in the beginning. He can help to change the mentality of the staff and to build up a good and co-operative relationship with the respective authorities. It is important to establish and maintain a good relationship with one's joint venture partner, and to seek the advice and recommendations of the local municipal government in finding one in the first place. It is very useful to gain them as allies. Then, they are happy to give good advice. Meanwhile, many Chinese potential partners become more capitalistic, more open-minded and more modern in their thinking. The investment partner should be made a real member of the team. Some people prefer their Chinese partner to be very passive, to not get involved, to just make them legal and leave them to it. But, this is not making use of the partner. An integrated local partner can help to manage the local staff and to take care of things while the expatriate is away. It is also important to understand the cultural differences. In China, business is more family-oriented, with the boss behaving like an emperor. To some extent we must let him carry on – we don't want him to feel that his status is diminished – but the business must also function in an international setting. It is wise to treat him as a friend and show him that the job is secure and you want him to be successful.

In China many people only think in terms of incremental change and cannot imagine dramatic change. It is important to keep the partner informed, even on minor matters, and to involve him in the decision-making process, particularly in anything to do with staff. It is also wise to listen to their thoughts; they will be more supportive and will be more forthcoming with details on what is going on. This also helps to understand their objectives. Many Chinese partners are obsessed with control and knowing about what's going on; sometimes they even install spies in prominent positions. It is also important to remember what is in it for them. The best way to deal with the Chinese partner is to be flexible, go along with them, give them face, let them take the lead, help them to get what they want – as long as the profit is not adversely affected. It helps to give them a bonus on achieved profits. The Chinese partners are looking for status as well as money in their dealings with western organisations. It makes sense to invite them to all the important functions, ask them to make speeches and introduce them to all key foreign visitors. This makes them more understanding and co-operative. Apart from all this the hard figures have to be checked. A thoroughly done diligent investigation helps in the understanding and selection of the most suitable investment partner. His finance and market performance as well as his reliability and management qualifications should be also cross-checked with reliable auditing firms, local banks, potential competitors and major suppliers.

Summary/Recommendations

The professional preparation of strategic planning for investment in China is a vital factor for success. Many invested entities with the appointed management have no chance of success due to poor strategic preparation and lack of support and understanding in the headquarters. Clear strategies regarding where and how to conduct one's business are essential before embarking on the adventure of trading successfully in China. The feasibility study must be well done with a realistic estimation of achievable quality, quantity, cost and price levels. The right product, service and marketing mix is important, too. This is the basis for the decision of the right target, size and legal structure of the investment. If a strategic co-operation is entered into with a local partner, the selection process and co-operation with him must be based on a good mutual understanding. His finance and market performance and intercultural behaviour must be built on a healthy basis. Ultimately, it will be in the hands of the appointed management to implement the strategic targets into operational success.

Further sources

Jones, S. (1997) *Managing in China*, HK, B.H. Asia.
Moser, M. (ed.) (2000) *China Troubleshooter*, HK, Asia Law & Practice.

2.2. What are the most important factors for success and failure in the operational implementation of the strategies?

Many investors have a clear vision and a well-prepared strategic approach for successful entry into the Chinese market. The gap between success and failure in business can be quite small. The failure rate is especially high in cases of poor co-operation with a chosen investment partner and the authorities or where there is weak support from the head office. However, even otherwise successful business operations can suffer through intercultural misunderstanding and inappropriate working approaches by the appointed management. Therefore, it is important to be aware of the most important obstacles to a successful business operation in China. This chapter evaluates the major factors contributing to failure in business operation.

The most important factors for failure

- Poor operative implementation of set strategic objectives.
- Lack of co-operation with an investment partner.
- Weak understanding and support from the headquarters.
- Expatriate and management problems.
- Cultural, ethical and leadership problems.

Poor operative implementation of set strategic objectives

Experienced investors have strong business development departments for the investigation, evaluation and defining of suitable strategies, establishing which best suit the global expansion and development activities of the group. It is then the responsibility of the appointed management of the new entity in China to implement the agreed strategic objectives on schedule, within the set budgets and in a most professional way. All departments of the new entity have to be set up, co-ordinated and managed very efficiently, and be customer-oriented. The professional implementation of the fixed strategic objectives is a very difficult task for the local management and is often the main cause of management turnover. It is a good idea for the management to keep the board of directors fully informed about whether targets will be met and all relevant business issues in order to secure understanding and support should problems arise. Good co-operation with investors on all relevant strategic issues is essential for a successful business development and accordingly one of the key factors determining success or failure.

Lack of co-operation with the investment partner

Potential sources of conflicts with the Chinese partner are matters on which he will not or cannot shift, such as capital contributions, rate of market expansion, downsizing or just the product quality. The relationship may also become difficult if there is lack of working capital or there are frequent delays of sub-supplies from the joint venture partner's workshops. Personnel issues can also be quite sensitive. Joint ventures normally pay higher salaries and total compensation packages than state owned factories. This may have a negative impact on the morale of the employed staff and sometimes also on that of the non-transferred staff of the Chinese investor. Also the working attitude and performance of local staff is not always compatible with international standards. The production and marketing of premium and high-quality products is quite different from low-cost and poor-quality ones such as are produced in many state owned companies. It is difficult for the management to reconcile the different approaches to business philosophy and to maintain the understanding and support of both the joint venture partner and western headquarters. It is a difficult task to adapt and accommodate to Chinese and western business perspectives.

Weak understanding and support from the headquarters

It is usually the top management team of the western headquarters that makes the strategic decision regarding investment into a new entity in China. Such new business platforms can expand the global sales and service network of a company, increasing total business volumes. But such globalisation strategies can sometimes also cause conflicts with the existing business units at home. The production manager in the headquarters may fear that he will loose some production capacities in his workshop, with a negative impact on employment for his workers. The export manager may lose influence and sales volumes from preliminary protected markets. If two such managers are closely involved in the support of the newly invested entity in China, in close touch with the local business situation, conflicts may be averted. Sales and distribution channels are best co-ordinated from the operation platform in China, thus avoiding friction and price evasion. Unrealistic deadlines and targets set by the head office are also aggravating to the expatriates and the local Chinese employees. Many differences between foreign and Chinese partners in a joint venture result from pressure from the foreign partner's head office. Chief executive officers and their management teams don't like surprises, especially bad ones, so it is recommended that close contact with them is maintained, and that they are kept up-to-date with good and bad news. Visits from the headquarters should be welcomed and superiors should be informed about the situation. The management should neither exaggerate nor play down their problems, but show factual evidence to support the arguments. The boss should be introduced to the staff, and the importance of the visits should be impressed upon the staff. The staff should wear good clothes and try to avoid negativity. They should be encouraged to show their enthusiasm and commitment, but their circumstances should portrayed realistically. However, it is also important to understand the headquarters' concerns in connection with their investments in an insecure, expensive, volatile and unpredictable environment. It helps to have a spokesman in the head office and ensure that the intercultural differences are fully explained. The ability to educate the home office about China is essential. Convincing the head office of the causes of poor results or missed deadlines is a challenge, but it is something that senior expatriates who already have some clout and credibility in their own companies can succeed with more easily than a local or even a third-country national. An expatriate who knows the politics, mindset and priorities of the head office has an advantage over others. Otherwise, the response of head office to disappointing results can be to step in and start 'micro-managing', which results in greater stress and frustration for the expatriates and less localisation of expertise, having a negative influence on the overall success of the invested entity.

Expatriate and management problems

Expatriates often fail for a number of management reasons. Those who think they know China, and actually do not, often fail. Those who put too much trust in their secretary, interpreters or local assistants often get ripped off and also fail. It is essential to really know what is going on and to cope with the working hours and pressure, which are often greater than in the home country. Unsuccessful expatriates in China often suffer from one of two extremes: either they are too dependent on headquarters, or they lose contact with head office. Some experts even believe 'the single greatest source of stress in China is not China but head office.' The headquarters' business policies as well as their delegated expatriates in China sometimes change frequently. But the basic problems are only shifted, not solved. Nobody really wants to hear bad news and the responsible decision-makers of the early days of the establishment of the entity often deny responsibility. Such a situation may catch the expatriate in the middle of a lose-lose battle. Sometimes the local and expatriate management staff don't co-operate well due to intercultural problems or misunderstandings, which are avoidable. An expatriate, for instance, cannot implement completely western accounting and travel expense calculation policies in China. Small bookkeeping profits may cause huge opposition and respective losses in other fields of co-operation with the local management. Such mini-wars can even be responsible for the final closing of a potentially promising entity. The board of directors must keep a special eye and focus on such intercultural management issues. Simultaneously, the management of the company has to do their best to co-operate well and to motivate the local staff.

Cultural, ethical and leadership problems

Another cause of failure, is not adjusting to different cultural traits, value systems and ethical or moral standards. Westerners brought up to operate by Christian values, which have shaped most of western thought, law and government, find it difficult to cope with behaviour they see as wrong. Corruption, stealing and lying, coupled with or under the banner of *guanxi*, the Chinese system of relationships, are not uncommon in Chinese society. That is not to say that the Chinese are all dishonest and corrupt, but it is true that issues of 'face' and *guanxi* create a different perspective on the question of truth and honesty. Unless an expatriate can adapt to these issues, and not prejudge them from the standpoint of western morality, they will fail. When two variant cultures come together, the approach to equanimity is to identify the non-negotiable elements from both. For example, a company may be absolutely opposed to bribery or 'grease money', while in some cultures this process is normal. If a western company cannot accommodate grease money, it must suffer the consequences of that position. But, if paying grease money is a negotiable ethic, then an accommodation to this activity will be justified. Although some would see this as compromising the integrity of the corporation, some do not see it as such. Expatriates who find themselves in an environment of graft and corruption must evaluate this condition with company and personal ethics and find the common ground. If this is not possible, the expatriate is unlikely to be successful. An expatriate, or indeed, an external company, that is rigid is likely to fail. The applied management methods and the respective intercultural understanding are also a potential source of success or failure. China requires strong leaders, who are goal oriented, have initiative, and are fair, flexible and opportunity driven. They must work on their own and deal with far more responsibility to solve problems. However, they must also delegate a major part of their responsibility and coach their employees in a very patient and persistent way in order to meet the Chinese way of democracy and consensus orientation. The Chinese management culture requires the ability to deal with bureaucracy, gossiping, internal cliques and to cope with a common family atmosphere. Responsible managers have to be firm yet flexible, build confidence and create control mechanisms within a traditional strong and autocratic culture. The interests of the company should be balanced with those of the employees to promote trust and team spirit. This makes the staff loyal and committed to the intercultural company needs and reduces the risk of failure for the whole business operation.

Summary/Recommendations

There exist many potential reasons for success or failure in business operation in China. However, only few of them are really sensitive. The management must understand the set strategic objectives of the company and implement them efficiently. Good communication with the Chinese investment partner and their own headquarters may also help to succeed. On the other hand, the local management of the entity must also co-operate well and in a most practical way to solve critical issues. Expatriates need to master huge difficulties including intercultural, language and professional management issues. For expatriates, China is still a huge professional and personnel challenge in an environment where the difference between success and failure in business operation can be quite small.

Further sources

Jones, S. (1997) *Managing in China*, HK, B. H. Asia.
Moser, M. (ed.) (2000) *China Troubleshooter*, HK, Asia Law & Practice.

2.3. What are the main objectives of Chinese and western investment partners?

The overall success or failure of an investment project in the long term often depends on simple questions related to the main objectives of both partners. A project can only be successful when the strategic and operational objectives of both parties fit together. A lot of manpower, money and time, or other resources might be wasted when investment partners do not properly evaluate or even ignore differing views about the future development of the joint venture. The basic foundation of a joint investment must have a real strategic chance to develop successfully and to fulfil set targets. The management of a joint venture can only optimise operational tasks within the set strategic frameworks of the investors, represented by the board of directors. Therefore, it is extremely important to analyse fully the existing and potential interests of the investing counterpart.

The major interests of joint venture partners and the Chinese government

- The western investor is mainly interested in the achievement of domestic market shares whilst maintaining his international management methods and business practices.
- The Chinese government wants to avoid high and rising unemployment rates and improve the overall efficiency and competitiveness of China's industries.
- The Chinese joint venture partner mainly wants to solve his own problems in the company and achieve profit and advantages for his people especially in short-term considerations. He may care less about his fixed assets, which in many cases still belong to the state. Therefore, he also prefers longer depreciation rates of the assets. On the other hand he also wants to employ as many of his personnel as possible in servicing the joint venture. This increases the workload of his staff and creates further income.

The major interests of Chinese and western investment partners

The interests of the Chinese and western investment partner differ to some extent. The knowledge about their major objectives is an important factor in the failure or success of an investment in China.

Table 3 Interests of western and chinese joint venture partners

The major interests of western partners	The major interests of Chinese partners
• To be present in the Chinese market, to achieve respective market shares and to participate in the growing Chinese economy	• Western technologies to modernise as quickly and as cost-efficiently as possible their own firm and the Chinese economy
• Control of business operation and definition of the business strategy	• To participate in decision-making and strategy-defining in order to represent their own interests as much as possible
• To achieve quick profits and to reinvest them into the expansion of the business or to transfer profits back home	• Quick and continuous profits and keeping them in China

Table 3   (continued)

The major interests of western partners	The major interests of Chinese partners
• Using special investment advantages in China such as low salary levels, investment subsidies and tax holidays	• Learning from western technical and management know-how
• Limited release of own know-how in order to keep the strong position on the market	• Improvement of quality and competitiveness of Chinese products with the help of a western partner
• Minimising of the investments and risks	• Attracting of western investment to build up the Chinese economy
• Minimising of the employment risks by the engagement of fewer, but more highly qualified people	• Creation of many high-qualified jobs with respective personnel training and development programmes
• Transfer of most of the methods	• Keeping of own habits and identity
• Building up of a long-lasting position in China	• To quickly become independent by learning from western counterparts
• To use China as a platform for the penetration of other Asian markets	• Increase of international competitiveness of Chinese products, earning of foreign currencies and access to international markets
• Co-operation with China as important step within the international portfolio development	• Co-operation with a western partner as important step within the reform of the Chinese economy

Source: Reisach, U, Tauber, T. and Yuan, X. (1997) *China – Wirtschaftspartner zwischen Wunsch und Wirklichkeit*, Ueberreuther, Vienna, p. 173.

Major assumptions of western and Chinese board members

Internal communication and intercultural understanding of each other's assumptions on board level is very important for a successful co-operation. The different approaches of each should be understood in order to promote harmony and success from the top to the lower levels of management.

Table 4   Communication between the board of directors

Assumptions of western board	Assumptions of Chinese board
• The board is the highest decision-making body in the company	• Decisions are not made in the boardroom, rather this is a place where views are revealed
• Directors must have the interest of the joint venture company as their highest priority – over allegiances to the companies they represent	• Directors have the interest of their Chinese parent as their highest priority

Table 4   (continued)

Assumptions of western board	Assumptions of Chinese board
• Board members are empowered to make decisions in their own right	• Decision-making is only possible after approval from outside authorities
• Issues can be discussed resulting in changes of perception within the boardroom by directors	• There is little or no ability to change minds without outside approval
• Directors need to maintain a hands-off approach to management. Directors should focus on policy issues and react primarily to information and matters brought to their attention by the chief executive of the joint venture	• Directors feel free to involve themselves in operational details. Policy is discussed and agreed outside the boardroom, often in social or informal situations. The directors feel obligated to gather information directly from all levels of the organisation
• Board meetings are totally confidential	• Board meeting information is fed back to many levels of the organisation and into the Chinese partner without due consideration
• Directors are fully aware of their legal obligations in the West and are selected for their direct contribution to the operation, mainly without fear or favour	• Board membership is often viewed as a reward for loyal services without any legal obligation, only obedience in carrying out the directions of the person(s) charged with responsibility for the joint venture within the Chinese partner
• Human resources issues are largely the responsibility of the senior executives and not the board	• Board directors like to become involved in operational issues associated with human resources hire/fire, remuneration, benefits etc.

Source: Moser, M. (ed.) (2000) *China Troubleshooter*, HK, Asia Law & Practice, Chapter 4, pp. 5–6.

Summary/Recommendations

The key objectives of investors or stakeholders in a joint venture project might be the same. Both parties want quickly realised profits and to develop the joint business towards a bright future. In the euphoria of the beginning, they might neglect the impact of the different business cultures and post-pone potential questions on how to achieve the set targets. The risks of the joint venture can be reduced and better controlled when both investors pay special attention to the evaluation of the different objectives from the beginning. If discrepancies are too great, it may make more sense to start a wholly foreign-owned entity instead of a joint venture, although this might involve increased risks and higher costs.

Further sources

Huang, Q. (1997) *Business Decision Making in China*, Amazon.
Moser, M. (ed.) (2000) *China Troubleshooter*, HK, Asia Law & Practice.
Reisach, U., Tauber, T. and Yuan, X. (1997) *China – Wirtschaftspartner zwischen Wunsch und Wirklichkeit*, Vienna, Ueberreuther.

2.4. How do I select a Chinese partner?

The success of an investment in China is very dependent on the Chinese local partner. Reliability and basic mutual understanding are very important. The reputation and competence of the potential partner has to be checked in advance. This has huge influence on the future success or failure of the co-operation. The due diligence evaluation has to be done very carefully. Hard facts, such as technical and economical competence are as important as other factors, such as market know-how and *guanxi* networks. It is important to define key objectives of the co-operation. Production joint ventures concentrate more on quality standards and technological competence, whereas service-related joint ventures focus more on quality of management, existing sales and distribution networks and customer relationships. The financial situation of the partner is also a critical factor for success. A poor financial background may delay the start-up and disturb a smooth business development.

The most important features for the selection of a Chinese investment partner

- Financial background and reliability of the partner.
- Qualification and flexibility of the management.
- Product technology and quality competence.
- Specific relationships, *guanxis*, to authorities, key customers and suppliers.

Financial background and reliability of the partner

It is important to check the real value of fixed assets, open amounts of receivables and payables, bank loans, availability of property rights for used land and contributed machinery and equipment. Independent consultants can help in evaluation of the real value of contributions. The arrangement of bank guarantees for loans have also to be approved. There is not yet any existing reliable data information source about Chinese enterprises. Since 1995, Hoppenstedt and other consultants such as the Sinotricist Business Risk Management Company have been collecting such financial and business data for 50,000 enterprises in China. The major problem is the reliability of such data. Most of it is simply reported by the local enterprises themselves with subsequent lack of accuracy and reliability. Therefore, it is important to visit and check such potential partners personally or with the help of a competent consultant. Then, the due diligence investigation comprising of the balance sheets, the profit and loss accounts, the organisation and management as well as the realistic business activities and the site conditions can be checked thoroughly. Sophisticated controlling instruments and computerised accounting procedures and software often do not yet exist. An important question is also the reliability of the presented data such as the real production and sales quantities and the profit margins. Some financial data may be manipulated for fiscal or political reasons. Therefore, such data has to be cross-checked with other sources such as tax offices, banks and authorities. The evaluation of such material has to be done very carefully.

Qualification and flexibility of the management

An important success factor is the willingness and capability of the Chinese joint venture partner to adopt new products, strategies, organisational structures, customers and suppliers. He must fully support new levels of efficiency and targets for the achievement of better profit margins. The salary and compensation packages for the employees often have to become more flexible and individually performance-oriented. A strong will is needed for supporting the profit-oriented development of the venture. Arising problems should be solved in a most flexible manner. Experience in international management is often non-existent. Therefore, the operating control should be held in the hands of the western partner. However, the existing experiences of the Chinese managers and the intercultural differences must also be taken into consideration. The appointed Chinese senior managers should be innovative and aggressive, but not conservative and too cautious in decision-making and general business behaviour.

Product technology and quality competence

Technology and quality levels of the manufactured products and related services must be comparable to the western ones. Otherwise, the reputation of the joint venture will suffer and prices for the products will drop with negative effects on the saleable quantities and achievable profit margin. Both the qualification level of the staff and the technical level of the production equipment must be improved in order to avoid such problems. Many western investors prefer to import production equipment and to build new buildings to assure quality in production and to project a positive and innovative image to employees and customers. Another important consideration is the availability or importation of raw materials of a consistently high quality. Sourcing has become steadily less problematic over recent years.

Specific relationships *guanxis*

In China, it is not only important to know the value of fixed assets of joint venture partners, his product know-how and qualification of the management. It is sometimes even more important to know his *guanxi* network to authorities, key customers and suppliers. However, the existing relationship network is not necessarily the same as for the introduction of the planned new products. The marketing and distribution of premium products, the supplier network for high-quality components and the addresses of responsible authorities may be very different. Further, new circumstances may arise in debt management with customers. The supplier network has to be selected according to a different set of requirements than in state owned enterprises. Competitive pricing, on-time deliveries and stable quality levels have to be guaranteed in the long term without resorting to bribes. Imports of high-quality 'completely knocked down' (CKD) components are often still required to fill the local gap in supply. The *guanxi* network is, thus, not as critical and sensitive as in the past.

Summary/Recommendations

The selection of a suitable Chinese investment partner is a quite difficult and sensitive task. It takes some experience to know the respective market players with their weaknesses and strengths. Nowadays, major selection criteria for a suitable Chinese investment partner are his financial background and competitive influence due to respective high market shares in target segments. In restricted business areas such as telecommunications or automotives, the relationship network still plays a major role. However, with WTO membership, the business will increasingly follow international regulations. Therefore, in many ordinary markets and business segments, it may make even more sense to establish a wholly foreign owned entity (WFOE) or a trading or servicing company in a free trade zone. However, the number of professionally operating and high-potential Chinese business partners is increasing, too. A thoroughly done due diligence investigation in combination with an open ear to major competitors and sub-suppliers also help in finding a suitable partner for a successful co-operation.

Further sources

Reisach, U., Tauber, T. and Yuan, X. (1997) *China – Wirtschaftspartner zwischen Wunsch und Wirklichkeit*, Vienna, Ueberreuther.
Wang, Y. (1996) *Investment in China*, CITIC, NY.

General considerations

David Murphy

After years of trying to live together many joint venture partners are rethinking their marriage vows. 'The ideal partner is one who knows nothing about your business,' says a foreign executive who has been doing business in China for 20 years. For most foreign enterprises, business partnerships in China are more like shotgun weddings than love at first sight. Therefore, many investors are getting out of unhappy partnerships. New investors are seeking to avoid partnerships. For the past several years, wholly foreign owned entities (WFOE) have been the dominant method of foreign investment entering the Chinese market. The preference for independence is important for many investors against a background of many loss-making enterprises. An experienced American investor remarked that

> in most cases just the business license is of interest in order to make and market a world standard product, the experience of a failing state owned company is not an asset to such an operation. In most cases good local employees – one or two with good government connections – can bring more to your firm than a joint venture partner.

Local partners may know quite a lot about manufacturing a product, but they are unlikely to know much about product branding and marketing. 'When I need local expertise, I prefer to hire it rather than marry it,' says one investor who is currently buying out partners in many joint ventures around China. Misconceptions on both sides often poison the joint venture even before it gets off the ground. The foreign investor sees an able local partner who can offer access to distribution networks and government influence. The Chinese side sees a cash cow, which can provide technology transfer, foot old welfare bills and bring instant profitability. Neither side can deliver on these kinds of expectations. The resulting disappointment can produce massive problems over business strategy and methods and lead to bitter personality disputes. Better follow the old rule: opposites attract.

There are also many good examples of joint ventures. Profitable firms install special interest groups who are doing everything possible to support the firm's operations, but not their own interests. Powerful partners, no matter where both of them come from, can work strongly together using the advantages of both parties with significant contributions to the Chinese economy (i.e. Volkswagen and Sino Santa Fe). Good partners don't need to copy the foreign partner's products and compete against him. The co-operation with a local partner especially makes sense in still-restricted areas such as the automotive industry or when a partner really can help with his relationships to major distribution channels (e.g. Qingdao London International Latex Co. Ltd).

2.5. What kind of organisational structures fit the specific situation in China?

In general one must say, there is no one best way of organising either in western countries or in China. The best organisational design depends on the circumstances an organisation faces. Major determinants include the environmental conditions, the technology the firm uses, the firm's strategic goals or objectives, its size, the point in the lifecycle of the firm in question, and its culture.

The most important features

Regardless of the particular organisational design selected (i.e. functional designs, output grouping according to products, markets or geography, matrix design or forms of virtual organisations), the design should have certain characteristics to be effective:

- efficiency and innovation;
- flexibility and adaptability;
- facilitation of individual performance and development;
- facilitation of co-ordination and communication;
- facilitation of strategy formulation and implementation;
- respect for culture-specific peculiarities;

Efficiency and innovation

The design should encourage the efficient pursuit of goals and ensure that the right things will be done. Already in the start-up phase of doing business in China you should figure out and equalise the different goals of the participating partners (e.g. Chinese joint venture partner, western investors, Chinese authorities) and anchor it in the organisational structure, otherwise your effectiveness and efficiency always will suffer.

The organisational design should support innovation by providing the pooling of resources and the necessary communications for innovation to take place. The organisational design should facilitate the representation of the organisation to the outside world. In China good connections, *guanxi*, to external decision- and opinion-makers play an even more important role than in western countries, so you should establish in your organisation positions/functions that ensure a suitable lobbying and PR policy.

Furthermore your organisational design should support the gathering and interpreting of important environmental information and the introducing of the results of analyses into the organisation's strategic planning process in order to reduce the amount of environmental uncertainties and to react to the specific peculiarities of the Chinese market.

Flexibility and adaptability

Nowadays in China there is very dynamic economic development (changing legal rules and regulations, fierce competition in all key markets, etc.); fewer industries can be classified as simple and stable. Therefore, the organisation must be able to change and respond to new organisational conditions. Effective designs must balance the needs for consistency and predictability with the needs for flexibility and responsiveness.

As local Chinese managers – because of their socialist background – often shrink from taking over a wider range of responsibility all of a sudden, your organisational design has also to provide possibilities to transfer responsibilities step by step to your local Chinese staff. One way could be to introduce a kind of 'godfather concept'. That means an expatriate guides – in a 'transition phase' – as a mentor to a Chinese colleague, who will be his successor in due course. Step by step the westerner can introduce him to his new job and can hand him over more and more responsibility. This is a proven method for localising management positions.

Facilitation of individual performance and development

The organisational design should offer the individual the opportunity to perform at his or her highest level of ability in areas of interest and competence. It should encourage employees to grow by learning new skills and accepting more responsibility. Chinese managers generally are eager to learn. Showing them a clear career path in your company can strengthen their loyalty more than monetary incentives. Therefore your organisational structure should explicitly respect the issue of personnel development and training. But be aware that pre-produced solutions in those fields have to be adapted to the special needs of your Chinese employees (e.g. to the different educational background, culture, motivation, hierarchy of needs).

Facilitation of co-ordination and communication

At the core of structuring and designing organisations is the effective execution of tasks. It must facilitate co-ordination and communication in the times when it is needed most. You should be aware that in China – even more than in western countries – there are always a lot of informal channels of communication and informal opinion leaders. It is best to try to win the confidence of these informal leaders in order to gain their support for your company goals.

It is advisable to introduce a reporting system in your organisational structure that serves as a feedback and early warning system, as Chinese employees often shrink from telling you bad news and developments at an early stage.

Facilitation of strategy formulation and implementation

Structure and design are both key factors in the development of strategies and are key outcomes of the strategy formulation process. Organisations must be strategically designed so as to transmit strategic information to top-level managers. It is, however, amazing how many – some well-known – western companies still enter the Chinese market and run their business there in a kind of 'muddling through' way, without having a clearly defined strategy.

Strategy and design are tightly linked, and as organisations adapt new strategies, they may need to modify their designs. In China a change of strategy is often necessary, if you are starting or ending strategic partnerships such as joint ventures, sales or purchasing networks. In these cases professional support could be advisable in order to avoid problems resulting from the different cultural and economic systems.

Respect for culture-specific peculiarities

While it is true that doing business in China has been influenced a lot by western management tools and techniques, the influence of the Chinese culture is strong. There is a long tradition of family and communal values. You can find a lot of family-centred companies. But unlike the Japanese *Keiretsus* (Mitsubishi, Mitsui, Sunitoma etc.) or the Korean *Chaebols* (Samsung, Hyundai, Daewoo etc.) that are huge family-based powerful holdings, supported by the government, in China there are smaller companies. As soon as a company has reached a certain size, another company will be founded, usually managed by a member of the family, a close friend or a deserving employee. These people get some company shares to ensure, that they are motivated and loyal and feel responsible for the company. By this so-called 'mushrooming' some families control quite a few companies, without making their ownership too evident in public. That way they can avoid attracting too much attention that could cause envy and over-the-top control by public authorities. If you don't need a certain size in order to run your company in China, you should consider whether you cannot learn from the Chinese, adopting some of their management principles.

Summary/Recommendations

Building up your own organisation in China, your top priority should be to get a realistic view of the market potentials. On that basis you should start up step by step, giving your organisation the chance to grow by diligently planned packages to enlarge the structures. The ideal size for a company in China is about 50–300 employees. However, sometimes a bigger size is, necessary in order to get a reasonable input-output relation.

Further sources

Bartlett, C. and Ghoshal, S. (1999) *The Individualized Corporation: A Fundamentally New Approach to Management*, Portland, Diane Publishing Co.

Daft, R. (1992) *Organization Theory and Design*, Minnesota.
Hodge, B., Anthony, W. and Gales, L. (1998) *Organization Theory – A Strategic Approach*, NJ, Prentice Hall.

2.6. What are the sensitive issues that still may cause intercultural problems?

Although there has been enormous economic development over the last decade and the Chinese have adopted a lot of western technologies and management tools, we should not forget they have a very strong cultural background and structures that influence all aspects of their lives, their decision-making processes, their working style and the way they interact. Knowing the most crucial intercultural differences can help you to avoid major conflicts working together with Chinese partners and colleagues or negotiating with Chinese authorities.

The most important areas that could cause intercultural misunderstandings

- Listening and observing.
- Informing and being informed.
- Agreeing and rejecting.
- Recognition and mutual respect.
- Individualism versus collectivism.

Listening and observing

In China you have to invest a lot of time in having conversations with your Chinese employees, partners, clients etc. in order to get to know them and to create a base of understanding and confidence. You should try to explore the situation and the mutual needs, desires and expectations. The more you know about your Chinese counterpart the more easily you can interpret his indirect means of communication (see also chapter 2.7).

Therefore you should use a pragmatic way of communication with Chinese people. Listen patiently and carefully, observe attentively and ask yourself: What kind of guy is my interlocutor? What emotions does he signal? What intentions does he have? Try to go deeply into your interlocutor's thinking and to figure out what is most important to him. Pay attention to indirect signals in the statements and to the gestures, mimics and body language of your partner. Attend especially to those things that have not (yet) been mentioned. Often these are the most crucial points.

Note that there may be different attitudes regarding the best way to do business. Westerners, on the one hand, follow strict, proven rules such as the classic controlling approach that provides you clear criteria and regulations. There are for instance fixed accounting routines for travel expenses, overtime premiums, entertainment costs, incentive bonuses etc. The Chinese, however, often follow their own more flexible, pragmatic and person-focused way of handling such issues. If they think something may help to improve *guanxi* and networking it is not so important for them to follow formal western rules and regulations.

If the different approaches of western and Chinese business partners (i.e. of a western GM and a Chinese deputy GM) are clashing, it is best to work out a detailed, reasonable compromise on which both parties can agree. Otherwise you risk that the Chinese side is blocking your other activities, holding back information, building up a front and undermining your authority. It is important, therefore, that you avoid causing loss of face wherever it is possible and necessary!

You should also listen carefully to the proposals of your Chinese partners, interlocutors and employees; how they would handle certain problems, topics, business processes and strategic issues. Even if it seems to you quite weird or strange at the first glance, there is usually a certain reason in it, which describes the reality with which the Chinese partners or employees are familiar and which they live with and accept. As mentioned above, it is important to read between the lines and to consider carefully to what extent you should accept those approaches. Never forget that the Chinese have a social and cultural background that is influencing their thinking and acting. Check self-critically the advantages of the Chinese approaches and try to find solutions that result in synergy and contentment on both sides.

Informing and being informed

If you, for your part, want to communicate or obtain something, you should direct the conversation slowly but persistently towards your target – the Chinese do the same. In this case slowness is not seen as indulgence or weakness. Avoid putting your interlocutor under pressure. You will risk losing his confidence or you will get an answer designed to terminate the disagreeable situation without your interlocutor losing face. This answer, however, is often a wrong answer, given purely to satisfy you for the moment. Avoid asking direct questions that can just be answered with yes or no. Better is to ask open questions that give the chance to explain things from a different point of view.

Try to promote an atmosphere that encourages frank, open communication with your Chinese partners. Avoid being at cross-purposes when everybody conducts themselves without consulting and understanding the other party. Show your willingness to compromise in order to find a consensus both parties can live with. We recommend finding 'informal leaders', to convince them of your ideas and to gain their loyalty. These opinion leaders might be employees who play the role of a *laoshi* (teacher) and are respected by all the other staff. But members of business associations or design institutes or university professors etc. can also play such a role.

Note that many employees are trained to fulfil a plan, but not to name problems on their own initiative. They fear to be seen as incompetent themselves or as grumblers that always bring bad news; in ancient China bringers of bad news were something even executed. Therefore you should always double-check/monitor at least once, preferably more often, at every stage of a project whether you are still on track or if there are any obstacles that may prevent a successful realisation.

Agreeing and rejecting

For westerners it is often hard to recognise whether a Chinese interlocutor agrees or doesn't agree with the things that were said. The 'famous' Chinese smile and the reserved mimics seem to leave few conclusions. A 'yes' or 'hm' mostly does not mean anything other than that the opposite member has listened to you and understood what you have said. This and the nodding are an encouragement for you to continue. It does not mean, however, that you have full agreement with the content of what you have said. For the most part you can't expect a direct answer to your proposals, because decision-making in China is a complex process. It is not usual and most interlocutors are also not authorised to make 'lonely' decisions.

On the other hand you, for your part, should also avoid making prompt assents or concessions, even if wishes and requests seem to be reasonable and easy to realise. Coming round without getting something in return will often be interpreted by the Chinese as weakness, especially if there is not a well-established, mutual binding relationship existing between the partners yet. Moreover it could arouse the feeling that there is still a lot of unused elbow-room for negotiations.

If the Chinese party calls one of your proposals 'interesting' (instead of good or instructive) you can assume, that your Chinese interlocutors do not appreciate it very much. If you are confronted with demands you do not want to fulfil, you should do the same. You can say, for instance: 'We will study your interesting proposals and wishes intensively and let you know our decision as soon as possible.' Or you can deny your responsibility. Anyway, Chinese people in general don't believe that somebody can decide something without consultation. 'A very good proposal, I will discuss it with my boss and my colleagues' is therefore an elegant way to decline or postpone a request without making anyone lose face.

In general you should avoid the main goals being threatened because of dissent over minor issues. There are topics which are essentially important for the Chinese side, whereas for westerners they are just side issues. In this event, you can easily make some concessions to your Chinese partners to ensure their loyalty regarding the overall goals. Sometimes you can find solutions for problems of your Chinese counterparts, which do not result in any cost for you. So, for instance you can help your Chinese employees to find cost-effective social security services by bypassing FESCO, to get tax advantages or to raise housing funds from the government etc.

You have to be quite strict, if international standards such as quality management are to be met. Also internal control is a major topic, in the purchasing and sales department in particular there must be strict cost transparency ('four eye principle'), otherwise there is danger of *guanxi*-deals, which may not be the best choice for your business.

If positions seem irreconcilable it can be a good idea to adjourn the negotiations and to try new approaches that help you to reach your goal step by step. Sometimes it also makes sense to call a neutral mediator in, who is accepted by both sides. This might be a long, time-consuming and nerve-reacting way, but it can save you a lot of money and disappointment on both sides and will help you to build up a long-lasting relationship that is characterised by a win-win situation and mutual satisfaction.

Recognition and mutual respect

Western negotiators tend to say frankly and bluntly what they like or dislike. They are focusing on hard facts like success, products, technical details, costs or prices and are often neglecting the wishes, problems and indirect desires of their counterparts. What we think is simple, clear, precise and efficient, Chinese feel to be impersonal, harsh/rude and humourless. We are used to looking for direct eye contact, to give a quick feedback and even to interrupt other partners in a conversation – in China, however, respect and deference, especially towards superiors, is seen as polite. Our ways of reacting (intensive eye contact, frankness, showing of emotions) will be considered aggressive, immature or even cheeky. Also be careful not to criticise your own company, your superior, politics, government or other authorities. You should try to demonstrate 'harmony' as a group (company, delegation of negotiators, department, etc.). A devaluation of others always has a negative effect on the one who is criticising too.

At any rate you should take your Chinese counterparts seriously, respect them and motivate them to co-operate in a proactive and productive way. You should promote examples of extraordinary performance by awarding, for instance, the 'employee of the month', 'dealer of the year', 'most creative or productive team' etc. (see also chapter 4.3., monetary and non-monetary incentives). A conjoint appearance for the management team (e.g. western general manager, Chinese deputy general manager) ensures acceptance with your staff and helps to avoid the formation of different informal groups rying for control.

In China it is common practice to foster the relationship with clients and functionaries by providing incentives for them and sometimes also for their families; trips, support for family members to get a place in a western college or university, gifts for the Chinese New Year festival, etc.

Individualism versus collectivism

The western 'culture of debating', for instance between politicians or scientists, is a phenomena that is hard for Chinese people to understand. In China the opinion and the personality are always closely related. Criticism is likely to be taken personally. Therefore a dispute over different opinions should never take place in public, but, if it is really necessary, face-to-face in a very polite form. Otherwise the relationship of the respective partners can be damaged seriously. Even with legal or political debates the Chinese try to find a solution on friendly terms before a public debate starts. Therefore what seems to westerners like the influencing of a judge or political manipulation on camera, in China is seen as the 'golden way' in order to find a consensus and to avoid conflicts.

However, in the last couple of years there has been a trend towards an increasing individualism amongst the younger Chinese people, especially if they hold middle or higher management positions. Also the Chinese government supports a turning away from the 'iron rice bowl' philosophy. Driven by economic necessities they encourage thoughts of profitability and the capitalistic way of acting. Thus the government strongly promotes the purchase of flats for owner-occupation, for example.

The roots of Chinese history and culture show that the Chinese are actually not averse to capitalistic thinking, as they traditionally always have been people who love to deal and to bargain and who have strong hierarchical structures. Only elderly people, workers on a lower level and some institutions of public life (such as hospitals, universities, public administration offices, etc.) still stick to the socialistic ideas.

Summary

There are three rules of thumb that help you to communicate without losing or causing loss of face:

- Enhance the prestige of your partner by praise, votes of thanks and appreciation (for the work that has been done, the success that has been realised or generally about the importance of China, the economic boom etc.) or a polite request (e.g. for support or advice).
- Try to avoid disagreeable topics (like conflicts in the past, unsolved problems, failures, misfortunes or delicate political issues). If you have to mention problems or mistakes, try to show your appreciation about the co-operation in other fields first and avoid the delicate issues at least in the official part of the discussion and at the very beginning of the negotiations.
- Assume the perspective of your Chinese partner. Go deeply into his situation and try to analyse his interests and thinking. This way you get to know your interlocutor better and it is easier for you to be aware of misunderstandings and misinterpretations (affecting either party) (see also Reisach, 1998).

Further sources

Hofstede, G. (1991) *Cultures and Organisations – Software of the Mind: Intercultural Cooperation and its Importance for Survival*, London.

Hofstede, G. (1992) *Culture's Consequences – International Differences in Work-related Values*, Beverly Hills.

Reisach, U. (1997) 'Chinesische Denkstrukturen und Kommunikationsmuster', in *Personal*, 12, pp. 612–19.

Reisach, U. (1998) 'Konfliktvermeidung und Konfliktbereinigung', in *Wirtschaftswelt China*, 1, pp. 18–20.

Reisach, U. Tauber, T. and Yuan, N. (1997) *China – Wirtschaftspartner zwischen Wunsch und Wirklichkeit*, Vienna, Ueberreuther.

Table 5   Characteristics of western and Chinese thinking

Characteristics	Western world	China
Structure of thinking	Rational: systematic, mostly linear, respectively ramifying chains of cause and effect Emphasising of objectivity, conclusive thinking and inner consistency, absence of contradictions	Intuitively: arguing from analogies, multi-dimensional, respecting direct and indirect influences and reciprocal effects Emphasising of relativity and network connections, analogies and associations (including emotional)
Typical pattern of thinking	A → A1, A2; A1 → A11, A12, A13; A2 → A21, A22, A23	(network diagram)
Philosophy	Looking for absolute truth and logical explanations, theory of absolute ideas	Looking for concrete support to master the life, theory of relations between real things
Religion	Faith in a supernatural creating God that is the origin and the goal of all human being, tendency towards idealism and fanaticism	Subordinating of the human being under the community, harmony of the whole, piety towards living and dead persons, tendency towards realism and pragmatism
Science	(Abstract) theories about the world and its functioning, search for new perceptions and explanations; research targeting 'real big' innovations (technical revolution)	Investigation of relations and reciprocal effects targeting the support/improvement of the daily life; research of refined methods and new applications of well-known materials and principles (technical evolution)

Table 5 (*continued*)

Characteristics	Western world	China
Style of argumentation	Abstract and deductive: rational conviction by the power of the argument	Concrete and inductive: emotional conviction by the power of the person

Source: Reisach, U. (1997) 'Chinesische Denkstrukturen und Kommunikationsmuster', in *Personal*, 12, p. 618.

2.7. Do language problems really matter?

China and the western world – there are not only clashingly different economic interests, but also totally different language, thinking and communication structures. Irrespective of all the reformatory efforts, the thinking and behaviour of Chinese business partners will be strongly influenced by the peculiarities of this idiomatic and cultural sphere. For modernisation does not also automatically mean westernisation. In order to be successful personally and in business, it is necessary to interpret the verbal and non-verbal signals of your Chinese business partners the right way and also to take care to be correctly understood. You should never forget that success in business is closely related to personal esteem and mutual understanding.

The most evident barrier of understanding is the language. Only very few expatriates and negotiators have the opportunity and the time to study Chinese until they reach a very sophisticated level. Therefore English and interpreters dominate the business world. Nevertheless it is a big advantage to know at least something about the basics and the peculiarities of the Chinese language and character writing. The Chinese way of expressing themselves in a conversation as well as the way in which letters of intent, contracts and other agreements are formulated, are deeply anchored in the language and the mental structures.

Table 6 Contrast between language, writing and thinking

Western countries	China
• writing down abstract terms	• concrete, plastic marking
• construction of sentences and grammar according to strict rules, precise ways to express, clear-cut definitions	• no grammar, sense results of the context, strong appeal to the emotional sphere
• analysis, segmentation of thoughts	• transmitting of holistic mental attitudes
• Objective explanation of theories, not necessarily related to practice	• Suggesting of a way to act, not necessarily based on theory
• Rational explanation of the world	• Appealing, vivid mediation of the world

Real understanding of the Chinese language with all its metaphorical hidden meanings requires not only analytical thinking (as we are used to it from western languages), but above all it needs imagination and empathy.

Western writing means lining up letters and in doing so producing words that are totally abstract. In comparison to this by Chinese character writing nuances of a thought or of an impulse can be expressed in a very discrete way. The single symbols/characters – an average Chinese newspaper reader knows about 3,000 of them – are derived from pictures. Each of these pictures originally showed a specific object or idea (as computer icons do, for example). Therefore the Chinese language is much more graphic than Indo-Germanic languages. It appeals much more to the imagination, to the mind and even to the heart. Chinese characters aim to suggest a certain way to act and to convince the addressees.

In contrast to western languages there is nearly no grammar in the literal sense. Classes of words, singular and plural, persons, past tense, presence and future – these can't be seen by declinations and the inflexion of words (as it is usual with western languages) – they just become evident by the context.

Also in the oral language the context plays an important role. Of approximately 3,000 frequently used idioms, each is represented by its own character and all of these will be expressed by only about 420 syllables. A single spoken word therefore rouses a lot of complex associations with the addressee. Also ambiguities are pretty common and are often even intended or seen as very sophisticated. Therefore a Chinese sentence may have four or five English translations, all of which are correct. On the other hand important details can often be lost if a text is translated into Chinese.

Particularities of the Chinese language

- All Chinese words are monosyllabic (today they are usually combined into double words).
- In Mandarin Chinese all syllables end with vocals, 'n' or 'ng'.
- There is no accumulation of consonants possible (i.e. no 'st', 'pf' or 'nd').
- Each word has between five and 80 homonyms (words with the same sound).

As a result of the above mentioned you can find a multitude of associations and plays on words in the Chinese language. Only by the interaction of the single parts will the meaning of the whole become evident and make sense. In case of doubt the Chinese write the characters in question into their palms or in the air.

In the Chinese language we frequently find sequences of words that seem to westerners to be just an empty phrase (i.e. in contractual texts), but to Chinese counterparts they are of such importance, that the absence of them can even wreck a whole contract. These problems often pertain to the relationship between the partners; these formulations are seen as essential by the Chinese and transmit a whole bunch of feelings and mental attitudes that should regulate the general character of the co-operation. Precise detail is not deemed necessary; in fact, each detailed statement of a contract can be invalidated by reference to general formulas. The Chinese side practises this very often.

The Chinese language directly influences the mental attitudes of the Chinese people. Understanding Chinese characters and their meaning mainly utilises the right side of the cerebral hemisphere, the area responsible for the contextual and plastic thinking. The decoding of western languages, in contrast, addresses more the left side of the cerebral hemisphere, which promotes formal, analytical thinking and that recalls the meaning of the codes in our language memory. Not least because of their writing, Chinese are masters in combining whereas the westerners are masters in abstracting.

Summary/Recommendations

The conditions of the Chinese language and thinking don't primarily target analytical, segmentative thinking, but composing, synthetic thinking, that depends a lot on the specific cultural and social background of the Chinese. Chinese expressions are not as limited as western ones. They leave a lot of room for concrete associations and starting points for further thinking. Westerners often can't understand Chinese allusions or games on words because they are not familiar with the contextual peculiarities of the Chinese background.

Keeping all this in mind, you have to be aware that it needs somebody who is really familiar with all the peculiarities of the Chinese language and thinking in order to avoid overlooking or misinterpreting messages that Chinese counterparts intend to transmit to you. That means in important business meetings, you need a native speaker or a real expert of the Chinese language, who is familiar with all these kinds of plays on words, background intentions and allusions.

If you hire an interpreter or a consultant you should not just check his/her language skills and the knowledge of your branch of industry and of other special matters, but also whether he or she is able and willing to transmit these hidden messages to you. The last is a matter of confidence, because for Chinese people it is often difficult (and sometimes also a bit embarrassing) to explain these kinds of things to foreigners with a different cultural background and understanding. You should listen very carefully to annotations your interpreter makes and should not reject it as mere word splitting. It may help, if you ask your interpreter frequently during a negotiation how he/she would understand the intention of the things that have been said.

Further sources

Granet, M. (1985) *Das chinesische Denken – Inhalt, Form, Charakter*, Frankfurt am Main.

Hofstede, G. (1991) *Cultures and Organisations: Software of the Mind: Intercultural Cooperation and its Importance for Survival*, London.

Hofstede, G (1992) *Culture's Consequences – International Differences in Work-related Values*, Beverly Hills.

Reisach, U. (1997) *Chinesische Denkstrukturen und Kommunikationsmuster*, in *Personal*, 12, pp. 612.
Reisach, U., Tauber, T. and Yuan, X. (1997) *China – Wirtschaftspartner zwischen Wunsch und Wirklichkeit*, Vienna, Ueberreuther.

Table 7   Different styles of communication

Criteria	Western countries	China
Main focus	Subject (project/job instruction, product, price, technical issue etc.)	Persons (client, supplier, partner, employee, authorities) and their relations
Target of the conversation	Explaining the subject, solving a problem, improving the performance	Building up relations/*guanxi* (confidence, benevolence, harmony), stabilising and intensifying it, not losing or causing loss of face
Gestures and mimic	Vitality, spontaneity, individuality, frankness and expression of feelings, eye contact	Being chary of gestures and mimics, high level of self-control, no direct eye contact
Language	Direct, frank, authentic, focused on the subject (will be seen in China often as cool, harsh and humourless)	Indirect, very ritualised, focused on persons ('empty phrases of courtesy', creation of positive associations)
Voice	Emphasising of important things enforces the persuasive power and creates authority	Modulating of the voice is very rare and happens mostly in a ritualised form; a melodious sound plays an important role
Style of communication	Dynamic, vigorous (Catcher-style)	Reserved, 'wait and see attitude' (Judoka-style)
Readiness for conflicts	High: competition of ideas and performance principle	Low: respect and a face-keeping style of communication help to avoid conflicts
Behaviour when there are different opinions	Polarising: emphasis of the contrasts	Balancing: emphasis of the common interests and aspects
Behaviour in case of conflict	Power-driven, often emotional and aggressive, persisting in one's own point of view, sometimes dramatising	Evasive, playing down, postponing or exchange of participating people (= uncompromised new start)
Solution of conflicts by	Factual arguments: numbers, facts, pertinent compromises, reference to legal rules/con-tracts, appeal of neutral instances (experts, law courts)	Persons: intermediaries, authorities, proofs of loyalty, new formulations, amicable, whenever possible extra-judicial solution of disputes

Source: Reisach, U. (1997) 'Chinesische Denkstrukturen und Kommunikationsmuster', in *Personal*, 12, p. 616.

2.8. What are the most common legal business structures in China?

Since the 1970s, with the development of commercial law in China, a number of different vehicles for foreign investment have emerged. Each of the options available to foreign investors is described briefly below. Most of these structures are also available to Chinese enterprises as a means of investment. Most international companies may begin with an export business to China. After achieving sales in the region of 2 million US dollars, it may make sense to open a representative or even a branch office. With further development of the business, a joint venture or wholly foreign owned company on the basis of limited liability is recommended. Then the demand for the product, distribution and service-related activities could be set up according to customer need. Larger companies can also be financed by the Shenzhen or Shanghai stock market.

The most important types of business structures

- Representative office
- Branch office
- Foreign investment enterprises
    limited liability company
    company limited by shares

Representative office

The first representative offices were established in 1980 under the Provisional Regulations Regarding the Control of Resident Representative Offices of Foreign Enterprises in China. This form of investment has been the most common means through which foreign companies have established a permanent presence in China. The main disadvantage of the representative office is that its activities are usually restricted by the central government and by the terms of the business licence, which needs to be obtained in order to carry out activities in the PRC. As a general principle, representative offices may engage in promotional activities but may not carry out direct business operations. However, many of them do undertake such operations, although it is forbidden according to law. The general attitude of the government is also interesting. As long as the operation pays relevant taxes, the government does not punish such activities in general. No funds other than those necessary for the maintenance of the representative office itself should flow through the bank account of the office. In practise, however, there are numerous areas in which the distinction between permissible and prohibited activities are blurred.

Establishment of a representative office entails three main steps: finding a Chinese sponsor, formal application to the relevant authority and registration with the local Administration for Industry and Commerce (AIC) in the city of proposed operation. Chinese sponsors are usually state owned enterprises specialising in the business of the applicant. However, general sponsors are available. The Ministry of Foreign Trade and Economic Co-operation (MOFTEC) is the relevant authority for most applications. The representative office must also register with the tax authorities. A representative office must have at least one official registered representative, who may be local or foreign. An office may employ additional local staff but only through one of the official foreign service organisations such as the Foreign Enterprise Service Organisation (FESCO).

Branch office

The Company Law of PRC, promulgated on 31 December 1993 and effective from 1 July 1994, introduced the concept of branches of foreign companies within China for the first time at a national level. Registered branches, unlike representative offices, are permitted to engage in direct business activities. A branch does not have legal person status but bears civil liability for its acts. The parent company must provide funds for its branch operations and will be held liable for its related liabilities.

Foreign investment enterprises

When the PRC began encouraging foreign investment in the late 1970s the concept of Sino-foreign joint ventures was introduced with the objective of helping China develop, with the aid of foreign management and technology, based on the principle of equality and mutual benefit. Foreign investment enterprises (FIEs) are the traditional form of foreign direct investment involving the creation of a new legal entity in China. The three forms of FIE are as follows:

- equity joint venture – a limited liability company in which the foreign investor has a minimum 25 per cent investment;
- co-operative joint venture – a co-operative arrangement that may be established either as a separate legal entity or as a purely contractual arrangement;
- wholly owned foreign enterprise – an enterprise established as a subsidiary of the foreign investor.

Each of these three forms of investment is subject to minimum amounts of registered capital, which is not divided into shares. The key difference between the two types of joint venture is the legal status of the venture and the provisions for distribution of profit. An equity joint venture is a separate legal entity, whereas, in its pure form, the co-operative joint venture is not. The co-operative joint venture is established on a contractual basis with each party bearing its own costs. One of the key advantages of the co-operative joint venture over the equity joint venture is the ability to distribute profit according to a joint venture contract rather than in accordance with requisite capital contributions. The government encourages joint ventures in specific fields, generally those involving export, import substitution, technology and skills transfer. In many cases a minimum level is established for the proportion of goods which must be exported by a Sino-foreign joint venture.

Wholly owned foreign enterprises are foreign investment enterprises owned exclusively by one or more foreign investors. Foreign ownership offers the potential for stronger control over management and know-how. However, the lack of a Chinese partner is sometimes a weakness given China's complex legislation, governmental structure and regional differences. In addition, there are a number of industry sectors such as retailing and service industries which are open to joint ventures but are prohibited or restricted to the wholly foreign owned enterprises. Approval procedures for wholly foreign owned enterprises often require newer technology to be used or higher quality products produced than would be by a similar joint venture.

Limited liability company

The new Company Law of PRC of 1994, introduced the concept of the limited liability company. This is an entity that does not have capital divided into shares, and the liability of the investors to foreign investment enterprises, described above. However, the law stipulates that the regulation regarding FIEs will continue to apply, thereby creating a different regulatory regime for non-FIE limited liability companies.

A limited liability company must have between two and 50 shareholders and minimum contributed capital of between RMB 100,000 and RMB 500,000, depending on the nature of the business. All capital contributions whether in cash or kind must be made, valued and audited by a registered accountant before the company can be approved.

Company limited by shares

The new Company Law of PRC also provides for companies limited by shares in which the liability of the investors is limited to their share subscriptions. The key difference between the company limited by shares and the limited liability company is that the shares of a company limited by shares may be publicly traded. These companies are similar, in concept, to joint stock limited companies, which were created under the Securities Law of PRC, which came into effect on 1 July 1999. This law has been used as the basis for creating companies currently listed on the Shanghai, Shenzhen, Hong Kong and New York stock exchanges. The Shanghai and Shenzhen authorities have yet to state whether the local legislation allowing the creation of joint stock limited companies is superseded by the new national legislation. To set up a limited company there must be more than five participants, more than half of whom must be resident in China. The paid up capital of the company must not be less than RMB 10 million. The promoters may subscribe all the shares for themselves or, alternatively up to 65% of the shares may be offered to the public. State Council approval is required for public offerings outside China.

Lately a new trend has emerged: Western firms have ventured into the merger and acquisition business, buying Chinese SOEs. Just as is the case in joint venture companies, it is difficult to get a clear picture of the Chinese company. The biggest difference: While in a joint venture Chinese partners try to hide their assets, they will overvalue them in the case of M&A so as to increase the selling price.

Summary/Recommendations

The market entry and establishment of a business in China can be done through different means of legal entities. The most appropriate one depends on the product and size of the business volume with the Chinese customer. The traditional method is beginning with exports to China through agents and import companies. The next logical steps are one's own representative offices and the establishment of local production enterprises on the basis of limited liability. (See also chapter 10.7.)

Further sources

Cooper & Lybrand (1994) *Guide to Reporting and Accounting*, HK.
Ernst & Young (1994) *Doing Business in China*, HK.
Reisach, U., Tauber, T. and Yuan, X. (1997) *China – Wirtschaftspartner zwischen Wunsch und Wirklichkeit*, Vienna, Ueberreuther.
Wang, Y. (1996) *Investment in China*, CITIC, NY.

2.9. What are the advantages and disadvantages of the different ways to enter the market?

Most of the internationally operating medium- and larger-sized companies want to participate in the long-term perspectives of China, one of the largest-growing markets in the world. The market penetration mostly begins with some kind of export business activities with the advantages of high operational convenience and low risks. Major disadvantages are the still relatively high customs duties and complicated import formalities, and the fact that the end-user of the products can not make his special requirements and complaints known. This makes it difficult to develop tailor-made products and related after-sales services and, as a consequence, to further develop the business.

This motivates many foreign investors to build up a production and service facility in China. China's major objective is to strengthen the domestic economy and to avoid extensive foreign currency expenditures as far as possible. Therefore, the Chinese government is promoting foreign investment and technology for China.

Possibilities of market entry

- Import/Export of raw materials, semi-finished and finished goods
    through purchasing and sales agents (see Chapter 9);
    through own representatives in China (see chapter 2.8);
    through own representative offices (see chapter 2.8);
    settle down in a special free trade zones (see chapter 2.11).
- Licence agreements with a Chinese enterprise.
- Contractual co-operation with a Chinese enterprise
    purchasing co-operation;
    sales and distribution co-operation (see Chapter 9);
    research and development co-operation (see chapter 8.9).
- Equity joint venture with a Chinese partner (see chapter 2.8 and 8.4).
    with majority shares;
    with minority shares.
- Establishment of a wholly foreign owned enterprise (WFOE) (see chapter 10.4).
- Holding companies (see chapter 2.10).
- Trend to stock companies (see chapter 2.8 and 10.7).

Imports and licence agreements

In the past, all imports to China and the respective prices had to be approved by licences from the Ministry of Foreign Trade and Economic Co-operation (MOFTEC) in order to guarantee an adequate balance of foreign exchange trade. Recently, MOFTEC has lost full control over all imported products. Foreign trade companies have the right to decide their quantities and prices by themselves. Also a 'one year licence' is no longer needed for most ordinary products. However, the import of a few products is still limited by special quota systems in order to protect the local industries and to control the trade balance with some countries. With the recent approval of participation in the WTO, further improvements and liberation in trade can be expected. The average rates of customs duty have already been reduced remarkably within the last few years in preparation for WTO entry.

All imported products have to be inspected and approved by the State Administration of Import and Export Commodity Inspection (SAIECI) organisation. They have subsidiaries in most western countries. SAIECI is controlling the contracted terms with international standards and regulations due to quantity, quality, specification, packaging, weight, safety and hygiene. Sometimes, such regulations are aimed at protecting the domestic industries or acting as counter-measures in the case of restrictions to the import of Chinese products to a western market. In 1998, for instance, the internationally acknowledged ASME and TÜV standards for the import of pressure vessels were no longer accepted. The certification for the additional Chinese inspection now costs up to DM 50,000, to be paid by each importing company. The export business can be further promoted through counter-trade arrangements or through a licence agreement with Chinese partners. Such arrangements combine the Chinese low labour cost and the lack of foreign currency with the possibility to import high-quality machinery and equipment as a basis for the production of high-quality products. The Chinese government is heavily promoting the importation of the latest technology by granting duty and tax subsidies.

Foreign invested enterprises (FIE)

China is looking for the transfer of latest and highest technology standards at the lowest cost levels. Many Chinese customers don't want to accept reduced quality levels or a downsized scope of supply. This urges potential foreign investors to compete by the combination of lower labour costs, better energy efficiency, longer product durability, more reliability and better features for environmental protection. In joint investment projects, the Chinese joint venture partner mostly supplies land, buildings, labour force, machinery and equipment. The Chinese government is promoting projects which support the balancing of foreign exchange or which represent a high-tech status. Such high technology projects are also promoted by tax and customs duty subsidies or by reduced costs for land and buildings. MOFTEC defined the regulations for attracting foreign investment in 1995. These regulations define four categories of foreign invested projects: promoted, permitted, restricted and not permitted. Limited or prohibited are products with a high saturation grade in the domestic market, monopolistic products of state owned companies and products of the service industries such as telecommunications, insurance, banking, publishing and law firms. Such restrictions of foreign investment have been loosened will be only step by step or not completely removed with the present entry to the WTO.

Chinese criteria for approval of foreign invested enterprises (FIE)

- Transfer of technology.
- Investment of foreign capital.
- Increase of profitability and efficiency.
- Transfer of management know-how.
- Training and qualification of Chinese staff.

- Improvement of product quality levels and international competitiveness.
- Reduction of environmental emissions.
- Improved energy and raw material consumption.

Source: Reisach, U., Tauber, T. and Yuan, X. (1997) *China – Wirtschaftspartner zwischen Wunsch und Wirklichkeit*, Ueberreuther, Vienna, p. 131.

Joint ventures

Joint ventures have been an important tool for market entry to China for many years. Major advantages are reduced import duties, lower labour costs, possibility for tailor-made product and service solutions, more effective marketing and distribution activities, no foreign exchange problems, governmental subsidies, quicker delivery times and more flexibility on meeting the customers' individual requirements. The registered investment depends on the final total investment. The paid in capital at the beginning of business operation has to be 70 per cent for joint ventures with a total investment of less than 3 million US dollars. The paid in capital ratio can be reduced to 50 per cent for total investments between 3–10 million US dollars. In case of even higher investments the ratio can be further reduced to 33 and 40 per cent. Most joint ventures and wholly foreign owned enterprises (WFOE) are registered as limited liability companies in order to limit the financial risks for the investor. The applicable laws are similar to the German limited liability companies regulations. The minimum levels of investment amount to RMB 500,000 for production related companies, RMB 300,000 for trading companies and RMB 100,000 for service related companies. Equity joint ventures can be also registered as joint stock companies. Then, the company is liable for the whole equity and the shareholders according to their kept share ratio. The de-investment or reduction of the invested capital is not possible for a joint venture during the approved period of operation. Only contractual ventures have such possibilities. However, this is subject to governmental approval. The distribution of the paid in capital is possible through the ending of the joint venture or by special approval through the respective authorities. With the end of the joint venture, all open accounts with debtors, employees and governmental bodies have to be compensated. The rest can be paid out according to the shares of the investors.

Wholly foreign owned enterprises (WFOE)

The Chinese law of 1986 also permits the establishment of wholly foreign owned enterprises. However, the scope of business is limited to special products and activities. So far, WFOE are not permitted in media, insurance, banking and telecommunications, infrastructure, real estate and leasing. Further restrictions are the requirement for a 50 per cent export rate and the respective balancing of the needed foreign currencies. The approval of such enterprises has become much easier within the past few years. This has resulted in a much higher quantity of such foreign owned enterprises. Most of the foreign investors have now much more experience in how to start up and operate their business in China. They also prefer to make their own decisions, without the time-consuming process of negotiations with a local counterpart.

WFOE are recommended if:
- the investor is operating within a relatively well-developed infrastructure with a reliable and efficient local government that is supporting the enterprise development;
- the investment project is small or medium sized;
- the investor is producing high-tech products. He will want to protect his sensitive manufacturing and product know-how – no huge transfer of know-how is required;
- the headquarters has a very individual business culture and doesn't want to mix it up with one of a local state owned company;
- the manufactured products are only supplied to a limited and special customer circle, which is well known to the investor. The sales, marketing and distribution efforts don't need the help of local investment partners.

Source: German Chamber of Commerce (1995).

Holding companies

Holding companies often take the form of WFOE investment. However, theoretically, holding companies can alternatively be an equity joint venture according to the relevant regulations promulgated by MOFTEC. They are mainly installed to support services of several related local investments. Shares have to be consolidated within the holding company: then, they can offer finance, law, tax, accounting, human resources, information technology, marketing, sales and consulting support to the subsidiaries. The required total investment has to be at least 30 million US dollars. A holding is especially recommended for a larger-sized group of companies with extensive investment activities in the Chinese market.

Summary/Recommendations

There are different possibilities for market entry in China. Business activities should be developed step by step taking particular account of the individual nature of the investing enterprise with the special applications for the products and requirements of the key markets. In a long-term perspective, there should be well-planned strategies for the most efficient and promising market penetration. Combinations of several planned steps may also make sense. Sometimes, the establishment of a joint venture with a minority partner may make more sense than the establishment of a WFOE. Now the business opportunities will expand considerably with the entry of China into the WTO. This applies for the exporters to China as well as for investors in production facilities.

Further sources

Moser, M. (ed.) and Lauffs, A (2000) 'The Problems of Distribution, Salzer A. – Recruiting and Managing a Distribution Workforce', *China Troubleshooter*, HK Asia Law & Practice.
Reisach, U., Tauber, T. and Yuan, X. (1997) *China – Wirtschaftspartner zwischen Wunsch und Wirklichkeit*, Vienna, Ueberreuther.
Wang, Y. (1996) *Investment in China*, CITIC, NY.

2.10. When does it make sense to establish a holding company?

Many international operating 'groups of companies' have already invested in several projects in China. Meanwhile, their investments often exceed 30 million US dollars. This is the initial amount of investment which is required as a minimum for the establishment of a holding company. Most of the investors appreciate the benefits in creating a holding body for their extensive business activities in China. The holding can support their entities in strategic and operational matters and supply extensive legal, fiscal, finance, human resources and sales support services in combination with the representation of the political interests of the group of companies.

The most important activities of a holding company

- Representation
  maintaining contacts with the Chinese national, local and city governments and with all the Chinese joint venture partners;
  representing the strategic and political interests of the foreign headquarters operative divisions;
  keeping contacts to major suppliers and key customers.
- Co-ordination
  not managing, but co-ordinating all of the operational business activities in China;
  support in consolidation and restructuring of the various investment activities;
  co-ordination and support in the implementation of the overall strategic marketing and management concept as well as in the positioning of the headquarters' products and activities.

- Supporting services
  support of the entities without or against the payment of service fees;
  financial, legal, fiscal, human resource and R&D services;
  due diligence investigations of new investment projects;
  standardised finance control and reporting on behalf of the group of
    companies;
  marketing and sales support co-ordination.

Formalities for the establishment of a holding company

The legal framework for the establishment of an investment holding company was first formulated in 1995 with additional regulations in August 1999. Meanwhile, several holding companies have been established with a wider basis of experience. The required minimum registered capital for the establishment of an investment holding company amounts to 30 million US dollars. In addition, there is a 'debt-equity' regulation, which fixes the ratio of self-paid in equity to debt financed equity. Since 1999, the self-paid in equity must amount to at least 20 per cent of the total equity. The total investment is comprised of the self-paid in equity and the debt financed one. Therefore, it can be financed up to 80 per cent of the total equity. Consequently, it can be understood that the self-paid in capital is more important and relevant than the total invested equity. The main purpose in the future is the fixing of maximum debt limits in relation to the invested and paid in equity. The new regulation is similar to the relevant laws for domestic Chinese companies.

A holding company is permitted to deal with transport and warehousing or stock keeping for it's own domestic subsidiaries. However, the holding must hold at least 10 per cent of the invested shares in such activities. For all other related services for the own invested entities, the holding must hold at least 25 per cent of the shares as in the past. Board resolutions are required for the approval of such outsourcing services, signed and approved by all directors. Furthermore, investment holding companies can now establish their own R&D centres. This could be a possible method by which to apply for governmental subsidies or tax holiday arrangements. In the past, this has been only possible for production enterprises.

Representation

For many huge groups of companies with several or few larger investment activities in China, it is very important to have a legal body for the representation of the overall economical and political interests of the group. On the other hand it is also important for officials in China to know whom to contact in case of specific issues.

Co-ordination

One further major task of a holding is to support the improvement of the overall performance and efficiency of the several investments of the group in China. The strengths of the several business activities have to be worked out and weaknesses eliminated as much as possible. Obvious threats to the business have to be realised in advance and new business opportunities be followed up as a basis for the continuous developing and the implementing of strategic planning processes. A benchmarking analysis helps to improve products and services as well as to reduce cost in the various business operation activities. For the fulfilment of these tasks it is recommended and usual practise for the management of the holding to be represented in the various boards of directors of the local entities and to keep close contact with the appropriate management.

Supporting services

A further important question is related to the possible services an investment holding is permitted to carry out on behalf of its invested entities and the respective headquarters' sub-divisions. Possible supporting services include legal advice in labour and commercial contract law or in all kinds of investment-related issues such as capital increase, changes of the joint venture contract or articles of association or when legal opinions are required on special issues. The fiscal advice can help in optimising the tax payments for investment projects or business operational activities. The finance-related services can support cash flow or loan arrangements with required bank guarantees. The holding Siemens China Ltd has formed it's own financial services company. However, this status also required a total investment level of 80 million US dollars and was subject to approval by the People's Bank of China (PBOC). Management or service fees can be paid for the supplied services from the related invested entities or its headquarters. But, the Chinese law requires a specific board resolution from the board of the invested entities for authorisation.

A further important question for foreign investors is the possibility of carrying out sales, marketing and service co-ordinating activities for the related local entities or the foreign subsidiaries of the group of companies or other manufacturers. The active trade and sales of imported products in the name and the account of the holding companies with the additional convenience of Renminbi billing is quite limited or often not possible in China. Therefore, the formulation of the fixed scope of business with the Ministry of Foreign Trade and Economic Co-operation (MOFTEC) in China is very important. The experiences of existing holding companies seem quite different with respect to the approval of this important issue. However, the holding at least can install sales co-ordination and promotion people to do liaison work. With this instrument, the total marketing, sales, distribution and service business activities can be optimised in favour of the holding and it's representation of the whole group of companies. Now, investment holdings are also permitted to be active in export business. They can purchase domestic products and export them in their own name and account. There are only limitations when export quotas for the respective products exist. These new opportunities might be quite interesting in special cases, but don't fit the strategic objectives of most western investors.

Summary/Recommendations

Before the second half of the last decade, most of the multinationals just started their business in China with the establishment of smaller investments. Meanwhile, several of such smaller platforms have expanded into more profitable business volumes and performance. Now, it is important to increase the overall efficiency of the several investments and to make use of all legal, fiscal, finance and strategic possibilities which are given in China. The establishment of a holding company can help to fulfil this difficult but important task. Most of the international operating 'groups of companies' have opened a holding company for such reasons.

Further sources

Cooper & Lybrand (1994) *Guide to Reporting and Accounting*, HK.
Moser, M. (ed). (2000) *China Troubleshooter*, HK, Asia Law & Practice.
Schulte C. (1992) *Holding Strategien*, Wiesbaden, Gabler.

2.11. When does it make sense to locate in a free trade zone?

Free trade zones (FTZ) were designed to assist in the opening up of China to the outside world so as to develop international trade and promote economic prosperity. In China there are presently 15 FTZs of which 13 are operating. The free trade zones are governed by two laws, these being from the State Council for Customs Regulations which applies to all FTZs and from the local municipal council. For this reason policies vary between the different FTZs. Tax rebate for companies in Shanghai Waigaoqiao free trade zone is 25 per cent. However, in other FTZs this might be less. When choosing a FTZ in which to locate, not only the position should be considered but also the preferential policies. Companies operating in the FTZ can have various legal forms. The most common are wholly foreign owned enterprises and equity joint ventures. FTZs are not attractive for representative offices (i.e. cannot issue receipts for tax refund). The first and most famous FTZ, which has attracted the most foreign investment, is the Shanghai Waigaoqiao free trade zone.

Standard application process

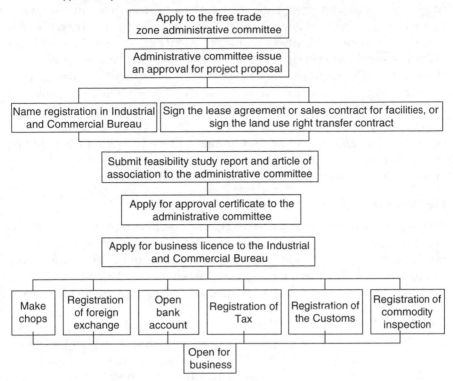

Chart 2   Application process for locating in a free trade zone

Source: Fiducia Management Consultants, HK, 1999.

Shanghai Waigaoqiao FTZ

Shanghai Waigaoqiao FTZ was established in June 1990 and was the first of its kind. Waigaoqiao is located 20 Kilometres from the centre of Shanghai on the east coast of Pudong. A major part of the port is located inside the free trade zone. The free trade zone was developed to encourage certain types of investment. These consist of 'manufacturing, processing and assembling', 'bonded warehouse, commodity distribution and part maintenance' and 'international trade'. Goods that are sold from the FTZ to China proper are considered as imports and goods that enter the FTZ from China proper are considered as exports.

Companies, which are located in Waigaoqiao FTZ can take part in trade with the Chinese domestic market and issue their own VAT invoice. However, legally the FTZs are not considered as part of China. In China the standard level of value added tax is 17 per cent. The companies located in the Waigaoqiao FTZ are refunded 25 per cent for trade with the Chinese domestic market. Furthermore, companies can open both Renminbi and foreign currency accounts, depending on which business categories the company is in. They can also convert their Renminbi sales into foreign exchange. Of the three different categories mentioned previously, only companies active in selling goods from the FTZ into China proper are restricted as to how they can convert their Renminbi sales into foreign currency. However, if the trading company uses an intermediary (i.e. an import/export company), then it can still obtain foreign currency, but with a reduced margin. Companies also can have their own bonded factory and warehouse. In this aspect, there is no limit regarding the time and category of goods. However, for this you first need to obtain the approval of the Waigaoqiao FTZ administrative committee.

Establishment requirements

Companies active in production and logistics, must have more than 200,000 US dollar in registered capital and they must rent or purchase more than factory buildings or warehouses of at least 400 square metres in the FTZ. Pure trading companies must also have a minimum registered capital of 200,000 US dollars. However, they only have to rent a minimum of 20 square metres of office space.

Duties and other importing costs

- Imported manufacturing equipment, construction materials and office appliances for self-use (except for vehicles) are free of duty and import VAT.
- Companies that import raw materials, parts, components and packaging materials into the FTZ are required to pay duties on the goods. This varies according to the product.
- When selling goods from the FTZ to the Chinese domestic market the agent costs will be approximately 1 per cent of the import value. When purchasing raw materials from the Chinese domestic market for the purpose of export the agent costs will be approximately 1 per cent of the export value. However, companies will also encounter a few other costs.

Income tax

Although there is an income tax rate of 15 per cent, processing companies receive a tax break, which lasts up to the second year of profit. After this period, for another three years, the company will only have to pay half of the 15 per cent; after this full payments required. Exceptions to the rule are made if the processing company's exports exceed 70 per cent. Then, it can enjoy an income tax level of 10 per cent. Logistic and trading companies receive a tax break, which lasts up to the first year of profit. After this period, for another three years, the company will only have to pay half of the 15 per cent of the full payment.

Summary/Recommendations

The advantages and costs of locating in Waigaoqiao (Shanghai) have been explained above. The advantage of locating in the FTZ is that it is possible to have a trading company that is wholly foreign owned. From this you can gain more control over your China activities such as standardising promotion and distribution. Trading companies are not restricted to trading in their own goods i.e. those produced in the FTZ or in China proper, but can also trade in products manufactured abroad. Furthermore, advantages arise with regard to companies who sub-contract to local producers, but wish to give the impression that these goods are made by themselves. Waigaoqiao also offers a solution when a company wants to import products into the FTZ and 'polish them up', i.e. put the company's name on the product and then re-export it back to China proper. The purchaser has the impression that it has been made by the foreign company and tax is only paid on the percentage of the goods which did not originate from China proper.

Further sources

China Briefing (2001) *Dezhan Shira*, 10, HK.

General role of business

Company A fulfils the application and registration for the import (registration pamphlet for bonded goods)

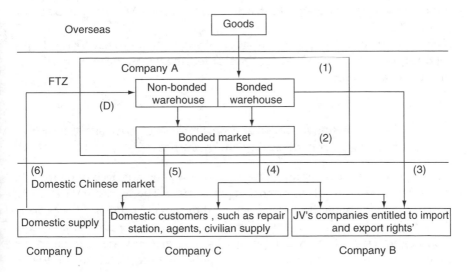

Chart 3 Example of a trading company and its functions
Source: Fiducia Management Consultants, HK, 1999.

- No time limit for bonded warehousing.
- Direct transaction with company B:

    commercial invoice and foreign currency settlement;

    company B goes through the customs formalities for bonded goods transactions including paying duties and VAT;

    company B commissions an agent.

- Bonded market acts as the import agent and company A, after paying duties and VAT, sells to company B using RMB with the official VAT invoice titled company A:

    domestic goods and bonded goods can be stored in separate parts of one FTZ warehouse. Company A pays RMB and gets VAT invoice;

    in the case of direct sales to companies B and C, bonded market issues the VAT invoice titled company A.

Spare parts and components for repairing can be shipped before monthly customs declaration; VAT issuance can also be allowed once a month.

Taxation

(1)–(2)–(3)

Company A pays no tax. Company B's purchasing from A is regarded as importing from overseas. Customs duty is based on A's selling price.

(1)–(2)–(4)

In this case, A pays the duties and VAT. (Bonded market acts as import agent.) A is allowed to sell the goods directly to B and C using RMB after paying taxes.

(6)–(2)–(4)

A buys domestic raw materials and sells to B and C. A has to pay VAT of 17 per cent. However, A is allowed to get the VAT rebate by taking company D's VAT invoice as verification.

2.12. What major advantages and problems are most likely to arise when investing in central and western China?

The Chinese central government has followed a policy of decentralisation in political and economic decision-making since 1999. The success in developing the coastal areas should be further expanded to the other provinces, especially the central and western regions. Remarkable amounts of financial and fiscal subsidies are granted in order to attract more foreign invested capital to the various provinces. In June 2000, MOFTEC published the 'Catalogue of Advantageous Foreign Investment Industries in Central and Western China'. This lists 255 industrial branches, such as agriculture, textile, environmental protection, tourism, bio-pharmacy, infrastructure, high tech and others. In addition, in

December 2000, the State Council published the 'Circular Regarding the Implementation of Various Policies and Measures Concerning the Great Western Development' for further promotion. Most important for success is the building up of a good and close relationship with the local government and the respective leaders as well as a good infrastructure and the availability of potential customers and sufficient qualified labour. Most local administrations are quite co-operative and flexible. However, the infrastructure for business operation and the recruitment of qualified staff and management are more difficult to solve.

Subsidies for attracting foreign investment
- Improved general tax subsidies
  reduced income tax – 15–20 per cent instead of 30 per cent, depending on location;
  there is no 3–10 per cent additional tax based on the income tax level – only reduced income tax;
  no industrial or trade tax for exported products.
- Additional possibilities for subsidies for Chinese foreign production ventures
  no business tax for the first two profit-making years;
  50 per cent business tax reduction for the third to fifth profit-making year.
- Additional subsidies for reinvestment of profits of foreign investors
  40 per cent return of the already paid business tax for the reinvested part of the profit for a period of at least five years.
  return of up to 100 per cent is possible, when the reinvestment is used for the establishment of an export-oriented company with the latest technological products.
- Custom duties
  exemption of industry and trade duties for imports of raw materials and for the import of production equipment.
- Other subsidies
  reduced fees for land use rights for buildings and land;
  convenient access to public infrastructure;
  more flexible administration for the approval of project proposals and feasibility studies;
  subsidies for development of infrastructure, environmental protection, agriculture and tourism;
  subsidies for education and training;
  preferable loan policies of Chinese local banks and state governments;
  loan subsidies of international organisations and governments;
  foreign banks are permitted to open branch offices with improved licences for local currency (RMB) business.

Follow high potentials to the central and western regions?

Investments outside the booming regions do involve some problems. Most of the local people are not yet highly enough qualified and the infrastructure is less developed in general. Many of the high potentials have been leaving such regions in recent years in order to find better universities or job opportunities in more developed regions. The central and local governments must do a lot to improve this situation and to attract qualified people to remain in and return the central and western regions to. High potentials receive 30–50 per cent higher salaries and bonuses such as regular home flights to their families, if they accept work in remote regions. This worsens the gap with the low salary levels of locals which impacts on relationships with their new colleagues. Beside several bureaucratic obstacles, high potentials from Beijing or Shanghai face further problems. They may lose their social insurance funds and existing rights or even their work permit (*hukou*) in their more developed hometown. The Chinese authorities already acknowledge such problems and are working on feasible solutions and more flexibility for the future. It is a good idea to negotiate respective cases with the local administration. Further obstacles are the huge differences in culture and business behaviour. Locals are still reluctant to accept preferential treatment of colleagues from developed regions. Therefore, it is important to promote and communicate the cross-cultural understanding and to accept short-term labour contracts (two to three years) with highly qualified employees. Such labour issues are important considerations for the strategic expansion planning into central and western regions.

Summary/Recommendations

China has made a huge step forward over the last 25 years, since the country started to open to foreign investment. In that time, many of the formerly state owned industries have been modernised and transferred to more efficient private investors. The Chinese government also made huge efforts to attract foreign investors with their advanced technologies and management methods. Substantial tax breaks and other subsidy programmes have been initiated and the whole infrastructure improved in order to attract more foreign investment. Meanwhile, many larger and medium-sized cities in the eastern coastline regions have better development than Beijing had one decade ago. This success should now be extended to the western and other major regions in China. The local authorities are keen to co-operate with new investors and offer quite attractive packages; they can provide more efficient support as they have fewer incoming investors than the very popular Shanghai Waigaoqiao free trade zone with more than 4,000 settlements. However, the impact of infrastructure, labour and cultural issues is also an important factor for consideration when 'Going West' strategies are developed and implemented.

Further sources

German Business Association (2001) *China Contact* 3, p. 35.
German Business Association (2001) *China Contact* 5, p. 9.
Reisach, U., Tauber, T. and Yuan, X. (1997) *China – Wirtschaftspartner zwischen Wunsch und Wirklichkeit*, Vienna, Ueberreuther.
Wang, Y. (1996) *Investment in China*, CITIC, NY.

Table 8 Attractive regions for investment outside the booming coastal areas

City, region or province	Advantages of the location
Shenyang, Jilin, Harbin in the Northern provinces Liaoning, Jilin, and Heilongjiang	Relatively good infrastructure: traditional region of heavy industries. Rich oil, gas and natural resources. Important location for the coal, iron and steel industries as well as for automotive and machinery manufacturing
Chengdu and Sichuan province	Centre for research and technology, trade, finance and transport in southeast China. New high-tech zones. Convenient climatic and soil structure. Mining, mechanical and chemical industries, construction materials, food, textile and wood industries
Hefei and Anhui province	Convenient infrastructure through the near proximity of the Yangtse delta
Yantai and Weihai and Shandong province	Important harbour and convenient old and new high-tech and special economic zones. Light mechanical and electronic industries
Suzhou and Jiangsu province	Close to Shanghai. New industrial park
Wuhan and Hubei province	Solid industrial basis. Important traffic junction in central China (railways and shipping). Growing area through the Three Gorges project
Haikou and Hainan province	Largest special economic zone in China. Attractive investment subsidies. Strong harbour. Rich natural resources. Attractive location for tourism

Source: Reisach, U., Tauber, T. and Yuan, X. (1997) *China – Wirtschaftspartner zwischen Wunsch und Wirklichkeit*, Ueberreuther, Vienna, pp. 92–3.

3

What are the Most Relevant Issues in Recruitment of Personnel?

Christine Boos

3.1. What requirements does an expatriate have to fulfil to work in China?

The wrong choice of expatriates for China may prove expensive. There are not only costs associated with repatriation/calling back or for contract termination of the unsuccessful expatriate, but even more important are losses because of wrong personnel decisions such as shrinking turnover, declining revenues and market shares, negative company image, distrust of the Chinese business partners and employees etc. Expatriates may fail because of incorrect assessments of the technical, economical and political surroundings, but also because of a lack of specific leadership and co-operation qualities or because of an insufficient information exchange within the different departments of their company.

Therefore you should select and train the expatriates you want to send to China very carefully. The first step is to be aware of the nature of the requirements an expatriate has to fulfil in order to be successful in China. The following should help you to figure out the most important qualification criteria.

Requirements an expatriate has to fulfil

- Functional/professional know-how specific to China.
- Teaching quality.
- Social and leadership competence.
- Self-competence and intercultural sensitivity.
- Personal and professional environment.

During the late 1980s and early 90s, when the euphoria of doing business in China reached its peak, there was suddenly an enormous need for people willing to work in China. In those days there were not many people with relevant experience and the 'China business' was still a 'black box' for lots of the western companies. Therefore, in the building up phase, many western companies tended to hire as China expatriates people who studied Chinese language, literature and culture.

During this start up phase *guanxi*-making was one of the major duties. Nowadays, however, processes of restructuring and consolidation are usually necessary to survive in the highly competitive Chinese markets. That requires a new generation of China managers, who show not only intercultural sensitivity and leadership qualities but also are familiar with the latest western management tools and who have already gained experience in optimising and consolidating business processes.

Personnel selection for China should target expatriates that fit the specific requirements of a job in China. The requirements can be classified in the categories functional/professional know-how, social and leadership competence, teaching quality, self-competence and intercultural sensitivity as well as compatibility with the personal and professional environment.

Functional/professional know-how specific to China

When it comes to professional competence, it is very important to have the capability to transfer one's own knowledge and to judge the value of western technologies and methods in different surroundings. In China an expatriate often has to cope with obsolete machines and production lines, difficulties in spare part purchasing, delivery bottlenecks concerning raw materials, an insufficient infrastructure and similar obstacles, that are unusual in industrialised western countries.

In the administrative field expatriates are confronted with similar problems: planning, management and controlling tools – as far as they are existing at all – seldom comply with western standards. Often bookkeeping as well as the whole organisation, process control and marketing are still in their infancy. However, one has to admit that especially in the last five years there have been massive changes in all these areas.

Western and Chinese ideas concerning the use of technical specifications often match as little as the ideas about calculation methods. Mutual misunderstandings are pre-programmed.

A solid knowledge about the technical, economic and political situation in China, about the level of education and the background of their Chinese partners and about their expectations of the western managers therefore is an important qualification criteria for expatriates. The Chinese expect western managers and engineers to be able to solve technical problems and difficulties. They are called experts and should not only be well informed in their special field of expertise but also in other areas.

Teaching quality

For the Chinese the most important goal of the co-operation with foreign experts and expatriates is the know-how transfer; in other words to learn more about modern technologies and management techniques. Western managers and engineers often are seen as 'teachers'; therefore they should consider the teaching activity as part of their work. In China teachers (*laoshi*) are models, and it is expected that they act prudently and deliberately.

Respect the fact that the teaching styles in China are pretty different from the western ones; methods of conveying information should be adapted accordingly (see also chapters 4.3, 4.4, and 4.5). As the Chinese way of thinking is more inductive (i.e. based on a lot of concrete examples), you should not explain in a too abstract way. As already mentioned, teachers are very much respected and esteemed in China. Therefore expatriates should try to be good teachers.

Social and leadership competence

A western manager, who is working in a leadership position, should consider his employees, get to know them, gain their confidence and motivate them. More than in western countries a 'solicitous', personal and employee-focused leadership style is necessary.

On the other hand in China a superior should have a high level of authority, follow a clear line and give concrete instructions. An expatriate that shows a great deal of decision-making competence is seen as an authority and a person who deserves respect. As there are lots of technically well-trained people, one should gradually transfer more responsibility to the Chinese employees. However, an expatriate should respect that the development of independent thinking has not been promoted by Chinese education for a long time, and that the Chinese employees have to get used to making decisions by themselves and taking over responsibility.

A superior in China has more duties than in western countries. Thus, he sometimes has to take care of private matters and family affairs for his employees (children's education, marriage problems, sickness of family members etc.). However, despite this, the interests of the company always have to be in focus.

Expatriates have to be moderate, flexible and willing to make compromises. At the same time, they have to make it clear, that certain rules and standards of professionalism have to be met and are not negotiable. They should be able to solve problems. In case of conflict they should not put the screws on their employees, but try to reduce the conflict. Not loosing or causing loss of face is very important; there is a Chinese saying: 'The tree has a bark, the man has a face.'

At any rate superiors should have team spirit and a profound knowledge of human nature. Calm, self-controlled and moral behaviour is essential for a good leadership style. The capability and readiness to adapt oneself to different roles, new situations and conditions of the environment complete the profile of requirements.

Self-competence and intercultural sensitivity

Self-competence is focusing on the expectations, behavioural patterns, values and mental attitudes of an expatriate. It emphasises the capability to recognise that one's own ideas and ways to react are neither the only possible ones nor the only right ones. Self-competence therefore is the basis for intercultural sensitivity. One should be open towards new ideas and developments and be ready to learn and to rethink and put into perspective other habitual patterns of thinking, actions and reactions as well as points of view. Foreign staff, for example, will sometimes switch language during meetings to say things they do not want their Chinese partners or colleagues to hear. Although convenient and often unintentional, it is obviously impolite towards the Chinese people who are present.

For an expatriate it is very important to get to know the Chinese customs, habits and mentality in order to gain an understanding. He should know what it means to live in the Chinese culture group and how to react properly. Adaptability is in great demand. He should understand the principles of the Chinese code of behaviour, but he should also keep his own identity. It is rather negatively interpreted if a foreigner tries frantically to behave like a Chinese. Some flowery phrases out of courtesy, however, may be of advantage.

As there is often the need for quick decision-making that does not allow time-consuming further inquiries at headquarters, expatriates have to be able to think and plan strategically as well as to decide and act efficiently. Therefore in China a sense of what is realitic is needed as well as readiness for risk, talent for improvisation, the capability to handle stressful situations and sometimes also to deal with frustrations.

Personal and professional environment

The physical condition of an employee is relevant here as well as his/her family situation. The latter is especially significant if the future work place of an expatriate is far away from the big Chinese cities or from the dynamic coastal regions. What in Beijing, Shanghai or in the hinterland of Hong Kong is not a major issue may become a problem in remote areas quite quickly. In the Chinese provinces, accompanying partners have hardly any chance of finding a job or an assignment of their own and are often socially isolated. There is a lack of an international community and language problems as well as inter-cultural barriers often prevent expatriate families from contacts with locals. In addition there is often still a poor infrastructure, particularly with regard to transport, streets, shopping centres, kindergartens, schools and other western-style leisure activities (sporting facilities, discotheques, cinemas etc.). These factors often lead to dissatisfaction of the expatriates' partners and to family conflicts. This might effect the professional performance of an expatriate.

Therefore you should include the family of an expatriate in his/her preparation for China. A first 'get to know' trip to China and to the future work place for the whole expat family and an explicit explanation of what living and working in China really means by other expatriates are proven means to help avoid later disappointment or unpleasant surprises. If possible and agreeable to the partners of the expatriates, a company should also try to offer them a job. Supra-company co-operation as well as the mediation of embassies and chambers of commerce could be suitable means to reach this aim.

Interview worksheet for potential expatriates

According to most of the HR managers, interviews are the best instruments for selecting expatriates for China. By an interview you can try to get information on the CV, the personal field as well as on the values and targets of a candidate. Furthermore by the behaviour of the interviewed person you can draw conclusions about his/her social competence in new surroundings. In practice you often use interview guidelines in order to structure the process of interviewing.

Table 9   Interview worksheet for China candidates

Motivation
- Investigate reasons and degree of interest in wanting to be considered.
- Determine desire to work in China, verified by previous concerns such as personal travel, language training, reading, and association with foreign employees or students.
- Determine whether the candidate has a realistic understanding of what working and living in China requires.
- Determine the basic attitudes of the spouse/ husband towards a China assignment.

Health
- Determine whether any medical problems of the candidate or his family might be critical to the success of the assignment. (Respiratory tracts must be quite stable, no allergic reactions to sulphurous particles of coal dust and other pollution factors in the air of Chinese cities and industrial centres.)
- Determine whether he is in good physical and mental health, without any foreseeable changes.

Language ability
- Determine potential for learning at least the basics of the Chinese language.
- Determine any previous language(s) studied or oral ability (judge against language needed on the China assignment).
- Determine the ability of the spouse/husband to meet the language requirements.

Family considerations
- How many moves has the family made in the past between different cities or other countries?
- What problems were encountered?
- How recent was the last move?
- Are there children and if so what are their ages?
- Has divorce or its potential, death of a family member etc., weakened family solidarity?
- Will all the children move; why, why not?
- What are the location, health, and living arrangements of the grandparents, and the number of trips normally made to their home each year?
- Are there any special adjustment problems that you would expect?

Table 9 (*continued*)

- How is each member of the family reacting to this possible move?
- Do special educational problems exist within the family?

Resourcefulness and initiative

- Is the candidate independent; can he make and stand by his decisions and judgements?
- Does he have the intellectual capacity to deal with several dimensions simultaneously?
- Is he able to reach objectives and produce results with whatever personnel and facilities he has available, regardless of the limitations and barriers that might arise?
- Can the candidate operate without a clear definition of responsibility and authority on a foreign assignment?
- Will the candidate be able to explain the aims and company philosophy to the local managers and workers?
- Does he possess sufficient self-reliance, self-discipline and self-confidence to overcome difficulties or handle complex problems?
- Can the candidate operate effectively in a foreign environment without normal communications and supporting services?

Adaptability

- Is the candidate sensitive to others, open to the opinions of others, co-operative and able to compromise?

- What are his reactions to new situations, and efforts to understand and appreciate differences?
- Is he culturally sensitive, aware and able to relate across the culture?
- Does the candidate understand his own culturally derived values?
- How does the candidate react to criticism?
- Will he be able to make and develop contacts with his peers in China?
- Does he have patience when dealing with problems?
- Is he resilient/ can he bounce back after setbacks?

Career planning

- Does the candidate consider the assignment anything other than a temporary China trip?
- Is the move consistent with his progression and that planned by the company?
- Is his career planning realistic?
- What is the candidate's basic attitude towards the company?
- Is there any history or indication of personnel problems with the employee?

Financial

- Are there any current financial and/or legal considerations, which might affect the assignment, e.g. house purchase, children and college expenses etc.?

Source: Adapted from Ronen, S. (1986) *Comparative and Multinational Management*, New York, p. 537.

Summary

Expatriates are facing different demands from the parent company, the local workforce, and in case of a joint venture, the Chinese partner. The home company expects the expatriates to represent the company's interests and management philosophy. Besides, it is the expatriate's task to develop a harmonious co-operation with the Chinese partner. The Chinese partners usually pay great attention to the expatriate's attitude over and above the interest balance of the enterprise, while local employees are more concerned about their foreign manager's professional know-how, his behaviour with the local workforce and his policies of compensation, training and career opportunities for the local employees.

The combination of all these factors requires that expatriates possess a solid professional know-how, a rich management experience, a fair and objective personality, cultural sensitiveness, ability to adapt to a foreign environment and very good people skills. They have to be able to adapt to the cultural conditions and peculiarities of China, without being manipulated by them.

Further sources

Mendenhall, M., Dunbar, E. and Oddou, G. (1987) 'Expatriate Selection, Training and Career Pathing: A Review and Critique', in *Human Resource Management*, vol. 26, no. 3, pp. 331–45.
Reisach, U. Tauber, T. and Yuan, X. (1997) *China – Wirtschaftspartner zwischen Wunsch und Wirklichkeit*, Vienna, Ueberreuther.
Ronen, S. (1986) *Comparative and Multinational Management*, New York.

3.2. How do I prepare expatriates for their job in China?

Sending a western expatriate to China means that he will be confronted with surroundings that are quite different from the social, technological, cultural, political and economic situation in his home country, where he grew up and has worked so far. Therefore thorough preparation for the job in China is essentially important for your company as well as for the expatriate candidate. Up to 40 per cent of expatriates abandon their assignment earlier than intended because of a lack of adaptability to the new cultural surroundings. Furthermore, lots of the expatriates that are still in China are not as effective as they would be with better training and preparation.

The most important aspects

- What managers should learn before going to China?
- 'Get to know trip' for the expatriate and his family.
- Preparation in the headquarters.
- Close links between the expatriate and the headquarters.
- Reintegration into the headquarters.

What managers should learn before going to China?

An investigation of the European Centre of Leadership showed that the majority of European companies that do business in China emphasise the importance of intercultural management know-how, including negotiation and communication skills.

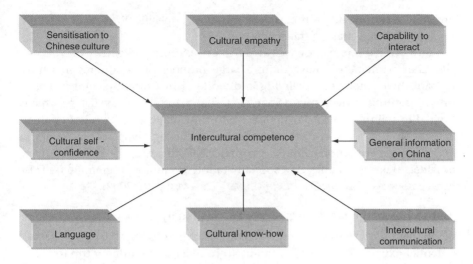

Chart 4 Components of intercultural competence

American companies, on the other hand, often see intercultural training as wasted money and time. They assume that good management is good management, and therefore an effective manager in New York or Los Angeles will do fine in Beijing or Shanghai, too. But management behaviour is not identical everywhere and a manager who acts successfully in one culture may not necessarily succeed in another.

Management and professional know-how is taken for granted in an expat job by most western companies. Therefore, in general, the companies don't provide a special training in this field. However, there often will be a China-specific training targeting critical fields of communications, such as contractual law, personnel management, project management as well as marketing and sales. Also western employers rate knowledge about the political situation as relatively important.

An integral part of the preparation for both the candidate and the accompanying partner should be not only the basics of the Chinese language, but also a good understanding of the cultural, political, economic and social situation in China. Furthermore the expat candidate should get detailed information on the present standing of the company in China and in the region in particular, as well as on the living conditions.

To ensure that the future expatriate can put his increased knowledge into practice, training methods should be used that require the candidate not only to listen but also to respond. The powers of recollection with active doing are around 90 per cent, far above those of mere listening (20 per cent). There could be, for example, a simulation of a specific negotiation situation that makes the different economic interests as well as the culture-specific differences of behaviour and decision-making transparent.

Multinational companies such as Ericsson, Motorola, Siemens or Volkswagen, that permanently have quite a large number of expatriates in China, prepare their employees for living and working in China by comprehensive intern training programmes. Some external courses are available, usually limited to training sessions of about two to three days. These kind of seminars in general focus on history, mentality, negotiating skills or on economic reforms, legal conditions and JV experiences. Comparing the different offers/providers helps you to design a specially tailored training programme (see also further sources: *Training Services in China – Directory 2001/2002*).

'Get to know trip' for the expatriate and his family

Besides language classes and seminars, it is highly recommendable to enable a potential expatriate and his/her family (!) to make a preliminary trip to China to give them the chance to get to know his future colleagues as well as the surroundings and the living conditions. Such a 'live' impression is the best way to test whether the Chinese reality really meets their expectations and demands. It helps to reduce exaggerated fears or illusions and to judge whether one is capable of living and working for a couple of years in China. Experience has shown that China-specific training measures are much more effective if attended *after* a trip to China.

Preparation in the headquarters

In the headquarters itself there are a variety of measures that can contribute to effective preparation of an expatriate. First and foremost every potential expat should get the chance to speak to all departments of the headquarters that may be relevant for his/her future job in China. Thereby existing contacts will be strengthened and both parties – the future expat as well as his colleagues in the headquarters – get to know who can help them in the future, dealing with different types of problems.

For an expatriate it is not only important to build up a system of *guanxi* in China, but it is as important not to neglect the connection network in the headquarters. This also includes plans regarding repatriation. A frequent exchange of information and regular communication with all relevant people from the headquarters is essential for the success of an expatriate in China.

Close links between the expatriate and the headquarters

As an expatriate contract usually runs for about three years, after two and a half years most of the expatriates start to become nervous. They worry about their future career development subsequent to their job in China. Lots of them are worried about being in China, too far away from the network of connections and communication that is normally imperative for professional advancement. Senior expat managers especially often complain about being cut off from the headquarters' important strategic decisions.

Therefore linking the expatriates to the headquarters and informing them regularly about the latest technical, economic, organisational and personnel developments should be a firmly established component of the company policy. Of course China expats have to be included in the company's reporting system and must be on the list of people that get a copy of all important notices.

A high-ranked personal 'coach' in the headquarters, who keeps regular contact by phone-calls and visits helps to reduce the feeling of isolation and to keep the expat informed on the latest developments at the headquarters. The personal and individual touch is very important: by direct communication you can often more nuances and also more of the informative, internal company gossip than pick up a highly official circular.

Paying close attention to the needs of the expatriates prevents them from feeling ill-informed, raises their job satisfaction and their identification with the company. Furthermore it makes reintegration easier and reduces the risk of future candidates being put off.

Reintegration into the headquarters

A fairly long stay in China is advisable; still, expatriates will have to go home one day and a company should think in advance about further employment of its expats and provide them attractive offers for when they return. Someone who has succeeded in China, confronted with pretty different cultural, economic and social conditions, is well prepared for other demanding leadership roles. He has learned to think and act in a way that goes beyond the usual behaviour patterns and to find innovative, situation-specific and realistic solutions. Furthermore he is able to co-operate with people that have different values and targets and often also quite different educational and experience backgrounds.

An investigation of Hay & McBer shows that, on average, when it comes to analytical and conceptual thinking and to leadership and decision-making qualities, internationally experienced managers are performing much better than their colleagues who have never been abroad. Therefore it should be a priority task of the international personnel management to guarantee optimal follow-up employment for staff with expatriate experience. This includes offering the expatriates attractive career paths subsequent to their job in China in time, and assuring them that care will be taken for their successful repatriation. Otherwise you may lose your expatriates to competitors.

Summary

Before an expatriate is sent to China he should get special training that gives him the necessary information, skills and attitudes to adjust to and function productively in China. A reconnaissance trip prior to the final move to China is highly recommended. Also regular communication and exchange of information with the headquarters should be ensured. And last but not least, it is necessary to solve the problem of reintegration/ repatriation in advance, giving the expatriate a promising perspective of the next step in his career, where he can use the specific experience he gained in China.

Further sources

Beijing You and I Software Development Co. Ltd (ed.) (2001) *2001 Directory – Training Services in China: Company Profiles and Training Capabilities*, Beijing.

Eichler, U., Grössl, L. and Neumeyer, C. (1995) *Chancen und Risiken im Zukunftsmarkt China*, Munich.

Mendenhall, M. and Oddou, G. (ed.) (1991) *International Human Resource Management*, Boston, MA.

3.3.   What are the special features of expatriates' labour contracts?

Most western investors employ one or several expatriates in China, especially in the starting-up phase of their sales business, their legal services or their production entities. Expatriates normally know the products and markets of the headquarters quite well and most of them have already proved their ability to manage and establish an entity in difficult environmental conditions. Therefore, most investors rely on such experienced people in order to safeguard a smooth business development. However, the investment in the employment of such expatriates is also quite high and the risk of failure due to different reasons for both parties huge (see also chapter 3.4). Therefore, it is important to formulate proper conditions in the labour contract in order to protect the mutual interests of both parties. This chapter evaluates the major terms of the main labour contract with the headquarters as well as the side letter for local employment in China. Further consideration is given to the early termination of such contracts.

Common terms in the main labour contract with the headquarters

- The job description: comprising job position and location, tasks and responsibilities, set targets, reporting line, power of attorney, date of starting of the employment and responsibility.
- Corporate communication, promotion of management training, in-house job promotion.
- Confidential issues, publications, prohibition of insider business.

- Side employment as consultant or teacher, work for non-profit organisations.
- Intellectual rights, inventions, software development, branding.
- Confidential personnel and business data.
- Salary comprising fixed and variable bonus payments, taxation, working hours, term of salary payments after serious accidents, illness or death.
- Vacation arrangement and its application procedure with superiors.
- Social benefits (pension fund, unemployment insurance, health and accident insurance), shared payments of employer and employee, promotion of health-keeping activities.
- Information and in-house communication with superior business unit and human resource department, possibility of cross-check on own personal files.
- Car for business and private use (car type, taxation and operational costs and fees) or an appropriate monthly compensation. Due to high import taxes, cars are up to 150 per cent more expensive in China than on the world market.
- The standard term of contract is normally three to five years; however, companies often reserve the right to transfer somebody to an adequate position within the group at short notice.
- The regular termination of contract normally has to be advised in writing six to 12 months in advance or the contract will end according to the preliminary fixed period of time, but at the official age of retirement at the latest. Then, all company belongings have to be handed back.
- The probation period is normally six months.
- The applicable law and place of arbitration has to be fixed.
- Confidential and anti-competition clauses are sometimes included.
- Note that all changes and agreements have to be established in writing.
- List of attachments.

Side letter with benefit package for the most common fixed labour terms in China with reference to the master employment contract with the headquarters

- Health insurance in China in addition to the national insurance policy for the employee and his family is normally borne by the employer.
- Travelling (business, home and green leave, emergency home leave) is usually paid according to the international travel regulations of the headquarters. Normally, one annual home flight for the whole family is borne by the employer in business or economy class. Some companies agree to accept a budget regulation, which can be flexibly spent for home flights by the employee, independent of the using family member and chosen flight status. Refund of unused budgets is not possible. Home flights also should be used for visits to the headquarters.

- Home transportation after termination of contract or on special request by the employer. Most companies pay the transportation costs for personal effects and belongings (up to 50 to 80 cubic metres) to the home country including the home flights for the family, if used within six months after termination of the contract. The respective clause may also depend on the time of employment in China.
- Some companies agree to pay home flights for private emergency reasons such as illness or serious accidents within the immediate family.
- Vacation in China is normally limited to a maximum of 28 days for expatriates. However, some companies agree longer or only shorter vacations according to their national laws.
- Tuition fees for children under the age of 18 (school and kindergarten) are usually paid by western employers.
- Memberships for sports, recreation or country club facilities are often borne by employers, depending on the social status, individual circumstances and personal responsibilities of the job.
- Housing is mostly borne by the employer within a fixed budget. Rents are still relatively high. The housing subsidy is still a tax-free income for the employee.
- Sometimes also a budget for furnishing the apartment is agreed. The budget may have to be paid back in case of early termination of the contract.
- Travelling in China is mostly paid according to the regulations of the company.
- Purchasing power offset: for expatriates, life in China is more expensive than it is back home (usually between 30 and 40 per cent). Several global companies (such as Lufthansa) make an annual purchasing power comparison that can be used as a basis for calculation.

Early termination of the labour contract in China

- The agreement on an early termination of contract should be done on a mutually agreed basis.
- Memberships in boards and official bodies should be terminated simultaneously and any remaining vacation be taken before the end of the contract.
- Payment of salary is usually continued till the agreed date of termination. Bonuses are normally paid in same amount as in previous years.
- Severance and compensation payment depends on the remaining time of the contract in China as well as on the total working years in the organisation. Mostly, a one-year full package continues to be paid, sometimes as a lump sum at the end of employment. For each year in the organisation, there may be added a half or one month's basic salary, if the employee is leaving the organisation for good.
- Rental agreement, tuition fees and use of company car is usually continued for up to one year.

- Health and accident insurance is normally stopped after leaving the company.
- Home moving and transportation costs are borne by the employer according to the agreed master contract for working in China.
- Rights and duties of both parties end or continue according to the wording of the master contract when leaving the company.

Official procedures for termination of labour contracts

Legally responsible general managers or chief representatives need a letter of resignation, which has to be approved and duly signed by the board of directors. Normal employees can settle the termination respectively with the responsible legal representative of the company. In this case the labour relationship must be settled and terminated with the local labour bureau. They will take back the green permanent resident card and hand over a receipt for the tax bureau to terminate officially the personal income tax payment. The whole application procedures with the authorities begin again in the event of starting a new job in China, including registration with the labour bureau, the public security office, the tax authority, the official obligatory health check and the human resource department of the new employer.

Taxation of personal income

Taxation of the salary income has to be done according to Chinese regulations. The tax rate depends on the individual income and is progressively increased to a maximum rate of 45 per cent of the paid salary. The taxation issue is quite

Table 10 Table of taxation rates (2002)

Monthly taxable income	Tax rate	Amount of rapidly calculated deduction
Not exceeding RMB 500	5%	0
The part exceeding RMB 500 but not exceeding RMB 2,000	10%	25
The part exceeding RMB 2,000 but not exceeding RMB 5,000	15%	125
The part exceeding RMB 5,000 but not exceeding RMB 20,000	20%	375
The part exceeding RMB 20,000 but not exceeding RMB 40,000	25%	1375
The part exceeding RMB 40,000 but not exceeding RMB 60,000	30%	3375
The part exceeding RMB 60,000 but not exceeding RMB 80,000	35%	6375
The part exceeding RMB 80,000 but not exceeding RMB 100,000	40%	10375
The part exceeding RMB 100,000	45%	15375

complicated and depends on the type and annual sequence of work in China as well as on the individual type of compensation package. Some countries have signed bilateral agreements on taxation issues with China in order to avoid double taxation. Hence, that issue should be discussed with appropriate experts/consultants.

Summary/Recommendations

The formulation and termination of labour contracts with expatriates is a very sensitive and important issue. Many jobs in China are still quite hard for expatriates and their families to fulfil. The language and intercultural issues as well as the professional general management tasks and requirements are also difficult to manage for many senior managers. Many colleagues in the headquarters don't understand the situation and circumstances in China. As a consequence, they often don't give the needed support to the delegated expatriates. Therefore, many expatriates still have to be recruited in the market. For such reasons, the expatriates' labour contracts must be attractive enough to motivate good managers to move to China, but also protect the interests of the employer in case of the request of early termination. This chapter has summarised some of the most common terms in labour contracts with expatriates. But ultimately it is always a case by case decision on which terms both parties finally agree to co-operate or to terminate the business relationship to best mutual benefit in order to fulfil the set targets and to smooth the operations of the company.

Further source

Lauffs, A. (2001) 'Human Resources Management', in Shaw, A. (ed.) *Operation China: An Investor's Manual*, Baker & McKenzie, HK, pp. 123–40.

3.4. Does the localisation of senior management positions make sense?

For companies looking to cut costs in their China operations, sending the expats home is an attractive option. Whilst many have tried localisation, few have met success, and failure can be extremely damaging. Therefore you should weigh the pros and cons of localisations very carefully and decide in every single case whether and when a position should be localised.

The most important aspects

• Which aspects influence the localisation discussion?
  Cost aspects
  Continuity of leadership

Cultural aspect
Management and functional know-how
Consideration of Chinese officials
- How can localisation best be realised?
  Personnel development plan
  Mentoring and coaching concepts
  Perspectives for expats after a successful localisation
- Options for filling management positions in FIEs
  Western expatriates
  Local Chinese managers
  Hong Kong, Taiwan or overseas Chinese expatriates
  Locals that worked or studied abroad

Which aspects influence the localisation discussion?

Cost aspects

The salary of an expatriate in general will be calculated according to the 'balance sheet method'; that means the basis is the salary in the country of origin plus a purchasing-power compensation. The expat bonus is around 10–25 per cent of the contractual salary. Additionally there is – according to circumstances and location – another 15–35 per cent hardship allowance. That means the basic salary may rise by up to 60–100 per cent. Furthermore it is common practice that the company bears the expenses for housing (although rents are decreasing in China's cities they are still between 1,500 and 9,000 US dollars per month), as well as the cost for medical care and the school and kindergarten fees (5,000–20,000 US dollars per child per year). There may also be costs for family home leaves and green leaves as well as for club memberships for the whole family. This can easily mount up to 200,000 US dollars or more.

In the last couple of years, however, more and more western companies have begun to tie bonus schemes tightly to performance. As many firms consolidate their China operations and take on a new sense of realism, they are cutting back not only on expat staff, but also on the fat perks that foreign executives traditionally enjoyed in China. Last year, for instance, only 40 per cent of FIEs provided hardship allowances to expats. Other areas have seen benefits cut marginally. More executives now have to pay, for example, running costs on their company cars. But there is still plenty of silver left in this economic cloud.

According to a report of the HR specialist Watson Wyatt all companies surveyed by their recent investigation continue to provide housing benefits; and more than 90 per cent subsidised home leaves, while 95 per cent provided life and personal accident insurance cover.

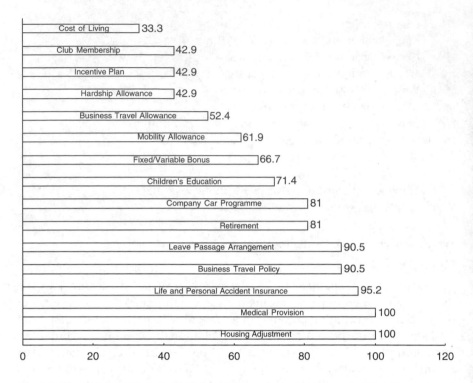

Chart 5   Benefits for expats in 1999 (percentage of companies)

Source: Murphy, D. (1999) 'Expats Feel Pay Squeeze', in *China International Business*, November, p. 66

Although salaries and packages for expats are being cut, companies are increasingly hungry for Chinese employees educated in universities in the US and Europe or for experienced local Chinese managers of their China subsidiaries to replace westerners. Investigations showed that, on average, for the cost of one expatriate you could employ about four equally qualified locals.

Continuity of leadership

Another argument western companies often mention in favour of their localisation policy is that expats don't convey a sense of continuity as they don't stay for a long time. On average an expatriate stays around three years in China, which is too short. The first year he/she is not fully productive, because the familiarisation, the settling in and the vocational adjustment are very time- and energy-consuming. In the third year expatriates are often already starting to look around in order to find a job to move on to after their China assignment. This may distract them from their duties in China. Therefore – for continuity's sake – lots of companies want to gradually substitute western expatriates with local Chinese colleagues.

Cultural aspects

Cultural proximity of local Chinese managers to their home country. Supporters of localisation also say that local Chinese are potentially more effective in what, for a foreigner, is an alien business culture. Foreign managers often push their way into China instituting practices and policies that may work at home but do not necessarily work abroad. According to a human resource development journal cited in the *China Trade Report*, about 70 per cent of western-Chinese JVs fail within the first five years due to fundamentally different approaches to management.

In general local Chinese employees better understand their own culture and way of thinking than their expat colleagues. Therefore locals are often the better choice in sensitive areas, which demand a lot of dexterity dealing with Chinese partners, clients and employees. Examples are tasks in the fields of personnel management, sales, marketing, public relations or the way to deal with authorities such as tax or custom bureaus.

Besides, Chinese employees are often involved in quite elaborate *guanxi*-networks to which westerners in general don't have access. Contacts going back to the times of studying or of working in state owned companies, or just out of personal acquaintances may provide valuable information and support to western companies and may help to open various doors (long-lasting approval procedures, insider information on orders the Chinese government is placing and so on).

Cultural proximity of an expat to the western headquarters. On the other hand expatriates know the corporate culture of their western headquarters and are familiar with the relevant strategies, processes and methods of the company. Their cultural proximity to the central office enables them to realise overall decisions and targets of the company in China. For western expatriates communication with the headquarters is often easier than for their Chinese colleagues, not only because of the common mother tongue, but also because of in-house contacts that grew over long years of co-operation.

Management and functional know-how

Nowadays there are two types of Chinese managers: the old and the young. The image of the old generation of leaders still dominates the idea western managers get of their Chinese counterparts. Because of their socialisation and because of the Chinese education system, they seem to miss essential attributes that characterise a good leader, or at least these attributes are less marked than with western managers. Often the ability for creative, conceptional thinking, the development of innovative approaches and the readiness to take over responsibility with Chinese managers are not yet as developed as with their western colleagues. Therefore tasks of strategic planning and realisation are still best transferred to western expatriates.

However, the younger generation of Chinese managers is making up in these fields pretty fast. In western companies they become familiar with western methods of problem-solving. Furthermore they get experience in terms of taking over responsibility and analysing facts critically. The new Chinese management generations are increasingly dedicated to learning deductive processes of thinking.

Also the educational system in China – especially in the field of management training – has seen mayor changes during recent years. Today intensive language training in English and other foreign languages is quite common at Chinese schools and universities. Furthermore more and more Chinese top universities (such as Fudan, Tsinghua, Beijing or Jiaotong) as well as subsidiaries of American (Rutgers University, Newport University, University of Maryland), European (CEIBS) and Australian (Eliza Monash University) business schools offer junior and executive MBA programmes.

Gradually the language skills and management know-how of the Chinese employees will align with international standards.

Consideration of Chinese officials

One of the major goals of the Chinese government is to profit as much a possible from the know-how of western experts and to get training for the local Chinese to take over management responsibility as soon as possible. Some joint ventures such as AMECO, a JV of Air China and the German Lufthansa, have already stated in their JV contract the time-schedule for localising the different expat positions.

However, local Chinese firms are in a different position as they seek to recruit more foreign entrepreneurs as managers. The introduction of foreign brainpower into China is seen as important for future achievement in local Chinese companies. Lots of Chinese companies nowadays say that if local Chinese enterprises want to compete for market shares in China and the world after China's accession to the World Trade Organisation (WTO), they have to hire entrepreneurs who are familiar with international management and skills. All this is good news for expats, who thought their days in China were numbered.

How can localisation best be realised?

Personnel development plan

If you are considering localising management positions, you should design a concrete personnel development plan for this project at an early stage. Working out such a plan for localisation we recommend consideration of the following steps:

- select the local Chinese employee you want to promote as the successor of one of your expatriates very carefully – prior consultation with the expatriate to be replaced is a good idea;

- make sure that all parties, the expats and the local Chinese manager, really agree with your plan and that they are equally enthusiastic. Don't try to force them to co-operate, otherwise the whole project could be threatened. Therefore it is essentially important to give both of them clear, attractive perspectives for their professional future;
- work out together with the expat and the Chinese employee the steps that are necessary for a successful localisation;
- develop a realistic time-frame that respects the needs of both the expatriate and the local employee;
- try to introduce a 'mentoring and coaching' system.

Mentoring and coaching concepts

Mentoring in this context means that a senior expat transfers his knowledge to a local Chinese colleague. This concept targets the training of long-term capabilities and know-how and the transfer of knowledge in specific areas. The ideal way is to realise a kind of 'godfather concept'. That means the expatriate takes the role of a mentor as well as that of coach.

Thus, the expatriate tries:

- to optimise the readiness to perform and to promote self-responsibility with his future successor;
- to discuss problems together with his Chinese colleagues;
- to define targets, develop strategies, think about interventions, choose suitable methods, etc. together with his Chinese successor;
- to fill his Chinese colleague with enthusiasm for the success of the company and to inspire him to design his own programmes and concepts;
- to activate the individual resources of his Chinese colleague in order to let him develop potential and to be aware of his own weaknesses and finally to handle them the right way;
- to motivate his protégée to explore creative talents and new perspectives;
- to define roles and rules as a common basis of understanding and to promote effective teamwork.

The measure of success of an expat coach is the rapidity, quality and extent of the transfer of the external company's business style, non-negotiable requirements and skills possessed by the expatriate that are not endemic in the local employees.

To introduce this kind of 'godfather concept' successfully, you have to point out the advantages for the parties, the expatriate and his local successor, right at the beginning of the localisation process. For the Chinese the perspective of replacing the expatriate colleague is such attractive prospect that he tries his very best to contribute in positively. The expatriate, however, also has to be motivated by incentives for successful localisation and an attractive follow-up assignment. His performance assessment should also contain targets relating to building up a local Chinese as his successor.

Perspectives for expats after a successful localisation

The expatriate, who represents his company in China is the pivot point for an effective localisation plan. The success of localisation turns on the expatriate's ability to mentor local staff, to recognise when staff can handle the job them-selves and finally, to release control at the appropriate time. Good coaching skills are a differential between an outstanding and just a good expatriate, and that should be recognised in pay and performance measures as well as in perspectives for his further career. The reward process should take into account the answers to the following questions:

- To what extent did the expatriate manager develop his staff during his assignment, especially his potential successor?
- To what extent were staff/the potential successor given the opportunity to work on different areas of projects?
- Have the staff/successor learned from participation in projects?
- What upward feedback has there been from his subordinates?

The future for expatriates once their position is localised, of course, depends on the company's needs and the individual's interest. Make sure that you can offer him an attractive perspective after the expatriate's own position has been successfully localised, otherwise the expatriate may block the whole localisa-tion process. Show the expatriate alternatives for his career beforehand – in your companies headquarters, in China or in another subsidiary – when you are initiating the localisation process.

More and more expats are putting down really long-term roots in China and are choosing to stay for a long period. Hence, there are lots of examples of people, whose role changes over the period of the expatriate assignment. They may come in at one level, localise that position, train up and coach their successor, move on to another different job, and do the same again, maybe several times. In some ways, this is one of the more successful examples of expatriation, where coaching is an integral part of the assignment.

Options for filling management positions in FIEs

Western expatriates

A common policy is that foreign managers will be brought in until local managers are more familiar with some of the management practices used by the western headquarters and then nationals should replace them. The very top positions, however, such as the president of a holding in China, will mostly, even in the future, be held by experienced expatriates who have the backing and years of experience in the headquarters.

Local Chinese managers

More and more ambitious Chinese local managers qualify themselves to replace western expatriates. These people often work very hard and are keen to gain special western management know-how, language and computer skills and other useful knowledge, studying hard in private night shift studies after their day job.

As lots of local Chinese have worked already for more than a decade for foreign invested companies (FIEs), they've already got a lot of experience in western management, culture and thinking. That makes localisation nowadays easier than it was just a couple of years ago.

Hong Kong, Taiwan or overseas Chinese expatriates

Hiring Hong Kong, Taiwan or overseas Chinese expatriates often seems to be an ideal choice for FIEs entering the Chinese market, because these people mostly speak Mandarin and know a lot about the Chinese culture; on the other hand they are also familiar with the western way of living and business practices.

However, local talent often resents overseas Chinese expatriates. They face the additional problem that they are expected to know the system because they look and speak Chinese. So, for instance, compared to overseas Chinese, a 'white-skinned' westerner is praised for minimal Chinese language skills, whereas a foreign born and raised Chinese, who might not speak Chinese fluently, finds it hard to be accepted.

Chart 6   Advantages and disadvantages of different types of senior managers in China

Locals that worked or studied abroad

Locals that studied and/or worked in a western country for a couple of years are in a similar situation to Hong Kong, Taiwan or overseas Chinese expatriates. Often, there is an element of envy, because locals couldn't get the privilege to study abroad and therefore they are generally paid much less although they (especially technicians) often have the same or even a better professional qualification.

Used to the western style of life, Chinese returnees don't want to live like their local colleagues any more. They are in-between the two cultures, the Chinese and the western one. That makes it difficult for them to reintegrate in China. On the other hand they often don't even want to come back to China, because they see better and easier ways to have a good career in western countries.

Summary/Recommendations

The goal of most foreign companies is to reduce their number of expatriates in China. They are driven by the lower costs of local employees and the fact that more and more qualified local staff are available in the Chinese labour market. A prerequisite for a successful localisation policy, however, is a comprehensive localisation plan. It should respect the needs and skills of both the expatriate and the local Chinese who will be his successor. The localisation plan should contain selection criteria for a suitable local candidate, a comprehensive time-frame for the localisation, and the single steps of the localisation process as well as 'after localisation' perspectives for the expat who is going to be replaced. It is best to fix the coaching role in the expatriate's contract and to include his performance in coaching and mentoring in his assessment.

Judge each case on its own merits; whether and when to appoint locals and when expatriates, local expatriates, overseas Chinese expatriates or locals that worked and/or studied in western countries for a couple of years. In practice you have to check (as everywhere in the world) case by case whether an employee – no matter where he/she comes from – fits your company and your expectations.

Further sources

'The expatriate in China – a dying species?' (1999) in *China Staff*, November, HK, pp. 21–5.
Localization in China: Best Practice (2000) HK, Asia Law & Practice.
Murphy, D. (1999) 'Expats Feel Pay Squeeze', in *China International Business*, November, Beijing.

3.5. How can I find qualified local staff?

In the last decade there have been enormous efforts by the government and the private economy in the field of education and professional training. As a consequence you can find more and more young aspiring local Chinese people with western management know-how and language knowledge in the Chinese labour market. Also senior managers got the chance to gain lots of experience in western companies. Nevertheless there is still a limited supply of qualified and experienced professionals in the local recruitment market. Therefore it is essential that you use different recruitment channels in looking for new local staff. Depending on the legal status of your company, your mid- and long-term goals, the lifecycle phase of your activities in China and the experience of your HR department there are several options to find qualified local Chinese staff. Only a couple of years ago you just had two alternatives for hiring local Chinese staff – an ad in *China Daily* and FESCOs: today there is quite a variety of possible ways to look for qualified people.

The most common ways of recruitment

- Foreign enterprises service corporations
- Takeover of Chinese partner's workforce
- Recommendations/networking
- Recruitment firms/'headhunters'
- Ads in newspapers and magazines
- Search via Internet/e-recruitment
- Talent fairs
- University liaisons/recruitment

Foreign enterprises service corporations (FESCOs)

For a pretty long time the Chinese labour market was not affected by economic reforms. It had been a sensitive field that was closely linked with the socialist system. Nowadays, however, the settling rights for cities have been abolished (in 1994) and the monopoly of the state owned employment bureaus for university graduates has been given up. Theoretically this has brought about a nationwide labour market. In practice, however, there are still enormous problems realising it.

So far the monopoly of recruitment services for foreign representative offices and WFOEs has been with the foreign enterprises service corporations (FESCOs). Formally the personnel for representative offices still have to be hired by FESCOs, however, it is possible to choose employees by oneself and just regulate the employment formalities via FESCO.

FESCOs are still active in most of the major cities, but they have competitors in other publicly permitted employment bureaus. The new agencies can only offer their services to joint ventures or WFOEs. These companies have to register their need for personnel with the respective public offices. Afterwards they can – respecting some restrictions – look for employees in the labour market.

Takeover of Chinese partner's workforce

Some JVs are facing restricted freedom of recruitment as a result of the involuntary takeover of the Chinese partner's workforce. The personnel heritage was agreed as one of the conditions at the start of co-operation and accepted by the foreign investors as the 'second best choice'. The transfer of workers from former state owned companies to a joint venture without going through any selection process may lead to difficulties for human resource management. Instead of recruiting the needed personnel from the labour market, the joint venture management has to put great efforts into improving the technical and managerial qualification as well as the working attitude of the existing workforce. Another disadvantage of workforce takeover is the inherited personnel surplus, which could be partly reduced through some extremely limited possibilities such as early retirement. The personnel surplus burdens the personnel cost and may have a negative influence on the working satisfaction and motivation of capable employees.

Reviewing their experience from this point of view, some enterprises that started a business in China through a joint venture, today would definitely prefer a WFOE (wholly foreign owned enterprise) relying entirely on foreign capital right from the beginning.

Recommendations/networking

Up to 30% of all vacancies in China will be filled in an informal way. That means loyal employees, content clients, business partners or other persons who are closely related to the company recommend friends or family members, whom they are convinced will master the respective duties and are good, reliable employees.

In China such a recommendation will not be given carelessly, as one would lose face if the protégé does not fulfil the expectations. As one does not want to risk the good relations with the company, one only promotes the hiring of a friend if one is really convinced of his/her capabilities and his /her strength of character.

This way, via recommendation, is naturally one of the most effective and cost-saving methods to hire staff. The main disadvantage, however, is that the Chinese staff could start building up internal networks that might turn out to be uncontrollable for the foreign management.

Recruiting firms/'headhunters'

Another possible way of finding new employees is to hire a recruiting or 'headhunting' firm. All big personnel recruiting and consulting firms have subsidiaries in Beijing or Shanghai and Hong Kong. Furthermore there are lots of small employment agencies that concentrate on special niches (i.e. automotive industry, IT industry, consumer goods industries, textile or chemical industries) and have an elaborate network within these industries as well as relevant experience.

In choosing an employment agency you should make sure, that it has some years – even better some decades – of experience in China and in the field of headhunting. Furthermore there should be Chinese native speakers who join the job interviews. Only these people are able – according to their language and cultural competence – to be aware of hidden nuances in interviews with Chinese applicants and to find the best candidate.

The big players amongst the employment agencies almost exclusively focus on the search for top managers. Often they place just two to four candidates per month, but there is mostly a success rate of over 95 per cent that they really find employees who fulfil the expectations of the employer in the long run.

There has been a noticeable increase in all-Chinese companies hiring professional employment agencies to fill their senior management positions. They offer attractive conditions in order to compete with western companies in the fight for the best employees. Sometimes they are also looking for western expatriates to support them with their special knowledge in promoting the tired out public enterprises.

Ads in newspapers and magazines

Another popular source of recruitment are advertisements in newspapers and magazines. If you are looking for employees in a specific region, it is advisable to advertise in local newspapers and magazines. With ads in nationwide newspapers the density of circulation is too low and the respective target groups are not optimally addressed. Because of family ties and the restricted freedom to settle everywhere in China most Chinese are inclined to look for a job in their immediate area.

In big cities there are newspapers published in English language that are targeting the international community such as expatriates, overseas Chinese people or mainland Chinese people who are interested in western culture, lifestyle, products and companies. Looking for 'local expats' (westerners who agree with a local labour contract) or English-speaking, western-oriented, local Chinese employees this type of newspaper (i.e. *Metro.zine Beijing, Shanghai Community, Beijing Scene, City weekend*) is an ideal medium.

There are also regional newspapers and special interest magazines. Lots of special interest magazines are edited by industrial associations (such as those of the pharmaceutical industry, automotive industry, textile industry etc.). It is worth the effort to contact these associations directly, as they often have huge databases and sometimes they also know suitable candidates who are willing to change their employer.

Search via Internet/e-recruitment

As the use of Internet in China is growing explosively, companies have recently been able to choose e-recruitment as a way of looking for new employees. Websites that focus on job offers and applications already have more than 100,000 CVs in their databases and offer vacancies worldwide (see also chapter 5.6). A quick check on the Internet already shows seven of these websites in Beijing, eight in Shanghai and eight in Guangzhou. The most popular of these sites – all of them are designed as Chinese language or bilingual – get up to 220,750 hits per day.

Some job centres recently began to put video sequences of the applicants onto the Net together with the results of elaborate tests the applicants had to pass in order to be accepted in these virtual job markets.

The big advantage of recruitment via Internet, is not only the extensive variety of employees but also – compared to traditional channels – the higher velocity. As the labour market becomes more and more dynamic, this will be an important criterion for the future.

Talent fairs

Visiting talent fairs is one of the most popular weekend occupations of young graduates and other Chinese people looking for a new job. Attractive talent fairs will be visited by up to 80,000 people who want to start their career or are looking for new career development prospects. These exhibitions are organised by local HR companies, which have been authorised by local authorities and will be announced by ads in regional newspapers such as *Beijing HR Market*, *China News Information*, *Shopper's Guide* or *Beijing Evening Post*.

Companies that are looking for personnel also can rent exhibition space (for about RMB 2,500 per day), where they can present their enterprises. Talent fairs mostly take place in autumn and springtime. After the Chinese New Year (end of January/beginning February) lots of Chinese want to change their job. In autumn university graduates have passed their final exam and are looking for a suitable start for their career.

University liaisons/recruitment

Companies that are interested in university graduates also can take part in so-called career days, which are organised by major newspapers, student organisations such as AIESEC or by international service companies. Companies get the chance to have direct contact with young graduates and students who will finish their studies in the near future. In special lectures representatives of the companies have the opportunity to present themselves and to create an image of their company.

Generally speaking university liaisons and close contact with faculties which train people for disciplines which are interesting for your company are

Table 11 Recruitment options

Strategy	Action	Dilemma
'growing'	• training • personnel development	• slow process • danger that the best employees will be hired by competitors after the training
'buying'	• FESCO or other job agencies • university recruitment • job fairs • recommendations • newspaper and Internet ads	• limited market, • lots of 'non-suitable' candidates with a lack of education and know-how
'heritage'	• by the JV partner • prior testing is highly recommended • ask for a long trial period	• lack of education • know-how that is not exactly useful • divided loyalty
'hire from competitors'	• FIEs often look for suitable employees with competitors and • offer attractive salary packages and conditions	• inflation of costs • solution in the short run

Source: Fiducia Management Consultants, Hong Kong.

recommended as good measures to recruit junior managers. Guest lectures, granting scholarships, awards for extraordinary research achievement and internships as well as common research projects give you the chance to get to know capable students before they finish their studies and to offer them a suitable job after they have graduated.

Professors often can provide you with valuable information for finding qualified employees. More than in European countries, university graduates in China stay connected with their *alma mater*. Over decades they stay in touch with their former teachers and fellow students and let them know if they want to change their job.

Recent trends in the Chinese labour market

As already mentioned, the Internet boom also has reached the People's Republic of China. New start-ups attract lots of talented, well-trained young Chinese who have already worked for multinational companies.

Only one year ago a career in a well-known international enterprise was seen for almost every Chinese as the most promising way to professional success. The image of the multinational trusts, the possibilities of career development and training, the resources of these enterprises and the attractive salaries and benefits were enough to attract high potential Chinese employees.

Recently, however, the new generation of Internet companies advertise career chances that often seem to be more attractive to young talents. Furthermore, there may be the possibility to realise additional income by stock purchase warrants for employees, if a company is quoted at the stock market. These perspectives motivate many Chinese employees of multinational companies to change to promising start-ups of the Chinese 'new market' (i.e. to new-comers such as Netease, Eachnet, Alibaba, Elong, Etang or Renren).

Despite the recent breakdown of the 'new markets', in the future western companies of the classical industries are not only competing with other multi-nationals for highly qualified Chinese employees, but also with young private Chinese companies.

Summary/Recommendations

To concentrate on classic recruitment practice is often not efficient enough in the highly competitive Chinese labour market, where qualified people are frequently facing different job offers. In other words, the decision of a potential employee to accept an offer is influenced by many factors not directly related to the job itself. These influential factors include the reputation and the appeal of the employer. Companies should learn how to sell actively another kind of 'product', namely the image of their enterprise, to a special circle of 'customers', the potential employee. The principle of human resource marketing is similar to the one of product marketing. The purpose is to build up familiarity that leads to a long-term acceptance, trust and desire. This process takes time and cannot be realised through a simple recruitment advertisement when there is a vacancy.

Further sources

Looking for local Chinese staff, the following websites may be helpful:
www.alliance-china.com,
www.asia-net.com,
www.china-hr.com,
www.ChinaHR.com,
www.chinese.yahoo.com,
www.cjol.com
www.fescochina.com,
www.jobchina.com,
www.jobs.com.cn,
www.jobs.cn.net,
www.zhaopin.com

Note that Web-sites are subject to frequent change!

3.6. How can I evaluate the qualifications of local Chinese staff?

Chinese applicants are very interested in western employers, especially the younger generation, which is quite income-driven and sometimes also very focused on western lifestyle. Therefore it is no wonder that international companies with a good image in China get lots and lots of direct applications. However, even if the choice may seem huge, it is a hard job to identify those people that really fit your company and your expectations.

Basics for a successful applicant selection

- Preparing the selection process
  clear definition of the job requirements;
  respect the peculiarities of the Chinese education system and Chinese culture.
- Leading a job interview
  be careful with western interview and evaluation methods without any adaptation;
  find out details of prior behaviour to assess possible future behaviour;
  double-check the candidate's data carefully.
- Multilevel evaluation of the applicants' data and the job interviews

Preparing the selection process

Clear definition of the job requirements

Before you look for new staff you have to analyse carefully the exact requirements of the specific vacancy. There are two ways to do this:

- by a complex analysis of the specific job and the related workflow, finding out most important behaviour patterns that are necessary for a successful handling of the job-specific tasks;
- by a 'criteria defining meeting'. During such a meeting superiors and possibly the prior jobholder discuss together with members of the HR department the tasks of a potential candidate and the resulting requirements he has to fulfil for the particular job.

Then one has to cluster similar types of criteria under one generic term (for the sake of clearness eight to ten such terms are enough) and define these terms (such as self-initiative, leadership, reliability, ability to take stress) properly in order to make a priority list that becomes the so-called requirement profile (see also Table 12 on page 150). These requirement criteria are the basis for your interviews with the applicants. They define the aspects that should be emphasised in order to get as much useful information as possible.

Designing this requirement profile and setting respective priorities, you always have to respect that Chinese employees' reactions differ substantially from those of westerners and that the criteria for judging employees in China may vary in certain respects significantly from those of the western world (see also chapters 2.6/2.7).

Respect the peculiarities of the Chinese education system and Chinese culture

Selecting Chinese employees lots of western managers underestimate the Chinese way of thinking and its use, especially its intellectual meaning. They note disparagingly, that the Chinese are not able to abstract, that they prefer rote learning to independent thinking and that they are not very creative.

Doubtlessly the western way of thinking, which is familiar to us, has its advantages. During the last centuries we succeeded by those skills in becoming the world-leading nations in terms of economical and technical development. On the other hand we have to consider that the Asians – and especially the Chinese – had been the leading culture for a much longer time in history. And examples like Japan, Taiwan, Singapore and Korea have shown us over the last decades that the Asian way of thinking can't be totally wrong or basic. The Chinese way seems to be particularly strong, as most business in Southeast Asia is done by people of Chinese origin.

Why do we westerners look down on Japanese, Koreans and Chinese and say that they just copy everything? How can it happen that those people, who allegedly are only able to imitate, could so often gain economic success with slightly modified copies? It's not only the cheaper production costs; it is rather that the Asians know how to use what they learned and copied to suit market requirements. And this is exactly the success of their mental strategy (see also chapter 2.6).

A quote from Confucius summarises the advantages and disadvantages of both ways of thinking, the western and the Asian way: 'Rote learning, without thinking is useless; thinking, without [prior] learning of facts, is dangerous.' Both culture-specific types of learning are in their unfinished form not very effective or may be even damaging. The ideal, therefore, in both cultures is somebody who carefully understands all aspects of his work and now is able to handle it independently. There are just different starting points, at the end of the day the results may be pretty similar or will lead in combination even to synergy.

Chinese university graduates, who are described as theoretically very well trained, but who lack the ability to transfer their knowledge into practice, therefore, have just not reached the final level of their education yet. Doubtless this is a result of the Chinese learning and thinking style. Conversely there is also the idea that practitioners are seen as inferior to theorists. However, there are many practitioners in China who have acquired a lot of skills without any formal education.

You should keep these facts in mind when interviewing potential employees for your FIE in China. It is up to you to promote suitable candidates by specific personnel development measures.

Leading a job interview

Be careful using Western interview and evaluation methods

You should be aware that you cannot simply transfer western selection processes to China. Because of the different culture, socialisation and education, western-style aptitude tests are confronting Chinese applicants with undreamed-of difficulties. Also intelligence tests that are allegedly made for universal use have been proven to be culture-specific, as they presuppose western thinking in terms, categories and abstractions. Most of the Asian patterns of thinking, however, are based – not only because of totally different language approaches – on a completely different system. The concrete, that means the thinking in examples and in wired structures, is dominant. This, however, is not necessarily a disadvantage, as western mono-causal or linear thinking – as we have seen – also does not meet all needs one can imagine.

Western managers often blame the hierarchical orientation as well as a lack of self-initiative of their Chinese employees. They often describe their Chinese colleagues as shy of taking over responsibility and not experienced in long-term, systematic planning. At this point the question arises whether for a job in China employees should be hired that are totally westernised or whether in these surroundings the traditional Chinese strengths could not be a bigger advantage.

Western managers often are impressed by Chinese that meet the western patterns of behaviour as much as possible: Chinese, who speak a lot (often without being asked), who don't want to play a subordinate role in a group, but always attract attention one way or the other, and who are looking for direct contact to their western colleagues and bosses. Those persons, however, who always step into the limelight and tend to give their own interests precedence over the group interest, are not necessarily appreciated very much in China. Therefore if this type of person is promoted to higher management positions, they may get into difficulties with their Chinese compatriots.

It is worthwhile to think about the question a Chinese HR assistant asked to her expatriate boss: 'How can it happen that westerners always just hire and promote hot-air merchants?' Suitable candidates for leading positions and promotion are Chinese employees who handled the transferred tasks to the full satisfaction of their bosses and colleagues. To be able to do this they have to have analysed everything in detail and they have to be sure of the backing of their Chinese colleagues.

Find out details of prior behaviour to assess possible future behaviour

The behaviour of an applicant in critical situations in his prior job or during his education can provide a lot of interesting information to the interviewer. Therefore he should concentrate on asking the applicant for details of such critical situations; let him describe the situation explicitly, and also the measures and actions the applicant took and the results or changes that were realised by his behaviour. That way the interviewer checks the so-called behaviour triangle: description of situation, action and results. The interviewer should be able to get the desired information by targeted and focused questions.

There are two types of questions that are especially suitable for this purpose:

- concrete, behaviour-oriented questions;
- open questions (first and foremost the so-called 'w'-questions: who ... why ... when ... where ... which way ...).

Closed questions such as suggestive questions or 'yes' or 'no' questions should be avoided as the statements of the applicant may be misleading or bring only very little information.

The interviewer should behave in a suitable manner and respect the self-confidence of the applicant, possibly trying to influence the interview positively by:

- expressing understanding (direct or indirect) and appreciation;
- offering explanations (for prior failure or unfavourable behaviour);
- changing the topic when there is the danger that the candidate may lose face.

Furthermore the interviewer should steer the speed of the interviews and the volume of information by:

- summarising and leading over to other topics;
- interrupting, if necessary;
- promoting short answers;
- asking for explanations;
- encouraging or being silent where it is appropriate.

Double-check the candidate's data and explanations carefully

Be aware that very often Chinese applicants write their CV according to the profile you are looking for (in your job advertisement or job description) rather than according to their real knowledge and skills. Chinese don't see that as a lie, but as a necessary adaptation of the reality. They think they will be able to learn the respective skills as soon as they are hired (before starting the job).

Chinese certificates and reports are hard to interpret, especially if you don't know anything about the particular schools/universities. In general the reports are written in Chinese language. That makes it even more difficult to evaluate them, as you have to rely on interpretations. Also the files that every state owned company holds of each employee will not usually be handed out to a new western employer and they are not a great help anyway because the appraisal factors for good employees in state owned companies may differ remarkably from the western ones. The assessment often is based more on functionary merits than on business-related skills/performance. Therefore it is even more important that you build up your own picture of the applicant, his qualifications and his personal strengths and weaknesses. Verify the specific skills (language, computer, accounting, technical or management skills) he mentioned in his CV during the job interview by asking specific questions and letting him provide samples of his work.

Multilevel evaluation of the applicants' data and the job interviews

The final selection of the best candidates is not an easy task. An enterprise may fail to choose the most appropriate applicant not because of the inability to identify the best one, but because of some personal considerations of the managers participating in the selection and hiring process. Some Chinese managers involved in the selection process may tend to consider the applicant's family background and his social connections as more important criteria than his educational background and his professional skills. Another aspect is, that some managers – even expatriates – avoid choosing candidates with better qualifications than they hold themselves, in order to eliminate potential threat and competition. Therefore it is highly recommended that at least two or better even more interviewers speak with a promising applicant. In the first place the information gained by the interviews should be systematically evaluated by each individual interviewer. In order to increase the objectivity of the evaluation process, as a second stage there should be an evaluation session, in which all the interviewers from HR and the relevant departments take part.

The interviewers have to verify their judgements by concrete examples of the applicant's behaviour. Each criterion of the requirement profile must be discussed and the interviewers have to agree on one common judgement.

If there are more applicants with similar scores/assessments, you should take the following aspects into consideration:

- importance of the criteria within the requirement profile (priorities);
- correlations between the criteria (i.e. which strength may eventually compensate which weakness);
- possibility of training in certain areas (no problem/big problem, can be trained with enormous effort/with just a little effort);
- behavioural tendencies.

Summary/Recommendations

To avoid selections based on ineffective criteria, meaning that your company takes only second- or third-best candidates who will often lack some of the knowledge or skills needed for the respective job, a systematic, multilevel selection process has to be developed. First, in order to reduce subjective influences, the selection should begin with an analysis aimed at the identification of the specific attitude, knowledge and motivations needed for the job. Second, both HR and line managers should interview the candidates and exchange viewpoints with each other. It should be noted that the participation of HR managers might contribute a more objective judgement. As 'outsiders', most of the HR managers aren't 'threatened' by a better-qualified candidate; this, however, can be the case for some of the department heads. Third, candidates for certain key positions should be interviewed in the last round by the top managers of the organisation. Sometimes it also makes sense to hire external service providers who develop special tailored assessment centres or interview guidelines which cater for the different approach of the Chinese applicants.

Further sources

China Staff (ed.) *China Staff Case Study Compendium* (1997) HK Asia Law & Practice.
Kleimann, L. (1998) *Human Resource Management: A Tool for Competitive Advantage*, Beijing (Reprint), pp. 110 ff.

Table 12   Important criteria for interviews with applicants

Professional knowledge	Know-how, abilities and experience of the specific job and routine in necessary working methods/ techniques
Sense of responsibility	Readiness to take over responsibility, to vouch for the resulting actions and to bear the consequences
Team-playing	Behaviour towards superiors and towards other colleagues of their own and other departments. Ability to talk to others in a constructive way and to work in international teams
Creativity/Initiative	Capability to develop a sense of pioneering fantasy in order to see new opportunities, to evaluate them and to promote promising innovations
Decision-making	Capability to recognise problems, to analyse them and to introduce adequate, future-oriented measures. Capability to decide at the right time
Independency/Working technique	Ability to design own working area. Planning and organising own working and recreation phases

Table 12   (*continued*)

Sociability	Capability to express oneself clearly and convincingly in spoken and written form. Capability to deal with clients, providers, colleagues and superiors in the right way
Stress resistance	Psychological and physical ability to be a high performer and to deal with sudden difficulties and failures
Attitude towards learning	Ability and willingness to recognise own mistakes and to acquire new patterns of behaviour; readiness for life-long learning and to deal with intercultural differences
Planning and organisation	Ability to delegate tasks, responsibilities and competencies, to control and to co-ordinate
Leadership	Ability to give one's time and attention to colleagues, to respect their knowledge and their experience, to appoint them to the right tasks and to influence them in a suitable way
Delegation/Promotion of subordinates	Ability to delegate tasks, responsibilities and competencies, to control and to co-ordinate

3.7. What are the special matters concerning employment of local Chinese staff?

The employment of local staff in China can be a quite complicated issue. There are many regulations and local circumstances to be followed up. The labour relationship between the employer and the employee should be fixed in an 'employment handbook' as a guideline for the HR department as well as in the 'employee handbook' as a guide for the employee. The terms and conditions of the labour relationship are fixed in the 'individual labour contract' as a legal document for the relationship between the company and the employee. In case of the existence of a labour union the 'collective labour contract' as a legal document between the company and the labour union is also required. It is strongly recommended to comply with the implemented regulations and laws of the PRC. If a company ignores current regulations fines might be imposed on the enterprise or other rightful claims might be denied in case of legal proceedings. If there are any uncertainties concerning employment matters, especially in regard to legal issues, external professional help should be requested. Some of the regulations may differ between cities.

Important matters concerning labour contracts to be fixed in an employment handbook

- General conditions
- Duration of the contract
- Probation period

- Working hours
- Overtime
- Remuneration
- Bonuses and motivation packages
- Violation of labour discipline
- National social benefit
- Holidays and leave entitlement
- Termination of the contract
- Rescinding the contract
- Confidentiality agreement
- Non-competition clause

General conditions

Except for the foreign representative offices, recruitment of Chinese staff can be done through the FIEs themselves. Even if the company's contribution to welfare benefits might be higher than an arranged fixed amount payable to service firms like FESCO or CIIC, the company should consider such direct employment, as reward for outstanding performance or for Chinese staff who have already worked as FESCO employees for the company for a long time. By doing so, the benefits an employee might get are much higher compared to service agency payments and therefore the employee might be attracted to stay with the company long term and see his/her performance being rewarded. There must be an individual labour contract concluded with the particular employee and a collective labour contract with the labour union, if existing. Below is some information to enable the HR departments to employ the employees through the company itself and to provide them with some background information regarding problems or risks.

Two forms of labour contracts exist. The collective contract is a binding contract between the labour union, which represents the employees and the employer. The individual contract is a binding contract between an individual employee and the employer. According to labour law, relevant labour authorities must approve collective contracts whereas individual contracts do not require such approval. Preconditions for any contract imply that the contract has to be concluded in writing and that the employee first has to terminate the labour relationship with other employers before the new company can employ him/her.

The contract has to contain clauses such as the term of the labour contract, the job description, labour protection and work conditions, remuneration, labour discipline, the conditions for termination of the labour contract and the liability for breach of the labour contract. In addition, the parties may consult and agree on other items such as the probation period, confidentiality agreement, pay back of training costs in case the employee changes his/her job, the establishing of a labour manual system or a non-competition clause. The labour contract has to be registered by the local labour authorities within 30 days.

FIEs are required to keep employment records of each employee. Such records should include information on the employee such as name, ID number, marital/family status and home address, employment commencement date, probation period, job title, wages plus bonuses, leave entitlement, notice period and date of termination. FIEs are also required to submit their employees' handbooks to the local labour bureau and retain copies for their record. The contents of the handbook outlines the benefit provisions the employee will be able to enjoy and serves as a guide to the employee's code of conduct. Local regulations could provide additional standards.

Duration of the contract

The labour contract can have either an open term or a fixed term basis or even a term terminated on a job basis. Generally, a fixed term contract should be drawn up because of the problems which might arise from an open term contract (for example, severance pay). Fixed term contracts lasting from one to three years are the best option. Under certain conditions, however, open term contracts can be workable; if an employee insists on such a contract you should ask for legal advice.

Probation period

The probation period should not exceed six months. This is the standard time for the probation period so the employee can show his/her ability for the new job. Within the probation period both parties can terminate the contract without giving any reasons. If the employee does not have the abilities required for his/her new job the employer can terminate the contract without any difficulties.

Working hours

The normal daily working hours, should not be longer than eight hours, with 40 hours a week.

Overtime

Employees can work a maximum extra three hours a day beyond the normal working hours, with no more than 36 hours of overtime a month. Employees will receive overtime pay based on the following scale:

Table 13 Types of overtime and its payment

Type of overtime	Overtime pay
Overtime hours worked on normal working days	150% of normal pay
Overtime hours worked on the employee's rest day	200% of normal pay
Overtime hours worked on the statutory holidays	300% of normal pay

Payment of overtime depends on prior approval by the head of department or the person in charge and in general will only be paid when overtime worked exceeds half an hour. In order to prevent any uncertainty, clear regulations should be set up in the internal regulations of the company. Instead of paying overtime wages it is also possible to give the employee an appropriate 'time off'. In general there are no overtime wages for sales people. The handling of overtime for receptionists and drivers should also be included in the internal regulations. For drivers working overtime, meal allowances can be granted or costs can be refunded by turning in a receipt. According to the needs of the employer it is possible to have more flexible working hours. Such a system of flexible working hours has to be approved by the local authorities. There are two different systems possible which are acknowledged by the labour authorities. Both systems have to be approved by the authorities in advance.

System of open working hours

With this system a particular day of the week is deemed as regular working hours. For example, a Saturday is deemed as a normal working day and only normal remuneration has to be paid. What matters is that the total duration of the single employee's work shall not exceed the statutory duration, i.e. eight hours per day, 40 hours a week. When obvious that the new employee will have to work overtime, the contract should comprise a clause about the implementation of overtime hours (for example, a certain amount of the remuneration should be paid as overtime compensation; the basic payment has to be reduced in that case).

System of total costing

The total amount of the working hours must not exceed the permitted total sum for a certain period of time, e.g. three months. But within those three months the employer is free to distribute the permitted total working time. With this system, it is possible to have staff work more than 36 hours in one week for normal wages. In order to balance this 'overtime', during another week fewer hours will be worked.

Remuneration

According to the labour law, all workers must receive the minimum wage of the region where the enterprise is located. The minimum wage is usually set by the local labour bureau and is based on criteria such as cost of living expense for the employee and his/her family, the local economic environment and the average national minimum wage as well as on the local labour and employment situation. As part of the contract the salary should always be set very precisely, whether it is before-tax wage or net wage and the implementation of income tax. There should always be a very precise differentiation between the basic salary and the bonuses. All allowances stipulated by laws and regulations should be included as a lump sum in the monthly salary.

Bonuses and motivation packages

Bonuses are commonly included as part of the employee's remuneration. The conditions regarding how to qualify for this bonus and the amount paid vary. Bonuses paid among the subsidiaries can be up to three additional monthly salaries per year. Other established bonus systems are based on the planned turnover and are only paid when planned figures are exceeded.

Meanwhile various ways of motivating and encouraging the employees have been established. In order to attract excellent staff to stay longer with the company and to improve the relationship between the company and the employee, every company should set up its own motivation packages. A quite popular motivation package in some enterprises is the housing fund. Apart from the mandatory contributions, the company and the employee can contribute an additional, voluntary amount, for example 10 per cent each, to this fund. If the employee leaves the company, he will only get back the voluntary amount he paid in (10 per cent). Further possibilities are free loans for house purchasing, extended annual leave for long-term staff, medical insurance for family members (especially children), training or company outings (see also chapter 4.2).

Violation of labour discipline

If an employee has violated labour discipline, this should be recorded in writing and, if possible, some witness reports should be kept. In the interests of the enterprise, a ban on the employee on entering the company should be considered if the employee has access to sensitive information.

Offences which entitle the employer to immediate dismissal

- Use of alcohol or drugs on the job.
- Assault on other staff members, supervisors, co-workers or guests.
- Theft or attempted theft of any kind.
- Falsification or attempted falsification of the company's documents and other signed documents.
- Provision of false information on employment application documents and other signed documents.
- Engagement in activities and practices that endanger the safety of the office, its occupants or other staff members.
- Damage to the office, building or their contents.
- Serious breach of the company's discipline.

- Disclosure of proprietary or confidential information to unauthorised individuals.
- Use of unauthorised software in violation of copyright or intellectual property rights.

Offences which entitle the employer to the disciplinary procedure described below

- Failure to follow instructions.
- Careless, negligent or low job performances.
- Abuse of company's property.
- Absences or tardiness not approved by the head of department.
- Misuse of sick leave.
- Inability to work with others.
- Activities during working hours other than the work that is assigned to the employee by the company.

Disciplinary procedure

- First offence: written warning.
- Second offence: written warning (also suspension without payment of salary and benefits may be applied).
- Third offence: dismissal without compensation.

National social benefit

Various cities have implemented programmes on the following social security provisions such as pension, medical, housing, worker's compensation and unemployment insurance. As these provisions vary by city, subsequent local investigations should be undertaken.

Holidays and leave entitlement

Except the statutory holidays that are enjoyed by all workers throughout China, other types of leave and holiday entitlement vary by cities. The following types of leave entitlement are usually leave with full pay (monthly base pay, not including bonuses or social subsidies), unless stated otherwise.

Statutory holidays

Holiday	Formal	Informal
New Year's Day on (1 January)	1 day	
Labour Day (1–3 May)	3 days	5 days
National Day (1–3 October)	3 days	5 days
Chinese New Year	3 days	5 days
International Women's Day (8 March)	1/2 day (women only)	1 day

Annual leave

An employee who has worked on a continual basis for more than one year is entitled to annual leave, which is usually ten to 15 days. Some additional extra days may be given to staff being employed throughout a longer period, for example, five years. During their first year of employment the employees can be entitled to annual leave on a pro rata basis. In any case, the probation period should already be completed before taking annual leave. However, some local labour authorities have promulgated their own annual leave provisions. The current regulations for the relevant cities are described below.

Personal leave

The labour law and other current regulations stipulate personal leave like marriage leave, maternity leave, nursing leave or domestic leave (including conjugal leave, matriarch/patriarch leave and bereavement leave). Especially when handling the domestic leave it should be clearly recognised that the employee is entitled to such leave by law. Annual leave can be included in any domestic leave taken.

Sick leave

Employees are entitled to non-occupational sick or injury leave. There is no national regulation stipulating the sick leave provision. So far, a variety of systems of sick leave have been established by companies. While some stipulate a fixed amount of days off for sick leave, for example, five days per year for minor diseases like a cold or flu, others don't grant any such days for minor diseases and will deem such days absent as days taken out of annual leave. Another possibility is to ask for a doctor's certificate from the first day of being absent. The current regulations for the relevant cities concerning sick leave provisions are described below.

Rest days

Usually there is a five day week system implemented. Rest days are Saturday and Sunday.

Termination of the contract

Generally, a 30-day notice is provided to the terminated employee. In addition, the enterprise must file a dismissal report with the labour bureau. The 30 days' notice is mandatory in three typical cases. The first one applies where the employee has fallen ill or has sustained injuries outside work and cannot engage in the original work or other work arranged by the employing unit upon the conclusion of medical treatment. The second case arises if the employee proves incapable after receiving training or being transferred to another post.

The third case arises where a major change in the objective circumstances under which the labour contract was drawn up has rendered such a contract incapable of being carried out and the parties have failed to reach an agreement regarding the contract after negotiations. Termination is not allowed if the employee has been disabled in an industrial accident or from an occupational disease or is on maternity or nursing leave or on non-work-related sick leave within a certain statutorily defined period. The contract can be terminated without prior notice:

- during the probation period;
- if the employee has seriously violated labour discipline or the rules or regulations of the employing unit;
- if the employee has committed an act of serious dereliction of duty, causing substantial harm to the interests of the employing unit;
- if the employee has been accused of criminal liability;
- if the employee is unable to fulfil the labour contract.

Arbitration

In principle, employees, who have been dismissed by their employers because of disciplinary violations will have the opportunity to defend themselves before the management of the enterprise. Furthermore, the employee may appeal against the dismissal to a labour arbitration commission or before the People's Court. Employers, who dismiss their employees because of redundancy, lay-offs or bankruptcy must inform their local labour bureau of the pending dismissals. Rallying support and acceptance from the labour bureau would certainly be to the enterprise's strategic interest; therefore, large-scale lay-offs should be avoided during negotiations.

Termination by the employee

Generally a Chinese employee is entitled to terminate the contract by giving 30 days notice in writing. A period of notice can be set with the employee and is valid if the local labour bureau registers the contract. An employee can terminate the contract without notice during probation period, or where the employing unit has coerced the employee into working by means of violence, threats or illegal restriction of personal freedom, or where the employing unit has failed to pay remuneration or provide working conditions as agreed in the labour contract.

Severance pay

Employees, who are dismissed for reasons that are not related to their performance are eligible to receive a severance payment. Generally one month's salary is provided for every year of service with the company. The severance pay is also provided for part-worked years. Salary is deemed to be the average monthly salary. It is not clear whether 'average salary' means the basic salary or the basic salary including bonuses. Because of opposing regulations the final decision is left up to the judge's decision.

Mutually agreed termination

The maximum payment is 12 monthly salaries if the employer initiates the mutually agreed termination.

Severance pay for fixed termination

In principle, this follows the same rules as above, except in the following cases; here it is not the monthly average wage of the employee that is counted but the monthly average per capita income of the total payroll, if this is higher than the monthly average salary of the employee:

- incapability of the employee;
- major change in the objective circumstances;
- major difficulties in the enterprise's business.

In case of incapability, there has to be paid a maximum of 12 monthly salaries, in the other exemptions no limit exists. If the employer terminates the contract on a non-notice base, no severance pay has to be paid.

Labour unions

The opinion of a labour union – if existing – has to be heard before the dismissal. The labour union should always be involved as early as possible in the dismissal process.

Rescinding the contract

It is possible to agree with the management staff a period of notice in the range from three to six months. In fact, this is not stipulated in the PRC Labour Law or otherwise, but if the contract was registered as such with the local authorities it can be referred to.

Confidentiality agreement

In the samples of the labour contracts (individual/collective) a general confidentiality clause is included. For staff, dealing with sensitive issues like know-how or finance, a separate confidentiality agreement should be signed. The employee should give back all internal documents of importance when the employment is terminated.

Definition of 'confidential information'

This includes any unpublished, patentable or unpatentable items or technical or non-technical information such as materials, tooling equipment, designs, processes, formulae, projects, products, costs, financial data, marketing plans, customer and supplier lists and business projections used by the company. The employee is under obligation not to directly or indirectly disclose or make available to anyone any confidential information, either during or after employment, as well as not to make use of any confidential information outside the company. Furthermore, he is required to safeguard all confidential information upon termination of the employment and to deliver all materials relating to the company business.

Compensation

If the employee fails to comply with this agreement a fine should be imposed on him as defined in the confidentiality agreement and he should reimburse the company for all economic losses.

Non-competition clause

A non-competition agreement should only be signed by those employees engaged in sensitive matters, who could therefore cause critical harm to the company, for example, sales people or a general manager. Every agreement has to be tailored to the employee's job position and the company's situation (what kind of and how many competitors etc.). Such an agreement is only valid if the company pays an appropriate reimbursement. A competition clause can be executed if the waiting period is appropriate or if the employer pays a severance pay. The total of the severance pay depends on:

- the period of time the employee needs to find another job;
- the difference between the amount paid to the employee in the new job and the salary he could gain with a competitor;
- the definition of the new job compared to the position the employee could gain with a competitor.

For example, there could be six months' salary payment as reimbursement for non-competition or from the beginning of the employment an additional 10 per cent payment to the monthly wages could be added as reimbursement. In this case, the company should take care to state clearly the meaning of this additional 10 per cent payment. Otherwise this agreement might not be valid if applying to a law court.

Summary/Recommendations

Each company has to follow governmental and internal rules and regulations regarding human resource issues. Such important matters concerning labour contracts and social benefit arrangements have to be fixed in an employment handbook as a guide for the management to follow. It is most advisable to comply with the implemented regulations and laws of the PRC. If a company ignores current regulations, fines might be imposed on the enterprise or other rightful claims might be denied in case of legal proceedings. In case of uncertainties concerning employment matters, especially in regard to legal issues, you should contact your legal or human resource department or one of the international law firms with subsidiaries in China that specialise in this field.

Further sources

Administration of Labour in Foreign Investment Enterprises Provisions: Art. 5; Art. 11; Art. 12
China Staff Employment Manual (1997) HK, Asia Law & Practice.
China Employment and Benefits Handbook (1999) HK, Asia Law & Practice.
Lauffs, A. (2001) 'Human Resources Management', in Shaw, A.(ed.) *Operation China: An Investor's Manual*, by Baker & McKenzie, HK.
PRC Labour Law: Art. 11; Art. 12; Art. 19; Art. 21; Art. 25; Art. 26; Art. 32; Art. 40; Art. 45.

3.8. How is the Beijing social insurance scheme for local employment regulated?

The social insurance scheme for local employment follows special regulations. Such regulations are fixed by the government as minimum standards and vary slightly in the different cities and locations of China. The differences are mainly expressed in the employer's and employee's contribution rates to the social insurance schemes. To give you some idea about the major issues of the Chinese social insurance scheme, we choose Beijing as a sample case. Therefore be aware that this section represents the situation in Beijing only. The summarised contribution figures for Shanghai are attached. For more details you should ask legal advice to ensure that you will respect the latest state of the regulations and specific local peculiarities.

The most important regulations of the social insurance scheme:

- Social Pension Scheme
- Social Medical Scheme
- Social Housing Scheme
- Unemployment Insurance Scheme
- Workers' Compensation Scheme
- Leave and holiday entitlement

Social Pension Scheme

Contribution rates

Employer contribution rate. Employers are required to contribute 19 per cent of their previous year's total payroll to the Beijing Social Pension Scheme.

However, each employee's monthly salary used in calculating the previous year's total payroll will be capped at 300 per cent of Beijing's previous year average monthly salary (PYAMS). Contributions are to be made in monthly payments.

Employee contribution rate.   Employees are required to contribute an amount equal to 6 per cent of their PYAMS to the Beijing Social Pension Scheme. However, for the purpose of calculating contributions, the employee PYAMS will be no less than 60 per cent and no more than 300 per cent of Beijing PYAMS. Contributions are to be made in monthly payments.

Portion of employer contribution allocated to EPA.   Of the employer's contribution, an amount equal to 11 per cent of the employee PYAMS will be allocated into the Employee Personal Account (EPA), while the remaining amount will be allocated to the social pool fund.

Portion of employee contribution allocated to EPA.   The employee's total contribution is to be allocated into his/her personal account.

Benefits

Retiring employees who have contributed to the Social Pension Scheme for a period of ten years or more are entitled to the following pension benefits.

Social pool fund benefit.   Employees who have contributed to the scheme for a period of between ten and 14 years are entitled to a monthly pension equal to 20 per cent of Beijing PYAMS. Employees who have contributed to the scheme for more than 15 years are entitled to monthly pension equal to 25 per cent of Beijing PYAMS.

Contributory-related benefit.   An employee is entitled to a monthly pension of 1 per cent of the employee-indexed salary for each contribution year. The indexed salary is the employee's salary used to accelerate contributions revalued up to retirement age and then adjusted for price increases to protect the standard of living after retirement.

Individual EPA benefit.   An employee is entitled to monthly pension benefit equal to the accumulated value of the EPA multiplied by 1/120.

Social Medical Scheme

Contribution rates

Employer contribution rate.   The required employer contribution rate per employee is 2.5 per cent of Beijing PYAMS for foreign invested enterprises (FIEs). All contributions are to be made in monthly payments.

Employee contribution rate.   The required employee contribution rate is 1 per cent of Beijing PYAMS for all employees. All contributions are to be made in monthly payments.

Social Housing Scheme

Contribution rates

Employer contribution rate.   Employers are required to contribute an amount equal to 10 per cent of the employee PYAMS, with a minimum payment of RMB 30, to the Beijing Social Housing Scheme. Contributions are to be made in monthly payments.

Employee contribution rate.   Employees are required to contribute an amount equal to 10 per cent of the employee PYAMS, with a minimum payment of RMB 30, to the Beijing Social Housing Scheme. Contributions are to be made in monthly payments.

Portion of employer and employee contribution allocated to EHA.   The employer's and employee's total contributions are allocated to the Employee Housing Account (EHA).

Unemployment Insurance Scheme

Contribution rates

Employer contribution rate.   Employers are required to contribute an amount equal to 1 per cent of their total payroll to the Beijing Unemployment Insurance Scheme. The contribution is to be made in monthly payments.

Employee contribution rate.   The employee contribution rate is RMB 2 a month. All contributions are to be made in monthly payments.

Both employer and employee contributions are allocated to the Unemployment Insurance Pool Fund. No individual employee personal account exists.

Workers' Compensation Scheme

There is no government-managed workers' compensation scheme in Beijing.

Leave and holiday entitlement

The Beijing Labour and Social Insurance Bureau has mandated the following leave and holiday provision for all employees in Beijing.

Rest days

Employees working in Beijing are entitled to two rest days a week. The usual rest days are Saturdays and Sundays.

Annual leave

According to the PRC Labour Law, employees with more than one year of continuous employment are entitled to annual leave. In practice, any domestic leave taken will be applied against the annual leave (see first point in 'domestic leave' below).

Sick leave

The Beijing Labour and Social Insurance Bureau has mandated the following minimum sick leave provision. It is interpreted that the sick leave provision reflects a short-term disability schedule and the sick leave period is granted on a per disability and/or re-occurring chronic illness (for example, back pain) basis. Therefore, common illness (for example, colds and flu) would not be applied against this sick leave provision.

Employees with less than ten years' employment are entitled to:

- maximum three-month sick leave with full pay, if the employee has less than five years' continuous service with the current employer;
- maximum six-month sick leave with full pay, if the employee has more than five years' continuous service with the current employer.

Employees with more than ten years' employment are entitled to:

- maximum six-month sick leave with full pay, if the employee has less than five years' continuous service with the current employer;
- maximum nine-months sick leave with full pay, if the employee has between five and nine years' continuous service with the current employer;
- maximum 12-month sick leave with full pay, if the employee has between ten and 14 years' continuous service with the current employer;
- maximum 18-month sick leave with full pay, if the employee has between 15 and 19 years' continuous service with the current employer;
- maximum 24-month sick leave with full pay, if the employee has more than 20 years' continuous service with the current employer.

Marriage leave

According to the Labour Law, newly wed couples are eligible to a full pay marriage leave of three days. In order to encourage late marriage, the marriage leave is extended to ten days if the groom and the bride are at least 25 and 23 years old, respectively.

Maternity leave

According to the Labour Law, a female employee is entitled to a 90-day full pay maternity leave for normal pregnancy (that is, one child and no complications). An additional 15 days is granted for any birth-related complications (for example, prolonged birth or malnutrition of the baby) or for each additional baby (for example, twins).

In the event of a miscarriage, the woman is entitled a 15–30-day miscarriage leave with full pay, if the miscarriage occurs within the first four months of pregnancy. Otherwise, miscarriage leave is 42 days.

Nursing leave

Two 30-minute nursing breaks a day are allowed to mothers with babies who are less than 12 months of age. Extra time may be granted to travel to/from nursing centres or homes.

Domestic leave

Conjugal leave. Married couples that live apart are entitled to a 30-day, full pay conjugal leave granted every year. Extra time may be allowed for travelling.

Matriarch/patriarch leave. Couples whose parents do not live in the same province are entitled to a 20-day, full pay matriarch/patriarch leave every four years. Extra time may be allowed for travelling.

Filial leave. A single employee whose parents do not live in the same province is entitled to a full pay 20-day filial leave every year or 45 days every two years. Extra time may be allowed for travelling.

Bereavement leave. An employee is entitled a full pay bereavement leave of one to three days on the death of any immediate family member. Extra time may be allowed for travelling.

Miscellaneous benefits provision

There are no government-managed or mandated benefit schemes for short-term disability or maternity in Beijing. According to the Beijing Labour and Social Insurance Bureau, pre- and postnatal medical expenses should be covered under the regular medical benefit scheme.

Table 14 Employers' contribution to Beijing social insurance schemes 2001

Type of benefit	Employer contribution (% of payroll)	Employee contribution (% of payroll)
Pension	19	7
Medical	2.5	1
Housing	10	10
Unemployment	1.5	0.5

Table 14   (continued)

Type of benefit	Employer contribution (% of payroll)	Employee contribution (% of payroll)
Education	1.5	No scheme
Welfare funds	14	No scheme
Workers' compensation	0.5	No scheme
Total	**49**	**18.5**

Table 15   Employers' contribution to Shanghai social insurance schemes 2001

Type of benefit	Employer contribution (% of payroll)	Employee contribution (% of payroll)
Pension	22.5	6; max. RMB 212.3
Medical	12	2; max. RMB 70.8
Housing	20	5; max. RMB 165
Unemployment	2	1; max. RMB 35.4
Education	1.5	No scheme
Welfare funds	14	No scheme
Workers' compensation	No scheme	No scheme
Total	**72**	**14**

Summary/Recommendations

Social insurance schemes are a quite important issue in each employment relationship with local staff. They regulate the social security of the local employees as they do in any other developed country. China is presently undergoing major changes and restructuring in their social system. Therefore, many changes and new regulations are coming up frequently. Legal entities in China have to familiarise their human resource departments with the latest state of the regulations. Representative offices are obliged to engage a service company such as FESCO (Foreign Enterprises Service Corporation) in order to deal with such social requirements against the payment of an additional service fee. FESCO runs offices in all major cities in China.

Further sources

China Employment and Benefits Handbook (1999) HK, Asia Law & Pracrice.
Lauffs, A. (2001) Human Resources Management, in Shaw, A. (ed.) *Operation China: An Investor's Manual*, Baker & McKenzie, HK pp. 125–42.

3.9. What are the special features of an employee handbook?

The employee handbook will be handed over to each new employee of a company. It should serve him as a manual and help him to understand the company, its organisational structure and internal regulations and standards of conduct. The purpose of this handbook is to provide the employee with the required information that enables him to take up the new job without any constraint. Therefore, the employee is asked to peruse this handbook carefully and to consult it whenever necessary.

The handbook contains the policy of an enterprise. This policy will assist in handling affairs in a highly effective and systematic manner. If the company and employee jointly apply themselves to one goal, they will be able to reap benefits. However, rules are necessary for working together to safeguard the interests of each person and the company. The handbook assists to preserve a co-operative, polite, effective and honest attitude at work.

Content of an employee handbook
- Welcome letter from the office of the general manager
- Introduction of the company
  - Company history
  - Company objectives
  - Company values
- Organisation chart
  - Board of directors
  - Management organisation
- Employment and duties
- Health and safety
- Training
- Promotion
- Inventions
- Remuneration and benefits
- Working hours
- Overtime
- Business trips
- Statutory holidays and other leaves
- Termination of contract
- Discipline
- Compensation at termination
- Confidentiality
- Use of software
- Non-competition

- Exclusive employment
- Labour disputes
- Personal files and records
- Governing law
- General and miscellaneous regulations
- Amendment of the employee handbook

Employment and duties (sample content)

The company employs the employee and the employee accepts such employment according to the terms and conditions of the individual labour contract and of this employee handbook and other internal regulations. The employee shall be employed for the term specified in the labour contract. Any extension or renewal is subject to the labour contract in accordance with the law. The employee shall undergo a probation period as specified in the labour contract during which all terms and conditions of the labour contract, the employment handbook and the internal rules will apply. The employee has to guarantee that he/she has terminated all other relationships with any other employers. At the end of the probationary period, if the company decides that the employee is qualified, he/she shall be formally employed as a full time member of staff. However, if the employee is deemed unqualified, he/she shall be advised that he/she will not be hired by the company. The company may at any time transfer the employee to other departments and assign him new tasks and responsibilities. The employee shall devote his/her full working time and attentiveness solely and with utmost effort to the performance of his/her duties. The employee's duties shall be those specified in the labour contract and this handbook as well as laid down in internal regulations by the management. The company expects each employee to observe the highest standards of business and personal ethics, to be honest and sincere in his/her dealings with government officials, the public, firms, other corporations, entities, or organisations with whom the company transacts, or is likely to transact. The employee shall have the right to participate in labour union activities according to the applicable laws and regulations, provided that such activities under normal circumstances shall not take place during work hours.

Remuneration and benefits (sample content)

The employee will be paid a monthly salary as specified in the labour contract and in accordance with the company's wages structure and system. Unless stated otherwise in the labour contract, the basic monthly salary is compensating a working time of 40 hours a week in accordance with labour regulations of the People's Republic of China and including all allowances paid as a lump sum. The salary structure for the employee is as follows:

Monthly salary (including basic salary and allowances)
-   Contribution to housing fund
-   Contribution to pension scheme
-   Contribution to medical scheme
-   Contribution to unemployment scheme
+   Overtime (if applicable)
+   Lump sum of applicable allowances
-   Tax
=   NET MONTHLY SALARY

The basic monthly salary of the employee may be increased, or he/she might receive honourable or material reward as a result of exemplary conduct, productivity, performance, job attitude, etc. Any decision on the above is at the sole discretion of the company and will require the general manager's approval. The company will withhold the income tax from the basic monthly salary and transfer the amount to the tax authorities on behalf of the employee and according to the relevant laws and regulations. The liability for taxes on the employee's income lies with the employee. The company shall participate in social insurance and pay social insurance premiums in accordance with applicable regulations. The company shall pay the housing fund of the employee in accordance with applicable regulations. The company shall provide allowances fixed by the company's wage structure and system, or as prescribed by law. The company shall withhold individual income tax, old age insurance premium and housing common reserve from the employee's wages in accordance with applicable regulations. The company shall pay medical expenses (less any amounts paid to employee by a medical insurance policy, if any, taken out by the company for employee) and one child allowance of employees out of the welfare fund in accordance with applicable regulations. Bonuses will be paid once yearly according to the economic situation of the company. Except as explicitly provided for in this handbook, in the labour contract or as required by law, the company shall not be responsible for providing any other compensation, benefits or subsidy to the employee.

Discipline (sample content)

It is the policy of the company to strive to achieve the highest possible standard of business and personal ethics. The company observes and complies with all laws, rules, regulations of the People's Republic of China, which affect the company and its employees. All employees are required to avoid any activities which involve or would lead to the involvement of the company in any unlawful practices and to disclose to the proper company authorities any conduct that comes to their attention which violates these rules and principles. Accordingly, each employee should understand the legal standards and restrictions they apply to his/her duties. The company also expects each employee to observe the highest standards of business and personal ethics, and to be honest and sincere in his/her dealings with government officials, the public, customers and fellow employees. Employees are to avoid any relationship with persons, firms, or other corporations, entities, or organisations with whom the company transacts, or is likely to transact, business which may involve the employee in a conflict of interest. The absence of a specific policy or regulations does not relieve any employee from the responsibility to exercise the highest standards in those situations. The company does business without favouritism. Purchases of materials or services will be competitively priced whenever possible. An employee's interest or his/her relationship to the company is not influenced by any transaction with a business organisation that furnishes property, rights or services to the company.

Employees are not to solicit, accept, or agree to accept, at any time of the year, any gift of value which directly or indirectly benefits them from a supplier or prospective supplier or his employees or agents, or any person with whom the company does business in any aspect. All employees are representatives of the company. This is true whether the employee is on duty or off duty. All employees are encouraged to observe the highest standards of professional and personal conduct at all times. The company pays particular attention to the appearance of its staff and company premises. No excuse is accepted for a lack of hygiene, grooming, condition of clothing including shoes etc. The same applies for the place of work and the company in general. The company telephones have been installed for the purposes of the company's business. The employee may not make personal telephone calls during working hours except in urgent or exceptional circumstances upon approval of his/her direct supervisor. In non-urgent circumstances, outside telephone calls to the company of a personal nature shall in principle not be transferred. Personal telephone calls may only be made during lunch or break time.

The company insists on utmost discipline. The employee's misconduct or unsatisfactory performance will be brought to the attention of the responsible head of department or member of the management when it occurs and will be documented in the employee's file. Some offences are reasons for immediate dismissal and disciplinary procedures will apply to other offences. Offences which are reasons for immediate dismissal include: use of alcohol or drugs on the job; assault on other staff members, supervisors, co-workers or guests; and theft or attempted theft of any kind. Further reasons are: falsification or attempted falsification of company's documents and other signed documents; the provision of false information on employment application of documents and other signed documents. Dismissal is also applied in case of engagement in activities and practices that endanger the safety of the office, its occupants or other staff members and damage of company property. Further reasons are:

serious breach of the company's discipline; disclosure of proprietary or confidential information to unauthorised individuals; and the use of unauthorised software in violation of copyright or intellectual property rights.

Offences to which the disciplinary procedures apply include: failure to follow instructions; careless, negligent or low job performances; abuse of company's property; absences or tardiness not approved by the head of department; and misuse of sick leave. Further reasons are: the inability to work with others; activities during working hours other than the work that is assigned to the employee by the company. The progressive disciplinary procedure follows three steps. The first and second offence result in a written warning and the third offence results in dismissal without compensation.

If a dismissal occurs, the employee will be given a dismissal letter. The letter should be signed by the employee. If the employee refuses to sign the letter, the head of department will be called in as a witness and note the employee's refusal to sign. The letter should then be signed by the head of department as witness. The dismissal letter will state that dismissal occurred in accordance with the policy on discipline of the company. The letter will cite the reason for the action taken and will also cite any previous warning letters that are currently in the employee's file if the dismissal resulted from progressive discipline. The security service of the company is responsible for safeguarding the properties of clients, staff and the company. Employees are to respect instructions given by security personnel when on company premises.

Personal files and records (sample content)

The personal files of Chinese employees will be entrusted to the company to be kept by its filing agent and must be transferred after the end of the probation period. After termination of the labour contract, the company will return the files to the responsible authorities. The employee is required to notify the personnel department of the following events or changes in status such as changes of address and telephone number, marriage, birth of child or change in identity card number.

General and miscellaneous regulations

General and miscellaneous regulations include issues such as the applied language, company keys and identification card, fire and fire prevention, injury at work, posting of notices, gambling, collections, literature and authority to represent the company or other points of interest for the company.

Summary/Recommendations

The employee handbook represents the 'bible for the working relationship' as fixed between the employee and the company. The employee should familiarise himself with the company's organisation structure, values and objectives as well as with the applied laws and regulations as the basis of a good and efficient co-operation. The detailed introduction to the content of the employee handbook to the employee is obligatory. However, it is usual practice not to hand over the handbook to the employee in written form. But, an employee can always have a look into the handbook on special request. He should consult his superior manager or the human resource department.

Further sources

China Employment and Benefits Handbook (1999) HK, Asia Law & Practice.
China Staff Employment Manual (1997) HK, Asia Law & Practice.

4
What is Important in Personnel Development?

Christine Boos

4.1. How do I handle evaluation interviews with my employees?

The evaluation interview is an instrument of the personnel development by which managers as well as their employees get the opportunity – apart from the usual day-to-day business – to analyse the conditions of their working environment and to agree on necessary changes and improvements. This should not only influence the culture of conversation in a positive way, but also raise the job satisfaction and provide a good relationship between the superior and his employees. Especially in China, where hidden problems often arise caused by intercultural differences between western managers and their local Chinese employees, performance appraisal interviews can be a valuable instrument for clarifying misunderstandings, becoming aware of problems, special interests and potentials of your subordinates and motivating Chinese employees (see also chapter 4.2).

The major contents of evaluation interviews
- Job environment and co-operation
- Performance-, behaviour- and qualification-oriented targets
- Agreement on targets

What is involved in evaluation interviews?

In an evaluation interview (also called appraisal or review meeting) you should speak about everything that seems to be important for both participants, the employee in question and his superior. Unlike western countries in China it is pretty common – and sometimes even expected – to mention your employees' private problems (like education of children, caring for the employees' parents, conflicts with partners, etc.) and to try to support your employees in this respect. As already mentioned, the superior is seen as a kind of mentor who supports and protects his subordinates in every aspect of life. However, you should not forget that young Chinese employees with a good, modern education and background also will often have valuable advice to give to expats.

The following guidelines suggest how to structure your evaluation interviews with your Chinese employees.

Job environment and co-operation

- In the first part of the meeting, speak about the direct and indirect work environment and the processes of co-operation.
- Together with the employee you should specify the positive and negative factors that influence the work environment and co-operation within it and plan improvements in order to raise job satisfaction for both parties.
- First, encourage the Chinese employee to describe the way he perceives the work and leadership situation. You should listen very carefully without interrupting your employee with discussions or justifications. Try to create a relaxed atmosphere and encourage the employee with respective gestures and remarks; for Chinese people it is a quite unfamiliar situation to converse in this way with their superior and they have to get used to it step by step.
- Possible topics could be:
  - Are you content with:
    your current field of work?
    the room that is left to you for own decision-making?
    the value placed on your efforts and performances?
    the industrial climate in your department (including circumstances that have influenced this)?
  - How do you judge the support by your superior regarding:
    your private situation?
    information?
    planning and organisation?
    job layout?
  - How do you judge the co-operation:
    between you and your superiors?
    within your department?

After this appraisal the superior should comment on the statements of the employee without valuing them, and should explain how he perceives the situation. Be aware that, unlike western employees, Chinese colleagues with a rather traditional background are not used to being confronted with direct criticism which is often perceived as 'face taking', even if it is not offensive but constructive. Therefore you have to find a diplomatic way of indirect allusion. Try to praise the good aspects of the work, the character and the co-operation of the employee first and ask them for the reason why they think something went wrong without criticising the person directly and let him/her propose alternatives to solve current problems.

Chinese employees expect that a superior has a strong, flawless personality and cares about all aspects of an employee's life. He should understand their problems and lead them to an effective, efficient way to work. Therefore avoid causing loss of face and try to act as a kind of 'godfather figure' who helps his employees to develop their strengths and to overcome their weaknesses. A HR manager of a huge American company once said: 'If Chinese employees change the employer, they mostly are not leaving the company but their superior.' Therefore a superior in China should be – more than in the western world – a role model and a point of contact: Chinese are not working for an abstract company but for a particular person, their direct boss. For them it is important that it is worth the effort to work for this boss, in a material sense as well as a human one.

A superior should always be patient. In the eyes of the Chinese he bears the responsibility for mistakes caused by his employees (because he did not instruct and guide them properly): therefore he should not scold them, but he should 'tirelessly show them how to do their job and encourage them' (Confucius). Constructive criticism – that we are used to in the western world – does not really fit the Confucian idea of 'instructing and encouraging'.

An 'open door' policy is one of the major practices a superior in China should follow. That means one should always be receptive to all professional and private questions from an employee. This can often mean that a superior has less time left for 'job-related' work than he had in western countries. But in China it is considered the mark of a good boss, that:

- he visits the workplace of his direct subordinates several times a day;
- he asks actively whether they are all right, whether they are ill or worrying about something, and cares about them;
- every now and then he invites them for dinner or lunch;
- if an employee performs badly, the superior supports him to improve his performance;
- by regular control the superior supports the motivation of his staff;
- he makes final decision, but prior to that he consults his employees;
- the superior is responsible for the welfare of his employees, including housing as well as medical care, places in kindergartens and training vacancies for the children of the employees etc. In Chinese companies these services will be offered by the enterprises under the guidance of the respective superior. In joint ventures the Chinese partner handles these kind of issues; whereas in WFOEs the situation still is not finally clarified.

At the end of this part of the evaluation interview you should figure out together with your employee which points you agree on and where there are still differences. Try to find out the reasons for eventual difficulties and after that discuss with your employee possibilities for improvement and state these at the end of the interview in a written agreement on targets.

Performance-, behaviour- and qualification-oriented targets

Employees should participate in the planning of targets of performance, working behaviour and qualification. As in the first part of the conversation, the employee should get the chance to bring in his own ideas. The superior should not set targets all alone, but he should agree on them in a discussion with his employees. By this kind of involvement an employee can be motivated to identify with the targets and to do his very best to reach them.

Tasks have to be written down in a job description; they define the way to fulfil the tasks as well as the quality and the quantity of work.

The following targets could be discussed:

- Performance-oriented targets:
    possibilities for maintaining and improving the performance;
    improvements by structural, organisational or technical changes;
    emphasising service orientation.
- Behaviour-oriented targets:
    improved information exchange;
    improved awareness of costs;
    possibilities for a reduction of failures and mistakes;
    effective networking.
- Qualification-oriented targets:
    suitable measures of qualification and training;
    transfer of special tasks/projects;
    personnel development/career planning.

Agreement on targets

With the formulation of targets that you gained by the discussions from the first two parts of the appraisal interview, you should appreciate that the targets should be:

- worked out together with the Chinese employee in question;
- embedded in a concrete time-frame;
- attainable and realistic;
- precise.

Agreeing on targets you should be aware that even small changes in the co-operation or the working environment might lead to very positive results for both parties in the long run.

Written agreement on targets

At any rate you should note the results and the discussed targets of an appraisal interview in a written form in order to:

- make arrangements binding upon both parties;
- support the realisation of the respective targets;
- prepare follow-up interviews and discussions.

Such written statements, however, are not to be understood as legally binding facts and documents with effects on a third party. The records should not render the full content of the appraisal interview, but just the results as the targets for the future (see pp. 178ff). Therefore those targets should be formulated by the superior together with the particular employee at the end of the appraisal interview. The aim of appraisal interview should be – as far as possible – an agreement between both parties involved. The content of the appraisal interview must be treated confidentially!

You can use a form like the one on page xx to note the targets you worked out. If there should be difficulties or disagreement at the end of the interview, you should look for a neutral middleman who should join a follow-up meeting, in order to find a fair solution, which is acceptable to all parties.

Personal training and development (see also chapters 4.3, 4.4, 4.5)

You should use an appraisal interview to show your employees ways for individual personal development, tailored to the actual needs of your company and the particular employee's talents and wishes. Organising training measures is one of the duties of a superior (incorporation, consultancy, training on the job, etc.).

Summary/Recommendations

The results of an appraisal process are often used for a number of different purposes, and frequently these purposes will conflict. Appraisal can be used to improve current performance, provide feedback, increase motivation, identify training needs, identify potential, let individuals know what is expected from them, focus on career development, award salary increases and solve job problems. It can be used to set out job objectives, provide information on manpower planning and career succession, assess the effectiveness of the selection process and as a reward or punishment in itself. The evaluation interview should lead to a common agreement on job targets and qualification measures. At the beginning this kind of interview should be held more often (every three to six months); later on once a year could be enough. You should allow at least one to two hours for the interview itself and an appropriate time for preparation.

Further sources

China Solutions (2000) HK, Asia Law & Practice.
China Staff (ed.) (1997) *China Staff Case Study Compendium*, HK, Asia Law & Practice.

Checklist for superiors and employees

Preparation phase of an appraisal interview

The success of an appraisal interview depends on good preparation. By the following checklist you can note important topics which can aid your memory during the appraisal interview.

Part A: Working environment and co-operation

- How content are you with:
    your scope of work?
    the freedom for autonomous acting and decision-making?
    the award of your performance?
    the industrial climate in your department?
    other factors?
- How do you assess the support by your superior concerning:
    information?
    planning and organisation?
    design of the working environment?
    other factors?
- How do you assess the co-operation:
    between you and your superior?
    within your department?
    with other parties?

Part B: Performance-, behaviour- and qualification-oriented targets

- What possibilities do you see to maintain/improve your performance?
- What improvements by structural, organisational or technical changes could you imagine?
- How can the service orientation be improved?
- What targets do you have concerning working behaviour (i.e. better information exchange, networking, improved cost-consciousness, possibilities to reduce misunderstandings, errors and mistakes)?
- In what areas do you see the need for further qualification for yourself (i.e. by measures of personnel development and training, by taking over special projects, career development)?

It is important that you check regularly whether these targets have been realised. An appraisal interview may only contribute to improved co-operation and performance if its conclusions are acted upon.

Agreement on targets

Between

Party A: Mr. .... (employee)   Party B: Mr. .... (superior)

The following targets will be agreed on:

Targets from part A:

Working environment: _____

_____

_____

Co-operation: _____

_____

_____

Targets from part B:

Performance-oriented targets:

_____

_____

_____

_____

_____

Targets concerning working behaviour:

_____

_____

_____

_____

Targets concerning qualification, training and personnel development:

_____

_____

_____

_____

Signatures

_____   _____

4.2. How can I motivate and retain my Chinese employees?

Western companies often deplore the fact that turnover of their local Chinese management staff is way above the average of western countries. In the past companies contracted away the best employees from each other and, since the salary level had been relatively low, some – especially US companies – doubled or even tripled the salary of the individuals that they wanted to gain for their company. Nowadays the situation is better, although in some industries there is still fierce competition when it comes to hiring specially qualified high potentials.

Therefore lots of companies see the need to develop effective policies to retain their staff by raising their job satisfaction and motivation as well as their loyalty. For this purpose they not only have to create monetary incentives but also non-financial motivators that make the employees satisfied with their working environment and proud of being a member of the company.

The most important motivators for retaining qualified staff

- Monetary or monetary-related motivators
- Performance-oriented, above-average salaries
- Provision of private loans
- Attractive extra bonuses/stock options
- 'Face-giving' status symbols
- Non-financial motivators
- Offering attractive chances for qualification and career development
- Intercultural, well-balanced leadership style
- Creating a positive working atmosphere
- Regular communication and information
- Individual training and personnel development

Monetary motivators

Performance-oriented, above-average salaries

Speaking about monetary motivators first and foremost one thinks in wages and salaries. These have to conform to common industry standards at the very least. In recent years the salaries of qualified local Chinese managers have risen rapidly and they will continue to adjust to comparable salaries in western countries.

Generally it is not wise to have a uniform salary system. A performance-oriented system that enables you to pay extraordinary salaries and benefits to the key performers amongst your staff is preferable. For really good employees you should pay very attractive salaries; young, ambitious Chinese employees especially, who are willing to show an above-average commitment, are interested in performance-oriented compensation. Therefore you should avoid the practices of most state owned Chinese companies, which still pay according to the time being with the company, the age or the employee's function in the party.

At least 30 per cent of the income should be performance-oriented. This, however, requires you to work out – according to the principle of MBO (management by objectives) – individual performance objectives for each employee. The targets and the related premium and bonus systems should be clearly formulated, realistic and easy to understand. This way everybody is able to measure his/her own performance and arbitrary judgements can be largely avoided.

Provision of private loans

An employer can offer incentives by providing loans on easy terms for the private investments of his employees, such as for the purchase of a freehold flat. This often retains employees for years in a company. Even if there are better offers from competitors, those employees tend to stay as they don't want to be seen as ungrateful.

Loans for free or subsidized housing in particular can retain an employee for a long time in your company. Changing the company would also mean leaving the apartment, the *danwei* and the whole social environment. Such a prospect makes Chinese employees hesitant to change their job.

Attractive extra bonuses/stock options

Nowadays in China proportional contributions to health, retirement and unemployment insurances are already part of standardised working contracts. Additional contributions in these areas (i.e. in company pension funds) might have positive effects on the employees' loyalty, especially if the amount of money that will finally be paid out depends on the time an employee has worked with a company.

Measures like working out, together with the employees, special tax-saving models, contributions to life insurances or reserve funds for the education of the employees' children as well as stock options can support your staff retention policy too.

There is also a tremendous demand for so-called cash allowances that may amount to up to 20 per cent of the actual salary. Even if it is, at the first glance, hard for westerners to understand, Chinese employees prefer to get some consumer goods provided by their employer rather than to get the amount of money it would cost to buy these goods by themselves. In the eyes of the Chinese, by providing goods such as clothes, newspapers, transport, hygiene articles like washing powder, toothpaste, shampoo and lately even condoms, an employer shows that he really cares about his people.

In personnel interviews you should try to find out what is most important for your key performers and try to meet their needs with a well-balanced, flexible and attractive compensation package.

'Face-giving' status symbols

In some ways the behaviour of Chinese consumers is very similar to that of the Americans and the Europeans in the 1960s. Then not everybody had a car of his own, a private telephone or a luxurious apartment; these were all seen as status symbols at the time, as they are in China today.

If a company gives an employee a mobile phone, a company car also for private use, a well-designed office or sends him to overseas training, it improves the employee's status with his colleagues and in his private environment. Such measures of 'face giving' are often seen as more desirable by Chinese employees than a raise of net salary. On the other hand such costs can be depreciated and also raise the efficiency of the employee; so, for example, a mobile phone or a laptop can be very valuable for the job of a sales-person.

Non-financial motivators

Although financial need still plays an important role in job satisfaction and motivation, for employees at management level non-financial motivators, such as a harmonious interpersonal relationship within the working group, the trust of the supervisors, career opportunities, involvement in the decision-making processes and interesting work have become increasingly important over the last years.

Doubtless money matters, but there are also other non-financial measures that help you to improve your staff retention.

Offering attractive chances for qualification and career development

Like their western colleagues, Chinese employees are looking for clearly defined career perspectives. If their company shows them a definite career path they are usually ready to put in greater effort in order to reach their targets. If there is, however, uncertainty concerning their future development within a company, the employees often tend to doubt the loyalty of their employer and are more open to offers from competitors.

Therefore there should be regular personnel development interviews, at least once a year. In such interviews the employees can discuss with their superiors their performance in the past and the progress of their career in the company. Thereby they get to know how their superior is judging their performance and together they can work out a plan for the individual future development of the employee in question (see also chapter 4.1). In this context there should also be a discussion on personnel development measures that are suitable to support the employee in reaching future targets. Precise development schedules and targets for the future should be formulated in order to show the employee clear perspectives, for example that a local Chinese manager will take the place of a western colleague within the next three years. The single steps of this process have to be pointed out and fixed in a written agreement. Only in this way a consequent pursuit of the objectives is possible.

Intercultural, well-balanced leadership style

In FIEs problems often occur that are caused by intercultural differences. Chinese employees often perceive their western colleagues as arrogant know-alls that look down on them in a manner reminiscent of colonial times. The local Chinese sometimes get the impression that the expatriates do not really try to understand the Chinese culture and mentality and that they want to transfer their western management style without any adaptations to China. In such cases the motivation of the Chinese employees sinks drastically and they tend to show passive, reactive behaviour instead of being proactive and bringing new, innovative ideas into the company.

Therefore it is essential that western expatriates seriously consider the Chinese way of thinking and mentality. They should accept the Chinese particularities and try to profit by combining the strengths of western and Chinese management and working style. It should go without saying that Chinese colleagues have to be seen as partners with equal rights (although experience shows it needs to be mentioned). Any kind of western arrogance should be avoided!

Accepting the Chinese culture and knowing that an expatriate also has to fulfil the role of a teacher are inevitable preconditions for working successfully in China.

Creating a positive working atmosphere

Physical as well as psychological well-being plays a major role, in retaining employees for a long time in your company. Therefore you have to ensure that the practical working conditions suit your employees' wishes and needs in the best way. The working environment must be designed according to ergonomic principles and each work place should be equipped with modern working tools (i.e. furniture, computers, software, lighting, heating/air-conditioning etc.).

Of course all western safety standards have to be respected and wherever possible the specific needs of the Chinese employees should also be respected (i.e. the kind food in the company canteen, aesthetic design of the office space and of the individual work places, installation of tea-making facilities, shower rooms for the employees in the company – in China not everybody has a bathroom of his own–break and holiday arrangements).

Especially for the Chinese spring festival/Chinese New Year, Chinese employees should get bonuses, small gifts and generous holiday arrangements, so that they can visit family members that often live quite far away and that they also have some extra money for gifts. These measures can have a positive effect on the image of a company.

If there are family members seriously ill or other extraordinary situations (children's exams, marriages, births or deaths etc.) in the family of an employee, it will be expected that the company cares about it to a larger extent than it is usual in western countries. Taking responsibility for the costs for surgery for family members or for burials is common practice in China.

Regular communication and information

To ensure that everybody becomes aware of changes and can react in an appropriate way, you have to promote an open culture of communication in your company and an effective exchange of information. By regular meetings and the involvement of the local Chinese colleagues with decision-making processes you can ensure that the Chinese colleagues will support the objectives of your company and their realisation and that they can identify with these targets.

Internal company personnel magazines and regular circular letters/e-mails with information on new developments can be very useful. You should also try to identify informal leaders, to start a dialogue with them and always have an ear for their problems and concerns. This way you can guard against intrigues and misunderstandings and prevent those situations which cause job dissatisfaction with the employees tapering off and influencing the working climate negatively.

However, if despite of all these measures, there arise conflicts in your company you should try to find – at an early stage – a neutral mediator who will be accepted by all involved parties. Some personnel development agencies, which are experienced in conflict management, offer such services to their clients and often they can prevent a conflict escalating. Always keep in mind that in China a feeling of harmony and mutual trust is much more important than a strict set of rules.

Individual training and personnel development

Owing to the scarcity of qualified personnel in China's labour market, some training and development programmes can represent a key to certain management positions in FIEs. The strong emotional involvement of many Chinese employees turns this issue into a very complicated and delicate matter. Training, originally a necessity for an enterprise and a right of the employees is now seen as a recognition and reward for the contribution in the past and a promise for career development in the future. The choice of trainees deserves careful handling, since training opportunities directly influence the employee's satisfaction and motivation at work. Well-designed and organised training can be one of the most effective motivators for the Chinese employees; if poorly handled, it can provoke unnecessary competition among colleagues and spoil the atmosphere in the company.

The link between training and retention is a problematic one. The training programmes – especially external training, MBA programes or overseas training – bring the Chinese employees not only technical expertise and management know-how, but also a higher expectation of their future career development. However, they also become more marketable in the workforce market after the training. Often companies, not fully realising the expectations and demands of their employees, let the trainees, who are eager to make use of their new skills, continue in the same job for the time being. As a result of the combination of disappointment and ambition, some of the trained people transfer to a new employer shortly after the training.

The problem of personnel retention after training is exacerbared as the Chinese recruitment market provides good conditions for job-hopping (see also chapter 3.5). Of two possible personnel development strategies – train your own personnel, or gain the personnel already trained by others – many newcomers in the Chinese market, eager to start operations, would prefer the second alternative.

It should be noted that better communication between employer and employees concerning the matter of training and the expectations of after-training position would be helpful for both parties.

Summary/Recommendations

Staff retention is one of the challenges of human resource management in China. The unbalanced demand-supply situation in the market creates some 'frequent fliers' who change their job often. Therefore more and more companies see personnel retention as a strategic issue. Providing a good working environment, well-accepted personal leadership, training and development opportunities and a competitive compensation package are proven retaining measures. In addition, different spare-time company activities, including company outings with the employee's families, are also useful for promoting a family-like atmosphere among colleagues and enhancing the loyalty of local employees.

In general one can say broad job satisfaction is more effective in motivating and retaining good local employees than pure money incentives. Money matters, but it is not the one and only aspect that makes employees happy. If Chinese employees change their employer they mostly are not 'leaving the company but their superior'.

Further sources

China Staff (ed.) (2000) *China Solutions*, HK, Asia Law & Practice.
China Staff (ed.) (1997) *China Staff Case Study Compendium*, HK, Asia Law & Practice.

Feng X. (1998) The Payment and Reward System in XMPMH, in Lichtenberger, B. (ed.) *Managing in a Global World – Case studies in Intercultural Human Resources Management*, Wiesbaden, pp. 35 ff.

Lichtenberger, B. (ed.) (1998) *Managing in a global world – Case studies in Intercultural Human Resources Management*, Wiesbaden.

Newstead, S.E. (ed.) (1986) *Cognition and Motivation*, Dordrecht.

4.3. According to which considerations FIEs should conceptualise their training activities?

The following provides you with a kind of checklist that helps you plan your training activities in China. It gives you a basic idea which steps of conceptualisation are necessary in introducing a training cycle for your Chinese employees.

Phases of the training cycle

- Needs assessment
- Programme design and development
- Programme implementation
- Evaluation

Needs assessment

- Strength and weaknesses of the company and of each potential trainee need to be assessed. Thus you can pinpoint the areas where training is required and signal to the individual that the company invests in the future and provides opportunities for personal growth.
- A training policy should be formulated to which all China-based divisions and offices adhere. Training records should be kept to track; first, what kind of training each employee has received; second, the relationship between training and productivity; and third, whether specific training programmes boost retention efforts.
- Provide opportunities for life-long learning and acknowledge the strong need for knowledge.

Programme design and development

- Clearly outline the goals of the training.
- Use China-specific examples and case studies and incorporate Chinese cultural values. Chinese managers are often reluctant to see their own values shunted aside and may resist making the very changes they are being trained to implement.
- Respect the Chinese learning styles: take a holistic, concrete, visual, product-oriented, relationship-focused approach and develop a collectivist framework (see also chapters 4.4 and 4.5).

- Start with concrete learning and promote long-term incremental learning where skills are learned systematically. Teach fewer concepts each time and focus on the 'on-the-job' use of those concepts.
- Some companies put their managers through a similar series of training courses every three years. Fresh ideas are bound to emerge in a new session and managers who have already been through the cycle can serve as mentors to newcomers.
- Chinese managers must understand why it is important to do something a certain way, not just what to do, or how to do it. Pre-training preparation is as important as training itself.
- The objectives of the training and the company's expectations as well as employees' expectations should be made clear.
- The translation of training material into Chinese should be accurate. This is often a difficult task as many western business terms and concepts lack equivalents in the Chinese language.

Programme implementation

- Carefully select the *laoshi*/trainer (see also chapter 4.4).
- Encourage group-forming.
- Motivate by building relationships.
- Encourage reflection, self-observation and self-evaluation (see also chapter 4.5).
- Show active support from management and headquarters.
- HR managers or general managers should participate in the training (at least in the start-up phase). Managers can act as mentors/coaches while evaluating how effectively trainees are absorbing new materials. Participation raises the awareness of management of how skills, gained during the training, can be applied in the daily operations.
- Carry through follow-ups periodically.

Evaluation

- Follow-up evaluations should be made. Participants should be interviewed about whether they believe objectives were realised. Questionnaires asking the trainees to analyse how they benefited from the training should be assigned after each workshop; review workshops might be conducted.
- Measure learning, to see what knowledge and skills were learned.
- Prepare the trainees to succeed and let them see how much they have learned.
- Management has to be involved in the follow-up process. An objective analysis is desirable through checks of sales figures and productivity before and after training. However, improvement may not become apparent immediately, as training has a long-term impact.

Summary/Recommendations

Before you can start working out a definite programme design, you have to clarify the actual training needs. In the phase of implementation you must take into consideration intercultural differences that influence the learning habits of your Chinese employees. On the chapters 4.4 and 4.5 you will find a more detailed description of the Chinese learning styles and teaching methods. A careful evaluation of the training will help you to optimise your training efforts in order to gain best on-the-job results. The described learning cycle, (analysis of needs, programme development, programme implementation, evaluation), should ensure feedback loops back into on-going needs assessment, in order to keep track of the latest developments.

Further sources

Ng, S.-H. and Pang, C. (1997) 'Structuring for Success in China', *Financial Times Newsletter and Management Reports*, HK.

'Training options multiply, but what about quality?' (1997) *China Staff*, September, pp. 8–11.

'Training the troops' (1996) *China Business Review*, March – April, Beijing, pp. 22–8.

4.4. Which learning styles have to be respected when teaching local Chinese employees?

The need to develop a new generation of Chinese local managers requires more creative management education and personnel development strategies that fit with the Confucian culture. Students in China are criticised for memorising much of their reading and commonly produce large fragments on their assignments. Rote learning is one of the most popular learning modes in the PRC. Learning abilities, including the development of memory, are rooted in the total pattern of society.

Teaching local Chinese people you have to be aware that:

- rote learning is consistent with Confucian values;
- plagiarism is not considered unethical;
- memorisation and recitation are rewarded at school and in traditional test situations;
- the huge number of Chinese characters promotes pattern recognition and rote learning.

Rote learning is consistent with Confucian values

As social stability is based on an unequal relationship between people, subordinates (in the case of learning situations – the student) are expected to follow the decision of superiors (teachers) without questioning. Students are expected to assimilate knowledge without critical assessment.

Plagiarism is not considered unethical in the Chinese context

The phenomenon is said to stem from the Confucian trait of showing respect for one's teachers and elders and the Chinese value of memorising and repeating great scholarly works, which are more or less treated as sacred texts. The objectives of an education which focuses on writings from the past are moral and normative: the young ones are to be transformed into people with a highly developed social conscience and adapted to the code of living accepted already by the elders.

Memorisation and recitation are rewarded during primary and secondary schooling

The traditional tests and course examinations encourage the memorisation of textbooks and therefore impede the development of effective reasoning skills.

Chinese characters

Furthermore, the written Chinese language, which is composed of between 3,000 and 15,000 complex characters of up to 23 strokes, develops children's ability at pattern recognition, but it also imposes the need for rote learning.

The learning habits of western and Chinese people differ enormously. As in western countries the instructor/teacher is seen as a partner, who provides inspirations, challenges critical questions and sometimes also provokes, in China the instructor/teacher is seen as a model. He lectures, shows how to do something, incorporates the ideal and – if needed – he also protects his trainees/students. He just asks rhetorical questions, names examples and provides detailed descriptions and explanations. Chinese people are not used to asking their teachers questions, discussing with them or opposing them. They rather listen very carefully, take detailed notes and learn what they have heard more or less by rote. In general Chinese are not very experienced in transferring knowledge and testing new methods and approaches. They have to be carefully guided to learn it step by step.

Therefore teaching methods such as working out topics in a group, critical study of secondary sources and other material analyses, discussions in the plenary, controversy debating, questions that lead astray, provoking statements or even so-called 'hot chair methods' don't always lead to the desired learning success.

Chinese people will not necessarily share the western conviction that reflecting statements critically is a valuable attribute. Critical reflection is rather seen as a fussy, awkward expedient for the case, that the teacher does not know all about a topic. Instructors who prefer a participative, interactive learning style, are afraid to be seen as ignorant or incompetent.

This, however, is not valid for all Chinese. Amongst the young elite there are more and more who love to try the western learning methods, especially if the

Table 16   Roles of the teacher/trainer and the student in western countries and in China

Western countries	China
Teacher as a partner • Inspires, provokes • Asks test questions	**Teacher as a model** • Lectures • Only the teacher/trainer speaks
Students as partners • Discuss, ask questions • Follow trial and error principle	**Students as imitators** • Listen carefully, take detailed notes • Learn by rote, repeat regularly • See conformity as their basis

Source: Reisach, U., Tauber, T., Xueli, Y. (1997) *China – Wirtschaftspartner zwischen Wunsch und Wirklichkeit*, Vienna, p. 225.

tutor is aware of the common Chinese learning mentality and introduces them accordingly cautiously to the new style. But even then you should not expect very many interpolated questions and contributions to a discussion.

Someone who nevertheless wants to know what his audience has understood and what they think, should insert lots of tea breaks as part of the training programme. This is the time when Chinese trainees ask the trainer questions or tell him their ideas. The advantage of this way is pretty obvious for Chinese students: they will not be seen to lose face if the question is stupid or the teacher does not know the answer.

The role of the Chinese teacher (*laoshi*) is distinctly different from the western teacher: *laoshi* signifies respect and deference. The teacher is not only an instructor, but also an educator with a parental role: his concern goes beyond intellectual and professional growth to the development of the student as a whole. He prepares students for all aspects of life; as a socially aware and responsible member of the community and a citizen of China. Students are expected to be submissive to their teachers. The student–teacher relationship is clearly a hierarchical one. In contrast, western education prepares each individual to be able to attain his potential within existing political, social and economic structures and fosters self-expression, self-reliance, self-motivation, individual initiative and personal achievement.

Summary/Recommendations

When training Chinese people you should consider the following aspects:

- Enrich the teaching materials with as many examples as possible.
- First give examples, then introduce the corresponding principles.
- Don't teach too abstractly and theoretically.
- Repeat often using different wording.
- Have regular tea breaks to enable an informal exchange of ideas.

The table below shows the incongruence in teaching and training between Anglo Saxon/Germanic countries and China/Asian countries. It summarises the students' expectations in training situations – contrasting large and small power distance cultures, and strong and weak uncertainty avoidance cultures. The left-hand side refers to the learning situation in China, as Chinese culture is characterised by large power distance and strong uncertainty avoidance.

If you want to train your Chinese employees you should always keep in mind that they have a different learning approach, which can't be changed all of a sudden. Western teaching styles and learning methods can only be introduced step by step in a well-balanced evolutionary process.

Table 17 Participants' expectations in training situations

Chinese students	*Western students*
Large power distance	**Small power distance**
• Instructor is seen as a 'guru' who transfers personal wisdom to the trainees and deserves respect	• Instructor is seen as facilitator of learning, and is respected if competent
• The trainee expects that the instructor initiates the communication and guides the instruction (instructor centred)	• The trainee expects to take initiative during and after instruction (trainee centred)
• The trainee refrains from publicly criticising or contradicting the instructor	• The trainee is willing to level with the instructor
• Older instructors are more respected than younger ones	• The trainee considers age less important than the teacher's competence
• The trainee prefers an instructor who lectures	• The trainee prefers an instructor who provides a mix of experiential learning and lecture
Strong uncertainty avoidance	**Weak uncertainty avoidance**
• The trainee prefers clearly structured learning situations, including precise objectives and detailed strict assignments	• The trainee is comfortable in unstructured learning situations, including vague objectives, broad assignments and open timetables
• The trainee expects the instructor to have definite answers to questions	• The instructor may admit that he does not know something
• Trainees and the instructor regard learning as a serious process	• Trainees and the instructor regard learning situations as a challenge which can be fun
• The trainee is primarily interested in accurate problem-solving	• The trainee is comfortable with innovative approaches to problem-solving
• The instructor and the trainees find the expression of strong emotions acceptable	• The instructor and the trainee try to keep own emotions in check

Source: Saner R., Yiu, L. (1994) 'European and Asian resistance to the use of the American case method in management training: possible cultural and systemic incongruence', in *International Journal of Human Resource Management*, vol.5, no.4, December.

Further sources

Hofstede, G. (1991) *Cultures and Organisations: Software of the Mind: Intercultural Cooperation and its Importance for Survival*, London.
Hofstede, G. (1992) *Culture's Consequences – International Differences in Work-related Values*, Beverly Hills.
Reisach, U., Tauber, T. and Xueli, Y. (1997) *China – Wirtschaftspartner zwischen Wunsch und Wirklichkeit*, Vienna, Ueberreuther.
Saner, R. and Yiu, L. (1994) 'European and Asian resistance to the use of the American case method in management training: possible cultural and systemic incongruence', in *International Journal of Human Resource Management*, vol. 5, no. 4, December.

4.5. Which teaching methods are suitable for local Chinese managers?

The transfer of educational technology has encountered numerous problems in China. Management techniques and training packages developed in individualist countries are based on cultural assumptions which may not hold in collectivist cultures. Therefore one has to check carefully whether specific teaching methods fit local Chinese employees and how typical western teaching methods can be modified in order to be introduced in the Chinese context.

Innovative teaching approaches

- Case studies
- Games and role plays
- Coaching/mentoring
- Language of instruction

Case studies

Many business schools around the world have adopted the Harvard-style case study method in the training of managers. However, the skills to be developed through the traditional case method focus more on the process and less on the content side of business management. Those skills are analytical, application, communication, social and creative skills. Case studies demand a high level of tolerance for frustration and ambiguity, since there is no correct answer. The development of the solution is to be guided by the teacher/tutor.

The preferential Chinese mode of thinking is deductive, not inductive or operational. Unstructured cases force Chinese trainees to come up with their own solutions. Chinese students/trainees in general expect to find 'one best solution', so the outcome is fear of making mistakes, resulting in 'losing face' and looking ignorant. Chinese trainees tend to hold back with their ideas until the teacher provides them with the answer. Therefore the case teacher should explain the purpose of the case study, clarify the rules of the game and underline at the beginning that open disagreement is expected and that conflicts should be resolved through means other than conflict avoidance behaviour alone.

Case teachers who do not offer content information are perceived as incompetent. Chinese trainees expect the case teacher to provide relevant technical or even theoretical content, either before or during the case. Therefore the teacher should integrate the case into a larger theoretical framework and get involved in the discussion. Teachers whose classroom style is most admired are those who give clear structured lectures, with lots of information written in clear listed precursors with numbers and brief headings.

Group work provides a sense of safety as trainees take refuge in the team. Although some may not participate as actively as others, they still learn from both their peers and their teachers. Group discussions reinforce the trainees' understanding and enable them to develop leadership skills through working out and rationalising answers.

Games and role plays

Chinese enjoy games and friendly competition. Therefore they place a higher value on training based on group incentives than their western counterparts. This trait is particularly strong in societies that endorse collectivist values.

Friendly games provide participants with the safety of the group and force students to pay attention. In contrast role plays are often ineffective as conflicts don't get expressed or resolved, especially if participants have to sanction or manage other participants considered 'senior' to them, by either age or positional power.

Coaching/mentoring

One of the most promising methods for teaching local Chinese staff is coaching using mentoring. Capable employees are identified to act as assistant to senior managers with the explicit intention of succession. It is the duty of the senior manager – in most cases an expatriate – to transfer the knowledge and train the assistant to take over the senior role within a few years. Frequently, both the senior manager and the person identified to fill that job have the same job title. The success of this training method depends on the training ability of the coach/mentor (see also chapter 3.4, pp. 135ff).

Language of instruction

As language is a vehicle of teaching, the course language influences the learning process. Communication problems often hinder the understanding of taught material. Non-native language education affects the student's approach to learning: less confident students will continue to rely more on rote learning than attempting to gain profound conceptual understanding (see also chapter 2.7).

What is felt to be a 'message' in one language does not necessarily survive the translation process. Information is more than words: it is words that fit into a cultural framework. Having to express oneself in another language means learning to adopt someone else's reference frame.

The best medium of instruction for Chinese staff is controversially debated among HR managers and training providers. The requirements of both, company and trainee/employee, need to be taken into account. As a 'rule of thumb' many companies tend to conduct senior management training in English, as these people mostly have to act in a global environment. Therefore good English skills are a must. On the other hand the training of junior managers in functional areas such as sales or personnel management is conducted in Mandarin, as the reference groups of these employees are first and foremost other Chinese people. A good sales manager does not necessarily have to speak fluent English.

Summary/Recommendations

As a basis for successful training a climate of openness and trust has to be established and during in-house training participants should not be mixed with their superiors otherwise 'lower staff' will refrain from getting involved. As for Chinese there is a tremendous fear of 'losing face' (dignity, prestige, self-respect) among peers; any offence should be avoided. In mixed groups with participants from different companies, teachers should avoid case studies on companies the trainees work for.

Further sources

Hofstede, G. (1991) *Cultures and Organisations: Software of the Mind. Intercultural Cooperation and its Importance for Survival*, London.

Hofstede, G. (1992) *Culture's Consequences – International Differences in Work-related Values*, Beverly Hills.

Martinsons, M. (1996) 'Conquering cultural constraints to cultivate Chinese management creativity and innovation', in *Journal of Management Development*, vol. 15, no. 9, pp. 8–35.

Saner, R. and Yiu, L. (1994) 'European and Asian resistance to the use of the American case method in management training', in *International Journal of Human Resource Management*, vol. 4, no. 5, December.

4.6. Should I train in-house or should I outsource the training activities?

Multinational corporations and JVs in China are using a number of resources to carry out their training policies. One has to decide in every single case which source is suitable for the respective goals and structures of a company.

Options for staff training

- Internal training courses
- Company training centres
- Training overseas
- External training
- Training consortia

Internal training courses

Many companies are initialising in-house training resources as they feel that external trainers, unfamiliar with their business, do not understand their corporate strategy and therefore could not meet the needs of their corporations. Accordingly the demand for 'train-the-trainer' programmes is rising. Other companies establish links with Chinese universities and develop relationships with Chinese professors, who then become primary consultants responsible for conducting training sessions. Some FIEs hire outside consultants to develop specialised, on-site training courses for their employees. Ideally the development of such a course involves pre-training interviews with high-level Chinese and expatriate managers to help the trainers understand the company's operating procedures and training needs.

Also 'on-the-job training' by senior managers that take the role of a coach/mentor is becoming more and more popular (see chapter 4.5).

Company training centres

A growing number of FIEs (such as Motorola, Siemens, Mobil, Coca-Cola) are devoting substantial resources to establishing comprehensive company training centres in China aimed at employees from all the company's China operations, suppliers and key-account customers. In such cases, however, a huge initial investment for train-the-trainer activities, special tailored teaching material and general facilities is required. Furthermore the running costs (full-time trainers, actualisation of training materials, facilities, etc.) are often so high, that finally the outsourcing of training activities makes sense. Some companies (such as Henkel, BASF) have already given up their own training centres for cost reasons and now prefer training by external providers.

Overseas training

Employees find the option of overseas training attractive. Such programmes are generally considered effective because they offer exposure to company culture, at the same time as providing relevant training. Sending staff overseas, however, involves a considerable administrative effort and visas are not always obtainable. Often the companies also shrink from the supervising efforts that are necessary when a Chinese employee comes to the headquarters for a long period. If there is no stringent concept of overseas training, the effect of the training will be compromised.

In these cases programmes such as the SEMP (Sino European Management Programme) are recommended. The Chinese employees will be prepared in the first phase in China for the visit to Europe. In the second phase they take part for six weeks in MBA-level classes at a European university and finally in the third phase they work – supervised by university professors – on a project in the European headquarters of their company.

As experiences of FIEs show, the overseas training always involves the risk that a trainee does not want to return to China or is hired by a competitor just after having finished the training abroad. Nevertheless sending staff to overseas training is still popular among FIEs. This option is chosen by 75–95 per cent of FIEs to qualify their staff.

External training

Until recently, alternatives for external training were limited to training abroad at foreign universities, business schools and training centres, or to local training centres, run by Chinese educational or industrial organisations. However, the number of independent training providers has increased rapidly within recent years. HR managers no longer have to worry about where to find external trainers. However, as elsewhere in the world, the quality of the trainers may be quite heterogeneous. Therefore a critical check of the training providers is recommended.

In choosing an external training provider, the following aspects should be taken into consideration: the teaching and China experience of the trainers; the reputation and the references of the training provider; the suitability of the teaching style and the learning materials to specific Chinese needs (see also chapters 4.4 and 4.5); the possibility of getting specially tailored, modular courses; the teaching language; the results of course evaluations by your staff, etc.

Alternative training measures include object- and topic-related seminars, comprehensive management programmes as well as individual coaching. Short seminars are first and foremost suitable to impart specific operative knowledge in functional areas such as marketing, sales, financing, human resource management, productions and logistics or to gain a first insight into strategic topics. Also as an introduction to soft skills such as teamwork, creative and innovative thinking, conflict management, leadership, etc. short seminars are recommended.

However, if you want to give a Chinese employee a deep insight into all the operative and strategic areas of a company in order to prepare him/her for a responsible position as a senior manager in a global environment, more comprehensive management programmes are preferable. There are MBA programmes that can be booked as 'on-the-job courses' for selected local Chinese high potentials. Some American (Rutgers, Newport, Maryland), European (CEIBS) and Australian (Eliza Monash) universities and business schools are offering – partly in co-operation with Chinese universities – such Executive-MBA courses and the number of the MBA providers in China is growing steadily. However, as the quality of the different MBA programmes differs significantly, you should select very carefully the one that fits your specific needs best.

If you prefer shorter additional training for an employee, programmes like the above mentioned SEMP are recommended, which also enable the employee to get to know first-hand the corporate culture of your headquarters.

If a Chinese employee on mid-term should be responsible for a specific management position, it makes sense to give him a personal coach who intensively prepares him for his future duties, helps him to recognize his personal strengths, to use those effectively and also to accept his weaknesses respectively – as far as possible – to change them into strengths.

The type of training an employee should get should be discussed at least once a year in a review meeting with the employee inquestion (see also chapter 4.1). On this occasion a consensus should be reached between the wishes of the employee and the ideas of his superior. Only in this way will training be profitable for both sides.

Training consortia

To reduce training costs, to maximise the use of training resources, and to expose employees to more frequent training, some FIEs have formed training consortia. Usually based on geographic proximity and similar training needs, a consortium is a loose affiliation that actively explores ways of sharing venues and instructors, or aims at dividing the expense of outside training provided by consultants or universities. For example, in Beijing the Dutch-UK company Shell has participated in training programmes with both IBM of the USA and Henkel of Germany. In Shanghai the American companies Raychem and Intel have jointly hired a professor from Hong Kong to teach basic finance and accounting to local staff.

Summary/Recommendations

For larger companies in China there is the question whether they should train their employees in-house or they should outsource the training activities to external providers. An advantage of the in-house training is that company-specific specialities (i.e. concerning financing or sales) can be covered specifically and the corporate culture can be imparted to the participants of a seminar. Some – especially bigger companies – aim to introduce global training programmes worldwide in order to create unified standards.

On the other hand the outsourcing of training services is usually more cost effective than in-house training. External providers – not least for reasons of competition – have to keep track with the current developments in the training sector. In general on the external market new teaching methods, concepts and contents are available faster and more cheaply than by in-house developments. If the evaluation of a training course by your employees shows that the services of a provider are not satisfactory, it is usually not a big problem to change to another competitor. With in-house trainers, however, it is not as easy. Therefore from our point of view we recommend training only very company-specific seminars in-house. In all other cases small and mid-sized companies (in particular) should outsource training services to external providers.

Further sources

China Staff (ed.) (2000) *China Staff Training Manual*, HK Asia Law & Practice.
China Staff (1997) September, p. 9.
China Staff (1997) May, p. 4.
China Staff (1997) July/August, p. 11.
'Growing number of MBA providers in China', *Business China* (1997) 23 June, Beijing, pp. 12–16.

5

How Do I Get Reliable Market Information?

Christine Boos

5.1. How reliable are Chinese sources?

Almost all statistical data that are published by official Chinese sources, such as by the National Bureau of Statistics (NBS), are aggregated macro-economic data, limited to a few key figures. If you can find data about specific branches of industry, these are mostly very general data that just give you a very rough idea of the situation. Furthermore official statistics offer almost no consumer data that refer to psycho-graphic, emotional or lifestyle aspects. As large parts of China are still underdeveloped in terms of market research, there is a lack of the necessary precision and completeness of the data recording and of the registration system. The problems concern the bookkeeping of single (state-owned) companies as well as the statistics of the provinces. However, China's central government is fighting against these problems in order to get the relevant data from the provinces in correct, up-to-date and complete form.

Problems getting reliable and valid data from Chinese sources

- Manipulated data according to the needs of different target groups.
- Lack of the special know-how in doing professional, reliable market research.
- Translation and interpretation problems.

Manipulated data according to the needs of different target groups

A burden for the central government and its planning is the lack of reliability and validity of the figures that are delivered by the provinces and the state owned companies. The bad quality data is usually the result of economic interests. Sometimes a province or a village tries to avoid high contributions to Beijing; sometimes the career of leading cadres are accelerated by glossing over data. There is a familiar quotation in China: 'Figures make cadres, cadres make figures.'

The statistics you can get in China are still specially tailored to the needs of a centralised economy. They deal first and foremost with output figures rather than with costs, prices and returns, as is usual in market-oriented economies. Often there are also different figures for internal and external use. The 'unofficial' information is only available via good *guanxi*; therefore it may be worth the effort to have a Chinese counterpart who cares about these matters.

Sometimes the Chinese authorities also publish contradictory data, whose differences can't be explained in an adequate way. Take, for example, the exact method of calculating the Chinese price index and hereby also the deflator for the calculation of the real economy growth. This method remains a secret of the National Bureau of Statistics that still changes, adds or eliminates statistical categories quite arbitrarily without any further comment. The low published rate of price increases, for example, may possibly falsify the real economic growth. Though Chinese statistics are often said to be highly unrealistic, China can less and less afford to forge numbers if it wants to be taken seriously by the international business community.

Lack of market research know-how

As professional market research still is quite a young discipline in China, there is often a lack of experience and special know-how regarding recording and evaluating statistical data. For different reasons it is hard to get really valid and reliable empirical data:

- Because of the cultural differences between China and the western hemisphere, it is not possible just to transfer proven market research methods and instruments from western countries directly to the situation in China. Because of different habits, lifestyles, behaviour patterns, ways of thinking and answering questions etc., western techniques of asking questions have to be modified to get reliable answers. Otherwise lots of information gets lost in between the lines (see also chapters 2.6 and 2.7).

At present market researchers are still in a kind of testing phase in order to refine market research tools for the Chinese market. They have to evaluate data acquired by empirical research and cross-check this several times with the results of prior studies. Only by trial and error can they create reliable and valid market research tools for the future that ensure the quality of market research in China.

- There are still very few experts in the Chinese bureaus of statistics. However, over the last couple of years there have been several co-operation projects between the Chinese National Bureau of Statistics (NBS) and statistic bureaus of European countries. This way the employees of NBS get familiar with western market research tools and together with their European colleagues they can work out research instruments which are adapted to the needs of the Chinese markets and consumers. However, despite the enormous efforts to improve statistical data in order to take the internal and external needs of information into account, the learning process and market research in China still shows some major defects.

- Aggregated economic data are mostly based on random sampling in single branches of industry and provinces. Their extrapolation to all of China by weighting factors can be manipulated almost arbitrarily. Thus, multiple counting will raise success figures, which falsifies, for example, statements of production and foreign investment. So, the National Bureau of Statistics has had to revise down the aggregated data of the industrial growth several times during the last few years.

- On the other hand there are still quite a lot of non-measured markets that seem to be a black box for the researchers. One challenge for the future is to find methods to also cover these areas and to handle the very fragmented market situation in China. The development of systems and research tools which meet the needs of the Chinese market is a major task for the future.

Translation and interpretation problems

An additional burden analysing original data sources may be the language. Not only are the statistical figures often totally differently defined by the Chinese authorities than is usual in the western world, also the language of the comments may be equivocal or ambiguous. Often you find more in-between the lines than in the actual text (see also chapters 2.6 and 2.7). The official translations are limited to a few key figures that are intended to represent a kind of prestige value. Therefore they are not always reliable. Very often data that had been recorded by international institutions differed noticeably from those published by the Chinese government.

Summary/Recommendations

Market research in China is a very special story: there is neither detailed data as we are used to in western countries, nor, if it is available the data is as reliable as the investors would wish. On the one hand there is a lack of market research know-how with the Chinese researchers; on the other hand data is still often manipulated according to the needs of specific groups of interest. Furthermore, there are often problems in translating and interpreting the data correctly. Therefore you should not rely exclusively on official Chinese data. It is highly recommended to use other sources as well to get realistic, reliable information about the Chinese markets (see also chapters 5.2, 5.4 and 5.5).

Further sources

Jimmerson Peng, J. (2001) 'Advertising and Marketing,' in Shaw A. (ed.) *Operation China: An Investor's Manual*, by Baker McKenzie, HK, p. 1–30.
Reisach, U., Tauber, T. and Yuan, X. (1997) *China – Wirtschaftspartner zwischen Wunsch und Wirklichkeit*, Vienna Ueberrenther.
Worcester, R.M. (1986) *Consumer Market Research Handbook*, Amsterdam.

5.2. What do you have to consider when doing market research in China?

Market surveys are necessary for every company wanting to be engaged in the Chinese market: no matter whether a company plans to encounter the Chinese market, wants to review its already existing China engagement or requires permanent observation of relevant markets and their main factors of influence. A well-founded market survey provides the information needed to develop a tailor-made and effective marketing strategy in China. As the market situation in China is changing constantly it is also imperative to analyse the market continuously with respect to trends in demand, pricing, packaging, etc.

The most important considerations when doing market research in China
- Size of the country and regional differences.
- Goals and contents of a market analysis in China.
- Methods of executing market research in China.

Size of the country and regional differences

China is nearly the size of the European Union although it is one country! Therefore it must be noted that a region in China is normally the size of a European member state. Whereas, however, nobody would suggest that consumers' behaviour in Stockholm (Sweden) and Palermo (Italy) are alike, lots of people still think that China has quite a homogeneous population with nearly identical taste, consumer behaviour and lifestyle. Often all Chinese consumers/buyers are lumped together.

As a matter of fact there are enormous cultural differences between the Chinese provinces.

- There are more than 200 spoken languages/dialects in China. Even within one region often communication is only possible in Putonghua (the official Chinese standard language) because of the enormous language differences.
- The biggest ethnic groups are Han (92 per cent), Manchu, Mongols, Uighurs and Tibetans.
- 30 per cent of the population lives in urban areas whereas the rest (70 per cent) lives in rural areas of China.

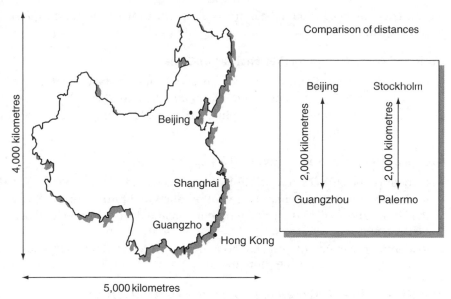

China is with an area of 9.6 square kilometres, nearly as big as the European Community

Chart 7   Comparison of distances

- There are 22 provinces, four municipalities (Beijing, Shanghai, Tianjin, Chongqing), five autonomous regions (Guangxi, Tibet, Xinjiang, Ningxia, Inner Mongolia), two special administrative regions (Hong Kong and Macau) and around 834 cities.
- There are totally different lifestyles, consumer habits and cultural backgrounds. In the north of China the philosophic orientation is based on Lao Zi and Chung-Tzu; that means a kind of passive attitude and no belief in authorities. In the south life is determined by Confucianism; that means orderly conditions, hierarchy and the reign of a caring sovereign. At the same time ways of thinking and acting are influenced by different religions such as Buddhism, Taoism, Islam and Catholicism.
- There are immense differences concerning social-economic aspects such as purchasing power, logistics, investment climate, the competitive situation and product requirements. Also geographic considerations such as density of population, infrastructure and natural resources play an important role.

As these facts and figures show, you find a very fragmented market situation in China. Therefore it is highly recommended to analyse the Chinese market per region. This will enable you to be more focused. The Chinese 'prototype buyer' does not exist!

Goals and contents of a market analysis in China

Careful market analysis may help you to avoid vital mistakes that lots of investors made before, because they didn't do their 'homework' properly. Therefore they got trapped in some pitfalls they could have avoided, if they had been prepared adequately.

Possible goals of a market analysis in China can be:

- to identify the chances and risks for your products in China;
- to identify the level of demand for your products and future trends;
- to identify and analyse the level of production and distribution by competitors in China;
- to identify the main potential buyers and their anticipated buying trends as well as the respective purchasing power.

An initial analysis and overview of the Chinese market includes an evaluation of:

- the region and the attractiveness for investment;
- market prices of relevant products;
- current levels of production, quality and demand;
- the competitive situation in the market (over-supply or a shortfall in supply);
- future trends for the level of production and demand;
- the regions that are the most attractive for you based on the level of demand;
- import, selling and production regulations/restrictions relevant to your business.

Methods of executing market research in China

Nowadays in western industrialised countries many marketing managers get lucky and find most of their information needs can be satisfied by internal or external data in a general marketing information system; they can fall back upon secondary data used by marketing but gathered for some purpose other than a current marketing information need.

In China, however, because the markets are still quite young and the marketing data published by various official and unofficial channels is not very reliable, there are often times when only the results of primary market research will be useful. That means data have to be specifically collected and organised for a particular marketing information need or to solve a particular marketing problem. In this context the importance placed on interviews is very high. Through interviews it is possible to collect up-to-date and accurate information and compile data about future trends from people who specialise in their field of business. Furthermore through interviews it can be established whether the potential competitors or buyers are genuine.

Since 15 August 1999 there have been new regulations for foreign invested companies carrying out market surveys in China. These stipulate that only special authorised market research agencies are allowed to collect primary market data on behalf of FIEs (see also chapter 5.3). We really recommend complying with these rules, as otherwise you may have serious problems. Unlike western countries, you can't go with your questionnaire in a shopping centre, in the streets or to other public places and ask people for their opinion. At worst you could go to jail for this.

Summary/Recommendations

In the past, lots of foreign investors failed to explore the Chinese market properly. Dazzled by 1.3 billion potential consumers and in order not to miss the chance or to lose time, they started to do business in China without an intensive prior market investigation. For many of these investors this ended with disaster. To avoid those pitfalls you should try to get as much information as possible about the Chinese markets, your target groups and their habits before you start or continue to invest in the PRC. Because of the enormous size of the Chinese market and the heterogeneity of the population you have to segment very deeply. Consider that market research in China is still a quite young discipline and that therefore research systems or methods that fit the need of the Chinese market are often still under development. At any rate you should respect the PRC's regulations for market research. Don't try to do any primary data collection on your own without prior permission!

Further sources

Media Com/Grey, (2000) *China: Market Research – An Overview of China*, December, HK.
Worcester, R.M. (1986) *Consumer Market Research Handbook*, Amsterdam.
http://www.fiducia-china.com

5.3. What impact do the new market research regulations have on FIEs?

On 15 August 1999 new regulations came into force regarding carrying out market research projects on behalf of foreign invested enterprises. These *Provisional Procedures Governing Foreign Related Social Surveys* have an enormous impact on international market research agencies (such as AC Nielsen, AMI Ltd, Gallup China Ltd, Roper Starch Worldwide Co-op.) as well as on companies with foreign investment, which are looking for reliable primary market data.

The most important features
- Contents of the new regulations for market research.
- Consequences of the *Provisional Procedures Governing Foreign Related Social Surveys*.
- Reactions of the affected parties.
- How do FIEs handle these regulations in practice?

Contents of the new regulations

The *Provisional Procedures Governing Foreign Related Social Surveys* include:

- Only specially licensed companies are allowed to carry through market research for FIEs. Foreign passport holders or companies are no longer allowed to do primary market research on their own. They rather have to hire a specially licensed Chinese or international market research agency to collect the desired data. As demanded by law the international market research agencies have to be joint ventures with local Chinese partners.
- A draft of the respective questionnaires has to be granted by the National Bureau of Statistics (NBS).
- Until May 2000 the market research agencies had first to submit the results of such an investigation to the NBS before they could hand them over to the respective customer. The European Community, however, succeeded in negotiations about China's access to the WTO, meaning that Beijing changed those rules, which could endanger the secrecy of the results of market investigations. In the future, only a copy of the questionnaire has to be sent to the authorities, but not the results of investigations.

Consequences of these regulations

By these new regulations the Chinese authorities can not only check the extent, the content and the time-frame of a market research project, but also they are able to forestall all points that are – from their point of view – 'sensitive' ones. According to the NBS these are mainly topics such as the protection of the interviewees' trust, religious questions, aspects that concern the status of minorities and political questions; they also want to prevent investigations already carried out by the Chinese government being 'duplicated' by foreign enterprises.

Lots of foreign investors in China who want to conduct primary market investigations are concerned about the questionnaires they have to submit to the NBS. The type of questions often reveals quite a lot about future strategies and plans. Of course, the Chinese authorities emphasise that the questions handed over to them will be treated as strictly confidential; but the National Bureau of Statistics does run its own commercial market research institutes.

Reactions of the affected parties

International market research agencies which run offices in China such as Asia Market Intelligence Co. Ltd (with clients such as Coca-Cola and Nokia) or Roper Starch Worldwide Inc. have, in the past, avoided asking political sensitive questions in order not to annoy the Chinese authorities. For that reason in 1998 Roper Starch rejected a client's wish to ask in a market research project whether Chinese consumers see the future with positive or negative feelings.

So far the market research business only has a value of about 80 million US dollars. However, considering the enormous potential, the international market research agencies have to accept that they must work within these restraints when doing business in China.

AC Nielsen Media International, which worked closely with the Chinese authorities even before the new regulations came into operation (i.e. with the inquiry of audience data for the Chinese TV), sees something positive in these regulations: by the forced close co-operation the authorities are more likely to become up-to-date in their knowledge and know-how of market research. As a consequence the usual international standards of market research can be reached in China sooner as a result of the new regulations.

On the other hand some members of the Delegation of the European Committee complain that these new regulations violate one of the WTO's basic principles, the equal treatment of domestic and foreign companies. According to the *Provisional Procedures Governing Foreign Related Social Surveys* foreign companies and persons are not allowed to carry through direct market research in China. All-Chinese companies, however, do not need special permission for their market research.

The situation in practice

On 29 July 2000 the National Bureau of Statistics (NBS) gave 29 market research agencies registered in China a licence to carry out market investigations for overseas companies and organisations (including those from Hong Kong and Macao). Ten of these licences were handed out to companies with foreign investment. Further licences are under preparation.

Those foreign market research agencies that got a licence joined the positive arguments of the Chinese authorities. AC Nielsen, for instance, emphasises that the new licence system made the response figures rise drastically, as the Chinese people now trust more in the market researchers that are approved by the government; Nielsen praises the NBS for the quick handling of applications for approval of surveys.

Since the *Provisional Procedures Governing Foreign Related Social Surveys* came into effect, the NBS has consented to thousands of drafted questionnaires and rejected only very few cases. Amongst the latter were, for example, questions concerning products for which China had refused foreign investments.

Summary/Recommendations

The new regulations regarding market research prescribe that only licensed market research agencies may carry through primary market surveys on behalf of FIEs. Be aware that you should under no circumstances do market research yourself by asking Chinese consumers in the streets, in supermarkets or elsewhere. That is strictly forbidden in China and may have very serious consequences! As market research still is a very young discipline in China we recommend co-operating with one of the international research agencies rather than with all-Chinese agencies (see also chapter 5.4.). In practice the *Provisional Procedures Governing Foreign Related Social Surveys* allow the government access to any information gathered by a company in the course of conducting a market research. Naturally this may adversely affect the type of information which a company decides to collect, its ability to collect it, the associated costs, the time-frame and the use of information. In addition the existence of this regulation and people's awareness of it may affect the data's reliability.

Further sources

Austrian Chamber of Commerce Beijing (ed.) (1999/2000) *China Nachrichten*, 3/2000, p. 47, 4/1999, pp. 127ff, and 2/2000, p. 119.
Jimmerson Peng, J. (2001) 'Advertising and Marketing', in Shaw, A. (ed.) *Operation China: An Investor's Manual*, Baker & McKenzie, HK, p. 1–30.

5.4. What can market research agencies do for me?

A number of international market research agencies have established operations in China and have a special licence to do research work for foreign invested companies (see also chapter 5.3.). Depending upon the type of information a client needs, they can offer different levels of specialised research or general information. They also can give you detailed information, which kind of market research – according to the Chinese laws and rules – are permitted and what differences – compared to western countries and consumers – you have to consider when conceptualising and carrying out a market investigation.

Services market research agencies can offer you

- Off-the-shelf reports
- Syndicated research
- China-wide permanent data collection
- Completely tailor-made services
- Test-marketing

Most of the big players of the international market research agency scene such as AC Nielsen/SRG, Gallup China Ltd, Frank Small & Associates, Asia Market Intelligence Ltd, Roper Starch Worldwide Co-op., Tyler Nelson Sofres or GfK Market Research have founded offices in Beijing, Shanghai and/or Hong Kong. They offer a wide variety of services that may help you to optimise your marketing efforts.

Off-the-shelf reports

Many market research agencies offer off-the-shelf reports at relatively reasonable prices. Companies that are thinking about starting business activities in China or in a special region of China often find a report that is available for their particular market. For example, AC Nielsen/SRG offers ready-made reports on markets including beer, shampoos, air fresheners, furniture etc. This can be a quick and easy way to find out whether a market exists for a company's product before any major work is done. These kinds of market reports are offered for nearly all major Chinese cities such as Beijing, Shanghai, Shenzhen, Nanjing and Guangzhou, and also for important provinces and regions.

Besides the market research agencies, departments or affiliated companies of big ad agencies (i.e. Grey, J.W. Tomphson, Saatchi & Saatchi, Mather & Ogilvy, Team BDO) often also offer quite a number of such off-the-shelf reports. So, it is worth the effort, first to look around to find what kind of material is already available before starting something on your own.

Syndicated research

The next level of research offered by these marketing research firms is syndicated research. In this type of research project, also called omnibus surveys, a number of clients club together to pay for the agency's research. During the survey, the agency's representatives ask members of the public questions set by each of the clients. Clients are required to pay a fixed fee according to the number of close-ended and open-ended questions requested. The client can ask for its questions to be directed only to a certain consumer group, for example only females, only males, or only household decision-makers. The groupings are by necessity quite broad because of the wide range of clients for whom surveys are being carried out simultaneously.

Each participating company buys questions on the survey and receives only the results of those questions. Omnibus surveys are a way to share the costs of doing research, so they tend to be cheaper and more efficient. They are especially appropriate for a company wishing to ask a limited number of questions in a study of a large representative sample of consumers. AC Nielsen/SRG's China Omnibus service, for example, visits Beijing, Shanghai and Guangzhou three times a year and also goes to secondary cities, although less regularly.

China-wide continuous data collection

For a couple of years there have also been research projects that provide a continuous fieldwork. One of the most important is CMMS (China Media Marketing Services). It is a co-operation project between BMRB (British Market Research Bureau), Telmar (Software) and Sino-Monitor (Research Vendor).

Across 30 Chinese cities (including provincial capitals, special enterprise zones and other large cities) 71,000 people will be asked about standard demographics (region, sex, age, gender, working status, income, education, children etc.), their habits concerning the use of media such as TV, radio, magazines and newspapers (heavy/medium/light users), data on usage of 90 product categories and 3,000 plus brands as well as lifestyle and attitudinal data. By cross-tab-ranking and correspondence analysis (clustering, multivariate analysis) you can figure out regional differentiations as well as profile data of consumers. So you can get, for instance, information on how many males between 25 and 35 in Dalian or Harbin are heavy smokers of a special brand of cigarettes and which newspaper they prefer to read.

The results of CMMS are actualised every quarter on a rolling basis. So far CMMS is the most elaborate, complex and popular instrument for continuous market research and most of the major ad agencies are using this data for their daily work. However, other research companies such as AC Nielsen/SRG have initiated similar projects for a permanent market research. The future will show whether they can compete with the benchmarking CMMS.

Completely tailor-made services

Market research agencies can also offer completely tailor-made services for individual clients, including consumer profiles, advertising recall rates, assessments of the image of a product, and so on. This method enables much more detailed research and allows the client to target particular market sectors, such as middle-income females between 20 and 30. Questions to examine the attitudes of a much more tightly defined target market are possible. However, this method is significantly more expensive than buying off-the-shelf research or taking part in syndicated research groups.

Test-marketing

Companies that want to launch a new product in the Chinese market often want to conduct a field experiment to test the effectiveness of product offering under realistic market conditions. The complete marketing plan for the new product is tried out – distribution, advertising, sales promotion, point-of-purchase displays and so on – but just in one Chinese city or in a small geographic area. When choosing a geographical region or city for test-marketing purposes marketers typically try to locate a place which is most representative of the country and matches most closely the national average in terms of age distribution, income, mix of population, educational background etc. Market research institutes such as AC Nielsen/SRG can figure out a suitable test-region/ city for you and carry out your test-marketing.

There are a number of benefits and some problems associated with test-marketing. By offering a new product to a sample of Chinese customers, marketers can evaluate and improve their marketing programme. In fact, test-marketing may be the only way to see if all the technical and commercial elements work. Sometimes test-marketing leads to product improvements or adaptations to the taste and needs of the Chinese consumers. In other cases test marketing may warn marketers of probable product failure, allowing the company to save millions of Renminbi by 'pulling the plug' before the doomed item is introduced for real.

However, test-marketing is extremely expensive. Another hazard of test-marketing is that it allows the competition to get a free look at your new product, its introductory price and your intended promotional strategy. In China, which is one of the most competitive markets of the world, this can be deadly to a new product's success, because it enables other foreign as well as local companies to adjust their own strategies in advance of your product introduction. So you have to weigh carefully in every single case, whether test marketing really makes sense.

Difficulties of market research in China

Despite of all the progress of market research in China during the last years, there are – compared to western countries – still restrictions that make it difficult to get reliable and valid data:

- Compared to the western hemisphere the amount of money per capita that will be spent on market research is very small.
- Lots of people are living in 'unresearched' areas which are still blank spaces on the market research map of China.
- Because of Chinese regulations, asking psycho-graphic or emotional questions is quite restricted. There are no questions allowed that target judgements or opinions of present or future economic, political or social developments in China. Also asking for feelings and emotions is not very popular in China and people often hesitate to answer this type of questions (partly because of bad experiences in the past). Therefore market research and ad agencies often restrict their results to clustered consumer categories gained by observation, such as traditionalists, achievers, young achievers, modernists, untouchables etc.
- There are not yet existing reliable and valid tools and methods to evaluate the results of empirical investigations in China, as, so far, nobody can really

judge whether the methods we use in western countries are also adaptable in China with its totally different culture (see also chapter 2.6). Often there is much more to read in-between the lines. Therefore it's hard to say whether it really makes sense to use the evaluation tools that work well in western countries. Only by repeating investigations several times and comparing the results can you judge whether you really have reliable, valid research and evaluation tools.

Summary/Recommendations

During recent years almost all international market research agencies have opened offices in China. Gradually their services have become more complex and they have learned how to collect data on Chinese markets, consumers and investors. From off-the-shelf reports, syndicated research and continuous data selection to test-marketing and panel studies you can get almost any sort of information. However, as China is still a very young market in terms of market research and because of strict regulations from the Chinese government, carrying through a market investigation is often much more difficult and less effective, reliable and efficient than in the western hemisphere.

Further sources

Gijsen, R. and McLaughlin, B. (1997) *Reaching the Shanghai Consumer*, HK, Asia Information Associates Ltd.
MediaCom/Grey (2000) China: Market Research - An Overview of China, December, HK.
Solomon, M. and Stuart, E. (1997) *Marketing – Real People, Real Choices – International Edition*, Prentice-Hall.

5.5. Which institutions can help me to collect secondary data?

Getting qualified information is one of the elementary problems which may influence the success of your China activities. Information gained by secondary data influences feasibility studies as well as contracts, strategic planning and operative decisions of the management. The kind of information you actually need depends largely on the lifecycle phase of your China business. Reliable information is especially important during the start-up phase of your China engagement. It may save you a lot of money, time and frustration. For instance the knowledge of local conditions such as local product priorities or the general price-income level may help you to avoid inefficient business activities. Also in other lifecycle stages of your China business information plays an essential role. Market information, information about business partners (clients, providers, potential JV partners etc.), general conditions and guidelines regarding laws and regulations are indispensable preconditions for success. Good, reliable information can not only improve the interactions and help to keep face but also promote transparency, prevent frustration, reduce costs and improve efficiency.

The most important sources of information
- CCPIT and other official Chinese information offices
- International sources
- Newspapers, magazines and handbooks
- Internet as a data source

CCPIT and other official Chinese information offices

The following list gives details of the most important Chinese authorities and offices that offer different kinds of information services

CCPIT (China Council for the Promotion of International Trade) and the CCOIC (China Chamber of International Commerce)

CCPIT and CCOIC are nationwide organisations for trade promotion with 14 'industry sub-councils' and 46 'local sub-councils' in China's major provinces and cities.

The tasks of CCPIT are:

- to support foreign companies starting business activities in China;
- to exchange delegations in co-operation with foreign economic organisations;
- to organise trade fairs and exhibitions in China and abroad;
- to handle foreign patent and trademark applications;
- to offer economic information to foreign and local companies;
- to produce publications on Chinese and foreign economic development;
- to mediate if there are problems between local and foreign trade or co-operation partners.

The following departments and sub-divisions of CCPIT and CCOIC can offer foreign companies in China concrete support:

- Department of International Relations (acquisition of partners and care for companies)
- Economic Information Department (information services)
  Fax: 00 86 / 10 / 68 53 31 16
- Department of Legal Affairs (legal advice, arbitration in questions of trade and law of the sea)
  Fax: 00 86 / 10 / 68 51 10 69

- China International Exhibition Centre (trade fairs and exhibitions in China)
  Fax: 00 86 / 10 / 64 67 68 11
- China International Economic and Technical Co-operation Consultants
  Fax: 00 86 / 10 / 68 53 05 61

Contact address of CCPIT/CCOIC

- CCPIT Building,
  1 Fuxingmenwai Dajie,
  Beijing 100860, PRC
  Tel: 00 86 / 10 / 68 52 61 18
  Fax: 00 86 / 10 / 68 51 13 70

China Legal Consultancy Centre

- Television Service Building, Room 4184/F,
  20 Wanfujing Dajie,
  Beijing 100006, PRC
  Tel: 00 86 / 10 / 65 13 52 61

China Statistical Information and Consultancy Service Centre

- 38 Yuetan Nan Jie, Sanlihe,
  Beijing 100826, PRC
  Tel: 00 86 / 10 / 68 51 50 76
  Fax: 00 86 / 10 / 68 51 50 78

Foreign Enterprises Service Corporation Beijing (FESCO)

- 14 Chaoyangmen Nan Dajie, Chaoyangqu,
  Beijing 100020, PRC
  Tel: 00 86 / 10 / 65 01 66 77
  Fax: 00 86 /10 / 65 12 53 58

State Economic Information Centre – Economic Information Department

- 58 Sanlihe Lu, Xichengqu,
  Beijing 100045, PRC
  Tel: 00 86 / 10 / 68 35 25 28

Chinese Patent Office

- 6 Xitucheng Lu, Jimenquiao, Haidianqu,
  Beijing 100088, PRC
  Tel/Fax: 00 86 / 10 / 62 01 93 07

Ministry of Foreign Trade and Economic Cooperation (MOFTEC)

- 12 B Guanghua Lu,
  Beijing 100020, PRC
  Tel: 00 86 / 10 / 65 05 – 22 55 12 15
  Fax: 0086 / 10 / 65 05–15 17

State Administration of Taxation

- 68 Zaolinqianjie, Xuanwuqu,
  Beijing 100053, PRC
  Tel: 00 86 / 10 / 63 26 33 66
  Fax: 00 86 / 10 / 63 26 68 36

State Administration of Exchange Control

- Huibin Office Building, 13/F,
  8 Beichendong Lu,
  Beijing 100101, PRC
  Tel: 00 86 / 10 / 64 91 57 01
  Fax: 00 86 / 10 / 64 91 47 83

State Administration of Import/Export

- Commodity Inspection,
  12 Jianguomenwai Dajie,
  Beijing 100022, PRC
  Tel: 00 86 / 10 / 65 00 33 44
  Fax: 00 86 / 10 / 65 00 23 87

State Planning Commission

- 38 Yuetan Nan Jie, Xichengqu,
  Beijing 100053, PRC
  Tel: 00 86 / 10 / 68 52 72 68

Furthermore you also can get product and industry-specific information from the Chinese associations of the different branches of industry. Contact addresses are available from CCPIT (see also chapter 6.4).

Economic and financial studies are also often available from major Chinese banks such as Bank of China, Bank of Communications, China Construction Bank, Industrial and Commercial Bank of China and People's Bank of China.

Official Chinese statistics are available, for instance, in the form of national and regional statistical yearbooks. However, these statistics often contain contradictory data (see also chapter 5.1). The lack of reliability of Chinese statistics may be caused because the responsible authorities often tend to keep secrets;

furthermore the methods of calculation and evaluation may differ quite a lot from region to region, from period to period and from office to office. Therefore the calculation of statistical data is quite hard to comprehend for foreign analysts.

Information on internal planning projects of the government or of state owned companies is only available via very good personal contact networks (*guanxi*).

International sources

You can get aggregated economic data for China, which is the basis of all market research, by generally accessible international sources such as the World Bank or the International Monetary Fund etc. Often there is also quite good information available from the chambers of commerce or with the offices for trade and promotion at the western embassies in China as well as with international banks or with the national bureau of statistics in your country.

These sources increasingly fall back on Chinese statistics, translated into English, especially if they need to compare different Chinese provinces. In general, however, international organisations, which use official Chinese data, re-evaluate it critically and test its validity before they finally publish them.

More detailed investigations are necessary to analyse regional or product markets. Often the associations of the particular branches of industry in your country already have quite good information. However, if it comes to very specific products, you will quite soon reach a point where US, European or Hong Kong sources are not enough. At this point international market research agencies and consultant companies may be able to help you. They can try to get – via connections (*guanxi*) in China – the info you need. It is essentially important that the consultants you deal with have a good, widespread *guanxi*-network as lots of information in China is treated as confidential or, like aggregated economic data, exists in an official and an unofficial version. Therefore, in choosing a suitable consultant, you have to consider his/her specialist orientation and his/her system of existing contacts.

Survey on international sources

- *Embassies and consulates of your country*
  Department for Exhibitions and Trade-fairs
  Department of Economics and Commerce
  Department of Trade Promotion
- *Chambers of commerce*
  American Chamber of Commerce (AmCham)
  European Chamber of Commerce
  Australian Chamber of Commerce
  Single chambers of European countries

- *National and provincial ministries in your country*
  Ministry of Trade and Commerce
  Ministry of Foreign Aid
  Foreign Ministry
- *International banks and insurance companies*
- *National and supranational organisations*
  International Monetary Fund (IMF)
  World Bank
  Political and social foundations
  European Community Investment Partners (ECIP)
  Corporations for technical and economical co-operation (such as GTZ)
- *International consultants*
  International public accountants/auditors (such as Ernst & Young, Price WaterhouseCooper, KPMG, Delvitta Touche Tomatsu, etc.)
  International law fims (such as Baker & McKenzie, Clifford Chance Pünder, Haarmann, Hemmelrath & Partner, BBLP Beiten, Burkhartdt, Mittl & Wegener, etc.)
  International consultant companies (such as BCG, McKinsey, Bain, AT Kearney, etc.)
  International advertising and market research agencies (such as J.W. Thompson, Grey, Saatchi & Saatchi, Mather & Ogilvy, Team BDO, AC Nielsen, Gallup, Roper Starch, Sofres, etc.).
- *Institutions and associations of different branches of industry in your country*
- *Round tables for the exchange of experiences*
  'Joint venture round tables' in major Chinese cities (see also chapter 5.8)
  'Investor round tables' in your home country
  Meetings of business associations that specialise on China topics (such as German-Chinese Businesses Association)

Investigations show that institutions and organisations that are contacted are often not the most efficient and effective ones. Therefore, depending on the aspect you are interested in, smaller, less well-known institutions could prove most informative.

Newspapers, magazines and handbooks

In the last few years some very comprehensive handbooks have been published that cover the peculiarities and problems of doing business in China in general, but also special publications that focus on specific topics such as law, marketing, personnel development, finance etc. Also big consulting companies, banks or law firms publish articles or brochures on China-specific issues fairly regularly.

Table 18 Selection of relevant newspapers, magazines and periodicals

Title	Editor
Asia Law & Practice	China Law and Practice Ltd
China Banking and Finance	China Law and Practice Ltd
China Current Laws	Longman
China Daily	China Daily
China Economic News	External Services Division of Economic Daily and EIA Information & Consultancy Ltd
China Law and Practice	China Law and Practice Ltd
China Law Reporter	American Bar Association
China Newsletter	JETRO (Japan External Trade Organisation)
China Patents & Trademarks	China Patent & Trademark Publications Office (HK) and China Patent Agency (HK) Ltd
China Review	China Review Publications Ltd
China Trade Report	Review Publishing Company Ltd
Far Eastern Economic Review	Review Publishing Company Ltd
Intertrade	ITRI/MOFERT (International Trade Research Institute of the Chinese Ministry of Foreign Economic Relations & Trade) and Wide Angel Press
Intellectual Property in Asia	Shomei Ltd
South China Morning Post	South China Morning Post
Xinhua News Bulletin	Xinhua News Agency
The Asian Wall Street Journal	Dow Jones & Co. Inc.
The China Business Review	China Business Forum (US-China Business Council)
Trade Promotion	CCPIT and CCIC (China Council for Promotion of International Trade and China Chamber of International Commerce)

The most up-to-date sources of information are newspapers, magazines and periodicals. China-internal information can be taken from a great number (more than 5,000) of Chinese local newspapers. The table below gives details at the most important publications and periodicals.

Internet as a data source

The Internet is a convenient tool to collect current data quickly, target-specific, comprehensive and uncomplicated, independent of time and location. Especially in China this is major progress, as ten years ago, for foreigners it was really hard to get access to in-depth information or to find respective literature. In the following you can find some key web sites (see also chapter 5.6) that may help you to optimise your Internet search for China-specific information.

Table 19   China on the Internet
(subject to frequent changes)

General information	Internet address	Notes (language)
Survey on all China-related webpages	www.chinasite.com	
General information on China	www.china.org.cn	
Information on the Chinese provinces	www.china-window.com	
'Yellow pages' of China	www.chinabig.com	
News and information about specific industries	www.chinaonline.com	US Information Service, very good!
Laws and regulations	www.chinamarket.com.cn	
Chinese Yahoo site	www.yahoo.hk	
General information	www.insidechina.com	
General information	www.chinasite.com	
Business information	www.china-bis.com	
Business information	www.cbn.com.sg	
General information	www.chinavista.com	
List of companies	www.china-inc.com	
List of companies	www.cenpok.net	
Real-time Asian stock quotes	www.boom.com	
Chinese authorities	Internet address	Notes (language)
China Council for the Promotion of International Trade (CCPIT)	www.ccpit.org	English, quite comprehensive
Ministry of Foreign Trade and Economic Co-operation	www.moftec.gov.cn	English, best Internet performance of all Chinese ministries
Ministry of Electronics Industry/ Chinese Electronics Standardisation Institute	www.ceic.gov.cn	
Ministry of Finance	www.mof.gov.cn	English, quite interesting
Ministry of Foreign Affairs	www.fmprc.gov.cn	English, complex
Ministry of Information Industry	www.mii.gov.cn	Chinese, English planned
China Meteorological Administration	www.cma.gov	English, very good
Government Online Project	www.gov.cn	Quite complex, Chinese
Office for Special Economic Zones	www.sezo.gov.cn	Chinese, poor performance
Patent Office	www.cpo.cn.net	English, OK
State Administration of Foreign Exchange	www.safe.gov.cn	Chinese
State Administration of Taxation	www.chinatax.gov.cn	Chinese, poor performance

Table 19   (*continued*)

General information	Internet address	Notes (language)
State Bureau of Surveying and Mapping	www.sbsm.gov.cn	Chinese
State Economic and Trade Commission	www.sec.gov.cn	English, poor performance
State Information Centre	www.cei.gov.cn	English
State Statistical Bureau	www.stats.gov.cn	English, good performance
China-related media	Internet address	Notes (language)
Survey on media	www.readchina.com	
Xinhua News Agency	www.xinhua.org	State owned
China Daily	www.chinadaily.com.cn	State owned
People's Daily	www.peopledaily.com.cn	State owned
State Council News Office	www.china.org.cn	State owned
China International Broadcasting Station	www.cnrado.com	State owned
Hong Kong Standard, HK	www.hk-imail.com	Short news
Asian Wall Street Journal	www.wsj.com	Current information
Dow Jones News Report	www.djnr.com	
Information of the Government	www.chinainfo.gov.cn	
South China Morning Post	www.scmp.com	Hong Kong
China Central Television	www.cctv.com	English, OK
Foreign organisations	Internet address	Notes (language)
World Bank	www.worldbank.org	
International Monetary Fund	www.imf.org	
American Chamber of Commerce	www.amcham-china.org.cn	
Australian Chamber of Commerce	www.austcham.org	
Canadian Chamber of Commerce	www.cancham.org	
European Chamber of Commerce	www.ecd.org.cn/	
Swiss Chamber of Commerce	www.osec.ch	Swiss business guide for China
German Chamber of Commerce	www.china-net.de	
Austrian Chamber of Commerce	http://aw.wk.or.at/awo/markt/asien/cn	
Japanese Chamber of Commerce	www.cin.or.jp/Beijing/index.html	

For more websites related to links, portals, search engines, staff recruitment, Internet information, exhibitions, software and information technology, import and export in China, etc. see also chapter 5.6.

Summary/Recommendations

Doing business in China means that you have to continuously collect and evaluate information essential for your activities. This chapter includes the most important Chinese and international addressees as well as important newspapers, magazines and webpages. But remember, some information is only available by unofficial means. In this case you should leave it to your Chinese employees/partners, consultants or friends to make the necessary contacts. For foreigners the *guanxi*-system may be non-transparent, hard to understand and sometimes also dangerous to handle.

5.6. How can I use the Internet to get information and to promote my China activities?

Encouraged by reformist leaders such as Premier Zhu Rongji, Internet use is growing explosively. Three years ago only 640,000 Chinese were connected; now more than 8 million are. According to Computer Economics Inc., an information technology research company, Chinese 'netizens' will total 37 million by 2005, making it the second largest Internet market behind the United States. And while only 24 million US dollars in e-commerce transactions are expected this year, they could near 4 billion US dollars by 2003. English will remain the lingua franca of global commerce. But as the Web reaches the mass market in China and elsewhere in Asia, Chinese could become one of the medium's most used languages within five years.

The most important features

- China will be one of the most important Internet markets of the world and the Chinese language will play a major role within the Internet community.
- Chinese Internet-users represent a class of consumers with an enormous purchasing power and an educational level above the average.
- Internet provides a wide range of up-to-date data and information about the Chinese market and supports you with your acquisition, marketing, selling and purchasing efforts in China.
- E-commerce offers you the opportunity to deal with Chinese partners (suppliers, retailers and customers) directly bypassing cumbersome middlemen.
- Since 2001 panel data of Chinese Internet users has been available.

The veritable explosion of computer and Internet users in China promises also the vast expansion of Internet services like advertising, marketing and customer services (making reservations, ordering and purchasing goods etc.). While the mass market is still in its early days, some Chinese and western entrepreneurs are experimenting with business-to-business models. There are, for example, Alibaba's English and Chinese sites that feature the 'Bizman Club'. This is a bulletin board for companies that buy and sell everything from toys and sporting goods to textiles and chemicals. It gets around 125,000 page-views per day. The founders of sites like Alibaba profit by the fact that the same Web-based enterprise resource planning software used in the West spreads to China. Thus traders around the world can link directly with suppliers and retailers across the mainland, bypassing cumbersome middlemen. But payment for Internet purchases and services can only be done by credit card. The development of e-commerce therefore depends on the development of the banking and credit system as well as on the development of the telecommunication system (including technical aspects like telecommunication networks and speed thereof).

Since June 2001 panel data about the use of Internet directly via the net has been available in China. This means, on the computers of a representative sample group of Chinese Internet users special software is installed. This software enables you to get information on hits of webpages and on images that will be clicked on in preference. Furthermore it provides you with the demographic data of the respective Internet users such as age, gender and educational background as well as about the time spent on a site and the search paths. So-called 'banner tracking', that is getting lists of the ad banners with the most clicks/hits in China, is also possible. This information allows you a target-group focused design and placement of your Internet performance and your advertisement.

Summary/Recommendations

In order to keep on track with the rapid spread of the Internet you should build up your Internet competence in China as early as possible to participate in the enormous possibilities that this technology offers. You can display catalogues, receive orders and negotiate prices via the Web. But overall you can get valuable information about the Chinese market, its consumers and its economical development. Don't miss the chance the Internet offers you to do business in China! A first starting point could be to visit some of the webpages listed below.

Further sources

Einhorn, B. (1999) 'China's Web', in *Business Week*, August, pp. 14–18.
Perkins, C. (1999) 'All the world's a...big web?', in *Beijing Scene*, June, Beijing, pp. 12–18.
Silverman, S. (2001) 'The Dragon online', in *CCN*, May, HK, pp. 32–6.

Table 20   China-related websites (subject to frequent changes)

A quick tour of China-based websites can give you an indication of the budding process. The sites listed below have plenty of links to other good sites.

Links, portals and search engines:

www.sohu.com.cn	www.chinatrading.com	www.cseek.com
www.cei.gov.cn	www.search.com.cn	www.chinabig.com.cn
www.china.org.cn	www.surfchina.com	(massive database of
www.chinahot.com	www.zhaodaola.com	Chinese companies)
www.sinanet.com	www.netease.com	
www.chinavista.com	www.gbchinese.yahoo.com	

English language China business sites:

www.wsj.com (*Asian Wall Street Journal*)
www.djnr.com (Dow Jones)
www.securities.com (Internet Securities)
www.asianwind.com/pub/hksr (Hong Kong stocks)
www.yahoo.hk

www.boom.com (real-time Asian stock quotes)
www.scmp.com (*South China Morning Post*)
www.chinaonline.com (news and information about specific industries)
www.insidechina.com

Bilingual sites with business info:

www.chinabig.com.cn	www. cbn.com.sg
www.china.com	www.chinavista.com
www.chinasite.com	www.moftec.gov.com.cn
www.china.bis.com	

Chinese language sites with business info:

www.chinabyte.com	www.moftec.gov.cn
www.xhinfo.com.cn	

Employment and staff recruitment:

www.chinese.yahoo.com	www.china-hr.com
www. asia-net.com (for bilingual professionals)	www.cjol.com
www.alliance-china.com	www.fescochina.com
www.jobchina.com	www.zhaopin.com
www.jobs.com.cn	www.ChinaHR.com
www.jobs.cn.net	

Lists of companies:

www.moftech.gov.cn	www.china-inc.com
www.mii.gov.cn	www.cenpok.net

Internet information

www.cnnic.net	www.netratings.com

Table 20   (continued)

Market information

www.chinamarket.com.cn   www.yahoo.hk
www.chinaonline.com   www.alibaba.com

Trade fairs and exhibitions

www.cecf-gz.com

Regulations and law

www.chinamarket.com.cn   www.moftec.gov.cn

Software and information technology

www.richsight.com   www.chinabyte.com

Import and export of textiles

www.chinatex.com

Books, magazines and newspapers

www.readchina.com   www.chinainfo.gov.cn

5.7. What are the most interesting consumer classes?

Since Deng Xiaoping proclaimed that consumption and money-making is compatible with the principles of the Marxism/Leninism, the demand for improved products and services increased dramatically, especially with the younger population. These new consumer trends are possible because of permanently rising income levels especially in the bigger cities in China's east such as Beijing, Guangzhou and Shanghai. In these three cities the average income per month nearly tripled in the last decade. This chapter is meant to provide the foreign prospector mining the modern-day China market with a basic introduction to the general trends and market segments. It should be a staring point for the initial understanding of this very complicated market.

The most important features:
- The myth of a market of a billion consumers
- Types of Chinese consumers
- Prudent spending of disposable income
- Consumption affecting macro-economic aspects
- Geography and wealth

The myth of a market of a billion consumers

Unless you are in the chopstick business, China cannot really live up to 1.3 billion consumers. In reality, wealth is highly concentrated in the major coastal

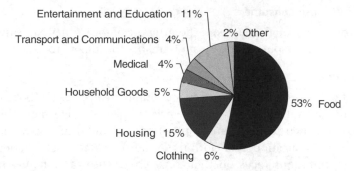

Entertainment and Education 11%

Transport and Communications 4%

Medical 4%

Household Goods 5%

2% Other

53% Food

Housing 15%

Clothing 6%

Expenditures of an average rural household in total: RMB 1577   197 US dollars
Per capita annual income (households) in 1999:   RMB 2210   268 US dollars

Chart 8   The average per capita living expenditure in 1999 of China's rural population

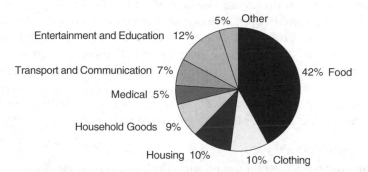

5% Other

Entertainment and Education 12%

Transport and Communication 7%

Medical 5%

Household Goods 9%

42% Food

Housing 10%

10% Clothing

Expenditure of an average urban household in total: RMB 4616   575 US dollars
Per capita annual income (households) in 1999:   RMB 5453   680 US dollars

Chart 9   The average per capita living expenditure in 1999 of China's urban population

cities. The 1999 national average income per rural household was RMB 2210 (268 US dollars) and China is still 70 per cent rural.

The good news, however, is that there is a growing group of professionals with significant disposable income in the coastal regions and the major cities, which can afford many mid-range consumer products. In total you still have a market of over 100 million legitimate consumers; still a significant market by global standards! Therefore it is no wonder that marketers tend to focus on specific groups, generally in urban areas.

Types of Chinese consumers

To give you a first, rough idea about the structure of the Chinese consumers, the following describes some of the most disamable consumer groups.

Little emperors

The effect of the one child policy is that children are making up less and less of the population but conversely these 'little emperors' wield more and more influence over their family's consumption of food and drink, books and toys, computers and education, and clothing. As all the parents' and grandparents' hopes and ambitions focus on their only child, the whole family tends to pamper him/her and to put all their efforts and most of their money into the education and the future of this child. He 'may be a pudgy little emperor whose grandparents treat him to McDonald's and his parents save intensively for his education' (see DSA, January 2001).

Young urban consumers

This generation grew up reaping the benefits of China's opening up and rapid economic development. They are open to foreign products, new ideas and are knowledgeable about product choices, trends and images. They often still live with their parents and thus have more disposable income to spend. It is no wonder that this group of 18–34 year olds is highly sought after by the foreign marketers. The 30-year-old sales manager at some JV factory in Guangzhou going off to play tennis with his Ericsson phone in one hand and a designer bag in the other exemplifies this category of consumer.

Lost generation (45–60 years)

Quite in contrast to our 30-something sales manager are members of the so-called lost generation, the 45–60 age group, who grew up in a society under constant flux. Many lost out as China moved away from a command economy. This group is exemplified by the cab driver – found in any major city – who lost his hard but stable job at a state owned enterprise. He probably has a picture of Mao on his rear view mirror and talks nostalgically about the good old days. Rather than carrying a mobile phone and a designer bag, he has a pack of smokes and a bottle of *baijiu* (strong Chinese alcohol) or a glass of green tea with a screw cap. Members of this generation are unlikely to try new brands and are mainly motivated by price. They are struggling to make it in an unfamiliar and rapidly changing modern society.

Age 65 and over

In 1985 4.9 per cent of China's population was over 65, today it is 7.3 per cent thanks to improvements in health care and nutrition. A growing elderly population of this scale translates into massive spending on pharmaceuticals and medical care. The members of this generation are often taking over the education of their grandchildren while both parents are working full-time – often far away from their children – to support the family.

Prudent spending of disposable income

Recently retention of consumption has been recognisable. Lots of Chinese are afraid that by new reform policies unprofitable state owned companies will be closed or at least restructured. That would mean that millions of Chinese would lose their jobs. Because of this fear for the future many Chinese have reduced their consumption expenditures and raised their saving quota. As a result China today, with 40 per cent, has one of the world's highest saving rates. More than 0.8 trillion US dollars are held in Chinese saving accounts. Anxiety about devaluation and price rises exacerbate this tendency.

All kinds of measures have been tried to stimulate spending. Large sums of government money have been allocated to public infrastructure construction. The People's Bank of China cut interest rates seven times. A law was passed to tax interest on savings. A policy was made to extend the term of housing mortgage loans from the usual 15 years to 30 years. Yet the public obstinately refuses to spend more money on commodity items.

Popular wisdom has it that rising incomes and greater access to credit will by themselves create demand for more consumer durables, automobiles and private housing. But even the most elementary economics should be enough to demonstrate that a society without decent services can hardly pursue ever-greater spending of goods alone.

Nowadays in China there is still an immense need for professional services such as property management, car repair service, providing Internet and tele-communication networks, children's education, medical services, organisation of cultural and sport events, travelling agencies, etc.

Consumption affecting macro-economic aspects

The country's macro-economic development and various reform measures have a close bearing on the people's livelihood. They include:

- whether the Renminbi will be devaluated under the grim international economic backdrop;
- how urban residents will be affected by the implementation of the welfare housing allocation;
- the shares individuals will have to pay following the reform of the public health care system for urban employees;
- whether state owned enterprises can ride the current difficult stage of reform;
- whether the employment situation will improve;

- whether commodity prices will rise or fall following the government's effort to stimulate domestic demand;
- how the local government restructuring will proceed after the reform of government departments under the State Council;
- whether the reform of institutions will lead to large-scale redundancy;
- the cost of students' tuition fees.

Geography and wealth

As even the largest consumer goods retailers can't afford to set up sales facilities in every major Chinese city, the trick becomes finding those areas that have the ideal mix of accessibility, saturation and ability to buy. The following is a rough guide to a market that consists of a quarter of all mankind spread out over almost 4 million square miles.

Table 21   Geography and wealth

First tier	Comments
Largest 16 cities with urban population over 2 million	5.3% of total population but 24% of GDP. Significantly higher incomes. Almost 50% of national urban retail sales occur in this tier. Workers in Beijing, Shanghai, Guangzhou earn an average of RMB 15,788 or about 1,925 US dollars per year. This is where most foreign firms first set up operations, making these markets the most competitive.
Second tier	**Comments**
65 major cities with populations over 500,000	On average, income levels drop compared to the first tier, yet they have relatively developed consumers and distribution systems. New infrastructure projects will increase access to these markets.
Xiamen, Ningbo, Nanning	These specific second-tier cities have income levels on a par with the first tier and are close to major hubs of transportation and production. Sophisticated consumers in these cities having had exposure to Hong Kong, Taiwan and Shanghai make them ideal stepping-stones into the second tier.
Tianjin, Qingdao, Dalian	These northern cities, due to a decent amount of disposable income and proximity to the Beijing area, are also attractive.
Third tier	**Comments**
Remaining cities of 500,000 and above	Average per capita incomes but less educated consumers. As competition increases in the first- and second-tier cities, opportunities may lie in the third tier.
Rural	**Comments**
The remaining 70% of the population	Low penetration of foreign goods. Minimal income levels (1999 average of RMB 2210 or 270 US dollars). Highly fragmented with limited distribution methods.

Source: DSMR, *China Briefing*, January 2001.

Summary/Recommendations

Although the average income in China is still much lower than in western countries, the steadily rising income levels lead to changes in consumer behaviour. Some producers are finding Chinese consumers already well aware of the most modern items in the world market and unwilling to accept older or obsolete items that some multinationals were hoping they could dump into the Chinese market. The age structure of the Chinese population is an additional advantage. In a country where so many young people live it is much easier to promote the consumption of new, innovative products and services (see for instance Internet or mobile phone users) than in countries with a higher average age. A minority of the population is making the majority of the wealth so the majority of luxury goods will be sold in few key coastal cities of the north.

Further sources

China Statistical Yearbook (1999) www.stats.gov.cn no.
'China's reluctant customers' (1999) in *Beijing Review*, Beijing, pp. 18–20.
Dezahn, Shira & Associates (DSMR) (2001) *China Briefing January 2001: Chinese Consumer Profiles*, Beijing.
Grey China (ed.) (1999) *Building Brand Loyalty in Turbulent Times*, Grey ChinaBase.
Holland, L. (2000) 'A Brave New World', in *Far Eastern Economic Review*, October, pp. 46–8.
Swiss–Chinese Chamber of Commerce (ed.) (1999) *Bulletin 3*, Beijing.

5.8. How can I realise competitive advantages through benchmarking in China?

All over the world the concept of benchmarking has changed the perspective of managers. Benchmarking is the art of revealing how and why some companies perform tasks much better than other companies. Recent evaluation processes in China show substantial differences in the quality, speed and cost performance of an average company versus a leading company – sometimes as much as tenfold.

The most important aspects

- Benchmarking – a valuable management tool in China.
- The systematic approach of benchmarking.
- Different dimensions of benchmarking.
- Joint venture round tables: a form of co-operative benchmarking.

Benchmarking – a valuable management tool in China

The aim of benchmarking is not to discover performance gaps in specific areas but to learn from the best practices of other companies. Japanese companies for instance used benchmarking assiduously in the post-World War II period, copying and improving many American products and practices. Later on western companies like Xerox analysed Japanese products through 'reverse engineering' in order to improve their own product's cost and reliability. These companies went on to ask further questions such as 'Are their marketing, salespeople and practices among the best in the world?'

Today many foreign companies ask themselves similar questions in China. What are the best methods to enter the Chinese market? Which regions should we target and how should we sell there? How many people (with what background) are required to set up an effective sales network? What does a fair remuneration system look like? And so on.

Due to a limited presence of foreign companies in China, benchmarking was rarely used in the past. There was little to learn from other companies. However, today's business environment is different. Many multinationals have moved aggressively into the market. To know one's own products and customers is not enough any more. Companies not only face huge challenges due to market size and restraints, but also due to international and increasingly local competition.

Yet not all companies are making enough effort to adopt the successful methods of competitors in China. Some companies think they know all about their competitors because they compete with them in other countries. However, knowing one's competitors and best practices is critical to success in production and marketing in China. A company must constantly compare procedures, costs and services with close competitors and leaders in other fields.

Benchmarking follows a systematic approach

- Determine which functions to benchmark.
- Identify the key performance variables to measure ('critical success factors').
- Identify leading companies in those areas (must not be direct competitors).
- Identify reasons for performance differences.
- Measure the company's performance.
- Specify programmes and actions to close the gap.
- Implement and monitor the results.

The first question in order to select the objective of a benchmarking study is: 'What factor has the strongest impact on the performance of the company?' Since a benchmarking study can be a long-term and expensive process, a company should make sure that the process would improve the performance significantly. A company should focus primarily on those critical issues that are deeply affecting customer satisfaction and cost structures and where the performance can be significantly improved. When looking for best performing companies, a good starting point is to identify the 'best practice' by asking customers, suppliers and distributors. When collecting this information, companies should verify the reliability and the source. In China, the accuracy of data needs to be ensured by cross-checking with different sources. After manufacturers with the 'best practice' have been identified, the company needs to collect information on their own performance with respect to cost, time and quality.

Benchmarking can take different dimensions

Companies are limiting their possibilities by only looking within their own organisation for successful methods (internal benchmarking). The same is true if a study only focuses on the company's main competitors (competitive benchmarking). This might lead to a short-term edge but not to a long-term competitive advantage. The real strength of benchmarking is that it focuses on best practices regardless of which industry companies are in (global benchmarking).

One of the best forms of global benchmarking is the so-called 'co-operative benchmarking'. It was first used in the Asian Pacific region when MTR (Hong Kong Mass Transit Railway Corporation), American Express, IBM China, Rank Xerox, Federal Express and Hong Kong Telephone joined together to benchmark each other's outstanding capabilities. This worked well because none of the companies competed against each other.

IBM provides the majority of its staff with techniques for process analysis. This enables them to look at internal procedures and characteristics and to suggest how the organisation can be streamlined. Although MTR already teaches problem-solving techniques to its staff, it believes the problem-solving skills taught by IBM helped its employees find new ways to improve. Rank Xerox's internal customer complaints system also impressed MTR. After ensuring that customers who complain are dealt with satisfactorily, Rank Xerox then follows the complaint internally to ensure the problem has been addressed.

Joint venture round tables: a form of co-operative benchmarking

Although benchmarking in China is nearly the same as in the West, there are some differences. Collaborative benchmarking – a group of firms in the same or different industries agreeing to compare certain business processes – is likely to remain more popular in China than competitive benchmarking; not least because data files, which are required for competitive benchmarking, seldom exist in China. The foreign chambers of commerce in China bring companies together to compare performance by organising 'round tables' which meet to discuss the best practices in production, marketing, sales, finance, personnel and management.

An important point is that benchmarking can be done without resorting to industrial espionage. Moreover, discovering trade secrets is not what companies need in order to compete successfully. They need tactical and strategic intelligence, which can be developed from information sources around its competitors. For instance, does Pepsi truly need to know Coke's secret formula? What it actually needs, is to know the method of its rival's new pricing or advertisement strategy, or its more successful distribution strategy in China. These are not trade secrets. These are examples of intelligence Pepsi can develop as it strives towards long-term success in China.

Summary/Recommendations

In China companies should make use of benchmarking before investing, to make sure they understand appropriate strategies and business practices in China. This can prevent a lot of misunderstandings. To get the best out of benchmarking, companies need to take advantage of their people's talent and say: 'We found this best practice. Now tell us, how we can implement it creatively here and even go beyond it.' Creativity is the key getting optimal benefits from benchmarking.

Further sources

Benchmarking in China, (1997) in *Fiducia China Focus, Reports–Analysis–Strategies*, HK.
Bendell, T. and Boulter, J. (1993) *Benchmarking for competitive advantage*, London.
Camp, R.C. (1998) *Benchmarking – the search for industry best practices that lead to superior performance*, Milwaukee.
Kotler, P. (1997) *Marketing-Management: Analysis, Planning, Implementation, and Control*, NJ.

5.9. How can I find a good consultant?

The market for consulting services has boomed in China during the last few years. Today you can find more than 40,000 companies wooing the clients' favour. There is a broad range from 'one-man shows' up to complex office networks of international global players of the consulting scene such as McKinsey, Boston Consulting Group, KPMG, At Kearny, Roland Berger, etc. offering a broad range of different services.

For the clients it may be baffling trying to judge the service quality of the various consultants and finding out which type of consultant is best suited for a current problem. As there are some 'black sheep' and also consultants that are not able to handle intercultural differences/problems, you have to select very carefully before you finally hire a consultant to support you in your China business.

The most important aspects

- Range of services
- Situation in the consulting business
- Selection criteria for a good consultant
- Future trends

Most important China-related services

Besides the common tasks of a consultant that are important in every part of the world, such as strategic management, operative support or economic advice, in China a consultant should also have some special skills and be able to:

- work out China-specific peculiarities;
- procure reliable information and contacts with relevant Chinese decision-makers and authorities;
- support western companies in questions of acquisitions and market access;
- prepare and adapt existing Chinese company structures to western technology transfer;
- select suitable management tools that fit the current needs of the Chinese market and the client's particular situation in order to promote a change of behaviour in an intended way (purchasing, quality, intercultural adaptability, etc.);
- transfer knowledge, know-how and experience and fulfil also a 'train the trainer' function, especially when it comes to the introduction of western management tools;
- take the role of a trouble-shooter and/or mediator; therefore intercultural sensitivity is very important for a consultant;
- support clients in questions of restructuring and consolidation, as these are areas in which advice will be most valuable in the future.

Situation in the consulting business

- In China you can find a lot of semi-professional consultants. Some of them used to offer their services (of variable competence) in the former USSR, in Vietnam or in other underdeveloped countries that were popular for a while in terms of making quick money. You may meet the same consultants today in China looking for an easy deal. However, as the Chinese market becomes more mature and investors get more experience in these markets, they are less inclined to trust this kind of consultants.
- If somebody pretends he is able to provide nearly every kind of consulting service, in general he can do no one thing really very well. You should look for specialists concentrating on core-competences!
- Sometimes you can find a lack of intercultural experience even with the big players of the consulting scene. Western management style and thinking is not always transferable to China without any prior adaptations. So, for instance, the American 'hire and fire mentality' that some 'genius' young egghead consultants from big, sometimes well-known consultant companies promote, is not always the right way to go in China. A good consultant

should be familiar with China-specific peculiarities and show a great deal of intercultural awareness and sensitivity.

- Subsidiaries of international management consultants in China are often business units of their own. Therefore they often can't afford to have one or more experienced expats in China. Also the quality of local consultants is not always satisfactory and often not comparable with international standards (i.e. educational background of auditors, etc.).

- A very particular type of consultants are the Chinese '*guanxi*-makers' you meet occasionally in the aeroplane, at fairs and on other occasions, telling you they have the very best connections to the authorities of your branch of business or to important Chinese politicians and functionaries, etc. If they spontaneously offer you their support to start a business in China or to solve your problems you should be very careful. Not everything may be true and lots of western investors who trusted in these people and promises, at the end of the day, realised quite big losses without any recognisable success. The only ones who made profits in these cases were the consultants.

Selection criteria for a good consultant

'Consultant' is not a protected title such as lawyer or accountant. You don't have to fulfil special admittance prerequisites for this profession nor do you officially need a respective study or an exam that qualifies you for this job. Anybody can start a career as a consultant founding his own company. As a consequence there are lots of so-called consultants that are not really professional. Furthermore the consulting market in China is even less transparent than in western countries. Therefore hiring a consultant you should select very carefully. The following questions and hints may be a useful tool in this process.

- Ask for references from other clients with similar projects or related branches of industry. Don't be satisfied with lists of companies that just mention the name of big enterprises like Coca-Cola, Siemens, General Motors, etc. without further comments. Ask for concrete reference projects that are similar to yours and for reference persons you can talk to.

- Ask for samples of studies a consultant has carried out and/or for consulting reports (these may have erased names/figures or invented 'Mickey Mouse' figures) to judge the quality of reporting and expertise. Furthermore you can ask for professional presentations that give you an idea of the range of services a consultant offers and of his consulting philosophy. It may also be helpful to study the homepage of a consultant company and to read – as far as existing – its publications (such as brochures, articles in magazines, newspapers etc.).

- Try to find out how long the consultant has operated already in China and whether they have China-specific know-how and experience. Ask test questions about Chinese daily life, culture, geography, economic development and so on, to check whether you are really speaking to a China expert. Also discussions about special operative and/or strategic management topics, which are related to the type of problem you have to solve, may be helpful.

- Ask for the management tools (e.g. portfolio analysis, trend extrapolation, managerial grids) the consultant generally uses in his job and let him explain exactly why he thinks these tools are suitable for the special situation in China.

- Make sure that there is a transparent system of billing/accounting. Show significantly which results you are expecting and set a time-frame. Ask for the professional background and the experience of the consultants who are members of your project team. Often big consultant companies tend to reserve their best people for projects of big, important clients and treat small- and mid-sized companies as second best. In these cases, it may be better to have first priority with a smaller consultant.

- Ask for co-operation partners and existing networks. But be careful if somebody tells you about his excellent *guanxi* to high-ranked politicians or authorities that are important for your branch of industry. Those connections – if they exist at all – are not always really good or relevant enough (see also the final point in the previous bullet list).

- Make sure that a consultant not only leaves you with a complex system of strategies, but that he is also able and willing to support you with the realisation of necessary operative measures. A good consultant in China must also be able to teach, being able to train the client's employees especially when it comes to the introduction of western management tools.

- Remember good consulting has its price! Often low performers tend to agree to lower the prices for their services. Think carefully about what you really expect.

- Ask your business partners, other western managers and/or the associations of your branch of industry for recommendations. Maybe one or the other already has good or either negative experience with a consultant. This kind of information may help you with your selection process.

Future trends on the consulting scene

- In the future the services of consultants will become more and more professional and their quality will approach international standards. China today is no longer the 'mystical' black box for investors and consultants. The experience of recent years and extensive research work will help consultants to develop new management tools or to adapt existing consulting instruments which take the peculiarities of the Chinese market into account. A professional consulting scene that is strongly influenced by the classical management know-how as well as by China-specific aspects will become established.

- Nowadays a change of focus in the consulting business is discernible. Whereas in past years market access and company start-up consulting dominated the work of the management advisors in China, today consultants have to concentrate more and more on restructuring and consolidation tasks. After entering the market and establishing business an optimisation of business processes, that had often been neglected during the start up phase, is a must in order to be competitive.
- The Asian Development Bank (ADB) wants to support the Chinese to bring more transparency in the Chinese consulting market and to get rid of direct political influence that still dominates the bidding procedures for consultant jobs in Chinese state owned companies. Together with the Ministry of Science and Technology they asked a consortium of one Chinese and two foreign management-consulting companies to work out guidelines for hiring consultants. In 2000 the China International Economic Consultants Co. Ltd (CIEC), Development Alternatives (USA) and Landell Mills (Great Britain) developed general principles for the awards of public consultant contracts.
- The Chinese government is planning that consultants should contribute more to Chinese tax revenue. The State Tax Administration (SAT) stated in its *Notice on Handling of Taxes Imposed on Foreign Investment Enterprises and Foreign Enterprises Engaged in Consulting Business* some basic rules of taxation that came into effect on 1 June 2000. Make sure that your consultant follows these rules; otherwise you may, as a client, be at a disadvantage because of potential omissions.

Summary/Recommendations

In choosing a consultant for your China activities you should select even more carefully than in western countries. Besides the classical management consulting know-how, in China a consultant must also have a profound knowledge about the specific peculiarities of this country along with a great deal of intercultural awareness and sensitivity. Also an insight into the complex network of connections and the complex decision-making mechanisms in China may be very useful. In hiring a consultant you should carefully check his references, professional experience and China-specific know-how. Otherwise you may be confronted with nasty surprises.

Further sources

Cockman, P. and Evans, B. (1999) *Consulting for real people – a client-centred approach for change agents and leaders*, London.

Harrison, R. (1995) *Consultant's journey – a professional and personal odyssey*, London.

Manager Magazin, DEG, *et al.* (eds) (1999) *Wirtschaftshandbuch China – Praxisnaher Ratgeber für Unternehmen*, Frankfurt.

6

How Do I Plan a Successful Marketing Campaign in China?

Christine Boos

6.1. How can I create an optimised company, brand and product image in China?

China's ad industry totalled 8.5 billion US dollars in 2001 and is quickly becoming the fourth biggest advertising market worldwide after the US, Japan and Germany. With tremendous double-digit growth over the last ten years, the comparatively young industry averaged 40 per cent growth in 2000, according to AC Nielsen figures. And even when recession hit in 2001, when advertisers all over the world were suffering losses, it saw a 12 percent increase in the first six months.

Advertising turnover is bound to grow even more despite the global economic downturn as China entered WTO in December 2001 and successfully bid for the 2008 Olympic games, which will add powerful growth to the industry. TV commercial minutes have more than tripled since 1998, while strong growth is expected from local brands. Of the top 20 brands, measured in terms of ad spending, in 2001, all were local except for Coca-Cola.

At the same time also the demands of the target groups concerning product quality are consistently rising. The label 'made in USA' or 'made in Germany' is not sufficient any more to guarantee high sales figures for western products in China. The demands concerning the technique and the aesthetics of advertising, regional concepts, increasingly costly campaigns and means to anchor a brand have drastically risen.

Important factors that influence the branding
- Good quality and reasonable price as prerequisites of successful branding.
- Lack of brand loyalty and inconsistency in style and taste.
- Lack of reliable information about consumers and markets.
- Building up a brand is always a regional business.
- Starting up with a test market is recommended.

- Components of brand building.
- Creating a suitable brand name.

Good quality and reasonable pricing as prerequisites of successful branding

A prerequisite for creating a strong brand image is that your products are of a very good quality, according to the latest technical progress. Don't think you can launch old, obsolete products/ models in China that are not any longer saleable in western countries. Chinese customers in general are very well informed about new developments and react quite defensively if you try to sell them 'old' products. Also good customer services (after-sales, distribution and spare part service etc.) should be offered.

The distribution channels and your pricing policy must fit in with your target groups. Be aware that local products have improved a lot (e.g. white goods, AV products) and the difference with western goods is often not significant enough to justify big price gaps. Some western companies (like Whirlpool) even started to sell their products in China under the label of a Chinese brand (like Kelong).

Foreign marketers are realising Chinese consumers are price-conscious. They are not willing to pay for western products if they can find a local equivalent of almost the same quality that is much cheaper. A modest premium (not more than 30 per cent), with an imported flavour, is the way to go for western companies, otherwise they are not marketable.

Lack of brand loyalty and inconsistency in style and taste

The difficulty of advertising in China is that as a result of many rapid changes consumers have not developed a solid taste or clearly perceptible style. People are still buying in a relatively indiscriminate and undifferentiated way.

Of course the 'class-conscious', modern Chinese with a salary above the average wants to buy Japanese entertainment electronics, French cognac, American cigarettes and German household goods. However, within these classes of goods he does not have any significant criteria to differentiate. Does he buy a TV set from Sony, Toshiba or Panasonic? Does he prefer Remy Martin, Martell or Hennessy? Does he prefer to smoke Marlboro Country or does he identify himself with the 'Camel-man'? Should his coffee machine come from Krups, Melitta, Roventa, Siemens or Phillips? Only by advertising does the consumer learn to differentiate, because he cannot rely on his own experiences or the experiences of other generations. Brand-consciousness does not have a tradition in China; brand loyalty still is very rare. The motto is to try every innovation that comes to the market. As there are no long-term relationships with a producer or brand, the abrupt change to a competing product seems very easy.

Lack of reliable information on Chinese consumers and markets

Another obstacle for branding is that there are no reliable findings about the 'average Chinese consumer'. Terms and devices that are traditionally used by advertising in western countries to address the customer, like definition of the target groups, investigation of the consumer's needs, market research or the regional launching of a product in a test market are still at a very early stage. There is no 'transparent consumer' as there is in western countries, where marketing specialists have already found out (nearly) all about consumers' needs by oral and written investigations, empirical tests, statistical definitions and computer-based evaluations. In China there is just a vague idea about target groups.

Nevertheless you should try to track changes in Chinese consumers' behaviour and attitude over time and to gather actual information about Chinese consumers and brands. Although the development of professional market research is still at its beginning, several international media consultants have set up offices in China (AC Nielsen, CVSC, Zenith-Media, CMM- Intelligence etc.).

Building up a brand is always a regional business

Generally in China it does not make too much sense to run nationwide advertising and marketing campaigns. The country is too big and the markets are too heterogeneous. The language, culture and mentality of the people in the provinces are too different. An advertising message that hits the taste and needs of the people in the northern Chinese provinces Liaoning or Heilongjiang, perhaps totally misses the mark in the southern provinces of Fujian and Jiangxi. Advertising is always a regional business that has to be adapted to the needs of the respective region. The horizon of experience, the confrontation with western consumer goods, the purchasing power and the general living standard of a relatively wealthy consumer class in greater Shanghai is totally different from the one of structurally weak provinces in the southeast of China. However, remember in your branding, that despite of the regional differences in buyers behaviour, there are national similarities when it comes to values and beliefs.

Starting up with a test market is recommended

To enter a new market in China it is a good idea to be cautious and start with a test market to check the acceptability of your product. Then, step by step, you can proceed into other markets. If you have avant-garde, trendy goods you can choose as a test market one of the big cities in the southern part of China like Shanghai or Guangzhou, as the southern regions are more affluent and they are generally more open to innovations, western thinking and creative ideas.

For more technically related investment products, however, Beijing would be the best first choice as a test market, because in Beijing are all the decision-makers of the government, the industrial associations and the major design institutes. As most Chinese companies are still state owned, the decision-makers are asked to buy preferentially products from providers that have a flawless reputation and contribute something valuable to the development of the country. If you sell investment goods, this fact should have a major influence on your brand-building strategy.

Components of brand-building

The principles of building up a brand are the same as in western countries. You have to create brand relations with the consumers in terms of their mentality and way of living. Therefore some sort of cultural contact is necessary (see also chapters 6.3/6.5). You can use the same components of the brand-building process like advertising, public relations, sponsoring, event marketing etc. A special focus, however, should be laid on relation marketing.

Your PR activities should emphasise values which are important for the Chinese public and personal life (e.g. support for ecological projects, activities around the Chinese spring festival, charity work as in help for the flood victims etc.). In advertising it is best to try to combine 'western lifestyle' (e.g. technical progress, high living standard, fashionable trends) with traditional Chinese values (e.g. old 'wise' Chinese man uses his mobile phone standing in front of the Great Wall to call western friends or overseas family members). Remember in your advertising that in major cities like Beijing, Shanghai or Guangzhou people have more exposure to cosmopolitan ideas and are more open to western humour and values, whereas in rural areas people are more information-oriented and price-driven than brand-driven.

How to find a suitable brand name in China?

Entering the Chinese market you first have to think about what name you want to sell your products under. Should it be a suitable Chinese name or should you keep your global western brand name? In practice a combination of both is best. That means you should choose a Chinese name, that sounds similar to the original western name, but which has also a metaphorical Chinese meaning that fits your product and promotes the image you want to create in China with your product or your company. Once you find a suitable Chinese brand name it is recommended to register the respective Chinese combination of characters and parallel the Latin characters as a trademark (according to the first to file principle).

Below are examples of the successful transfer of western brand names into Chinese ones.

Table 22 Chinese translation of western brands

Brand	Chinese translation/sound
BMW	treasure horse (Bao Ma)
Mercedes Benz	make headway, gallop (Ben-che)
Porsche	fast and time gaining (Bao Shi Jie)
Shanghai-VW	Shanghai–mass-car (Shanghai Dazhong Qiche)
Coca-Cola	you drink, you laugh (Ke-Kou Ke-Le)
Siemens	gate to the West (Xi-men-zi)
Kodak	gaining a subsidiary (Keda)
Quaker Oats	old man (Lao Ren)
Swatch watches	se-wa-shi (no meaning, but similar sound)
Apple Macintosh	apple computer company (Pinguo Diannao Gongsi)

According to the results of an investigation the Beijing Business Management Service (Beijing BMS) carried out in 2000 the most important Chinese brands are:

1. Haier (white goods)
2. Legend (computers)
3. Changhong (electrical appliances)
4. Shougang (Beijing's biggest company)
5. Founder (IT)
6. Stone (IT)
7. Shanghai Volkswagen
8. Konka (electrical appliances)
9. TCL King (electrical appliances)
10. No. 1 Automobile

The top-ten foreign brands are:

1. Microsoft
2. Panasonic
3. Coca-Cola
4. Motorola
5. General Motors
6. IBM
7. Toyota
8. Mercedes Benz
9. McDonald's
10. Sony

Summary

Reflect on brand-building activities in China:

- only if your product is competitive (quality- and price-wise) with other products in the Chinese market – it makes sense to build up a brand;
- there are regional differences in buyer behaviour but also national similarities in values and beliefs;
- opportunities emerge rapidly, but markets also quickly move towards maturity, therefore anticipation and taking leadership positions are the keys to success;
- to maintain growth you have to segment and differentiate and to sell the product/service relationship

Further sources

China Media Yearbook and Directory (2002) (ed. CMMIntelligence, www.cmmintelligence. com).

Grey China (ed.) (1998) *Building Brand Loyality in Turbulent Times*, Grey ChinaBase.

Rommel, C (1999) 'Die geheimen Verführer – Die Werbewirtschaft boomt' in *China Contact*, no. 7, pp. 6–9.

Taube, M. (1997) 'Schutz von Warenzeichen in der VR China', in *Wirtschaftswelt China*, no. 8.

General information on branding

ESOMAR (ed.) (1996) *The Big Brand Challenge*, Amsterdam.

Jones, J.P. (1986) 'What is a name?' in *Advertising and the Concepts of Brands*, Hampshire.

Murphy, J.M. (ed.) (1987) *Branding: a key marketing tool*, Basingstoke.

6.2. What legal aspects have to be considered in marketing your products in China?

For a long time in China product and company advertisements had been viewed as capitalistic decadency. In parallel with the progressive opening policy, however, marketing and advertising businesses became more and more. The new advertising law put into operation in February 1995 regulates the legal aspects.

The major reasons for introducing this law were the need to regulate the advertising industry and for consumer protection. Therefore the advertising law also contains aspects that support the trade supervisory authorities and similar institutions in order to prevent deception, exploitation of the clients such as exaggerated prices, poor quality, intentional wrong descriptions of products/services, usury, etc.

The new Chinese advertising law prohibits, amongst other things:

- presentation of national symbols (flag, anthem) and political allusions;
- sexual content and nudity as well as TV commercials for tobacco goods;
- comparative advertisement and advertising with superlatives etc.;
- content which may be injurious to public safety, present a danger to person or property or harm the public interest;
- content which is superstitious, frightening, violent or repulsive;
- content which discriminates on the basis of ethnic groups, race, religion or sex;
- content which is harmful to the protection of the environment and natural resources.

The advertising law states that anybody, who wants to market his products in China, must hold a business licence or a similar permit for the advertised product. This way the advertisements of faked or pirated products is prevented.

Furthermore documents have to be shown which will prove the asserted quality characteristics and advertising messages. This should at least ensure that no totally untrue messages influence the purchase pattern.

The advertising law contains extensive lists of prohibitions which forbid the use of national symbols like the Chinese flag or the Chinese national anthem. Also allusions to the Chinese government and politics or remarks that could threaten the public security and order are prohibited. In this context the terms 'public security and order' have to be broadly interpreted. Slogans or subversive expressions of opinion that could endanger the youth or threaten the social stability and other 'offensive' advertising messages (e.g. pictures that disparage women) are banned. This regulation applies to any form of presentation of nudity or erotic images. The Ministry of Education, the China National Advertising Association (a sub-division of the State Administration for Industry and Commerce [SAIC]) and the local counterparts of the National Advertising Association at the country level and above watch Argus-eyed, that the moral boundaries will not be infringed. For example recently a TV commercial for shampoo was criticised because of showing too much 'shoulder'.

The advertisement for some products, for example for medicines, cosmetics or agrochemicals such as fertilisers, are even subject to pre-censorship by public control authorities. Comparative advertisement is only allowed as long as it does not disparage competitors. See also the *Law of the PRC Against Unfair Competition* that came into effect in December 1993. It should be noted that there are a number of local unfair competition laws, as well as provisions in other national laws that may impose somewhat different restrictions and requirements depending on the circumstances of each particular case.

Superlatives like the 'best', or the 'highest' are forbidden as well as wrong listings of ingredients. For example, before Budweiser could publicly announce, that its brand is 'America's favourite beer', they had to prove this statement by statistical figures. Recently government officials have checked a couple of thousand TV commercials and advertising spots. The result was that more than 10 per cent were criticised because of inadmissible superlatives, comparisons, wrong declaration of ingredients or other irregularities. See also the *Notice on Halting the Publication of Advertisements that contain Arbitrary Comparative Appraisals, Arbitrary Ratings etc.*, issued by SAIC in late 1999.

Summary/Recommendations

According to the Chinese advertising law, the 'China National Advertising Association' must censor every piece of advertising. As this association has a tremendous influence on the different media you should seek its advice, if you are in doubt, whether an ad will adhere to Chinese advertising law and whether it meets the tastes of your Chinese target groups. The Chinese Advertising Association, however, does not give official permission in writing, that your ad is correct under all parts of Chinese law and regulations. They just call your attention to aspects they think they are violating the law, public regulations or ethical, cultural or social values.

The lack of specific advertising standards means that what is permitted by approval authorities in Shanghai may be rejected by those in Fuzhou. There is no nationally agreed standard as to how to interpret advertising legislation or how to judge the content of an advertisement. This often makes it difficult to initiate a co-ordinated, nationwide advertising campaign. In any case of doubt, therefore, we recommend seeking professional advice with law firms such as Baker McKenzie, Clifford Chance Pünder, Breiten, Burkhard, Mittel or Harmann, Hemmelrath & Partner etc. and/or with experienced ad agencies (see also chapter 6.9).

Further sources

Jimmerson Peng, J. (2001) 'Advertising and Marketing', in Shaw, A. (ed.) *Operation China: An Investor's Manual*, Baker & McKenzie, HK, pp. 1–30.

Reisach, U., Tauber, T. and Xueli, Y. (1997) *China - Wirtschaftspartner zwischen Wunsch und Wirklichkeit*, Vienna, Ueberreuther.

See also http//:www.moftec.gov.cn/moftec/official/html/laws_and_regulations/trade25.html

- The *Advertisement Censorship Standards*, 1993.
- The *Advertisement Law of the People's Republic of China*, which came into effect in 1995.
- The *Announcement on Regulating the E-mailing of Commercial Information*, which was issued by the Beijing Municipal AIC (BAIC) on 15 May, 2000.
- The *Law of the PRC Against Unfair Competition* that came into effect in December 1993.
- The *Measures for the Administration of Advertising Display Screens*, issued by SAIC in 1996.
- The *Notice on Halting the Publication of Advertisements that contain Arbitrary Comparative Appraisals, Arbitrary Ratings etc.*, which was issued by SAIC in late 1999.
- The *Provisional Measures for the Administration of Advertisements in Shops, Halls, etc.*, issued by SAIC in 1998.
- The *Provisional Regulations of the Administration of Printed Advertisements*, which came into effect in March 2001.

6.3. What kind of advertising messages appeal to Chinese consumers?

The development of the Chinese advertising market has followed a parallel course to the development of the markets for consumer goods. Latest figures, however, show an annual average growth rate of about 9 per cent; in the last four years the retail sales in overcrowded regions like Shanghai, Canton or Beijing reached growth rates of more than 25 per cent. The advertising market exceeds even these figures.

'Which media is the most suitable for which target group?' is one of the most urgent questions western marketers are confronted with. Because of the enormous size of the Chinese market and the regional differences you have to segment very deeply. You should try to learn as much as possible about your target group and its habits (see also chapter 5.2). According to this you can choose the media vehicles by which you can reach it.

The most important features

- Don't overestimate your market.
- Need of intensive market, media and purchasing power research.
- Belief in advertising messages and creating high aspirations.
- Watch your language – avoid misinterpretations!

Intensive market, media and purchasing power research

Be aware that not everyone of China's 1.3 billion population is a potential client for your products. As an optimistic guess you can calculate around 100 million consumers as a target group for western consumer goods. The rest of the Chinese population does not have enough purchasing power to afford your goods. Don't forget needs and wants of the Chinese will only be of interest to you, if they come along with a respective buying power that transforms them into demand.

Therefore it is advisable to do extensive purchasing power research together with the classical market investigations (socio-demographic analyses, media research and contact analyses) in order to get a reliable basis for your marketing activities. Be careful about overestimating the market and think of the heterogeneity of the Chinese consumer population! An Ogilvy PR survey, for instance, found that consumers in Guangzhou are price-sensitive and somewhat sceptical of the value of brands; Beijing residents prefer local brands and react strongly to nationalistic images, and buyers in Shanghai are less concerned with price and more enthusiastic about overseas brands. Thus marketing a product in different parts of China may require very different promotional approaches.

Belief in advertising messages and high aspirations

An advantage for marketers in China is that in general the Chinese consumer – unlike hypercritical, often sarcastic western consumers – still believe in advertising messages and respond to them. They think that if you can afford to advertise in the big, important media you must be a big brand.

If you want to advertise with western celebrities as opinion leaders you should make sure, that the person is also really well known in China and has a positive image (like Michael Jordan, Michael Schumacher or Steffi Graf.). Arnold Schwarzenegger, for instance, has become the advertising face of a big Chinese electronics producer. When choosing models/actors to feature, go for Asian-looking people rather than 'long-nosed' actors; the Chinese want be able to identify with them.

Chinese are in general quite aspiring consumers; that means, if you can project an image which is higher than the consumers' living standard really is, they want to be part of it (in the sense of looking up rather than looking down). You have to aim high, but your products must be affordable, otherwise you cause frustration instead of goodwill by your advertising messages.

Watch your language

Lots of western multinationals have had difficulties crossing the language barrier, with results ranging from mild embarrassment to outright failure. Seemingly innocuous brand names and advertising phrases can take on unintended meanings that are ridiculous or even offensive when translated into Chinese.

Careless translations can make a marketer look downright foolish to Chinese consumers. The classic language blunders involve standardised brand names that do not translate well. When Coca-Cola first marketed Coke in China in the 1920s it developed a group of Chinese characters that, when pronounced, sounded like the product name. Unfortunately, the characters actually translated to mean 'bite the wax tadpole'. Now the characters on Chinese Coke bottles translate as 'happiness in the mouth'.

A similar thing happened to a well-known German bank that opened a representative office in China. They also chose a combination of Chinese characters that sounded in spoken Chinese similar to their German brand name. The actual translation, however, was 'the bank that works particularly slowly'.

Such classic boo-boos are soon discovered and corrected, and they may result in little more than embarrassment and extra costs for the marketer. But countless other more subtle blunders may go undetected and damage the product performance in less obvious ways. As a multinational company you must carefully screen your brand names and advertising messages to guard against those that might damage sales, create an embarrassing image, or offend Chinese consumers.

Summary/Recommendations

To avoid fatal overcapacities and misjudgements you should try to get a realistic idea about the number of your potential clients. It will certainly not be 1.3 billion people but far less. In the past there have been lots of disastrous developments because of this mega-market illusion. The lack of purchasing power, however, brought them all back to cruel reality.

Similarly to western ad-markets of the late 1950s and early 60s you can often affect your target groups with the classic devices of 'me-too', status, opinion leaders and celebrity advertisements as well as by raising high aspirations that provide the consumer with reachable lifestyle targets.

You should carefully monitor your advertising messages to avoid misinterpretations, misunderstandings and classic boo-boos, that might be embarrassing or even counter-productive for your company and sales figures.

Further sources

Helin, D.W. (1992) 'When slogans go wrong', in *American Demographics*, February.

Jimmerson Peng, J. (2001) 'Advertising and Marketing', in Shaw, A. (ed.) *Operation China: An Investor's Manual*, Baker & McKenzie, HK, pp. 1–30.

Ricks, D.A. (1983) 'Products that crashed into the language barrier', in *Business and Society Review*, Spring, pp. 46–50.

6.4. Which Chinese institutions can help me to market my investment goods?

In western countries, a producer of investment goods can quite easily identify his target groups. Mostly they belong to other industries that need your goods to contribute to the value chain. The managers who are responsible for purchasing decide in general more according to objective criteria than the buyers of consumer goods. In China these decision-makers, however, are often still functionaries of the 'old Chinese type' so it is important to know their specific preferences and who actually makes the decisions. To address your target groups in an effective way, there is a great range of marketing instruments you will already be aware of from western countries. The following concentrates on China-specific ways to promote investment goods.

Table 23   Survey amongst dealers in China on the most effective marketing instruments

Marketing instrument	Rank
Personal sales	1
Invitations to the clients to visit the production facilities	2
Participation in exhibitions and trade fairs	3
TV advertisements	4
Advertisement in print media (newspapers, magazines)	5
Radio advertisements	6
Sending out catalogues and brochures	7
Billboard advertising	8

Source: Ho, S.-C., Sin, Y.-M. (1986) 'Advertising in China: Looking Back at Looking Forward', in *International Journal of Advertising*, vol. 5, no. 4, p. 311.

Try to get support from the associations of your branch of industry

As experience shows, Chinese associations of industry and design institutes can give you very valuable support promoting your products.

Associations as a source of information

Especially if you are a newcomer in the Chinese market, you should contact the specific associations that represent your branch of industry. It is worth the effort to create a close relationship with them as in general they know the market very well, have a widespread *guanxi*-network and an elaborate database with all the important facts and figures of their branch of industry. They can provide you with data about potential clients (e.g. liquidity, decision-makers, current needs, planned projects, existing purchasing channels etc.).

Placing your advertisements in the special publications of the associations

Most associations also publish a kind of 'yellow pages' with detailed information about all the companies of the particular field and/or special interest magazines that are read by your target groups. These publications are one of the best channels for your advertising messages. It is even better if you can convince the editor to write a public relations article, where your products and/ or your company are mentioned in a positive way. Therefore you should regularly provide the associations with current news of your China business (e.g. new products/techniques, successful projects, latest results of your R&D activities, special activities like seminars, technical training, new sales policies, anniversaries or social activities of your company etc.).

Associations' support with trade fairs and special seminars

The associations also can support you in distributing your company brochures and product catalogues as well as give you valuable advice – which trade fairs are relevant for you and how to present your company at these fairs (see also chapter 6.8). You can also ask them for advice on how to organise special in-house seminars for your (potential) clients. As experience shows, inviting clients and potential clients to special seminars at attractive locations is one of the best ways to do market communication in China. This way they not only have the opportunity to learn more about your company, your products, your service network and special topics like technical issues or western management tools, but at the same time they have a reason to make an agreeable business trip. Chinese managers generally don't travel very much; therefore they really appreciate an opportunity to come to big cities like Beijing, Shanghai or Guangzhou or to attractive tourist spots like Guilin, Kunming Beidahe, Hainan or Tsingdao to take part in a seminar. By hosting them generously, you show them your esteem and give them face – a good base for a long-lasting relationship. In general the participants pay for their travel and hotel expenses themselves. The host takes all the other costs like catering, sightseeing, little gifts and seminar facilities.

To address the right target group you could also ask the associations to choose and invite suitable candidates, sometimes the associations also like to show up as co-hosts.

Associations of related industries and design institutes

Associations of industries to which your potential customers and the customers of your customers belong may provide you with valuable hints, data and contacts. Therefore you should analyse precisely which groups of clients are directly or indirectly affected by your products. In other words, you should follow the specific value chains. (For example, a producer of condensing units for big supermarket cooling systems should not only concentrate his activities of market communication on companies that produce these cooling systems, but also on companies that buy this kind of system like big supermarket chains. If you have convinced the last group that your product is the best they can get, they put pressure on their providers to buy your products as a part of the cooling system.)

Besides the associations you should also try to build up *guanxi* with the respective design institutes that are responsible for your branch of industry. These are special institutions (mostly institutionalised by the government or universities) that set standards for products and services and give recommendations as to which products are best, taking quality and price into account.

Summary/Recommendations

As a producer of investment goods you are selling in niche markets. That means your marketing efforts have to be very targeted, addressing government officials and leading industrialists. In this context Chinese associations of industries and design institutes may be of great help. Therefore you should try to build up a good relationship with them. Generally the best means of communication to market investment goods are direct marketing, relationship marketing and special programme marketing.

A good way of gaining the goodwill of decision-makers amongst the official authorities and functionaries is sponsoring activities that support issues about which the Chinese are very concerned (e.g. tree-planting activities to support environmental protection or practical help for victims of natural disasters, such as flood victims). This way you show the Chinese that you don't only want to do business in China, but you also really care about the Chinese country and its people and you are willing to take over social responsibility.

Further source

Ho, S.-C. and Sin, Y.-M. (1986) 'Advertising in China: Looking Back at Looking Forward', in *International Journal of Advertising*, vol. 5, no. 4, pp. 307–16.

6.5. How do I plan and produce advertising material in China?

The question of what form your advertisement in China will take should be clearly defined right at the beginning of your China engagement. The more thorough your preparation is, the more mistakes and expensive redesigns can be avoided. In-house or associated text composers, layout designers, printers etc. should be involved at a very early phase. This way you can become aware of your China-specific creative potential and your technical compatibility. Check your own resources and ask your Chinese partners and employees for advice and support.

The most relevant questions about creating advertising media for the Chinese market

- Does your global corporate identity fit in with all aspects of the peculiarities of the Chinese market or are careful changes necessary?
- Could you do without your global worldwide brand and is it possible to install an independent regional identity (see also chapter 6.1)?
- Which existing means of marketing and presentation can be adopted for the Chinese market? Which parts have to be complemented or supplemented by Chinese materials? Do presentations only need to be translated into Chinese or are there special accentuations or logical sequences that make further adaptation necessary?
- What character does the existing advertising text have? Can you transfer the usual metaphors into Chinese without causing problems?

- Where can you get professional translations for technical as well as for advertising texts and how can you judge and ensure the quality of the delivered texts?
- Where and how can technical documentation and print media be produced and which partners can provide multimedia ads?
- Is your ad agency able to create a concept of flexible advertising ideas that considers right from the beginning a modification for the Chinese market (see also chapter 6.9)?

Globalisation versus localisation of advertising media

Multinational advertising usually develops in one of two ways. In some cases, a campaign is initially developed with the intention of distributing it globally. Pioneers of this approach were companies like Coca-Cola, Marlboro, Rolex, Nissan and Gillette. This global advertising works if the ad is published in cultures – especially in the industrialised countries of Europe, in Australia and in the United States – which share so many similarities that the same advertising campaign will work well for all of them. Some of these campaigns are very successful in China, too.

Standardisation also tends to be easier in trade advertising, where ads are more likely to convey specific information that is needed by industrial buyers rather than communicating a status image, sex appeal and so on. Furthermore, standardised advertising is successful for products that are strongly identified with a country which people want to identify with.

A few large companies have had success with standardised advertising, but most have found that the often subtle differences between western and Chinese consumers demand that advertising be tailored to the Chinese culture for maximum effectiveness. There are too many different customs and often Chinese customers do not necessarily even use the same product in the same way (e.g. in some of China's rural areas farmers also use their washing machines to wash their vegetables).

However, it is not a question of uncompromising, global advertising, which is totally unified, versus a total assimilation of local principles, but of the right mixture of both elements. In China there is the principle of 'as well as...' instead of the western 'either...or ...'. In other words, you have to bring global ideas into a local context!

Dominant values (like family, technology and youth) have to be taken into account by the advertising. Including elements of Chinese culture like proverbs, poems, traditional songs, texts of classical books, religious symbols, hints to historically relevant persons and happenings as well as to well-known movies may attract special attention. You should not underestimate the national pride of the Chinese, the intensive perception and the potency of the

Chinese identity and traditions. This demands an comprehensive exposure to the Chinese way of thinking, to folkloristic customs and rites and to language and mentality, with which western marketing strategists often are not familiar.

Differences in attitude towards advertising messages

The use of language elements is quite different. Western consumers judge advertisements pretty coolly and critically. They have recognised that advertising does not automatically mean information, but is more a massive subjective influencing. Therefore western advertising has become more and more subtle, discenning and differentiated, in order to attract the buyer. Humour, irony, funny puns and appeals to the subconscious are dominant.

In China the contrary is true: the Chinese tend to take advertising messages literally and they usually believe what they see and hear. Therefore clear and direct statements are requested that don't leave the consumer with a lot of open questions concerning the advantages of your product and why he should buy exactly your product and not a competitive one. As a result advertising for the Chinese market often seems to be superficial, clumsy and less professional.

But recently new trends have emerged. As consumers in the economically well-developed East Coast become more and more critical and discerning, they cannot be bluffed any more by stimuli in the foreground. This hyper-stimulated class of Chinese consumers need to be entertained by intelligent 'advertainment' and by satisfying their desire for technical kicks.

Summary/Recommendations

Creating advertising materials for the Chinese market, you have to be conscious of local attitudes and economics. But in fact up to 80 per cent of the emotional element is the same around the world. In general you can say that messages that focus on universal values, such as love of family, tend to travel fairly well, whereas those that focus on specific consumer lifestyles do not.

Further sources

Armstrong, C. and Kotler P. (1997) *Marketing – An Introduction*, NJ.
Boesken, G. (1999) 'Werbemittel für China – Konzeption, Planung und Praxis der Produktion', in *China-Contact mit Wirtschaftswelt China*, 7, pp. 10–11.

6.6. What are the essentials of effective media planning in China?

Planning an advertising strategy to reach China's burgeoning consumer market can be a baffling task. There are 2,049 different newspapers, over 8,000 magazines titles, more than 1,500 radio channels and 2,097 different TV channels. Most of them accept advertising. Furthermore nearly half a million billboards and thousands of neon signs and window displays are also available to carry your message at a reasonable cost. With so many options, the selection of the right media format is essential to the success of any company's advertising campaign. Generally western advertisers use more than one category of media in order to realise an optimal media mix.

The most important media vehicles in China

- TV – advertising vehicle number one in China with 40 per cent ad spend share.
- Radio ads reach even the regions in the deepest hinterland.
- Newspapers and magazines support very target-group-specific messages.
- Outdoor-advertising – a cheap way of regional advertising, becoming increasingly popular.
- Direct mail – traditional and via Internet – an optimal way for individual ad messages.

TV – advertising vehicle number one in China

The fact that via TV you can communicate in an audio-visual way is surely an invaluable advantage in a country like China, where the rate of illiterates still totals around 20 per cent. These days the television is the biggest and most important advertising vehicle in China. Around 89 per cent of the population have at least one TV set in their household; thus, by TV advertising you can reach an enormous part of the 1.3 billion people. No wonder that TV ads will have so much time and money invested in them, combined with high expectations. The number of consumers that watch TV is from 62 to over 80 per cent daily.

Producers of consumer goods and services in particular should try to take advantage of this enormous potential and the fantastic viewing figures that would cause tears of joy with western TV producers and advertisers.

With over 1,000 TV stations and 2,000 channels, China has in recent years started reforms of the broadcasting sector. Terrestrial and cable TV stations are being merged while radio is also being merged into provincial radio, film and TV groups. Still, there are many different TV channels to choose from. CCTV, the national TV station, reaches the whole country with its 11 channels, while it commands a total of 40 percent of TV spend. Other provincial satellite channels with footprints reaching the far boundaries of the country are, however, closing in on CCTV's monopoly. Other than that, city TV stations and local stations add to the complex picture. However, despite the abundance of channels and advertising time, lack of quality content, professionalism and reliability make advertisers flock to the major media owners; as a result advertising times are overbooked on the main channels. Over 70 per cent of TV ads are 15 seconds or less in length.

Table 24   Broadcasting areas, attendance figures and prices for 30 seconds of TV advertising

Channel	Broadcasting area	Estimated audience figures	Price for 30 seconds of advertising in RMB
China Central TV	National	600 million	100,000–160,000
Beijing TV	Beijing, parts of the Hebei province	20 million	35,000–40,000
Shanghai TV	Shanghai, Zhejiang and Jiangsu provinces and parts of Fujian and Anhui provinces	150 million	42,000–50,000
Guangdong TV	Guangdong province parts of Hainan, Hunan and Guangxi provinces	80 million	around 11,000
Hubei TV	Hubei province and surroundings	100 million	around 8,000
Liaoning TV	Liaoning province parts from Jilin, Hebei and Inner Mongolia	50 million	around 5,500
Sichuan TV	Sichuan province and via satellite to the whole of China	200 million	around 8,000

Source: MediaCom 1999 (these prices are subject to frequent change).

Advertising rates vary greatly. A prime time CCTV commercial can cost 20,000 US dollars and is only sold on the CCTV advertising auction. Beijing TV, one of the biggest regional broadcasters can also command 5,000 US dollars for a 30 second spot, while smaller channels will only achieve 1,000–2,000 US dollars.

One way to maximise the impact of a commercial is to place it at the beginning or the end of an advertising break in order to avoid channel-surf losses. However, attaining such a prized spot can be exceedingly difficult, particularly during peak viewing times. Even when advertisers are promised a slot at such an ideal point, things may not be as they seem. Often, advertisers, who have better *guanxi* with the television station, or who offer to pay more, manage to bump the original advertiser down the priority list.

One of the few ways in which an advertiser can ensure exposure at the right time is through sponsoring a programme rather than simply placing an advertisement. By sponsoring a suitable programme the advertiser can ensure that it puts across an appropriate message and that its commercials are broadcast at the beginning and the end of the show.

Choosing the right channel can be a dilemma for advertisers. Until the late 1990s, accurate ratings for TV programmes were not available. Since then, the multi-billion US dollar ad market has become much more sophisticated, demanding better market accountability. The market research agency Sofres in co-operation with the China Central Viewers Service and Consulting Centre (CVSC) is carrying out TV panel research around the country, where the panel participants fill in weekly diaries describing their television viewing. Also the internationally recognised research company AC Nielsen/SRG uses a system of 'people meters' in major cities, which electronically monitors the viewing patterns of the households in which they are installed. They give advertisers a much clearer idea of which programmes reached which audience and even of how many viewers saw a particular advertisement.

Companies only launching their products in a few major cities such as Shanghai, Beijing or Shenzhen are likely to get more relevant media exposure through advertising on local stations than through national stations. In addition, local advertising affords companies the opportunity to focus their advertising budget on those cities and regions they wish to target rather than wastefully advertising to people who will not have access to the product for a considerable time to come.

Radio spots reach even the regions in the deepest hinterland

Especially in the rural areas of China the radio plays an important role as an advertising vehicle. The media reaches of broadcasting stations often still surpass the television ones. You can't receive TV in every region of China yet, whereas the radio network was built up extensively in the past. Nowadays there are about 1,200 national, regional and local broadcasting stations with over 1500 different channels. The most popular channel is the Beijing located Central Broadcasting System (CPBS), which broadcasts nationally on two different channels and reaches around 750 million listeners.

Table 25   Broadcasting areas, attendance figures and prices for 30 seconds of radio advertising

Channel	Broadcasting area	Estimated number of listeners	Price for 30 seconds of advertising in RMB
CPBS 1+2	National	750 million	4,000
Beijing Radio	Beijing and surrounding	50 million	2,000
Shanghai Radio	Shanghai and surrounding	40 million	2,000
Guangzhou Radio (Cantonese language)	Guangzhou and surrounding	70 million	1,500

Source: MediaCom 1999, Siemens, Corporate Communications in China (these prices are subject to frequent change).

Newspapers and magazines support target-group-specific ad messages

When it comes to Chinese print media you have to investigate carefully the single newspapers and magazines in respect of their publication date and frequency, their circulation figures, the number of actually sold copies, the readership and their regional distribution. Such information, however, often is difficult to find. This is especially true for the circulation figures, as they influence the prices for advertisements. Not all newspapers and magazines are authorised to accept advertising.

The leading newspapers are:

1. *Renmin Ribao* (people's newspaper) is the official newspaper of the Chinese Communist Party and is read mainly by members of the party and leading decision-makers of industries and trade. By advertising in this paper you can reach important decision-makers on a national basis.
2. *China Daily* is the first and so far only newspaper in English language that is nationally published and mainly read by Chinese people who want to improve their English, or by foreigners. Primarily big hotels, airlines and property firms advertise in it.
3. *Gongren Ribao* (worker's newspaper) is published nationally and is mainly read by managers, businessmen and workers. It is suitable for ads for consumer goods as well as for investment goods.
4. *Beijing Bao, Guangzhou Bao* and *Jiefang Ribao* (which is published in Shanghai) are official party organs of the regional representations of the Communist Party. They are suitable advertising vehicles for capital goods, as party cadres or related people mainly read them.

Table 26   Prices for a half-page ad in some selected Chinese newspapers

Title of the newspaper	Distribution	Circulation figures	Price per half-page ads (for foreigners)
Renmin Ribao	National	3,000,000	US$ 34,560
China Daily	National	300,000	US$ 7,000
Beijing Ribao	Beijing and its surroundings	700,000	RMB 184,000
Beijing Wanbao	Beijing and its surroundings	1,000,000	RMB 127,000
Wenhui Bao	Shanghai and its surroundings	1,000,000	RMB 72,000
Xinmin Wanbao	Shanghai and its surroundings	1,730,000	RMB 72,000
Guangzhou Ribao	Guangzhou and its surroundings	800,000	RMB 76,000
Yangcheng Wanbao	Guangzhou and its surroundings	1,200,000	RMB 114,048

Note: These prices are subject to frequent change.

Placing ads in inserts or supplements, which are added to a lot of newspapers fairly regularly and cover special topics can be useful. Furthermore, special interest newspapers like *Wenhui Bao* (literature newspaper), *Zhongguo Tiyu Bao* (China's sports newspaper) or *Zhongguo Qing Nian Bao* (newspaper of Chinese youth) enable a relatively cheap, target-group-specific advertisement.

Last but not least there should be mentioned the more than 80 different TV and radio newspapers and magazines. These publications will generally be flicked through a couple of times during its one-week lifecycle. Their price is relatively low and therefore they have high circulation figures. TV programme guides like *Zhongguo Dianshi Bao* (TV Guide China) or *Meizhou Guangbo Dianshi* (Weekly Radio and TV guide) for example have an edition of more than 2.5 million copies each.

Most of the 8,000 plus Chinese magazines are special interest magazines with a recognisable target group. The spectrum reaches from fashion, sports, photography, business and youth to wildlife magazines. For multinational producers of investment goods the magazines of the different industry associations are recommendable. Furthermore there is a special magazine called *Products and Technology Abroad* published by the CCPIT, which informs about new technologies and products of foreign companies. It covers a wide technical spectrum and will be read by a large number of Chinese decision-makers.

Be aware that the question of quality of the printed publications is one of the major problems advertisers are facing in China. In many colour newspapers and magazines, colour reproduction is very unreliable. If colour is a key component of your brand, this can weaken your brand's identity. Even in black- and-white printed publications print quality is often very poor, which can serve to detract from the advertiser's image.

Outdoor advertising – a cheap way of regional advertising

Advertising on the roofs or façades of well-known buildings at central locations and on billboards along the highways as well as on busses, balloons or lightboxes is increasingly popular in China and now holds a 15–20 per cent ad spent share. Whereas in western countries there is just a static picture or message, in China ad messages jump in a diverting, colourful sea of lights. You also can rent the windows of some shops to exhibit your ad messages. According to the ad agency Saatchi & Saatchi the average price for billboard or window advertising is around 70–90 US dollars per square metre per month.

The opportunities for outdoor advertising are immense, but the control of the advertising space is disorganised. Approval can be granted from various councils and authorities. The vendor's relationship with the right authorities is important. Some companies have made the mistake of using outdoor advertising inappropriately. Producing posters or neon signs simply to display their brand name can be futile in a market where consumers are not even aware of the product associated with the advertised name. If consumers cannot identify what a company is trying to sell, there is little point in displaying a brand name without an explanation of the product.

Direct mail – traditional and via Internet – an optimal way for individualised ads

Sending personally addressed advertising messages via public mail or electronically via the Internet attracts a lot of attention in China as it is not very common yet. Especially for producers of investment goods this is a suitable way to make a first contact as often personal contact is not possible because of the country's enormous size. Postage is often not reliable in China; therefore it is recommendable to get mail delivered from Hong Kong.

An ad on webpages visited frequently by your target group could be a promising way to attract attention (see also chapter 5.7).

Summary/Recommendations

Producing the maximum impact for a brand through advertising involves creating the right campaign and using the right media to express the message. Being able to reach the broadest possible audience at the lowest possible cost is one of the key issues.

Although in China there is more advertising than in any western country, the standards have not yet reached an international level. More than in western countries you have to double-check and to secure that your advertising messages really reach the appropriate audience in the quality and at the time you wish. The poor printing quality of many Chinese print media and the untrustworthiness of some TV and radio channels sometimes may prevent you getting maximum benefit out of your advertising activities. Moreover media research is still a very young discipline in China and there are quiet a few non-measured markets, mainly in the rural areas.

To ensure professional media planning and buying it is therefore a good idea to co-operate with one of the major international media or ad agencies (such as Sofes, AC Nielsen/SRG, Grey MediaCom, Mind Share/T.W. Thompson, Saatchi & Saatchi).

Further sources

China Media Directory (1999).

China Media Yearbook and Directory (2002) (ed.) by CMMIntelligence, www.cmmintelligence.com).

Gijsen, R. and McLaughlin, B. (1997) *Reaching the Shanghai Consumer*, Asia Information Associates Ltd.

Grey Advertising (1999) *China Base 99 – Building Brand Loyalty in Turbulent Times*.

Saatchi & Saatchi (ed.) (1999), *Asia Pacific Market and Media Facts*, HK.

Sacra, E. (1998) *Die Bedeutung des kulturellen Umfelds für die Unternehmenspolitik multinationaler Unternehmen*, Munich.

Siemens (1999) *Corporate Communications in China*.

See also

- The *Announcement on Regulating the E-mailing of Commercial information*, which was issued by the Beijing Municipal AIC in May 2000.
- The *Internet Advertising Management Web*: www.sgs.gov.cn/gsweb/ggindex.htm
- The *Measures for the Administration of Advertising Display Screens*, issued by SAIC in 1996.
- The *Measures of the Administration of Printed Advertisements*, which came into effect on 1 March 2000.

6.7. Shall I produce my advertising materials in China or abroad?

According to the volume of your China activities, your branch of industry or your product range there are good reasons for one or the other alternative. The decision, however, also depends on internal organisational or company-specific aspects. At any rate you have to weigh it carefully. To produce advertising media of a reasonable quality in China, you need a solid knowledge about the possible suppliers and a lot of patience. Even Chinese insiders sometimes find it hard to separate the wheat from the chaff.

Table 27 Advantages and disadvantages of the production of advertising materials in China compared to western countries

Production in China	Production in a western country
Positive	
• Proximity to the target market	• Quality control in every phase of the production possible
• Cost advantages (toll, transport)	
• Local creativity-potential	• Recourse to an already co-ordinated team
• Being up-to-date	• Adaptation of existing advertising concepts
• No problems with Chinese characters	• Direct and quick influence
• No intercultural hurdles	• Cost control
• Efficient co-ordination with Chinese colleagues on the spot	• Time control and flexibility
• Quick reacting possible	• Better co-ordination of the realisation of multilingual media
Negative	
• Deficient technical quality	• Distance from the market
• Inadequate adaptation of western ideas	• Cost disadvantages (toll, transport)
• Poor translations	• Lack of professionalism because of a lot of translators
• Quality controls are laborious	
• Contents often difficult to judge	• Time and content problems when it comes to a co-ordination with the Chinese subsidiary
• Orientation according to American or Japanese models and measures	

Only with a lot of staying power and by intensive comparisons you can get a suitable performance of your advertising materials and good printing results. The Chinese market for production of advertising materials has a lot of unusual traps in store with which westerners are not familiar. Product liability for instance is excluded to a great extent. In practice even big international companies have to pay 50 per cent of the price for the production of advertising materials in advance. In the case of complaints because of poor or unsatisfactory performance the providers often refuse to make improvements. They rather prefer to waive the rest of the agreed remuneration because they don't want to keep struggling with 'finicky' clients.

Recommendations

If you hope to get good advertising materials produced in China for a lower budget than in western countries, you will be disappointed. Reasonable quality has its price also in China.

Further sources

Boesken, G. (1999) 'Werbemittel für China – Konzeption, Planung und Praxis der Produktion', in *China-Contact mit Wirtschaftswelt China*, 7, pp. 10–11.
Woods, R. (ed.) (1987) *Printing and Production for Promotional Materials*, NY.

6.8. How do I plan and carry out a successful presentation at Chinese trade fairs?

According to a recent investigation of the German Chamber of Commerce foreign companies see trade fairs and exhibitions as the most effective method of sales promotion in China. In order to realise an optimal performance with exhibitions there are some basic rules to respect, that may differ from western standards.

The most important aspects in preparing a trade fair in China

- Check carefully the reputation of the specific fairs and of their organisers.
- Plan carefully in which cities you want to exhibit.
- Use the services of the official agents.
- Send out invitations the right way.
- Make sure to send the right people over to represent your company.
- Bring along enough name cards, brochures and give-away articles.

Check carefully the reputation of the specific fairs and of their organisers

This is even more important than in western countries because there are too many exhibitions all over China and sometimes the organisers don't tell you the truth about the importance, the international orientation and the quality and number of visitors. You can get reliable information about the history and the reputation of a fair:

- by old participant-lists of recent years (if important players of your branch of industry exhibited over the last few years, the fair should guarantee success and the visitors you are targeting);
- from trade and promotion offices of western embassies, consulates or chambers of commerce in China;
- from Chinese associations of your branch of industry or of related branches.

As western organisers of trade fairs in China always have to have a Chinese host (like MOFTEC or other ministries) you can also judge the value of the exhibition by the reputation of the Chinese counterpart. Ministries that want to become organisers of exhibitions have to get approval from the CCPIT. These authorised exhibitions are the most interesting ones for western exhibitors.

Decide in which cities you want to exhibit

For high-tech products Beijing is certainly one of the best places, because among the visitors there will probably be some members of relevant ministries, associations and other officials. If you succeed in convincing these groups and get their recognition, they can serve you as multipliers.

But Beijing is not always the number one location for exhibitors. Since the increasing liberalisation of Chinese markets and the decentralisation of decision-making processes, Chinese customers from state owned companies don't have to come to Beijing for approval any more. Therefore nowadays exhibitors will often be forced to take part in more trade fairs in other Chinese cities apart from the capital, in order to reach their target groups.

If you are just starting to enter the Chinese market or a specific market segment, it may be useful to take part also in smaller, regional fairs and exhibitions. Possibly you also can share the fair stall/presentation with related companies, clients or companies that offer complementary products. This is not only cheaper for you but also creates the image of system-competence, which in China especially is very important.

Use the services of the official agents

Most of the qualified international and Chinese organisers of trade shows and exhibitions recommend that you use the services of the appropriate official exhibition agents, who are familiar with all the rules and specialities that have to be considered by the exhibitors (see table below). In general there are three types of official agents:

- Official freight forwarders handle all customs and transportation problems for you, which sometimes for foreign companies can be pretty complicated.
- Official stand fitters are familiar with the location of the exhibition and the specific rules (China-specific standards and norms as well as different aesthetic values of Chinese customers) and facilities (electrical supply, etc.) and ensure you an optimised presentation.
- Official travel agents can deal with all the travel arrangements for you as well as organising special receptions, conferences, business luncheons or dinners with important clients.

Sending out invitations the right way

In general the organisers of exhibitions send out official invitations to a fair to all the people they think they might be important as possible visitors. If a western exhibition organiser has an important Chinese co-organiser (like a ministry or a university), it is easier to attract 'high calibre guests'.

However, to make sure that all the (potential) clients you want to reach are really informed, it is recommended that you send out your own individual invitations. It is more personal and you can combine it with an announcement of a special event you are organising especially for your target group like a reception, a special conference with a well-known guest speaker or a business luncheon or dinner, where you host your important customers.

In order to attract high ranked decision-makers of state owned companies and representatives of the Chinese media you need to have high-ranking people to support you, i.e. as guest speakers or special guests of honour at your reception. To get somebody from a public ministry or a well-known university (like Tsinghua University, Beijing University, Fudan University or Jiaotong University) you can contact the foreign affairs department of the appropriate governmental institution/university. You could offer a Chinese institution the chance to share the stand at an exhibition with you or to act as a co-host at a reception or a conference. To convince the Chinese counterpart of such an idea you have to show them pretty clearly where their advantages are and that there are no costs for the Chinese partner.

Make sure to send the right people over

In Chinese state owned companies it is not usual for only one person to make a buying or a co-operation decision. This means representatives of all the departments that are involved in the decision-making processes need to visit a relevant exhibition. That may include functionaries as well as technicians and economists. Therefore you should send both *sales people and technical staff* to represent your company at a trade fair. Also make sure that you have enough *qualified interpreters*, because lots of relevant Chinese decision-makers still don't speak English or other foreign languages. Address the related ministries that actually do the same business you do and ask them to recommend capable interpreters who not only have excellent language skills but also have some knowledge about your branch of industry and the respective terminology. If possible, ask them for an interview beforehand to test their language and technical skills.

Bring along enough name cards and brochures

Because of the complex decision-making processes and the enormous interest in western goods and technology many more visitors attend trade fairs in China than in western countries. Make sure that you bring along enough name cards (with Chinese translation on one side) and brochures of your products and your company. If you are not willing to translate all your written materials into Chinese, you should at least provide a small brochure with a description of your company and your products in Chinese language.

As not all Chinese have business cards of their own, it is recommended to have a sign-up or registration book, where visitors can write down their names, their functions and how you can contact them. This makes an effective evaluation after the exhibition easier.

Some recommendations to present your company and your products effectively

- Build up personal contacts and relations with (potential) customers, officials, media representatives and other important parties.
- Mix Chinese and western styles of presentation; locals should feel involved (e.g. high-tech combined with traditional Chinese values). Show short video clips about your production lines or the use of your products with well-known international clients.
- Try to arrange impressive live demonstrations of your products or procedures.
- Make sure that your advertising material meets the demands of the Chinese laws of advertising (see also chapters 6.2 and 6.5).
- Try to attract visitors and media representatives by organising special events (presentation of product innovations, receptions and conferences with well-known guest speakers).
- If you meet potential Chinese partners at an exhibition don't jump to conclusions too soon! There could be a rude awakening afterwards.

Further sources

www.cecf-gz.com
Waterhouse, D. (1987) *Making the Most of Exhibitions*.

Table 28   Exhibition Agents in China

Abbreviation	Full name of the agent	How to contact the exhibition agent (Tel., fax, e-mail, homepage)
Adsale	Adsale Exhibition Services Ltd	Tel: +852/2811–8897, Fax:+852/2516–5024, E-mail:aes@adsaleexh.com, Homepage: www.adsaleexh.com
AIT	AIT Conventions & Exhibitions Co. Ltd	Tel:+86/10/6567–0273, Fax:+86/10/6567–0275, E-mail:ait@ht.rol.cn.net
Amarex	Amarex Exhibition Service Company	Tel:+86/10/68095671, Fax:+86/10/68095670, E-mail:AMAREX@public2.east.net.cn
B & I	Business & Industrial Trade Fairs Ltd	Tel:+85228652633, Fax:+85228661770,28662076, E-mail:amuse@bitf.com.hk
Coastal	Coastal Int'l Exhibition Co. Ltd	Beijing: Tel:+86/1068482648, Fax:+86/10/68482554, E-mail:csd@public.bta.net.cn
Coastal	Coastal Int'l Exhibition Co. Ltd, Hong Kong Office	Tel:+852/2827–6766, Fax:+852/2827–6870, E-mail: general@coastal.com.hk, homepage: www.coastal.com.hk
Coastal	Coastal Int'l Exhibition Co. Ltd, Shanghai Office	Shanghai: Tel:+86/21/58392818, Fax:+86/21/58392808, E-mail:csdsh@public2.sta.net.cn
Chain Assoc.	Chain Store Association	Tel:+86/10/68392260, Fax+86/21/68392210–802, E-mail:chainsch@public.east.cn.net, homepage: www.ccfa.org.cn
C Promotion	China Promotion Ltd	Tel:+852/25117427, Fax:+852/25119692, E-mail: cpexhbit@hk.super.net, homepage: www.hk.super.net/-cpexhbit
CCPIT	China Council for the Promotion of International Trade	Economic Information Dept., Tel:+86/10/68013344, Fax:+86/10/68011370
CCPIT Dal.	Dalian Sub-Council	Tel:+86/411/2815738, Fax: +86/411/2815739, E-mail:ccpitxly@mbox.dl.cei.gov.cn
CCPIT Xian	Xian Sub-Council	Tel:+86/29/7292734, Fax:+86/297291461, E-mail:mchllb@sei.sn.cn
CETCC	China Economic & Trade Consultants Corp.	Tel:+86/10/65051585, Fax:+86/10/65051582, E-mail:autoshow.consult@bj.col.com.cn, Homepage:www.coolshow.com
China Great Wall	China Great Wall Int'l Exhibition Co. Ltd	Tel:+86/10/68748906, Fax:+86/10/68748906, E-mail:chengy@cgwic.com
Chinastar	Chinastar Fair Co. Ltd	Tel:+86/10/68041566, Fax:+86/10/68346980, E-mail:ccpitbms@public3.bta.net.cn, Hompage:http://www.chinabuilding.cn.net

Abbreviation	Full name of the agent	How to contact the exhibition agent (Tel., fax, e-mail, homepage)
CIC	China Information & Communication (Int'l) Exhibition Ltd	Tel:+852/26081015, Fax:+85226080981, E-mail:cic@telecomn.com
CIEC	CIEC Exhibition Co. (HK) Ltd	Tel: +852/28275078, Fax:+85228275535, E-mail:ciecechk@hk.china.com
CIEC China	CIEC China	Tel: +86/1010/64671704, Fax:+86/10/64663204
CNAVS	CNAVS Trade Fair Office	Tel:+86/10/64988376, Fax:+86/10/64988374, E-mail:fair@public.ease.cn.net
CNTA	China National Tourism Administration (CNTA)	Tel:+86/10/65053207, Fax: +86/10/65053260, E-mail:cwtced@public3.bta.net.cn
CWTCED	China World Trade Center Co. Ltd Exhibition Division	E-mail: cwtced@public3.bta.net.cn
MF Sinoexpo	Miller Freeman Sinoexpo Intl. Exhibition Co. Ltd	Tel:+86/21/64371178, Fax:+86/21/64370982, E-mail: sinoexpo@public.sta.net.cn
Modern	Shanghai Modern Intl. Exhibition Co.	Tel:+86/21/63217522, Fax:+86/21/63295774
Neway	Neway International Trade Fairs Ltd	Tel: +86/20/83878255, Fax: +86/20/83872116
North Exhibit	North Exhibition & Advertisement Company	Tel:+86/106352 9988, Fax: +86/10/6354 7597
NTDC-Cast	New Technology Development Centre-Cast	Tel:+86/10/62170166, Fax: +86/10/6217 4946, E-mail: ntdccast@public.east.cn.net
OMY	OMY Exhibition Consulting Co. Ltd	Tel:+86/10/67184659, Fax: +86/10/67181941
Oriental	Oriental Expo Services (Beijing) Ltd	Tel:+86/10/68342703, Fax: +86/10/68337922, E-mail: oriental@public.bta.net.cn
Promotion	China Promotion Ltd	Tel:+852/25117427, Fax:+852/25119692, E-mail: cpexhbit@hk.super.net
Pudong IEC	Shanghai Pudong International Exhibition Corporation	Tel:+86/21/62723462, Fax:+86/21/62723463, E-mail: spiec@sh.east.cn.net
Qingdao IEC	Qingdao International Exhibition Centre	Tel:+86/532/3888927, Fax:+86/532/3888922
RAI	RAI Exhibitions Singapore Pte Ltd	Tel:+99/253/2722250, Fax: 2726744, E-mail: raispore@singnet.com.sg

Table 28   (*continued*)

Abbreviation	Full name of the agent	How to contact the exhibition agent (Tel., fax, e-mail, homepage)
Reed	Reed Exhibition Ltd	Tel:+852/28240330, Fax:+852/ 28240246, E-mail: emiltung@reedexpo.com.hk
Renjia	Beijing Renjia Science & Technology Co. Ltd	Tel:+86/10/64663941, Fax:+86/10/64663943, E-mail: jiwang@public2.east.cn.net
SEMI	SEMI China Secretariat, ELINT	Tel:+86/10/68273868, Fax:+86/10/68212801
Teamwork	Shenzhen Teamwork Trade and Exhibition Co. Ltd	Tel:+86/755/3203–311, Fax:+86/755/3203–131, E-mail: szexpo@public.szptt.net.cn
SCADI	South China Architectural Design Institute	Tel:+86/28/3310647, Fax:+86/28/3397313
SIECO	Shanghai Intl Exhibition Corp.	Tel:+86/21/63872828, Fax: +86/21/63869400, E-mail: siec@stn.sh.cn
Sinostar	Sinostar International Ltd	Tel:+852/2865–0062, Fax: +852/28042256, E-mail:sinointl@hkstar.com
STE	Guangzhou STE	Tel: +862/83548263, Fax:+862/83549078, E-mail: Ste@sti.gd.cn
Tianjin Kenwall	Tianjin Kenwall Intl Trade & Exhibition Co. Ltd	Tel:+86/22/23115536, Fax:+86/22/23310042, E-mail: kenwall@public.tpt.tj.cn
TianjinIEC	Tianjin International Exhibition Corp.	Tel:+86/22/2312–6054, Fax: +86/22/23301344, E-mail: tiec@ public1.tpt.tj.cn
CTS	CTS Intl. Convention & Exhibition Co.	Tel:+86/10/65598489, Fax: +86/10/65598487, E-mail: wyh.cj@ctsho.com
Da Northern	Dalian Northern International Exhibition Service Co. Ltd	Tel: +86/411/4809318, Fax: +86/411/4809312, E-mail: dlne@mbox.dl.cei.gov.cn
Fairlink	Fairlink Exhibition Services	Tel: +86/10/64663366, Fax: +86/10/64634950, E-mail: fairlink@public.gb.com.cn
Great Credit	Hong Kong Great Credit (International) Co. Ltd	Tel: +86/10/64205697, Fax:+86/10/64276928, E-mail:greatcre@public.bta.net.cn, Homepage: www.packchina.com.cn
Global	Global Exhibition Service	Tel: +86/21/64400036, Fax: +86/21/64400035, E-mail: globalex@online.sh.cn
HK Exhibit	Hong Kong Exhibition Services Ltd	Tel: +852/25283103, E-mail: exhibit@hkesmontnet.com.hk
HK Exhibit	Hong Kong Exhibition Services	Tel:+86/21/62095209, Fax:+86/21/62095210, E-mail: tmnchina@public6.sta.net.cn

Table 28 (continued)

Abbreviation	Full name of the agent	How to contact the exhibition agent (Tel., fax, e-mail, homepage)
HMI	Hannover-Messe International	Tel: +852/2147–9921, Fax: +852/2147/9925, E-mail: itep@hfasin.com, Homepage: www.hfchina.com
Hua Xing	China Hua Xing (Group)	Tel: +86/10/63582076, Fax: 10/63582077
IDG	International Data Group	Tel:+85225279338, Fax: +852 2529–9956, E-mail:dinah_chan@idg.com.hk
IECE&TC	Intl Exchange Center for Economic & Technical Coop. Of CWRC	Tel: +86/27/8282–0217, Fax: +86/27/8242–9722, E-mail: exchange@mail.cjwrc.edu.cn
IIST	Information Institute of Science and Technology	Tel: +86/10/6491–4809, Fax:+86/10/64018204, E-mail: tcs@iicc.ac.cn
INTEX	Shanghai International Exhibition Centre	Tel:+86/21/6275 5800, Fax: +86/2162757210, E-mail: intexcax@public4.sta.net.cn
Jetta	Jetta (Beijing) Exhibition Service Co. Ltd	Tel: +86/10/68039757, Fax:+86/10/68036111, E-mail: jetta@public.bta.net.cn
Krause	E.J. Krause & Associates	Tel: +86–10–8451–1832, Fax: +86–10–8451–1829, E-mail: ejk@public3.bta.net.cn, Homepage: www.ejkrause.com
Link	Link Exhibition Services Ltd, Hong Kong Office	Tel: +852/23111736, Fax:+852/23119067, E-mail: linkexh@netvigator.com
Link	Beijing Office	Tel: +86/10/84603025, Fax: +86/10/84603028, E-mail: linkbjo@hotmail.com
Look Ease	Look Ease Enterprise Ltd	Tel:+852/25270759, Fax: +852/28613523, E-mail: tso@hknet.com
Mack-Brooks	Mack-Brooks Groups	Tel: +1/707/275641, Fax: +1/707/275544
Together	Together Expo Ltd	Tel: +852/2890–2657, Fax: +852/28902657, E-mail: tgrexpo@netvigator.com, Homepage: www.together-expo.com
Top Repute	Top Repute Co. Ltd	Tel: +852/2851–8603, Fax: +852/28518637, E-mail:topreput@hkabc.net, Homepage: http://www.toprepute.com.hk
Union	Union Fair& Trade Co. Ltd	Tel:+86/20/87361889, Fax: +86/20/87361350, E-mail: gzunionf@public1.guangzhou.gd.cn

Table 28   (continued)

Abbreviation	Full name of the agent	How to contact the exhibition agent (Tel., fax, e-mail, homepage)
Vantage	Vantage Exhibitions Ltd (HK)	Tel: +852/28815889, Fax:+852/28902657, E-mail: tgrexpo@netvigator.com, Homepage: www.together-expo.com
WES	Worldwide Exhibition Service Co. Ltd	Tel:+86/2152340646, Fax: +86/21 52340649
Worldpo	Worldpo Exhibition Ltd	Tel: +852/21486989, Fax: +852/27547822, E-mail: worldpo@worldpo.com.hk
Worldwide	Worldwide Conventions & Expositions Ltd	Tel: +852/27502868, Fax: 852/2318–1641, E-mail:info@ww- expo.com, Homepage: www-expo.com
Xinyu	Shanghai Xinyu Exhibition Services Co. Ltd	Tel: +86/21/6428–4310, Fax: +86/21/6469–3337
Zhong	China Beijing Zhong Jinming Cheng Exhibition Corp. Ltd	Tel: +86/106381 9497, Fax: +86/10/6381 4601

6.9. How do I co-operate with advertising and PR agencies?

As a western *lao wai* (alien) who has grown up with a different cultural background you can't really judge whether an ad meets the taste and the value system of your Chinese target groups. Therefore you need a reliable, partner – like an advertising agency – which supports you in realising your marketing communication concept for the Chinese market.

In the first years after the opening of the Chinese market it was difficult to find a really professional agency. The Chinese officials had seen advertising, and hereby also agencies, as a reflection of western decadence and they were therefore not approved of. Not until 1992 was it allowed for foreign ad agencies to invest or to open a branch in China. In these early days of advertising there was a lack of professional experience on the Chinese side. Also, western agencies which started a business in China first had to learn about the peculiarities of Chinese culture and the value system in order to meet effectively the Chinese target groups.

Issues of the client-agency relationship
- State of the ad-agency scene in China.
- Selection of a suitable agency.
- Optimal co-operation with your agency.
- From advertising to integrated communication concepts.

State of the ad-agency scene in China

It is said that nowadays in China there are around 48,000 companies in the field of advertising. Amongst them, there are approximately 200 companies with foreign interests. Nearly all the global players of the international ad-agency scene have opened subsidiaries in China. As demanded by Chinese law, these are joint ventures with local partners. The leading agency in China in terms of advertising billing is Saatchi & Saatchi with an annual billing of about 230 million US dollars, followed by McCann Erickson with around 140 million US dollars. J. Walter Thompson, Grey/MediaCom and Ogilvy & Mather hold positions three to five.

The initial rapid expansion of the agency scene in China has slowed down now. Not least because of reluctant consumer behaviour, the slow-down of the Chinese economy during the last few years and the high running costs of an agency in China, European and American ad agencies incurred losses in their China business. However, in order to avoid the risk of missing potential chances in this enormous market, they continue doing business in China.

As China is still very new in terms of having homegrown ad agencies, you can only find a few local Chinese experts in the market to fill the key positions in agencies. Therefore expensive expatriates have to be hired. However, there are not many western expatriates in the senior management level of the agencies now; they have been replaced by Taiwan or Hong Kong Chinese or other Chinese speaking people with Chinese roots, who are culturally more communicative and also have years of experience in the advertising and marketing fields.

The most important target groups of the agencies are not western global players but Chinese clients. In 1999 Chinese companies spent eight times more on advertising in China than western companies. The most important Chinese advertising client is Gaizhong-gai, who doubled its advertising expenditure in 1999 compared to 1998. The most important foreign advertising client, Coca-Cola, ranks number 12 on this list. However, many local clients are not yet prepared to spend huge amounts on media planning and strategy, and don't think it is worth it. Often the 'more is better' strategy is applied, while sophisticated foreign media planning agencies are snubbed.

The Criteria for selecting a suitable agency

In choosing an ad agency you should follow the rules of the game; in other words, you should not judge the quality of an agency by a pitched presentation, but you should rather:

- look at the local set-up and the particular agency's client portfolio;
- check the agency's professionalism and their knowledge about how potential target groups consume media by references;

- ask to be shown some of the agency's credentials/presentations and ask Chinese friends or colleagues how they perceive them;
- check whether the agency has good *guanxi* with officials from TV stations, publishing houses, the China Advertising Association and other authorities.

It is not recommended that you hire so-called 'hot shops' (highly creative service providers which usually deliver very avant-garde ideas that show a certain kind of 'wildness' like, for instance, the Bennetton ads). In western countries this kind of creativity creates an enormous resonance, but as advertising in China still is in its developing stage, solid image building combined with a consistent market communication is necessary. You should not take the risk of shocking, irritating or understating ads.

Optimal co-operation with your ad agency

Optimal co-operation between you and your ad agency needs excellent people on both sides. About 30–50 per cent of all problems in this relationship occur because clients don't really know what they want. They often change their minds and do not have a working, well-tuned marketing and communication strategy.

Therefore you should train at least one of your Chinese employees in your marketing department how to translate technical advantages or other peculiarities of your products into a consumer benefit; that means, what the product offers the customer and why he should buy it. For example, for an average consumer the content of a chocolate bar is not important; he is rather interested in what it offers him/her emotionally, socially, etc. Make sure that there is a regular communication between your marketing people and the agency's contact people.

From advertising to integrated communication concepts

In their efforts to communicate with more fragmented and diverse target segments, marketers are employing a richer variety of more focused promotional tools. As a result Chinese consumers are being exposed to a greater variety of marketing communications from and about a company. However, customers don't distinguish between promotional message sources the way that marketers do. In the consumer's mind advertising messages from different media such as television, magazines, or online computer services blur into one. Messages delivered via different promotional approaches – such as advertising, personal selling, sales promotion, public relations, or direct marketing – all become part of a single overall message about your company. Conflicting messages from these different sources can result in confused company images and brand positions.

Therefore you should work out – together with your advertising agency – an integrated marketing communications strategy. This is a concept under which a company carefully integrates and co-ordinates its many communication channels to deliver a clear, consistent and compelling message about the organisation and its products. Fix the roles that the various promotional tools will play and the extent to which each should be used.

In co-operation with your agency you should carefully co-ordinate the promotional activities and the timing of when major campaigns take place. If there is no specialist in your Chinese branch, your agency should also – according to a fixed budget – keep track of your promotional expenditures by product, promotional tool, product lifecycle stage and observed effect in order to improve future use of the variety of promotional tools.

You may be interested in the fact that some agencies like Ogilvy & Mather are diversifying their service range by founding departments for interactive marketing. These can help you to design your Internet presence and integrate it into your overall marketing concept. Since the Internet in the future will play a major role as a communication media in China this might be an interesting aspect.

Recommendations

If you are thinking of importing your advertisements, made by agencies in your own country, to China, the Chinese will treat this as an imported commercial and you might be charged tremendous import taxes. In order to avoid these taxes and to build better links with the Chinese consumer, it is recommended to produce your marketing communication materials locally. Newcomers should – despite the enormous costs – seek the advice of well-established international ad agencies with a broad experience in Hong Kong and/or China. They are generally familiar with closing the gap between East and West.

Further sources

Armstrong, G. and Kotler P. (1997) *Marketing – An Introduction*, NJ.

Butterfield, L. (1997) 'Developing advertising strategy', in *How to Plan Advertising*, ed. by Cooper, A., London, pp. 29–47.

China Media Yearbook and Directory (2002) (ed.) by CMM Intelligence, www.cmmintelligence.com

Duckworth, G. (1997) 'Creative briefing', in: *Excellence in Advertising: The IPA Guide to Best Practice*, ed. by Butterfield, L., Oxford, pp. 147–69.

Rommel, C. (1999) 'Die geheimen Verführer – Die Werbewirtschaft boomt', in *China-Contact*, 7, pp. 6–9.

7

How Do I Create a Strong Sales Concept?

Engelbert Boos

7.1. How to co-ordinate different sales channels?

Many internationally successful operating companies operate different sales channels in China such as their own production facilities in China and their other international subsidiaries due to strategic considerations. The main reasons may be the request for a higher total sales volume, the realisation of a profit centre concept, the differentiation in cost, pricing, specification and service for the penetration of different market segments or just a specific profit contribution policy for the local enterprise. However, the potential higher sales volume may have influence on the general price level and image on the same brand's products. On the one hand, customers will use their purchasing power and negotiate lower prices between the different sales channels. On the other hand, the competing salesmen will reduce their reliance on teamwork and keep secret important market information. The advertising of competing sales channels may also cause customer confusion. Therefore, the products should be clearly differentiated one from another and the co-ordination of such activities should be done preferably in China.

Important criteria of success for the establishment of sales channels

- Balanced distribution channels through OEM (Own Equipment Manufacturer), project and dealer businesses.
- Fixed and stringent pricing and discount policy.
- Cost and profit margin calculation for the achievement of good market shares.
- Clearly defined differentiation or cost leadership policy.
- Efficient supply and debt management.

Balanced distribution channels through OEM, project and distribution businesses and fixed and stringent pricing and discount policy

Within China, the distribution channels should be balanced by comparable sales contributions through OEM, project and dealer businesses in order to reduce dependence and risks on individual customers. There should also be fixed a stringent pricing and discount policy for the distributors. This reduces dealer complaints and unbalanced or uncontrolled competition between them. It is a good idea to calculate the required average profit margin for one's dealers' business such as approximately 10–15 per cent on their purchasing prices in the case of investment goods. Their final sales prices for the end users on the market must include such margins and remain competitive for the dealers. Therefore, direct sales from the factory to the smaller end users must be more expensive than those sold through the dealers. The discount conditions for comparable dealers must be the same in relation to the sold quantities. Otherwise, it is very difficult or even almost impossible to motivate and manage them effectively. It should always be taken into consideration that most Chinese dealers are very open-minded and quick-footed. Project business mostly enables the realisation of higher profit margin. However, the acquisition, job implementation as well as engineering and contracting efforts for such businesses are much higher, too. The penetration of the classic OEM business with large demand in quantity is very important for the realisation of sufficient productivity and business success in the long term.

Cost and profit margin calculation for the achievement of good market shares and clearly defined differentiation or cost leadership policy

The balanced turnover through the different distribution channels or respective market segments represents the basis for a reliable cost and profit calculation. Therefore, such sales control figures must be analysed and monitored regularly. The mentioned cost and profit margin calculation also influences the saleable quantities. This is important for the production planning and the covering of the fixed costs. In the start-up phase, it is of greatest importance to penetrate quickly and as much as possible OEM business in order to achieve market shares and more influence on the market. The competitive environment with prices, market shares, quantities and sales policy – differentiation or cost leadership – must be analysed in detail and counter-attacks respectively planned and implemented.

Efficient supply and debt management

Payment methods are very important in China. Delayed supplying of goods and late payments have huge influence on sales, finance and business success. Effort required to subsequently collect money is very consuming of time and human resources. OEM customers especially are permanently close to liquidity and smaller companies are mushrooming and closing down frequently. It may be advisable to build up a close information network with competitors for money collection and to install a special bonus payment system for salesmen who are responsible for money collection. It can also help to install one company representative within the major OEM facilities to promote the interests of the company such as new orders, after sales services and money collection.

Summary/Recommendations

The composition of the distribution policy and the chosen distribution channels using one's own salesmen, dealers or agents depends to a huge extent on the nature of one's products and special business circumstances. Some manufacturers may prefer to rely mainly on their own distribution channels in order to safeguard their own technologies and system know-how, whereas others, who have more commodities or standardised products, may prefer to engage more cost-efficient external distributors. Different competing distribution channels only make sense in the case of products with a high potential for differentiation. However, these effects and product features must also be realised and accepted by customers, otherwise they could cause customer confusion and hesitation in the purchasing decisions. The competitive market environment in China is very heterogeneous and changes easily. Therefore, the distribution policy has to be quite flexible and regularly adjusted to the present market circumstances.

7.2. What are the critical success factors in selling?

To be successful in selling is one of the most difficult tasks when doing business in China. The defining of the most favourable market segments, the realisation of good local cost levels and quality standards and last, but not least, the meeting of good and acceptable pricing and service levels are very sensitive and critical success factors in order to sell well. The suitably defined and focused sales policy in connection with the establishment of an effective and efficient sales network are major prerequisites for success in the establishment of the sales business.

The most important success factors in selling

- Clearly defined marketing and sales policy.
- Pricing policy must meet market requirements and should be stringent and transparent.
- Flexible terms of payment.

- Quick deliveries through adequate stock levels.
- Management and co-ordination of the dealership network.
- Highly motivated and well-trained sales-people.

Clearly defined marketing and sales policy

A suitable sales and marketing policy should be defined before the selling business really starts. It is essential to have a clear concept on how to present and communicate the products to the market, because China's market is changing rapidly. The pricing policy is especially relevant. Business success ultimately depends to a large extent on the positioning of the products on the market. Every customer should have a clear understanding and realistic expectations of the offered products and services. This is particularly difficult in China because people have only been learning to think about competing products and brands since the late 1980s. The employees should be aware of the required contributions. The marketing and sales policy must also fit the chosen most promising market segment under consideration in the fast-changing and fierce competitive environment. This is an important prerequisite for successful selling in China.

Pricing policy must meet market requirements and should be stringent and transparent

Each newly established entity requires high growth rates in sales in order to achieve the required production quantities. It is very important in sales that the cost levels, profit margins and prices meet the market requirements. This is a prerequisite for success in the achievement of specific quantities; then the influence on the market can be increased too. A further important issue is that the discount policy to the distributors is stringent and transparent. To some extent, special bonuses for higher-quantity orders may be applicable to promote the sales. However, Chinese dealers tend to place pooled orders if the additional bonus is too high. In China, other competing dealers quickly learn about special price arrangements and complain if they are at a disadvantage. The prices are mostly well known on the market with the particular sources of supplies. Therefore, the pricing policy is a very sensitive success factor with regards to sales. Basically, every dealer should have the same chances for price and quantity arrangements. However, it must be also taken into consideration that the competitive pricing environment may differ between various regions. The boom cities along the east coast have much higher per capita income and purchasing power than the western regions, which are still desperately poor and underdeveloped. The local differences in pricing can be balanced to some extent by including free transportation or packaging in certain cases.

Flexible terms of payment

The terms of payment are also a sensitive tool and success factor in promoting sales. Chinese customers often complain about their lack of liquidity and ask for respective credits or delayed payments for deliveries. However, the collection of money without guaranteed cheques may cause big problems. It takes a lot of experience and time to know the more reliable customers. Entertaining distributors is also important. As mentioned before, networking and building up good *guanxi* is the nuts and bolts of business in China. Distributors have to be taken out for swanky meals and given appropriate presents. Larger OEM customers with their huge purchasing power induce the most favourable purchasing terms. It may make sense to install one's own part-time staff there. Such a company sales representative can keep regular contact with important departments of the OEM customer including purchasing, sales, financing, technical, service and production. In such cases, the readiness of the customer to pay is much more unproblematic and indications of major risks or further business opportunities can be spotted in time.

Quick deliveries through adequate stock levels

The adequate stock level for quick deliveries in smaller quantities is a critical decision factor in purchasing for many customers, and dealers too. This helps them to overcome short-term cash flow problems.

Management and co-ordination of the distribution network

The dealership should be visited regularly and be invited to an annual dealer meeting. Dealers are very interested in ads, catalogues, small gifts and posters etc. Some smaller exhibitions should be participated in together with the dealers. Special attention should be paid in case of competing sales channels of the headquarters' several distribution networks with the dealers. Such businesses must be co-ordinated and managed very carefully. Otherwise, a lot of confusion can occur on the market and the customer becomes dissatisfied due to different price levels and contradictory advertising campaigns or differing service levels on the market. Special or individually agreed arrangements within competing sales channels often don't work if they are only based on goodwill agreements. Typical salesmen use all their efforts to conclude deals without any special care for each other. This problem can only be managed in case of a strong differentiation in product and market segmentation or in the case of a strong co-ordinator with influence and decision-power being installed in China.

Highly motivated and well-trained sales-people

People, especially in sales and service, are a further key factor to success. They must be well trained in product and sales know-how, motivated and controlled efficiently. It should be noted that sales strategies in China work differently than in the West. A sales-person has to convince his Chinese customers, not the foreign GM. An attractive bonus system should be initiated depending on the achievement of set targets. A wide range of bonus systems is applied in China, depending on key measurements, which may be based on the achieved sales volume (in turnover or sold quantity), the realised profit margin or success in money collection or other important factors used to measure success in sales.

Summary/Recommendations

In most business activities in China sales are one of the most difficult tasks, especially in the beginning. Therefore, it is essential to figure out the critical success factors in selling. First of all, the quality and cost level of a product must be competitive in the fierce market environment in China in order to be able to achieve market share. This is important for the achievement of sufficiently high production quantities and for the fulfilment of required productivity levels in local manufacturing facilities. Highly motivated and well-trained sales-people must be employed to follow a stringent defined marketing and sales policy. Then a positive image of corporate identity and products which support a positive business development can be built up.

Further sources

Huang, Q. (1997) *Business Decision Making in China*, Amazon.
Krott, M. (1999) *Marktmacht China, Global Player lernen das Schattenboxen*, Vienna.
Zhang, X. (1996) *Erfolgreich Verhandeln in China, Risiken minimieren, Vertraege optimieren*, Wiesbaden, Gabler.

7.3. How to find an adequate balance between the stock level and the time and the capability to deliver on time?

In China many customers are very concerned about cash flow. Project confirmations and subsequent final and binding purchasing decisions depend very much on the availability of funds; therefore, many projects are delayed. After the final preparation of the budgeted funds, the customer wants to quickly realise the project and rescue the required sub-supplied components and products. In such cases, the estimated delivery time is important and decisive for the final purchasing decision. A successful supplier has to react quickly and flexibly with very competitive delivery times. This can be only achieved with flexible production management methods in combination with relatively high stock levels. This is a decisive competitive edge for the business in China.

The most important criteria of stock management
- To define sales promoting and cost efficient levels of stock.
- To control the ratio 'stock per monthly sales'.
- To promote and follow up local sourcing and to introduce stock management systems.

To define sales promoting and cost efficient levels of stock

High stock levels also mean high fixed costs and the requirement of appropriate liquidity. This liquidity has to be financed by additional bank loans or by longer sub-supplier credits. This may be handled more easily in the case of main component deliveries from the headquarters by negotiated special payment terms. However, a third party supplier may be much stricter in the payment conditions. Money collection in China is a very difficult job and the legal possibilities for money collection are very limited. This has a huge influence on business and the decision to have relatively high stock levels. (see also chapter 7.12)

To control the ratio 'stock per monthly sales'

International controlling standards seriously monitor the movements and size of stock levels. One of the most interesting ratio is the change in 'stock per monthly sales'. This figure is put in correlation with the time-frame window, lasting from the order of components for sub-supplies to the possible delivery time of the respective finished goods. Other special ratios and figures are the 'quantity of models in stock', the 'average order quantity of customers' and the 'competitors' stock availability'. In order to balance seasonal peaks, it is recommended to calculate the respective 'three-month average' figures of such monthly sales. Under ideal circumstances, 'one complete turn of stock' should be fulfilled at least in a time-frame of six months. Slow-movers should be sold out once a year through a special pricing action.

To promote and follow up local sourcing and to introduce stock management systems

The pressure of the contraction of delivery times and stock levels can be smoothed by local sourcing efforts (shorter distances for supplies) and acquisitions of larger customers with requirements for standard products (better basic loads of production and less influence of orders of medium-sized customers on the stock level). The stock management software can also help to improve the stock efficiency. Minimum and maximum quantities of finished goods, components and raw materials can be optimised according to the sales levels. However, the demand level for finished goods may fluctuate a lot. The cost calculation of the stock value, the production management in general and the interface between the different related departments can be optimised and sources of errors be reduced by the use of a sophisticated stock management system.

Summary/Recommendations

The definition and management of an optimised balance between stock level and possible delivery time is a quite sensitive and difficult task for the management of a company. Market demand fluctuates greatly in most cases. As a result, reliable forecasts of demand and respective stock levels become very difficult. The situation can only be smoothed by using a sophisticated control and monitoring mechanism to have a thorough overview of the market situation.

7.4. What are the most important issues that influence the decision-making process in purchasing?

Successful and professional working salesmen know in depth their customer's decision-making process with regards to purchasing and how these processes can be influenced in general. Many local customers frequently lack liquidity and suffer from shortages of funds for new investments. Therefore, they base their purchasing decisions mainly on the price, without the calculation of the relatively high running costs that may arise later for service, maintenance and less efficiency. Western oriented or quite profitable operating companies in China make their purchasing decisions also on long-term considerations including issues such as quality, service, energy- and cost-efficiency, safety in operation, tailor-made solutions and consulting with regards to complex system integration or application technologies.

The most important features to influence decisions in purchasing

- To realise the individual situation and needs of the customer.
- To fulfil the customer's requests as well as possible and to satisfy him more than he expects.
- To share mutual profits and advantages of a deal with the customer to the benefit of both parties in the sense of a win-win situation.

In China there exist mainly two types of customers. The first one is always lacking liquidity and purchases only the cheapest and locally made products with poor service capability. However, the market is now putting increased pressure on such manufacturers and demanding increasingly reliable products. Therefore, the quality and competence level of such local manufacturers is improving. They are also urged to introduce or copy international quality and technical standards. This can only be realised through the purchasing and use of high-quality components. The manufacturers with poor performance will disappear from the competitive market environment if they don't adopt to the new pressures. This applies especially to many state owned companies. The other type of customer buys only the best and preferably imported or at least joint venture products at very competitive price levels. The price levels of international suppliers are very close together in China. Therefore, the product features have to be differentiated from each other and must best meet customer requirements in special target segments of the market. Low cost levels have to be achieved through the realisation of high quantities to remain competitive. This has huge impact on the selling and purchasing process of the counterparts. The quoted price level seems to be the most sensitive and decisive issue when making a decision about a purchase. Lower operational costs such as energy cost savings and higher future service costs are not yet important to many customers due to their limited purchasing budgets. However, the purchasing behaviour is changing due to international standards with more and more requests for tailor-made elements.

There has been a big change in the purchasing decision-making process within the last few years. In the past purchasing decisions were always politic-ally motivated. Nowadays it is more important to offer a good after-sales service package. Help should be supplied quickly and competently, preferably within a 24-hour time range. The classic *guanxi* is not as important any more. This applies to both for investment goods and consumer goods.

To attract new customers it is important to have a good local customer base. It is also helpful to involve key opinion leaders in the promotion of the products and brand name. Such persons may be professors or high-level representatives of acknowledged market leaders from both suppliers and customers. However, there is also the risk that negative image campaigns may arise using such key opinion leaders. It is also quite difficult to keep reliable information like prices, new developments or customer relationships confidential. Therefore, it is important to sensitively manage such information and marketing activities.

Today it is more difficult to identify the decision-makers in the purchasing process. For more complex products and systems or in case of a large customer organisation, the decision-making process must be analysed and consequently a suitable sales strategy created. In a larger group of decision-makers, the customer tends to find a consensus on purchasing decisions. There are always a lot of contradictory views while negotiating. The participants come and go. The main decision-makers often are located outside the group. It is difficult to set time schedules for the final decisions. However, the decision-making process has become more efficient and is developing a more economical basis. Many purchasing managers have, in the meantime, been trained to perform professionally.

Rational and irrational purchasing decisions have to be evaluated. It is important to know, if only one person or a group of persons should be approached. There may exist a consumer chain. The purchasing decision structure and policy – within the different interest groups – have to be analysed. Such a process has become quite complex; the reputation of a product becomes more decisive. This applies for both politically and economically motivated purchasing decisions. It is important to participate in the decision-making chain. Today, there are 12,000 import/export companies with a huge number of potential customers. It is recommended to be well informed, well prepared, and to be patient. The objectives of the customer and his real requirements in the extensive environment should be analysed in detail. In the case of irrational decision-making, a worst case strategy should be prepared.

In the consumer goods market, experience nowadays shows that the consumer knows more and more about what he buys. He/she prefers to purchase better quality and well-known products. The purchasing decisions are very similar in the various regions in China, only the quantities are different. Many consumers already have a lot of money to fulfil their wishes. Market research is still difficult or even impossible due to the consumer market not being saturated and the rapid developments within it. The consumers still trust the media's view.

Summary/Recommendations

The purchase decision-making in China is still under development but more or less follows western behaviour. Nowadays producers must meet good or even the best-quality standards in order to cope with the fiercely competitive environment in China. Weak local manufacturers cannot rely any more on the automatic subsidies of the government, as in the past. They really depend on the right components for competitive prices. However, there are still some special circumstances which have to be considered while undertaking sales and purchasing business in China.

Further sources

Huang, Q. (1997) *Business Decision Making in China*, Amazon.
Zhang, X. (1996) *Erfolgreich Verhandeln in China, Risiken minimieren, Verträge optimieren*, Wiesbaden, Gabler.

7.5. How do I manage the relationship network?

Since the opening of China, the issue of *guanxi* the 'relationships network', has played an important role. While networking is important in business worldwide, it is indispensable in a country that changes rapidly and that lacks strong institutions and strict, reliable rules. Most decision-making processes are no longer centralised by major import and export organisations or by central government institutions. The preparation and achievement of most of the purchasing decisions are now decentralised in the various provinces, far away from Beijing. The investing companies are quite free to spend their allocated or self-earned funds as they like. The *guanxi* is now as important and useful as it is in most western countries. They help in making a deal but it is also possible to set up a distribution network or to sell a product quite successfully without *guanxi*.

The importance of *guanxi* and relationship networks

- *Guanxi* is important for collecting information.
- Well-established relationship networks help monitor and control the business and market environment.
- Communication with the Chinese distribution partner helps in building up loyalty.
- There are formal and informal impacts of *guanxi*.

Guanxi is important for collecting information

Guanxi is still quite important for collecting information. Indeed media news and statistical data are not always complete. They are officially controlled and often politically influenced. As a consequence, such data is sometimes not reliable. Many officially published data can just be used as qualified, but not as quantified indication of the whole situation. Therefore, so-called good *guanxi* can help to get a more reliable overview on the various issues of interest.

Well-established relationship networks help monitor and control the business and market environment

Because of the lack of legal security and low market transparency, business in China depends very much on the relationship network. Through this network it is easier to get reliable information and to put pressure on relationship members, if required, especially to control customers. Good *guanxi* help in collecting outstanding payments more successfully, avoiding delayed deliveries of sub-supplies or just creating the image of a good company. Many good business deals depend very much on established and maintained relationship networks. Regular visits to key players in the market are important. Good *guanxi* can also be built up by regular factory visits, by frequently organising seminars, attending national and international exhibitions, accepting private invitations or business dinners or joining a golf club. Good relationships also help in the long run to defend market shares.

Communication with the Chinese distribution partner helps in building up loyalty

Internal communications within Chinese companies are usually one way, generating minimal flow of information, since knowledge is power and not to be dispensed unless absolutely essential. However, there is selective feeding of controversial information often through people with whom the management has good *guanxi*. In order to influence a Chinese partner's distribution team directly, the western multinational corporation should seek to significantly influence or actually take over responsibility for information distribution. Such communication strategies may include posters, newsletters and regular meetings where the western managers control the agenda.

Table 29 Formal and informal impacts of *guanxi*

Formal impacts of guanxi	Informal impacts of guanxi
• Interests and companies are not transparent	• *Guanxi* are a tool for informal communication
• Institutions not flexible in decision-making	• *Guanxi* make changes possible by using short, informal channels
• No functioning rule of law	• Networks of trust are better than contracts
• Rules are changing during the game	• Networks are based on reliability
• Power not based on position, but on network	• Amount of power depends on connections

Summary/Recommendations

Guanxi are important tools in management, especially in China. This applies particularly for the collection and evaluation of market information. Collecting and maintaining such data is one of the important management tasks in China. Good relationships with key players in the market help control one's own business and promote success in the medium and long term. A stringent communication policy helps to control efficiently the distribution and relationship networks.

Further sources

Moser, M. (ed.) (2000) *China Troubleshooter*, HK, Asia Law & Practice, Chapter 4, p. 67.
Reisch, B. (1995) *Erfolg im China Geschäft – Von Personalauswahl bis Kundenmanagement*, Frankfurt, Campus.

7.6. How can I arrange sales activities and relevant documentation?

Marketing and sales is a difficult and sensitive management task in China. The competition is fierce and frequently changes in all of the markets. Penetrated big-sized customers sometimes lose their former importance overnight and other new consumers become rising stars within the same short time. The demanded product features are also changing from cheaper and lower-quality levels to competitively priced higher-quality or even premium-quality products and components. Such frequent, huge changes in customer demand also influence the arrangement of the sales policy and the management of the sales team. As a consequence, the arrangement, control and documentation of the sales activities are the most important tasks for the sales management. The sales management has to overcome the lack of reliable and up-to-date marketing data and the need for the establishment of a creative and flexible sales team.

The most important standardised documentation in sales control

- Customer visiting reports
- Customer satisfaction and opinion questionnaires
- Sales statistics for each salesman
- List of outstanding customers
- Income payment list
- Order income and total order backlog
- List of times of deliveries
- List of finished products in stock inventory and in transit
- Statistics of sold products in quantity, prices, profit margins, cost levels and competitiveness
- Price list for tailor-made additional packages
- Sales schedule per customer, market segment and salesman
- Granted discounts of the different market segments
- Analysis of warranty and repair cases
- List of exhibitions for visits to exhibitions and exhibition reports

Customer visiting reports and customer satisfaction

Visiting reports are one of the most important tools in market evaluation and sales control. They should be well structured and contain all general types of customer data including their turnover and size as the basis for the creation of a well-focused approach in the marketing and sales policy. In addition, it is important to collect and monitor intelligence about the major customers' products within his key markets and competitive environment. The evaluation of such data can give valuable hints on the present and future purchasing behaviour and decision-making process of consumers. Some general questions should figure out the customers' view on the suppliers' products and services. The visiting report can be concluded by some remarks on special requirements and the next steps of the business. Within the sales department there should be a computerised customer database covering important general information such as the customers' names and addresses, purchasing and visiting information as well as the agreed payment and delivery conditions. The external performance of the salesmen should occasionally be cross-checked to monitor customer satisfaction and opinion questionnaires should be filled in by some customers. The professional technical knowledge, presentation and sales competence, human competence and service orientation of the salesmen should be checked and monitored frequently. However, it will be hard for many good Chinese sales-people to get used to this. Sales structures in China are less formalised than in the West, and many sales staff have found their unique way of reaching their customers. Therefore, one should first give the sales people some freedom to show if they can perform what they promise. Later, their sales methods can be analysed and optimised.

Sales management and documentation

Further key data for sales management should be regularly collected, monitored and thoroughly documented by standardised lists. These recommended lists should comprise such data such as: customers outstanding payments, payment income, order income and total order backlog, times of delivery, finished products in stock and inventory in transit, analysis of warranty and repair cases, statistics of sold products in quantity, prices, profit margin, cost level and competitiveness. The price lists for tailor-made additional packages and the granted discounts of the different market segments are of further interest. The sales schedule per customer, market share and salesman also give valuable hints to a more focused product promotion, pricing and other general marketing activities as well as the establishment of a more result-oriented bonus system for the salesmen. Sales statistics for each salesman including key data such as the respective contract number, the sold product models, quantities with the granted discounts and price levels, help to control and follow up the performance database within the sales department. Travelling and customer invitation expenses should be broken down systematically on a daily basis for each type of expenditure such as accommodation, telecommunication, entertainment, tickets, stationery, gifts and others in order to keep an overview on budgeted cost levels. This increases people's regard and responsibility for costs of expenditures.

Internal and external sales activities

Regular sales meetings should be held and the topics well prepared. The monitored results and agreed plan of action schedule should fix information such as 'what to do by whom until when', including the order of priorities and remarks. The attendance of key exhibitions and the organisation of technical seminars for key customers should be well prepared and implemented according to an agreed strategy. The results of the interviews of exhibitions, customer visits and attended seminars should also be documented in suitable reports as a requisite for a more effective marketing plan. Competitors' product catalogues with price indications further support the analyses and establishment of an efficient sales and marketing policy. It can be of great interest to compare through a SWOT analysis the different marketing, product and service policies of the competitors in the market. This helps to define the most suitable target market segments.

Summary/Recommendations

In China, many companies start from scratch or very low local sales after the establishment of a local entity. Skilled sales-people must be found and well trained in sales skills and technological knowledge. The customer base is still relatively low and has to be developed step by step. The same applies to the image of a prospective brand. This sensitive task can only be solved through clearly defined and implemented sales plans. All sales activities should be well structured. The sales know-how and customer relationships must be systematically built up. This requires the collection of good and reliable sales data and information. Salesmen must collect and maintain this sales documentation as an important basis for success and efficiency in sales. Still, be prepared to give sales staff some freedom to work their own methods.

7.7. How should sales control be organised?

In China salesmen are used to working quite independently. The basic salary often amounts only to about 50 per cent of the total salary. The connections or relationships to customers and market players are their major personal asset, so they tend to keep market and customer information confidential, even at the cost of good teamwork. An adequate sales control system should be organised which takes into account the company's interests as well as the salesmens' personal preferences. A further critical point of sales control is connected to corruption within the sales and purchasing departments of key customers. Suitable measures and control mechanisms should be worked out to cope with that problem.

The most important control instruments
- Agreed route planning for the systematic visit of A, B and C customers.
- Reports on customer visiting with regular checks of all relevant customers' data.

- Data about turnover, sold quantities, average agreed discounts and payment income for each customer and overall.
- Installation of an efficient anti-corruption control system.

Important tools for sales control

The cost and time efficiency of salesmen must be frequently controlled, bearing in mind that they also require enough freedom to arrange individual business decisions quickly and flexibly. An agreed route planning is important with regards to the efficient penetration of new A, B and C-sized customers. Salesmen tend to visit smaller B or C customers more often. There they can negotiate more easily with decision-makers and get quicker sales contracts. 'A' customers require much more effort, cost, time and more specific product and market competence. For such reasons, they can only be penetrated in longer timeframes through regular visits of the salesman and by additional support through higher-ranking representatives of the company. The agreed route planning must be cross-checked after each business trip. Many salesmen tend not necessarily to visit all agreed customers and report only fragments of their business trip. Many are reluctant to produce clear, structured business reports with all the marketing and sales data which are required for a more systematic market approach. Therefore, the reporting procedure should be standardised with all marketing and customer-related information. This enables the management to have an efficient cross-check of the salesmens' activities and a respective overview on the market. Agreements on compensation packages with bonus payments should also be dependent on the submitting of such reports. Otherwise, the required time for the controlling and promoting of the salesmen may be too large.

Corruption in sales and purchasing

The problem of corruption may take many forms such as trading of influence and favours or approaching sales personnel to share their commissions with purchasing officers or even direct theft. It is possible to combat and eliminate or at least greatly reduce corruption within an organisation within China; external elimination is much harder. Action is required to match these practices in a company. Often the purchasing officers expect some reward for placing significant orders. They are aware that the salesmen will receive commissions and they expect this to be shared with them either in cash or in kind. The final purchase decision may be decided purely on the largest 'kick-back'. The finance department is often aware of and involved in the major scams in an organisation. Often the finance manager is the 'bag person' handling the distribution of the financial 'benefits' of any major corruption activities. These benefits are usually shared with the most senior Chinese management team. Other areas where the finance department can be directly involved in corrupt activities include all areas where cash is required, debt collection and payment prioritisation. In case of suspicion, it is important first to identify areas of major corruption. Then loyal staff should be identified and installed in all sensitive areas. The company must decide to eliminate corruption and work for full support of the shareholders, the board and key senior managers. In corruption cases, key personnel involved should be dismissed straight away. Strategic staff replacement could include the sales director and his key sales managers or purchasing manager. Even in such serious cases you should not be afraid to lose key account people. Everybody can be replaced, at least in medium term. Good internal communication and control should enforce the anti-corruption campaign.

Summary/Recommendations

It is difficult to properly check the work and attitude of sales-people in detail. The management must regularly check whether they follow a consequent route planning and how they spend money for travelling expenses or customer invitations. Sometimes it is also necessary to cross-check that they do no work for their own profit or for some other competitor's products. Trusting is good, but controlling is better. Efficient anti-corruption measures should be installed. Some reference ratio can be used to evaluate the performances of each salesman. However, it is also recommended that the senior management regularly visit customers to find out their opinion of the visits of sales-people. Sales people should be regularly trained in sales and product-related know-how to improve their results and efficiency in work.

Further source

Salzer, A. (2000) 'Recruiting and Managing a Distribution Workforce', in Moser, M. (ed.) *China Troubleshooter*, Chapter 4, pp. 69ff, HK, Asia Law & Practice.

7.8. What are the most critical terms and conditions in co-operation with distributors?

Most manufactured or imported products in China have also to be distributed on the domestic market. The local distributors are one of the most important channels for the selling of products. This especially applies for the penetration of medium- and smaller-sized end users in the case of quite standardised products. In most cases such distributors, dealers or wholesalers are privately run enterprises with fairly localised business relationships with the end users. Distributors in China usually compete fiercely with each other, but are also in close communication with each other in the case of overlapping interests. Therefore, it is important for the manufacturer to define clearly for the distributors the range and scope of activities as well as the terms of co-operation in general. However, such contracts should be aimed at equality and mutual benefit.

The most important features in contracts with distributors

- The length of validity and extent of terms should be fixed.
- The nationality and language of the dispute regulation should be mentioned as well as the applied regulations and laws.
- The agreement should remain valid in the case of the correcting of smaller modifications.
- Matters concerned with but not yet included in the contract can be further negotiated.
- Fixing of signed copies.

Note: Details should be worked out with renowned law or management consulting firms.

The co-operation between the manufacturer and distributors only succeeds when the agreed terms of contract such as the prices, discounts and product-related services are suitable to the market requirements within the competitive environment. The reputation and professional qualification of the potential distributors should be checked thoroughly and improved by intensive training programmes where required. While this is standard procedure in western countries, it is a relatively new concept in China and should be given enough time. It also plays an important role in evaluating the potential distributor's range of competitive products, which he sells. In the case of a distributor switching to a new supplier, his reasons for it must be checked. Questions should be answered concerning the sales volumes in the past, high level of outstanding debts to former suppliers or the qualification of his key staff; there may be former fiscal or other problems.

Both parties' objectives for the co-operation should be clearly defined. The sales regions should be fixed and the marketing policy agreed. Exclusivity should only be granted in connection with agreed specific sales figures. However, the planned and negotiated sales quantities, prices and turnover levels should be based on realistic assumptions under special consideration of the competitive environment. The used price list and applied discount policy, bonus payments and general terms of payment must be agreed. The granted discounts may depend on the sales quantity. The payment of transport cost and packaging should be fixed. However, there should be no doubt that the final sales prices to the end users are dependent on competition with well-known price and quality levels. Well-branded premium products may only permit a mark-up of approximately 10–20 per cent.

After-sales services and spare parts must be guaranteed as well as the granted warranty periods. The distributors' staff must be trained in the product and market features to convince the consumers more effectively. Technical and advertising material should be supplied in sufficient quantities. The means of media, seminars, shop design and displayed exhibits and samples should be agreed. The cost of after-sales services on behalf of the supplier should be paid at an agreed expenditure level. The distributor is recommended to appoint specific people to be in charge of the supplier's products and after-sales services. Such service and maintenance people should be trained and qualified in the suppliers' factory for a sufficient period of time. The distributors' technical staff have to pre-check and report back on the technical problems from the consumers' end. Smaller repairs of the products should be done on behalf of the supplier. More serious cases should be handled through the supplier's service people. The distributor should defend the supplier's high reputation and benefits by serving well. In many sectors, Chinese distributors are reluctant to give information about their strategies. Sometimes, it can be hard to find out if products have been sold at all.

It is advisable to:

- try out several distributors and trace their channels;
- constantly check the stability of distribution channels;
- use modern software solutions for organisation (such as EDI- web solutions by GEDAS or others).

Summary/Recommendations

Distributors are one of key sales channels for most of manufacturers. This applies to domestic manufactured products as well as to imported ones. Thus, the way of dealing with them most efficiently and properly is of major significance. Terms of contract are fairly similar to international standards. Conditions of co-operation should be solved more individually. The level of product and sales competence as well as the relationship and service network must be checked for each potential dealer. Existing deficits should be eliminated through additional training and other measurements. The co-operation should be developed on a basis of mutual benefit. This is a good basis for a long-lasting and successful business relationship.

7.9. How can I find and keep good salesmen?

The hardest point of most business activities in China is the difficult penetration of customers with respectable sales volumes and acceptable profit margins, those that urgently need to establish a profitable business. This task requires the establishment of an excellent sales team. However, the good and best salesmen on the market are difficult to find and to hire into a newly established or not yet well-known brand company.

The most important features to attract good salesmen

- Corporate identity
- Attractive salary and bonus systems
- Special non-monetary benefits
- Additional skills and functional training in the foreign headquarters
- Good relationships to key opinion leaders and decision-makers on the market

Finding good salesmen is not an easy task. The company must have a good reputation with attractive salaries including a good personnel development strategy. The location is as important as the type of management in the company. The better salesmen can be attracted by recommendations from competitors, distributors, suppliers, customers or opinion leaders in the company or similar branch. Networking with university departments and research institutes, national business associations, employment organisations and the Chinese joint venture partner are further quite successful alternatives for the sourcing of qualified and reliable sales-people. This is increasingly being used by major domestic companies. Some evening newspapers or talent markets are also suitable sources for recruitment, although not necessarily for the more qualified or specialised experts. For management-level positions it may make sense to involve a domestic or international recruitment or headhunting firm or to use good connections to local personnel service firms such as FESCO. Special and long-lasting relationships to the leadership of FESCO may also help to secure the best people beforehand. The same applies to graduates from premium business schools like the SEIBS. Their sponsors have the right for first interviews. The sales team should be a mixture of graduates from well-known universities and more experienced people. The background and age can also differ within the team. Some OEM customers require more technical background regarding the products and distributors pay more attention to the negotiation skills of the sales staff. Both types of qualifications are required.

The compensation package should be attractive enough to get and keep the best sales-people on the market. The remuneration system depends on the social status, educational background and personal interest of the various people. The payment of interesting basic salaries, attractive bonuses with commission elements and incentive packages are quite important. In China living costs are high; standard salaries are low and experienced salesmen are still rare. Consequently, the bonus system must be good enough to attract in the long term the best performance from the salesmen. In general, the package should be defined, performance-oriented, easily understood, transparent and be accepted by the sales team in order to promote harmony and teamwork. In practice, most companies pay a basic salary of approximately 50 per cent of the total payment package; the rest is dependent on the performance. However, the compensation package also depends on the specific industry and varies between 15–500 per cent. Several industry specific salary surveys are available for information.

Summary/Recommendations

Attracting good or excellent sales-people requires a good corporate identity, a competitive salary and a compensation package. However, for many high potentials, the non-monetary benefits are more important than the purely monetary ones. Further skills training in combination with business trips to foreign headquarters are attractive as much as a bonus system depending on sales volume. Good relationships with important opinion leaders in the branch also help when looking for valuable people. Therefore, the creation of both a positive image and a corporate identity is very important (see also Chapters 3 and 4.2).

7.10. What is the best kind of training for salesmen?

Young, experienced and dynamic sales-people with a proven success record, who understand how to present and sell successfully high-quality products at premium prices and good profit margin to a Chinese customer are quite rare. This applies especially if such sales-people are required also to explain technical details and product features. In fact, such superior people are seldom to be found in the sales department of any headquarters. Therefore, it is more appropriate primarily to look for motivated high potentials and to train them extensively to achieve the required knowledge as quickly as possible. Some soft parts of the training can be outsourced to one of the experienced training providers in China; the more product-related part should be done by in-house experts.

The most important requirements for good sales-people

- Product knowledge (technology and application)
- Presentation and negotiation skills
- Service and customer orientation
- Proper outfit
- Intercultural understanding

Knowledge of the product is very important; without it Chinese salesmen, who have not yet sold high-quality products, may have difficulties in understanding and convincing the customer. Chinese products often are only sold on a price basis, but not on the quality, efficiency and service. This is counter-productive, however, in the sale of high-quality products. Therefore, such training is very important for the salesmen. Knowledge and product skills can be taught by in-house experts in China or from the headquarters' main production or training facilities abroad. Presentation and negotiating skills are also very important for convincing customers of the advantageous features of the products and the image of the company. Such skills may lead to a higher premium price of 10–15 per cent above comparable products. However, customer satisfaction and convenience in application and service should be monitored regularly in order to maintain high levels.

The attire of the salesmen is also an issue in China. Two-thirds of the representatives of state owned companies and distributors as well as many salespeople of joint ventures do not wear proper western suits with a tie. It depends to some extent on the business and the situation of the customer, which one is most appropriate, but wearing a proper outfit helps in many cases to make a better impression and improve success in sales. However with China's sometimes rather casual dress codes, overdressing can also have the opposite effect, leading to estrangement rather making a good impression.

There are several external training providers on the market who specialise in courses for marketing and sales. It is important to train in Chinese and that the trainers have enough comprehension of the subject and experience; the right mixture between the western and Chinese professional method of selling is important. Western professional salesmen also require many years of experience and understanding of the products and markets before they become successful. Western sales professionalism is for the most part more important than knowing the Chinese intercultural habits, as the products present western technology. On the other hand, purchasing departments are also becoming more and more professional; customers already know quite well what they want. Going to karaoke bars with clients and joining in is quite acceptable.

Summary/Recommendations

A successful business requires a well-trained and competent sales team. These highly skilled sales-people are difficult to find. The best potentials must be found on the market and trained to fulfil the needed profiles and requirements. Meanwhile, several sources for recruitment are available in China as well as a wide selection of training providers with good references and reputation. The human resources department must create a concept of how to systematically recruit and develop new high potentials (see also Chapter 4).

7.11. What are the common payment conditions and guarantees?

The final fixed and agreed prices of a concluded deal depend to a large extent on the overall competitive situation of the market. The market price has to be accepted by the customer. Often there is much more time spent in negotiating suitable payment conditions. The purchaser wants to keep his limited funds in his own hands as long as possible to avoid paying interest on short-term bank loans. Sometimes he may even hope to be released from paying the final rate of payment at a later date. The seller wants to be sure that he actually receives the whole of the agreed purchasing price without risking losing money due to the fact that there are only very limited legal possibilities for money collection. Importers to China can use 'letters of credit', but these cannot be used by domestic businesses. The question of common payment conditions and possible guarantees is quite important in doing business in China.

The most important questions concerning payment
- What are the common payment conditions?
- What payment guarantees are common?
- How can I recognise a customer's credit-worthiness and attitude towards payment?

What are the common payment conditions?

Payment conditions depend very much on the nature of the business and customer. The main problem is the weak legal system for collecting outstanding money in China. Therefore, the payment conditions should usually be very strict for smaller or first-time customers. Best-selling products should be kept in stock until the customer has his money ready. It is quite common to do business based on cash against delivery. For specialist or less popular products, it is recommended to ask for down-payments of 10–30 per cent of the contract price. The payment terms may include a penalty for late or not-collected goods. The penalty may be based on a daily, weekly or monthly basis but should be limited to maximum of 5 per cent of the value of the goods.

Providers of normal commodity goods should ask for full payment on collection. Larger projects, or plants and equipment for projects with one-off customers are more difficult to handle. Payment terms are fixed according to preliminary steps of completion. An average rate of 5–10 per cent of the total value is frequently held back by the customer as a guarantee. In China, it normally takes a long time to get this huge amount of money. There may be long-lasting complaints and discussions before full payment is received. Often, some part of the money is lost. Therefore, the profit margin should be calculated and negotiated high enough to compensate, or some type of bank guarantees should be received.

Similar difficulties may arise with larger-sized OEM customers. State owned companies in particular suffer permanently through shortage of liquidity. Their required quantities are relatively high, therefore, they tend to squeeze the supplier as much as possible for credit and delayed payment conditions. Sometimes, the supply of the products even have to be stopped in order to press for more payments. For such reasons, it is important that a supplier doesn't depend too much on a few larger-sized customers. Companies with very late payment policies are mostly known in the market. They should be dealt with by arrangements for 'cash against delivery' payments. The situation can be also improved by more frequent and smaller quantities of supplies.

What payment guarantees are common?

Regarding debt collection matters, caution is always recommended. If in doubt, it is better to ask for full payment before delivery. The payment terms must have priority over all other conditions. The general business terms should be fixed. It is recommended that you consult a lawyer for the fixing and the standardising of such terms. A reminder system should be set up. This is uncommon in some companies. The finance department should issue the first reminder and the general manager the second one. The credit-worthiness of the customer should be checked thoroughly. Addresses for such information are available at the Chamber of Commerce or at the company's bank. Experiences with 'sconto' payments are not yet developed to a great extent, as payments are not necessarily done after invoicing. The delivered goods should be of the correct quantity and quality in order to avoid reasons for late payments (i.e. 100 pieces ordered, but only 99 delivered).

Bank guarantees are difficult to get in China unless the good reputation or convincing performance figures of a company are obvious. For import business the opening of a L/C is still quite common. Larger companies can issue cheques such as *chengdui huipiao*, a cheque with guaranteed payment through the bank, for domestic business. The agreed cashing date can be fixed. Such cheques can also be used immediately; interest can be paid up till the cashing date. There also exist *shangye huipiao*, trade cheques without a cashing guarantee through the bank. Such a type of cheque is only cashed by the bank when enough money is available in the bank account. However, heavy penalties may have to be paid by the issuing company if the cheque is handed over to bank by the due date but payment of the amount cannot be honoured. Such possible troubles may also have a bad impact on the business relationship with the customer. Larger-sized companies may negotiate complicated finance or leasing agreements with the customer and his house bank and/or a third party leasing company. This especially applies for larger projects or respected imported goods. In such cases the financing banks or institutions issue the guarantees and bear the risks.

How can I recognise the credit-worthiness?

At the beginning of a business relationship, one should insist on payment guarantees. Alternatively, other benefits for the customer should be negotiated such as deliveries in smaller quantities or better discounts. Information on credit-worthiness can be obtained through good relationships with local or international banks in China. Some trust companies and banks specialise in searching for such information. Other market players are also a good source of such information, such as customers, suppliers, competitors, business associations or other opinion leaders in the market. In any case it is always better to minimise bad debts from the beginning as described more in detail in chapter 7.12.

Summary/Recommendations

Questions about suitable payment conditions and guarantees are common and frequently under consideration in each entity. A customer's credit-worthiness and attitude towards payment have a huge impact on the success or failure of business development. Most entities know their special customers and are used to their way of tackling such problems. Establishing some kind of guarantee is recommended, especially in the beginning of a business relationship. There are also some external sources able to provide information about the reputation of a customer.

Further source

Baker & McKenzie (2001) *Operation China, An Investor's Manual*, HK.

7.12. How do I handle debtors and customers who are not willing to pay?

The collection of bad debts or outstanding payments for delivered goods is one of the main headaches when doing business in China. The legal possibilities are quite limited. It is also difficult to get the outstanding money with officially received writs from the court. Debtors who are unwilling to pay often find some creative way to shift their money to safer havens before the creditors finally succeed. For such reasons, even the banks are quite conservative with their credit line policies and they have strict policies regarding reliable guarantees. Therefore, companies must also be quite cautious in dealing with customers who have a reputation for bad payment. There are always some flexible solutions in dealing with customers who are frequently in lack of liquidity. Bad payment habits can be overcome by some 'Chinese ways' of dealing to success-fully collect money.

The most important questions
- How do I handle debtors and customers who are not willing to pay?
- How do I sue customers for the collection of bad debts?
- What are the chances of receiving such outstanding money?

How do I handle debtors and customers who are not willing to pay?

First of all, the reasons for the bad payment record of a customer should be checked. One major reason might be that there is no money available. How-ever, quite often it is just a bad payment habit, which was quite common during the former planned economy times, when payments were not so important. In other cases, the customer's employee may act according to the principle that it is good for his company not to pay or to delay. There are some practical ways to overcome such a problem. Most common are incentives for the salesmen or debt collector in charge of collecting outstanding money. If there are any expatriates, contacts with western business partners can also be helpful. The engagement of a lawyer and possible legal case is very costly and time-consuming and bears some risks. The case may last up to one year without a final guarantee that the payments will be made in spite of a legal order from the court. Therefore, all possibilities of minimising bad debt levels should be used, such as doing investigate work early by checking the company's credit history, using credit reporting agencies and credit reports or just collecting payments before delivery of goods and services. It is also important to ensure that the sales contracts cover payment in sufficient detail. Selling and/or credit terms should be clearly stated including possible provisions for penalties and time limits for payments. Provisions for repossession of the goods in case of late or non-payment should also be included, specifying the same name in the sales contract as mentioned in the company's business licence. It is essential to operate a proper billing procedure with the use of detailed sales invoices and delivery notes that include the name/type, quantity, specification, and price of goods and to ensure that the customer acknowledges delivery with its company stamp. In case of future disputes it is also important to keep and file all documentation and correspondence including regular reminders which have been sent out. The installation of a special debt collection team to monitor and possibly to chase the company's debts sometimes also helps to smoothout the problem. It may help to motivate the customer to pay in time by offering attractive incentives or extra bonus arrangements to him. A branch-specific and flexible payment system can be also a further attractive tool to avoid judicial action.

How do I sue customers for the collection of bad debts?

Involving a lawyer is only a realistic option for a relatively high outstanding amount or if several cases can be handled by one lawyer. The cost of lawyers, court procedures, wine and dine invitations for involved officials and time-consumption of one's own staff in charge or losses through final compromises means that it is only financially viable to pursue more serious cases where you have a very strong position. In many cases, a received order from the court cannot be cashed; the debtor may put all money into other unknown bank accounts after a deal with his bank, he may sell or transfer fixed legal assets to other persons or even just disappear to an unknown address.

In future, Chinese banks may become even stricter in their loan policy for Chinese companies. It is assumed that the quantity of circled money will be reduced. The extensive reform of state owned companies has led to mergers and dissolution of companies. The big question now is: what will happen about outstanding debts? Some creditors try to limit the financial impact of bad debts by issuing invoices later with delay. They can also postpone the payment of VAT. However, each company should fix clear procedures on how to proceed with bad debts. It is important to prepare all documents well according to the law. The debtor should not find arguments for delayed payments in his hands, such as missing documents, bad quality or wrong quantities of delivered products. Since December 2000, the Security Law of the People's Court has been enforced to cope with such problems. Granted guarantees by a bank or business partner are legally safer now. In the past contracts between parties often included few details and were frequently unclear about the duration of the guarantee. Now contracts are more clear and binding, if both parties have signed or a business deal has been entered into. The legal requirement for the final payment of the main and associated costs of a contract is limited to a maximum of two years now. A specialised law firm should be consulted if there are additional details or special circumstances.

What are the chances of receiving such outstanding money?

First, all legal documents such as the official contract (*hetong*), the taxable invoice (*Zhengshui Fapiao*) and the receipts of delivery (*yunhuodan*) must be handed over to the customer in order to legalise the business. After some overdue time, several written and phone reminders for payment should follow. The responsible salesman should make several visits to the debtor and try to urge the payment. After reaching the credit limit, further deliveries and services should be stopped and further pressure should be put on the debtor. A sitting-out policy may be the appropriate next step. One employee should visit the debtor on a daily basis and keep contact with all the respective departments to put constant pressure on them. Professional sitting-out people can be also hired on the market. Sending a young lady may influence the payment approval of the general manager. Alternatively, an elderly lady could follow the clear order to persistently stay for days or weeks until money is received. Some limited success may arise in case of visits of expatriates or by offering gifts to the responsible persons. Counter-trade business makes sense only in a few cases or special circumstances.

The next step of pressure may be the involvement of a lawyer. However, success depends very much on the availability of money or other fixed assets which could be auctioned to cover debts. In serious cases where higher debit amounts are involved, professional money collection firms can be engaged. They receive a special agreed percentage on the refunding money (10–30 per cent) or work on an hourly cost basis. However, such 'money collection' firms are illegal. None of them describes themselves as being in the 'money collection' business. A further effective alternative for money collection is the co-operation and information exchange with competitors.

Professional bodies

The Sinotrust Business Risk Management Company is engaged in credit management, payment management and business information. They are specialised in pre-legal activities before litigation. For this purpose they employ 100 people for the writing of company reports. Their data basis covers more than 50,000 Chinese companies, 90 per cent of all companies with an annual turnover of more than RMB 1 million. Each year 25,000 credit reports are added. Further credit rating companies are Dagong Global Credit Assessment in co-operation with Moody's Investors Service and China Changxin Security Assessment with a joint venture with partners China Commercial & Industrial Times Development Corporation, Fitch IBCA and International Financial Corporation.

Summary/Recommendations

Most operating entities sooner or later have to face the question of how to handle debtors and customers who will not pay. If several visits by sales employees and reminders do not help, the question of suing the customer for the collection of bad debts arises. The next question is to evaluate the chances of receiving the outstanding money and the risks of writing it off. However, China has many straight and indirect, formal and informal ways of achieving good results. Do not give up and write debts off too early; it is often a question of time, depending on how much pressure is put on the debtor. He should be squeezed step by step and then more seriously if he has money but refuses to pay. Nevertheless, the soft and patient alternative of putting pressure on him is more likely to be successful. When you build up business experience on the market, you will get to know the customers with a bad payment reputation; with them, the most successful business relationship is based on 100 per cent cash payments against product deliveries. Flexibility should only stretch to special additional discounts in case of full payment on delivery; any term of late payment should be not accepted.

Further sources

Baker & McKenzie (2001) *Operation China, An Investor's Manual*, HK.
German Business Association (ed.) (2000) 'The New Security Law', in *China Contact*, no. 4, Düssuldorf, p. 22.

8

What are the Most Relevant Production-related Issues?

Engelbert Boos

8.1. Which product-related standards have to be respected?

In China, customers often find poor-quality products. This is not only the case with many local products, but also for imported ones, especially if these come from other Asian countries. Only a few companies have enough experience to judge quality questions and to realise an effective total quality management (TQM). In order to support the manufacturers as well as their customers, special, full or partly state owned organisations have been established to set China-specific product standards.

Some reasons for China to set up its own standards

- Improvement of production processes.
- Promoting user-friendly products, which are produced in an ecologically and economically sustainable way.
- Guarantee that China-specific product design requirements are respected.
- Protecting the consumers and providing some transparency.
- Making money by implementing own obligatory Chinese product standards.
- Protection of its own industries.

There are few major types of standards

- CE and GS standards and their Chinese equivalents.
- Environmental management systems and ISO 14001 certification.
- ISO 900x standards for the improvement of production processes.
- Branch-specific standards (i.e. automotive industrial standard VDA 6.1).

Some reasons for China to set up its own standards

Many Chinese companies do not have the latest know-how in production and want to save money by producing in the cheapest way. Therefore, China has a big interest in improving and optimising their production processes to world market standards. They aim to increase the domestic and international competitiveness of their companies. The government also wants to make sure either by law or by standards from design institutes, that products will be user-friendly and are ecologically and economically sound. China-specific circumstances must be taken into consideration in product design, e.g. shortage of space in big cities makes low-noise-making machines necessary and space-saving products.

It is also important to protect consumers and to provide some transparency in the various markets as Chinese customers do not have enough experience and knowledge about certain products yet. Therefore, design institutes test products, check whether the instruction manuals are understandable and give recommendations on products with a reasonable price/performance relation and so on. Further motivations are the granting of some kind of protection for local Chinese products in the Chinese markets and opposing western standards like DIN or ASME, that also often prevent Chinese products from entering the western markets. This conflict will improve considerably now with China's joining of the WTO.

The objective of making money by implementing one's own obligatory Chinese product checks can sometimes also play a role. In 1998, for example a new regulation was published and implemented that meant international pressure vessel certificates for imports would be not accepted any more. They charged each importing manufacturer approximately 30,000 US dollars for the application procedures, including testing, inspection and permission. Within the last few years, however, China has made great efforts to adjust to worldwide standards and norms. They actualise their standards and regulations on a regular basis in order to meet current technical levels. As China wants to become an acknowledged export nation, they try hard to be up-to-date with international quality standards.

There are three major sets of standards

CE standards and their Chinese equivalents ensure that the use of products is not dangerous to consumers. The most prominent Chinese label in this field is the 'Great Wall' label. So far it appears on all electrical products that are sold in the Chinese market. It means the product has been checked according to rules on the low voltage norm. Soon the 'Great Wall' label will be replaced by the CCIB label that is already used for cross-border trade; products currently exported to China need the CCIB label. There are, however, relatively severe conditions to fulfil in order to get this label; audits are requested from the original place of manufacture plus other hassles. The *GS* label signifies the electrical and mechanical safety of a product. The product certification deter-mines whether a prototype meets the legal safety regulations and standards of a respective country.

Environmental management systems and *ISO 14001 certification* are required as the Chinese government insists more and more strictly on compliance with environmental protection. The observance of the ISO 14001 principles is of enormous importance for companies that produce in China. The introduction of the ISO 14001 system lasts in average one to two months, the related documentation around three to six months and the testing period about three months.

ISO 900x standards are awarded for the best production processes. All steps in production and related supporting departments are clearly defined and documented in a handbook. The ISO 9001 standards cover the areas of research and development, construction, production and quality inspection procedures. The ISO 9002 standard covers production and quality control and the ISO 9003 standard is related to the end control of products. In China there are already some companies that have an ISO9000 certification. Productivity can be increased noticeably by introducing this system. Many globally operating customers are insisting on the implementation of such ISO9000 quality assurance standards throughout the whole value added chain including their suppliers from China. Some international certifying companies such as Lloyds Register, TÜV Rhine and TÜV Bavaria have already established subsidiaries in China where professional advice is offered. Arising costs can be divided into costs for manpower and equipment that has to be bought as well as for out of pocket expenses and other fees for the certifying institution. Eventually additional fees may arise for consultants.

Product warranty

Quality management and product warranties are increasingly important issues for companies in China in order to improve competitiveness and customer satisfaction as well as to reduce the risks of liability in general. Product warranties also play a critical role in the localisation and local sourcing activities within China. The Chinese government enforced the product warranty law for manufacturers, dealers and quality inspection authorities in December 2000, due to huge product quality problems on the market in the past. The new law also better fits the WTO requirements. The rights and compensation packages for injured people have been expanded and the penalties for damages in the case of poor-quality products increased. Now, it is even possible to confiscate poor-quality products or to withdraw them from sale. In more serious cases the manufacturer may even lose his business licence. The required information on products such as a list of ingredients and quantities are enforced too. The inspection bureau is now authorised to publish results of poor-quality products and to close specific production lines until requested quality improvements are made. However, the inspection bureau is no longer allowed to invoice for their inspection work, to participate in product advertisement seminars or to recommend single products in order to secure independence. This code of the inspection bureau is also subject to legal penalty in case of violation.

Safeguard quality and security risks

Purchasing in China requires some experience and local presence to safeguard the right relationship of price and quality as well as a smooth execution of the supplies. Quality control is particularly important. It is recommended to have somebody in China to avoid products with faked certificates and to cross-check the originality of products in order to prevent or minimise later claims or damages of the image. Private consultants, the German TÜV agencies or the English Lloyds organisation can help to assure such quality and security checks. An installed 'import management system' further supports manufacturers and purchasers in quality and safety issues. Such a management system covers the whole purchasing process including the search for the right supplier, the manufacturing and certification of prototypes, the issuing of CE (electrical products) or LMGB (for products with contact to food) standards. Further services are related to product and manufacturing quality questions, inspection and evaluation of the supplier's manufacturing facilities and raw materials as well as packaging and transportation of the finished products.

Summary/Recommendations

There are good reasons for China to set up quality standards for products and production facilities in line with other countries. The interests and safety of the consumers must be protected; regulations have to be defined and implemented. Management and employees must be motivated to accept and obey such product quality standards. A successful manufacturing and total quality management system is characterised by the strong commitment of all employees. In China, there are about 20 consultants who can help you with the ISO 14001 and ISO 900x issuance and 40 official auditors. Only local certification institutes are permitted to operate in China so far.

Further sources

German Business Association (2000) *China Contact*, 6, p. 12.
German Business Association (2000) *China Contact*, 10, p. 42.

8.2. How do I define and run a reasonable product policy?

The definition of the product policy is a very important factor for success in entering the Chinese market. Only the most suitable technologies and competitively priced products and services have real a chance for success within the dynamic market environment of China. Obsolete technologies and resulting poor services or too-high prices may be not accepted by enough customers to maintain an economically viable market this is likely to have an adverse effect on the company's development. Later changes to completely different products require a lot of time and further investments. Therefore, market analysis for the most suitable product range should be done carefully.

The most important criteria for the formulation of a suitable product policy

- Analyse the existing market.
- Do a SWOT analysis of your own products and services.
- Analyse potential customers and whether there is really a market for your products.
- Provide the most technologically advanced products.
- Calculate carefully whether you can compete at the relevant price-level.
- React quickly and flexibly to customer requests.
- Check the most important factors for success.
- Build up a reasonable service network.

It is important to consider several steps and aspects for defining and running a reasonable product policy in the Chinese market.

Analyse the existing market

An analysis of the existing market includes local Chinese products as well as products from western or other Asian countries.

SWOT analysis of own products and services

A SWOT analysis of own products and services means to define the *Strengths* and *Weaknesses* of your own products and services and the *Opportunities* and *Threats* they are confronted with. Compare with products and services of main competitors.

Analyse potential customers and whether there is really a market for your product

It is important to figure out which customers buy what kinds of products and why they buy these products. Are there price or quality issues that play a major role in their decision processes or is there a special *guanxi* (personal relationship) between a customer and a supplier that competes with your own products in the market? Based on this information and the consideration of your own individual strengths, careful analysis should be carried out as to whether there is really a market for the products or not. Can an innovative product be launched? Do you face very tough competition? The product and marketing policy have to be defined according to these results.

Provide the most technologically advanced products

If a new product is launched, it should be the most technologically advanced product. If possible and necessary – according to the results of the market investigation – try to adapt it for the special needs of the Chinese market or particular market segments. China-specific issues should be considered, ergonomic factors, special eating habits, drinking, dressing etc., but also ecological and economical issues that are different from the western standards. Generally, it is important to be aware that the Chinese are pretty well informed about the products that are sold in western countries so don't offer products that have already become obsolete in the West. China customers look for top quality at a competitive price. This is especially true for investment and industrial products.

Calculate carefully whether you can compete with the relevant price-level

Before you start to launch a product you have to calculate very carefully whether you can compete with the relevant price-level that is offered in the market segment you want to penetrate. Many projects fail for this reason. Often it takes time to learn about market price levels and to reduce your own costs by higher quantities and better market acceptance of the products; market share will then increase, but prices must be right from the beginning.

React quickly and flexibly to customer requests

If an investor has decided in enter a special segment of the Chinese market, he should act quickly and be target-oriented. China is one of the world's most competitive markets with harsh rules of competition. Act according to the Chinese saying 'The early bird catches the worm.'

The most important factors in order to succeed

Pricing that is competitive with local suppliers is crucial in the Chinese market. Western companies are normally strong in the service quality and the service network; after-sales service, spare parts or delivery makes the difference between good and 'ordinary' companies. Chinese clients in general are not used to the highly sophisticated extras that Western target groups expect, but they like to get reliable and effective support in case of any trouble related to the products they buy. They don't care whether the problems are caused by themselves or by the nature of the product; typical problems include the wrong use of a product, lack of knowledge on how to install an investment-related product or consumer durables or on how to integrate it in their own production processes.

Many customers are even willing to pay more than the actual market price to get a good service. The operating instructions and user manuals for investment goods or consumer durables should take account of the fact that Chinese clients often don't have the same level of technical background as the average western client. Therefore, it's important to explain the use of the products in more detail and also to consider China-specific issues. Western companies often deliver a very poor Chinese translation of the English instruction manuals; this gives the Chinese client the feeling that they are not very important to the company. The western enterprise must put in enough effort in order to avoid difficulties for the client.

Build up a reasonable service network

In order to build up a reasonable service network in China the possibility of integrating a certain amount of local input into the production processes should be considered. A production line in China – at least on a CKD level (Complete Knocked Down) of production – could provide various other advantages like the possibility of invoicing in RMB and the production of smaller quantities. Stocked products improve the delivery times with the advantage that the spare parts and repair services are quicker. Application engineers, tailor-made solutions and people with local language abilities for better communication with the customers promote customer satisfaction.

Summary/Recommendations

The definition of the 'right product range' requires a preliminary analysis of one's own weaknesses and strengths compared to the competition. The market only accepts the right package of product, price and service. The better the market investigation and preparation of a production facility is, the more success is guaranteed. Obsolete models and technologies are no longer accepted by Chinese customers.

8.3. Which levels of product quality are feasible and saleable?

Many global manufacturers still think that they can just produce and sell obsolete technologies and products in China. They assume that the Chinese consumer follows a slow step by step development as the West has over the past several decades. However, in general, most consumers really want to switch from a bicycle straight to a car. Chinese consumers are well informed through aggressive western marketing campaigns and satellite television. Many of them have enough savings and funds to purchase even most expensive premium-quality products. Only people with low budgets or a lack of good information, for example from remote areas, still purchase lower-quality and cheaper products.

The most important sources of products

- Products from local Chinese companies.
- Products which are manufactured by joint ventures or WFOE.
- Imported premium products.

Products from local Chinese companies

The quality of local products is often still poor. Only some companies in each industrial branch or market segment have enough experience to judge quality questions and to do effective total quality management (TQM). Local Chinese companies often use components and raw materials of lower quality in order to save money and cash flow. Often, they can't afford production lines and machines that meet the latest technical developments. However, the situation is improving markedly; as higher-quality components are used and more experience is gained. More and more private Chinese companies are building new plant facilities on greenfield sites with good success. Many other companies with poor product, market and finance performance will disappear from the competitive marketplace.

Products manufactured by joint ventures or WFOE

For several years many foreign invested companies have undertaken huge efforts in the transfer of technology and management expertise to build up good-quality products, services and western management methods for business operations, marketing and sales. The achievement of market shares is of huge importance. However, these qualification measures require high investments and time to build up the experience curve. Therefore, such investments for the most part are only really profitable in medium to long term with quantities and brand awareness. The efficiency of a business operation can be improved by extending the product range and by building up supporting services for other of the company's products.

Imported premium products

A decade ago China still imported complete turnkey projects including all the equipment, machines and related engineering services. Today, no major project can be won without local content and localised co-operations. Otherwise, the costs are too high and the competitiveness too low. Former imports of whole systems are increasingly being replaced by imported premium components, which are required by the local OEM's (Own Equipment Manufacturers) customers. The pressure for localisation measures in production facilities is increasingly important in order to secure long-term success.

Summary/Recommendations

Before a decision to produce in China is made, the investor should be aware of which level of product quality he wants and can deliver. A detailed and reliable market investigation is required for a better understanding of consumer behaviour. The price and quality levels of each targeted market segment should be evaluated and estimates of quantities should be defined as a reliable base for the business plan. In China three major types of competing quality levels of products can be compared, comprising locally made, joint venture made and imported. The local and joint venture-made products are improving their quality levels rapidly, reducing the gap to the imported one. Such higher quality levels are essential for the even fiercer competition following China's entry to the WTO.

8.4. What manufacturing and assembly activities are suitable in China?

There are several important reasons for an investor to transfer manufacturing and assembly or service activities to China. The motivation may arise through cost reasons, on the special demands of customers and end-users or just by pressure from competitors. The transfer of such manufacturing and assembly activities should be planned carefully with long-term perspectives and implemented step by step. Such a project should also fit properly into an overall business development strategy.

Manufacturing and assembly activities for which transfer is advantageous

- Service- or application technology-oriented products
- Tailor-made products
- Locomotive effecting products
- Products with local cost advantages and good sales potential in China
- Products of strategic importance
- Internationalisation and the pressure to follow global customers
- Premium local and foreign investment customers that require key technological products and components
- Products with high import duties or high transportation costs
- Products which have lost competitiveness or profitability in western markets may still have some market potential in China
- Labour-intensive products with cost advantages

There are many reasons for the transfer of assembly or manufacturing activities to China. The individual circumstances of the company with its products and target markets can be decisive. There are many convincing reasons such as cost advantages, required related services or application technologies or just demand for tailor-made products. Locomotive effecting products of latest technological levels or with special application advantages which fit best to the special requirements of the Chinese market may also have good potential. This applies at least in long-term considerations. Products of strategic importance for end-users, such as the demand of global customers to follow them to their worldwide production facilities is sometimes a good reason. This applies especially to the automotive industry with their traditional high import duties and governmental pressure for quick localisation. Such products with high import duties or high transportation costs are often best suited for transfer to China. Another important reason may be to extend the lifespan of products which have lost competitiveness or profitability in western markets.

Summary/Recommendations

There are several convincing reasons for the transfer of assembly or manufacturing activities to China. It is of major importance to have a clear understanding of the individual reasons for such a strategic decision. A suitable product policy and marketing mix has to be worked out and checked against feasibility due to realistic implementation chances. The achievable cost and quality levels have to be combined with a competitive pricing and sales policy. A profound feasibility and market research study should clarify the market potential, saleable quantities and achievable market shares; then the transfer of such assembly or manufacturing activities is more likely to be successful.

Further source

Stevenson, W.J. (1999) *Production and Operations Management*, NY.

8.5. What are the major weaknesses in organisational controlling and production management?

Many FIEs (Foreign Invested Enterprises) in China were established in the mid-1990s from scratch and have since gathered extensive experience. The whole market has become more professional and put increased pressure on the participants. As a result, many FIEs now need to improve their efficiency and competitiveness. Organisation control and production management must be optimised in order to become more profitable by passing through a process of consolidation or restructuring. Flexibility, fast reactions and well-trained professional workers are essential for success.

Major internal weaknesses in operating a production entity

- Organisational problems
- Poor controlling
- Production management problems

Major weaknesses in organisational controlling and production management

Within the consolidation phase the efficiency of the organisation and production must be improved or even restructured in order to cope with the requirements of a growing company. It is important to prevent errors in inventories for raw materials, work in progress and finished goods. Such errors have to be rectified for both purchases and sales. Goods deliveries should be pre-numbered for later reference. The duties of the stock keepers should be segregated in order to minimise systematic mistakes in counting and valuing the stock. The reconciliation between the warehouse and the finance department is also a critical issue that often creates problems. Stock movements and quantity differences must be regularly documented and updated. Slow movers have to be written off; the Chinese GAAP allows one to write off a yearly 3 per cent of the stocked value.

The calculation of the real labour cost is important too, to define the right costs for the suitable pricing calculation in the sales department. The accruals for operational expenses (i.e. heating) or social benefits (i.e. retirement and welfare funds) or service fees should be well prepared according to the law. The existing and new fixed assets must be regularly recorded. Fixed assets should be serial numbered and classified in the right accounts. The amortisation and depreciation policy has to be optimised within the legal limits and possibilities.

Foreign denominated bank accounts should be translated on a monthly basis. Evidences of approval by the GM and appropriate department managers for expenses (i.e. bonuses and overtime or travelling lists and others) must follow a fixed procedure. Evidence and review of the production plan including quality control is also important. The evidence of sales reviews and receivable accounts analysis report are also significant. Approval and goods receipt notes for sales returns must be followed up. Over-or understatements should be avoided for any accounts, advances, payments owed or owing with customers and suppliers. The control of the narration for journal entries is also important. Payables denominated in foreign currencies should be registered with SAFE in time. The devaluation of RMB to foreign currencies position has to be adjusted on a monthly basis. Hedging is not possible in China. However, a few companies have recently managed to do so.

Initiation of a consolidating or restructuring process

The following important steps are required for the initiation of a consolidating or restructuring process:

- process mapping and process optimisation;
- set-up and optimisation of controlling measures;
- improvement of cost allocation and accounting;
- guaranteeing internal control systems;
- handling of cultural, organisational and personal barriers.

Professional management consulting or training firms can help in the application or implementation of such an analytical process.

Summary/Recommendations

Most entities established in the 1990s are working now on the improvement of operational efficiency. They are analysing their organisational weaknesses and building up more professional controlling measures. The control of their costs and the increase of the productivity levels and competitiveness of their products have first priority. In more serious cases even a major restructuring process of the whole entity could be required. The growing organisations also demand new and more experienced management staff in different functions in order to operate the entity more professionally. This is a challenging task for each investor (refer also to Chapter 10).

8.6. How can I optimise my local sourcing activities?

Local sourcing considerations and decisions have to be made by most of investors in China. An operative entity in China only really makes sense with a high degree of independence. This applies especially to production and purchasing. The average material costs or costs of sales easily amount to approximately 80 per cent of the total cost. The import costs are more or less one-third of the total material costs including risks of exchange rate fluctuations and other problems related to customs and transportation. Changes within the political and economical environment are also difficult to predict, especially with regard to a long-term base. Local sourcing is a major factor of success in strategic planning and operative implementation.

Major issues for consideration in local sourcing

- Local sourcing is of strategic importance for long-term business development in China.
- Finding suitable suppliers for achieving and maintaining reliability, quality and high technological standards of sub-supplies is a challenging task.
- Low quantities are a big problem for negotiating good prices on high-quality components and for cost efficiency and high quality levels for localisation decisions.

- Bribery must be minimised through control mechanisms.
- The contractual terms and issues are of increasing importance.

General situation

China is experiencing strong growth in export rates due to increasing global sourcing activities and the establishment of production platforms of international operating companies. Exports are growing especially for machinery and electrical equipment of medium technological quality levels. Exports are further promoted with the entry into the WTO, the liquidation of state owned monopolistic structures, increase in international competitiveness and the huge restructuring process within Chinese industry. Purchasing in China is an easy option for market entry of products. Experience can be gained regarding business practices, the competitive environment and the local sourcing of components. Such information can be used for strategic considerations. Suitable partners can be found at an early stage of co-operation; this can be also used for the promotion of your own sales and marketing activities.

Suitable products

Larger engineering and contracting projects in China require major equipment, machinery and components with a high percentage of local content. Restricted products with relatively high import duties, such as for the automotive, electrical or telecommunications industries are also quite suitable for local sourcing. Those industries must localise their products up to 80% within a few years. However, key and master components often still have to be imported from the headquarters, especially in the beginning. Cost efficiency and high quality levels are key issues for such decisions. The respective industries and sub-supplier markets have to be developed. The local sub-supplier market must be integrated and long-term relationships have to be built up. But, each supplier shouldn't rely for more than 30 per cent of his total production capacity on just one customer for its own safety reasons. Quality management according to QS ISO 900x is important, especially for production facilities of global players. Keeping a high quality level in the long term is also a big problem. Therefore, one's own experts should be installed into key positions to secure high-quality purchasing. The main problems in China are reliability, quality and the technological level of sub-supplies. Labour-intensive products may be most interesting, including products for the world market. Tax holiday arrangements for import/export business may support the competitive import of high-quality components. Sometimes it is recommended to help the sub-suppliers with their cost calculation and quality-control efforts in order to speed up the co-operation, because many local purchases for key parts are not competitive in price and quality. For such reasons, it is important to install a creative purchasing policy which meets the regulations of the joint venture contract of up to 80 per cent local content. In case of difficulties, a flexible purchasing solution might be to purchase through Hong Kong or Taiwan. These countries are considered part of China. The cost basis for such deliveries is approximately 5 per cent above world market prices. Local content parts in the electrical and electronic industry for instance, comprise up to 80 per cent iron sheets, frames, painting, packaging, steel, copper, aluminium for panel and raw materials for switches and transmitters. Some of these components and raw materials are still purchased through Taiwan and Hong Kong for quality reasons. However, such limiting factors will be of less importance now with entering the WTO.

Handling procedures in local sourcing

The major target of the purchasing department is to achieve lower costs than in the home country, preferably of up to 20–30 per cent. CKD imports are the benchmark for Chinese offers. However, low quantities are a big problem for negotiating good prices for high-quality goods. Problems may arise through high qualification costs for tools or models or in the case of products which are only available from one supplying factory. Cast iron products and tools for mechanical machining parts require high investment costs. This sometimes makes it difficult to initiate local sourcing projects. In many cases there are cheaper Asian sub-suppliers available. Target prices need to be up to 25 per cent lower than direct imports from the home country. Common payment terms are 10–15 per cent down payment and the rest as payment on supply.

Three-quarters of the German companies in China already purchase more than 60 per cent of their sub-supplies in China. However, the total value of such supplies is still much less than 60 per cent due to the poor quality of critical components, unreliability, transparency and flexibility of suppliers as well as too-long delivery times and too-high prices of particular products. It is a good idea to submit product specifications, together with samples, to the supplier to safeguard better understanding and to keep the required quality levels of proto-types and series products. The technical specifications and drawings should be in English, but it is even better to include a Chinese translation. However, DIN and DINISO specifications are not well known in China. Videos or pictures of the product or required production process also support better understanding and quicker procedures without too many questions. Bear in mind the need to balance the cost of production and the efforts for quality control. Personal relationships are still quite important in the supplying and purchasing business so the purchasing department must be controlled efficiently. The system of 'comparing three quotations' doesn't work in China. Bribery must be avoided by control mechanisms.

The purchasing process can be supported by experienced organisations such as GPS (Global Procurement Services). They are co-operating with the

Shanghai-based German Chamber of Commerce and take care of supplier search, auditing, job implementation, quality control and handling of complaints. A big problem is the frequent dynamic change on the market with subsequent difficulties in getting reliable information and market overview. Reliable suppliers may be found through recommendations, data banks and evaluations of the market. Local and central governments can be also involved in the purchasing policy, but they are fragmented and often in conflict of interest with each other. Other sources of information are exhibitions, business associations, authorities such as CCPIT and MOFTEC, local or international trading or import/export companies, research institutes and special magazines as well as few data banks such as Wan Fan Data (www.wanfangdata.com) or other Internet-based sources (see Chapter 5).

Legal and contractual considerations

China is becoming more and more important as an internationally competitive priced place for local sourcing. This applies especially in cases without their own production entities. The contractual relationship is quite important to secure and maintain high quality, competitive priced and reliable sub-supplies in the long term. The product quality can be safeguarded by frequent training and well-defined know-how transfer agreement in case of exclusive supplier relationships. Such exclusive agreements require some specific contractual terms such as the safeguard of delivery time and quality criteria, and procedures for handling claims and penalties. The sales contract should contain information on quality, quantity, pricing, date and terms of delivery and on penalties in case of delayed delivery or poor quality. The dispute regulation should be fixed in the contract including the calculation method for the compensation for loss. Otherwise, the violated party can choose between repair, renewal, monetary compensation and in serious cases even reject the products or cancel the contract according to article 117 of the new Chinese contract law as promulgated in 2000. The official calculation of loss is based on the actual loss including lost profits. Further contractual elements of importance are related to exclusivity and the protection of intellectual property rights. Intellectual property rights should be registered well before any samples, drawings and product specifications are handed over to a potential supplier. In any case, a confidence agreement should be signed, which is also applicable to Chinese law.

A further possibility regarding binding the supplier is to found a joint venture company with him. This makes it easier to place in long-term company experts in the supplier's workshop and to safeguard quality levels and delivery times, especially when there is a tight deadline. Profits could be used for the purchasing of more shares in the company. However, such an arrangement with a potential supplier should be well prepared by thorough market research and a due diligence investigation of the partner. The cost structure (materials, labour, quality control and inspection as well as business operation in general etc.) should be evaluated in detail in order to avoid any nasty surprises afterwards. Some of the costs of such a co-operation should be put on the purchasing prices of the products over a fixed period of time to improve the return on investment. The right to take over more shares in the company at a later date, with the accumulation of profit can be also negotiated. Such a smaller investment can also enjoy some tax holiday arrangements and the pay back of a percentage of the paid VAT. Another important point is the need to protect against risks of exchange rate fluctuation by appropriate terms in the contract or arrangements with banks or insurance companies.

Summary/Recommendations

Local sourcing is an important, but also quite complicated task in China. Especially in the beginning, it is not easy to find reliable suppliers with high-quality products and low price levels. Problems may arise through high qualifying costs of such sub-suppliers. It is recommended to help them with their cost calculation and quality control in order to speed up the co-operation. Real cost reduction and corresponding increase in competitiveness may only be achieved in the medium or the long term. Nevertheless it is very important to build up the local sourcing infrastructure as soon as possible, even at the price of higher costs in the beginning.

Further source

German Business Association (2000) *Wirtschaftsforum*, 6, pp. 6 and 34.

8.7. Under what circumstances is licensing and transfer of technology advisable?

There are different types of co-operation in China. A first and easier step for market entry can be achieved by a licence agreement regarding the transfer of technology. Such agreements can be negotiated for assembly and manufacturing as well as for sales and distribution co-operations. A major advantage is the minimum amount of one's own financial funding and manpower that has to be involved in the project. Maximum flexibility and limited time-frame is another advantage of the agreement. This minimises the short-term risks. However, the influence on the implementation of the project is limited, too. It is not easy to guard against the unauthorised copying of the products and violation of the agreement and transfer of technology. It is not necessary to build up an organisation with all the various functions and to employ local people. These are further advantages of a licence agreement in comparison to other investment forms in China.

Major tasks of a project leader in following up an agreement for transfer of technology

- Controlling of the project in accordance to a correct implementation of the contract.
- Exchange of technical documentation including specific changes on the drawings and specification of components.
- Calculation and offering of CKD kits or modules as required by the licensed product.
- Signing of annual contracts for CKD deliveries.
- Job implementation of the CKD deliveries.
- Checking of the availability and procurement of required sub-supplies of components to the licensed product according to the agreement.
- Decision-making due to changes on the licensed product.
- Proceeding with warranty cases.
- General communication with the licensee and intermediate agents or consultants.
- Co-ordination of training programmes with the staff and management of the licensee.

Transfer of technology

The negotiations for a licence or technology transfer agreement should be undertaken with at least three potential partners. For strategic projects the government should make proposals for potential partners and suppliers. It is important to choose the best partner. The detailed negotiation time-frame for a technology transfer agreement may take ten days. The Chinese authorities sometimes take as long as three months to approve such an agreement. Medium-sized partners or profit centre units of larger companies may proceed quickly and flexibly with the negotiations. Consultants may help in avoiding costs and saving time, using their high levels of competence, experience and qualifications. The following costs can be considerably lower when the localisation project is established more smoothly. The terms of a licence agreement normally last for ten years; the technology then belongs to the partner. However, in the meantime, newer product generations will already have been developed.

The choice of the most convenient products and technology is important. But, the latest technology is not always the most suitable; it may be more complicated and not as controllable as proven technology. It is important also to consider the use of environmentally safe products and production methods as well as energy efficient processes. The production line preferably should be built up according to ISO 9000 regulations. The product end-control has to be improved and the service network established. The spare parts stock must be built up and special production equipment procured. 'Quality first' requirements take longer in terms of building up local content. This can be a problem for the meeting of governmental regulations or agreed terms in the signed licence contract concerning the quick build-up of local content ratios. However, the quality level of locally procured parts and components must be first checked and approved by the foreign enterprise in order to keep a high reputation for the components on the market. Within three years, the local content ratio should achieve an average of 30–60 per cent under normal circumstances. Spare part deliveries or deliveries from Hong Kong or Taiwan can also increase the local content ratio. The transfer price is an important issue in the purchasing of imported products or CKD components. This issue has to be handled very carefully (see also chapter 9.12).

The co-operation may begin with the delivery of few SKD (Single Knocked Down) parts and the installation of the assembly equipment. Additional business through imports of key components and spare parts is possible. The establishing of qualified local sub-suppliers normally takes some years and has to be built up under the supervision of the foreign supervisor. It is also important to include training modules in the licence agreement. This can be a considerable cost block. In the long term, training requirements of staff must be followed up and future product generations initiated. Even at the end of the technology agreement, there may be placed following-up contracts or purchase orders as additional business. Sub-supplies are an interesting business also in the long term. The start-up and implementation phase may take approximately three years. The establishment of a service network and increase of local content are interesting following projects.

In the case of transfer of the ownership of technology, the major part of the licence fees should be negotiated as advance payment in connection with a fixed production quantity. There should also be paid guaranteed fees per produced and sold unit; 50–60 per cent of such additional fees may be paid in advance. If the foreign partner keeps the ownership of the technology, royalty payments must be paid. Such royalties may amount to approximately 3–5 per cent of the sales. In the past, such payments were subjected to full taxation. Now, this regulation has been changed for high-tech products. The royalty payments for the transfer of such high-tech products are tax free, if approved by the tax authorities. Such tax payables have to be first accrued before payment, if tax payments still are required. The maximum value of contribution of technology in comparison to the paid in capital is limited to the maximum value of 12–20 per cent to be amortised within a write-off period of ten years.

Franchising

Franchising is more and more common in China, especially within the food and fast food industry. Companies like Mc Donalds, Kentucky Fried Chicken, Schlotzkys, Starbucks, Australian Kebab, Subways, Walls, Buds, Baskin Robbins etc. have already been engaged in the franchise business for several years. Franchising is especially recommended for completely localised products in connection with large start-up investments. The establishment of a widespread distribution network in the local market requires many people and huge amounts of liquidity. The legal situation due to the free exchange of earned Renminbi profits has not yet been solved satisfactorily. Therefore, earnings are still mostly used for the expansion of the business with the hope of improvements in the future. The present entry into the WTO may solve that problem. Specialised lawyers and consultants are available for more detailed answers on this topic.

Summary/Recommendations

Licensing with technology transfer agreements or franchising is a good first-entry step into some key markets in China. This especially applies for projects with high raw materials, labour and know-how costs, or in connection with huge turnkey plants. Typical market segments are the steel, chemical and petrochemical as well as the automotive industries. A technology transfer agreement should fit into the overall individual situation and strategy of an investor and should be well prepared and implemented. Then, it can be good business for both parties. However, it should also be considered that the technology know-how is lost after the end of the licensing contract. New product generations should be developed before the end of the licensing period and a new project should be initiated in due course.

Further sources

Moser, M. (ed.) (2000) *China Troubleshooter*, HK, Asia Law & Practice.
Tamir, A. (1991) *Technology Transfer in International Business*, NY, Oxford University Press.

8.8. How can I avoid product and know-how piracy?

Most investments in China are connected with the transfer of fairly up-to-date product technology and production know-how. Local competitors often have weaknesses in such areas. As a consequence, many of them have difficulties in remaining competitive in the market. These circumstances motivate some of them to copy competitors' products and know-how. The foreign investor must take this matter seriously with consideration to the special circumstances of his product and market. Adequate strategies should be prepared to deal with this matter in the best way.

The general situation in product piracy

- The existing laws for product piracy in China are relatively good. However, the implementation through the court is often time-consuming, costly and uncertain.
- Product piracy cannot really be effectively avoided.
- The transferred technology should not be the latest world standards. Thus, more modern products will be on the market before the marketing of copied products begins.
- A visually identical copied product often has low quality levels due to missing production know-how, poor workmanship and the use of the wrong key materials.
- Required after-sales and spare parts services or related application technologies of faked products are mostly poorly performed.
- Small production quantities and poor manufacturing efficiency of copied products leads to rising total production costs with negative effects on competitiveness.
- Most companies resort to the administrative route rather than judicial route.

Ways of improving protection measures against piracy

- A WFOE (Wholly Foreign Owned Enterprise) can be better protected than a joint venture.
- HR policies should focus on retention, on keeping well-trained people in the company, and on vertical expertise. Don't employ people from your own supply chain.
- Set up non-disclosure and non-competition from agreements with suppliers and employees. While they are not enforceable, they send out a clear, strong message about seriousness.
- Security – control of access to the technology and encryption.
- Marketing efforts and a branding campaign should aggressively inform the market and key customers about the real advantages and differences of original products. Publicity and carefully placed press releases about the faking companies may have a positive effect.
- More modern products, which are less easy to copy, should be marketed.
- The confidential holding of production know-how and production equipment protects against potential piracy. Attention to detail – strict enforcement of policies and rules governing document classification and disposal.
- Local manufacturing or tailor-made services support the creation of an attractive product and marketing package.

- Special interest groups (in the automotive industry, for example) have been established to cope with this problem on all relevant legal and political levels. However, potential legal cases should be well prepared by mapping of cases, data collection, budget and staffing preparation for investigation expenses and frequent analysis of pros and cons for legal action.

General situation

China is a world master in copying. After the closing down of certain production facilities, they re-open shortly afterwards in the same or other place. Major European, American and Japanese companies don't accept such practice any more. They set up the Anti Counterfeiting Coalition (ACC) to represent their joint interests on a high lobbying level. ACC multinational members estimate their own losses between a range of 15–30 per cent of their sales in China. Some consumer goods may even reach a level of more than 40 per cent. Many cheated companies approached the State Administration of Industry and Commerce as well as highest politicians to complain and urge them to react. The membership of China in the WTO, including TRIPS (Trade Related Intellectual Property Rights), may be a basis to put more pressure on China. China has already a Copyright Law, a Trademark Law and an Anti Unfair Competition Law, but the application and implementation of such laws is still weak and the procedures are very time-consuming, causing huge costs due to the requirement of the burden of proof by the plaintiff. Sometimes it's also quite important to have *guanxis*. A huge American software house, for instance, had a law case in Shanghai against a local university which was using unlicensed software; it won the case. However, the legal costs for them amounted to approximately 1 million US dollars. The university's fine was only a few thousand Remmimbi. Product piracy cannot really be avoided effectively. But, in many cases it is not necessarily as serious as expected for several reasons. In the case of new product development, it is quite common worldwide for R&D departments to analyse the special features and patents of competitors' products. Many companies then copy, to a lesser or greater extent, the competitors' applied technologies. In China, many domestic competitors do so to some extent. Therefore, it makes more sense to follow a forward-looking strategy.

Applicable protection measures

A visually identical copied product often has low quality levels due to missing production know-how, poor workmanship and the use of wrong key materials. Required after-sales and spare parts services or related application technologies for most products are poor. Finally, the small production quantities in combination with poor manufacturing efficiency often leads to rising total production costs with negative effects on competitiveness. As a consequence, the marketing efforts and branding campaign should aggressively inform the market and key customers about the real advantages and differences of the original products. More modern products should also be marketed which are less easy to copy. Local assembly, mechanical manufacturing or service entities support the creation of an attractive product and marketing package, which meets most successfully the customers' requirements; This makes it more difficult for local pirates to compete. Tailor-made retention programmes and the installation of special security systems in the company also support protection against the loss of confidential business and technological know-how.

Summary/Recommendations

Product piracy can be a serious problem for every investor in China. However, in most cases it is not necessarily as dangerous it looks like from outside. The success of the marketing of a product is not only dependent on the technical and application features, but also on the production know-how, the composition of the used basic components with quality control procedures and the related service packages offered. Financial issues may also play an important role in making the product attractive. A successful company is at least 10% better off with regards to this. In the case of very sensitive technology, it is recommended that you do the business without a local partner.

Further sources

German Business Association, *China Contact*, 2, p. 49.
Moser, M. (ed.), (2000) *China Troubleshooter*, Chapter 5, HK, Asia Law & Practice.
Proceedings of The Economist Conference (2000), 3, p. 42.

8.9. Under what circumstances is it recommended to transfer R&D activities to China?

Many investors in China are considering the possibility of the transfer of research and development (R&D) activities to China. Motivational factors for the localisation of such R&D activities can be cost reasons or the requirement for more tailor-made product and service solutions by the customer or the end-user that have to be developed locally. The headquarters' products are normally designed and manufactured more on a standardised or a modular version. Other motivators for the transfer of technology can be legal reasons or special requests for high R&D labour-intensive projects and products.

The most important motivations for the transfer of R&D activities

- Labour-intensive R&D projects.
- Projects for software development.
- Cost-effective research and testing of new, labour-intensive pharmaceutical products.
- R&D activities which have restrictions in other western countries by governmental laws.
- Products which have to meet local specifications and regulations.
- R&D activities for products outside the core business.

Global players as well as many companies of the 'new economy' have already internationalised their R&D activities to major markets and close to the customers. They want to make use of cheap labour and get access to the global platform of R&D knowledge and tastes as well as better understand tailor-made product preferences of special market segments. International co-operations in R&D are more and more popular. Nowadays, market researches also can be delivered *ad hoc* by e-mail on demand. Labour-intensive R&D projects or applications can be carried out efficiently in China. Many graduates from China's premium universities are quite good in several R&D fields. Their theoretical background and working attitude contributes to the success of such projects. However, a co-operation in R&D only makes sense with western partners' help in funding and technological know-how transfer. Instructions and extensive training must be given throughout the implementation of such a project, including support in the evaluation of results. The governmental laws and restrictions in some fields of research may be more flexible in China than in some western countries. This is another reason for the transfer of R&D activities. It may also make sense to transfer such activities in the case of R&D-intensive products, which need to be adapted to the local circumstances. Product developments which do not belong to the core business can also be done more cost- and labour-efficiently in China. The German Business Association, for instance, has initiated the programme 'ProInno', financed by the German Ministry of Commerce, with the aim of supporting especially medium-sized companies to find suitable co-operation partners in key markets such as China. Nominated 'Area Technology Scouts' are available to support the search for suitable global partners within a huge local network (see also www.ihk.de/tam).

Summary/Recommendations

The most important reasons for the transfer or localisation of research and development activities to China are cost or strategic reasons. This applies especially for products with high labour-cost ratios in development and production. The demand pressure for such decisions may also come from the market or local investment partner. In special cases the joint venture contract may also require a transfer of research and development activities to China. Ultimately, it depends on the individual situation if a localisation of R&D makes sense or not.

Further source

Deutsch chinesisches Wirtschaftsforum (2000), 6, p. 40.

8.10. How do I arrange my supply chain management?

Today, foreign invested enterprises are allowed to control most parts of the supply chain. They can provide or outsource for themselves most of the supplies, transport, warehousing, distribution and IT networks as well as shipping services that they require. There are increasing numbers of suppliers of materials and services; road, rail and air systems, warehouses and inventory control systems are available. This makes the supply chain function consistently and more efficiently.

Market leaders tend to do the following in arranging their supply chain system

- Select logistics providers for strategic reasons.
- Make the decision to outsource or provide their own logistics by carefully assessing a combination of factors such as cost, cycle time and core competency.
- Make clear definitions of the providers' roles in the supply chain and delegate authority to them.
- Continuously monitor the performances of the provider using tangible measures and goals.

Source: The Economist Intelligence Unit (2000) HK.

General situation according to findings of A.T. Kearney and the Economist Conferences

In 1998, A.T. Kearney found that almost half of companies manage their supply chains without an in-country presence in China. Such established companies often limit the responsibilities of in-country staff. Some companies conduct such functions as purchasing, quality assurance and logistics from corporate headquarters, even as they source materials and finished products from China. Moreover, says the study, 'different business units of Western companies often operate independently in China, working with different carriers, forwarders and vendors. Companies frequently fail to leverage their overall purchases across multiple operations.' A.T. Kearney points to the use of third-party logistics providers, whose services have broadened substantially in China over the past few years, and cautions companies requiring such services against making their outsourcing decisions solely on past experience or simple cost comparisons.

Still another key finding of the A.T. Kearney study was the fact that while electronic links among supply chain participants in China are growing, electronic integration of major participants in the chain is still low by western standards, particularly in China's inland provinces. The consulting firm found that most companies shipping goods are linked electronically to their logistics service providers but usually the transmission is one way – they receive information from their logistics providers. Most companies shipping goods, A.T. Kearney says, 'do not have their own advanced IT tracking systems, nor are they comfortable sharing information online with service providers'.

In fact, some service providers act as electronic middlemen, receiving data from multiple sources in the supply chain and feeding what A.T. Kearney calls a 'consolidated "pipeline" of data' to the companies taking their services. Says the study: 'By logging onto their providers' system, shippers (companies shipping goods) get electronic access to information about export documents and order status, and on track shipments. Such a data pipeline is especially valuable to shippers with less-developed logistics systems in China.' Fairly rapid growth in these electronic linkages can be expected in China now.

Supply chain and e-commerce according to 'On-line Service, Asia Pulse Pte, 3/2000'

'Bizipoint.com is a business-to-business (B2B) internet trade centre. The vertical B2B e-commerce market, or "eMarket", offers industry – focused e-commerce applications for electronics and computer companies at any point in the supply chain – in Greater China and worldwide – providing the means to achieve online efficiencies with dynamic market pricing, developing into full supporting information, payment and fulfilment functions. With China Electronics Chamber of Commerce (CECC) as partner, Bizipoint.com has an immediate channel to more than 3000 mainland manufacturers as well as a brick-and-mortar presence throughout China. The B2B eMarkets are expected to generate nearly US$ 1 trillion in sales in Asia by 2004, representing 13.6 per cent of the projected global B2B sales of US$7.3 trillion, according to the latest forecasts from the Gartner Group. A study by Goldman Sachs shows that computer and electronics will be the first – and third – leading sectors, respectively, in global B2B sales by 2004. In China electronics and machinery accounts for 40 per cent of all foreign trade, and CECC members alone did over US$ 15 billion of business in 1998. The active participation of CECC and the professional, focused vertical business approach means that Bizipoint.com members everywhere can obtain the latest industry news and market trends and gain access to a growing supplier/seller database and product range, without the need to search through a mass of other industry data.' The development of e-commerce concepts are quite volatile and subject to frequent change.

Logistics and transport situation

The EIU (Economist Intelligence Unit), in its on-line service 'ViewsWire China', commented on the transport situation in China that manufacturers can obtain the services of foreign invested haulage companies or they can establish an in-house fleet of lorries. Foreign invested haulage companies have been permitted in China since 1996, though only as joint ventures. A handful of foreign invested haulage and logistics firms offer scheduled runs, mostly on the eastern seaboard, using fleets of trucks they own or sub-contract from local haulage companies. According to the EIU ViewsWire China, TNT Logistics China offers regular haulage services as part of its supply chain management for clients, as well as domestic road express and long-distance haulage services. Maersk Sealand, through its Orient Trucking joint venture, offers specialised services including refrigerated container deliveries to major cities. In addition, to the multinationals, a number of small Hong Kong companies operate haulage services in the south. However, most of the transportation is still done by smaller-sized local companies, still mostly equipped with trucks of poor reliability.

Both joint venture and wholly foreign owned production enterprises are allowed to own and operate their own truck fleets for deliveries within their home provinces. Many companies take advantage of these maintaining fleets for local deliveries from their factory warehouse. Today, most international manufacturers mainly rely on third-party logistics providers for short and long-distance transport. The fleets of trucks owned by its individual factories are mainly used for local transport.

Summary/Recommendations

Supply chain management in China is a quite crucial and important issue. Most trading, servicing and manufacturing entities in China rely on imports and spent a lot of money on transportation, warehousing, distribution and other supply chain-related services. The huge quantities of components and products must be handled in a professional and cost-effective manner. Several highly reputable logistics and service providers are now operating on the market. The experience and supporting capabilities of such providers should be integrated into the local and global strategic and operational considerations. However, the performance should be frequently monitored and controlled by clearly defined targets.

9

What are the Most Crucial Finance-related Issues?

Engelbert Boos

9.1. What kind of costs are decisive?

The success of an investment depends very much on a competitive cost structure of the products and an efficient business operation. Lower costs are a prerequisite of attractive sales prices and hence better competitiveness. A high level of competitiveness is the basis for higher sales figures and lower costs in general. As a consequence, the business will achieve better profit margins with positive impact on the investment. It is one of the major tasks of management to improve the business efficiency by an intelligent overview and management of the cost structure.

The most decisive cost factors in the operation of an entity in China

- The depreciation and amortisation of tangible and intangible assets.
- The major cost-driving factors within the 'general and administrative' cost block are the depreciation of assets, salaries and social benefit expenses, travelling expenses, insurances, taxes, land occupancy fees and amortisation of intangible and other assets.
- The important selling expenses are the salaries and wages of employed staff in the sales department, office expenses, commission payments, transportation and packaging, travelling expenses and advertisement costs.
- The major manufacturing costs comprise salaries and wages of production department, depreciation of related equipment, supplies consumed and transportation of goods.
- The main finance department costs are interest payments for loans, profit and loss of exchange rate fluctuations for foreign exchange account positions and writing-off of receivables and inventory positions.
- The cost of sales (COS) expenses – purchasing of the production raw materials including transportation and importing costs – are most crucial

to business operation. Local sourcing and local production activities help the realisation of lower material and labour costs.

- Product promotion costs are quite high in China.
- High costs in the collection of receivable debts may arise if a sales manager whose job it is to collect them is leaving the company. Many local customers are not very willing to pay such money to successors.

The major cost blocks due to balance sheet and P&L issues are the depreciation and amortisation of tangible and intangible assets such as buildings, production equipment, licences and royalties for know-how transfer and other services. The cost of sales (COS) expenses often amount to more than 80 per cent of the total cost in business operation. Therefore, special cost-reducing activities are required in the purchasing of production raw materials. The very price-driven sales situation in China also requires low cost and high productivity levels for the achievement of required competitiveness. The minimisation of import costs through local sourcing and local production activities helps the realisation of lower material and labour costs. Some markets or products have special circumstances due to their individual cost structure. Pharmaceutical enterprises often suffer from high R&D costs; high-tech or consultant services companies tend to face high personnel costs due to the requirement of a certain number of highly qualified expatriates and local staff. Consumer goods manufacturers have enormous costs involved in product promotion. In case of high investments for production-related equipment or the establishment of an extensive distribution and service network, the financing costs may also play a big part in the total cost situation of an investment. The management of an entity has the difficult task to overview and control the cost structure and to initiate suitable measurements for cost control.

Summary/Recommendations

An efficient finance control of the company is important for the achievement and maintenance of lower cost levels. Special consideration should be given to the optimisation of the purchasing and raw materials costs and on the investment expenses with depreciation and amortisation. Labour costs of the employed expatriates can be particularly high. The business strategy including the budget plan for business operation should take account of these circumstances. The prospects for business success can be significantly improved in this way.

Further source

Cooper, R. (1991) *The Design of Cost Management Systems*, NJ, Prentice-Hall.

9.2. How do I organise budgeting and an efficient cost and liquidity management?

Companies can get into huge operational difficulties or even run into bankruptcy due to badly managed cash flow or a lack of efficient cost control. It is of essential importance that the set budgets and cash flow within the entity are efficiently controlled. The balance of inflow and outflow of money must always be positive. Otherwise, cash shortages may arise. This results in the need for short-term loans, which have to be financed by the headquarters or bank. Such short-term loan agreements are quite expensive and difficult to get from Chinese banks. The management must make an enormous effort to avoid the need for short-term loans whenever possible.

Cash flow calculation method

Cash flow calculation is based on the following balance of income and expenses:

- cash inflow and outflow from/for operating activities;
- cash flow balance of investment activities;
- cash flow balance of financing activities;
- effects on the amount of cash through changes of exchange rates.

These points reflect the net change of cash
The following situations have no direct influence on income and expenses, but do affect liquidity:

- investment and financing activities;
- balance of net profit to the cash flow of operative activities;
- depreciation and amortisation as well as changes in inventory, taxes, receivables and payables;
- changes in cash level and others.

Note: The budgeting calculation should be done according to the structure of the Chinese GAAP.

The professional management of cash flow and liquidity is an essential and critical factor of success, especially for a newly started foreign invested enterprise. Therefore, incoming payments and payment terms have to be planned and followed up carefully by the responsible management. For each customer individual credit limits have to be fixed. These credit limits depend on the planned turnover of the current fiscal year and on the experiences with the customer's attitude to payment in the past. Information from banks and competitors also has to be taken into account. The period between payments should be as short as possible in order to minimise risks. Payments in advance and 'goods against cash' agreements should be proposed to the customer together with prompt payment discounts. The standard payment term should be 30 days or in exceptional circumstances 60 days. Periods of payment exceeding this time-frame must be approved and justified by the general manager and payment reminders should be sent out at least every two weeks. The management must be informed about outstanding debts by the end of each week at the latest and about all customers who have been sent a third reminder for payment. Delivery to the customer must be stopped in case of payment delays of more than two months. Other decisions have to be agreed upon in detail and in written form and credit limits must be fixed for each customer. Further arrangements have to be made for pending guarantees, letters of credit and other finance-related obligations.

Summary/Recommendations

The management of an entity must be always aware of the financial positions with their influence on the net change of cash and liquidity. This knowledge is important to achieve balanced cash flow. The efficient management of outstanding debits and the payments of credits are essential for a well-run company.

Further source

Hohenstein, G. (1990) *Cash Flow – Cash Management*, Weisbaden, Gabler.

9.3. Which key ratios are essential for the finance control of my China investment?

In finance control and the controlling of business operations systems you can find many finance or general business control ratios. However, only a few of them are important for the management of an entity. A reliable overview of business development can be represented accurately enough by the use of some key ratios. The reader and analyst of the ratios should understand the special business environment and circumstances which such monitored data and ratios are based on.

Key finance figures and business control ratios

- Sales volume, cost of sales (COS) level and respective gross profit ratio.
- Expenses of the departments (administration, production, sales, finance etc.). Expenses are booked according to Chinese GAAP. Only sophisticated software packages calculate the expenses separately according to

international GAAP. The expenses should be followed up and compared to the previous months and last year in order to see a reliable development of the business.

- Total profit and profit from normal business activities.
- Inventory level and range (inventory level within the period of three months' sales) and stock turnover in days (inventories multiplied by 360 and divided by the cost of materials for a period of one year).
- Trade payables per inventory and payables to headquarters.
- Advance payments and receivables.
- Sales receivable debts, the age structure of sales receivables and the frequency of reminders, sales receivables per month and the average sales receivables per three months, ratio of sales per employee.
- Following-up of each customer's credit limits, agreed discounts on price lists, payment conditions and payment receipts from customers.
- Order income per month, order backlog and average orders in hand per three months' sales.
- Average cost per employee (personnel expenses per number of employees).
- Liquidity ratios such as current assets/current liabilities in order to know how quickly assets can be cashed.
- Return on equity (ROI, net income per average equity plus liability).

The listed figures and ratios represent a good basis for budgeting, cash flow planning and finance control. The figures can be understood and accepted by the management and employees who will work with them. Most of the figures and ratios should be evaluated on a monthly basis and be followed up throughout the year.

Summary/Recommendations

The shareholders and the management of an entity have a strong interest in what is happening with their investment. The use of controlling tools with figures and ratios is of critical importance for the control of the entity's development and for the evaluation of profitability. The more important figures and ratios are listed. Others may have to be added according to the special nature of the business in question.

Further source

Hax, H. (1999) *Corporate Finance and Corporate Control*, Tübingen, Mohr Siebeck.

9.4. How can I optimise business and finance control in the invested entity?

The efficient management and controlling of a company is a key factor for success. The control of finance and general business operation data is one of the most important tasks of the management and supervisory board of an entity. Key business data must be regularly monitored, analysed and be reported in a suitable form to the shareholders or their appointed representatives. The actual figures must be compared with the planned and budgeted ones. In the case of major discrepancies, the management can decide what operational or strategic adjustments are required.

The most important features for efficient finance and business control

- It is important to understand what has to be controlled.
- Controlling is important for the improvement of the cost structure and for the increase of efficiency in the company.
- The controlling tools used should be limited and be accepted by employees and managers.
- The software package used for finance control should fit the company's size and budget requirements and be flexible to use.
- Controlling the transparency and the quick availability of key data is as important as accuracy.
- The use of software programs and relevant information is very important.
- Good finance control software helps to build up profit centres with control over the origin of costs, types of costs and the payer of costs.
- The calculation of the real costs helps towards better budget planning and the limitation of cost escalation.

Potential sources of weakness in business operation

- Reconciliation of the correct quantity and the cost of the different inventories.
- Harmonising of the different departments such as production management, accounting and sales.
- The controlling of cost calculation, bookkeeping data and deliveries of goods and internal material flows.
- The issuance of bank cheques and the controlling of them have to be done by separate people.
- The booking of costs has to be done in time.
- The authorisation of payments with particular limitations has to be fixed and followed up.
- The bank revenues have to be reconciled against the book values on a regular basis.

- The physical reconciliation of stock and raw material flow has to be done occasionally.
- Purchase invoices must be cross-checked against the goods received notes.
- Sales invoices must be cross-checked against the goods delivery notes and be acknowledged by the receiver.

It is important to understand what has to be controlled. Controlling is important for the improvement of the cost structure and for the increase of efficiency in the company. The controlling tools used should be limited and be accepted by employees and managers. In controlling the transparency, the quick availability of key data is more important than perfect accuracy. The use of software programs and relevant information is very important for the receiver of the finance control data. Otherwise they may not be happy about working with them. Long discussions are normally required to convince internal people to use such finance and data control systems.

Good finance control software helps to build up profit centres with control over the origins of cost, types of cost and the payer of costs. Then, the averaged costs can be analysed in greater detail and the production costs be more precisely evaluated. The knowledge of the value of a product helps to estimate the time when it might become profitable. The calculation of the real costs help for better budget planning and the limitation of cost escalation.

There are several multilingual software packages for finance control available in China such as Anyi, SAP, Scalon, Sun Systems or Forth Shift etc. introduced and recommended by auditing companies such as PriceWaterhouseCoopers, KPMG and others. The cost level for the purchasing of such software systems and corresponding hardware varies between 10,000 US dollars (bilingual – but only following PLC GAAP) to up to 200,000–300,000 US dollars (multilingual – following PLC GAAP, International GAAP and US GAAP). Such highly sophisticated and expensive software packages can also be ordered step by step in modular portions, fitting the company's development requirements and budgets (each module may cost approximately 40,000–60,000 US dollars).

The management must take care with the control of some potential sources of weaknesses in the business operation. The reconciliation of the different inventories should be cross-checked with regards to correct amounts completed and the right cost cover. The business operation activities of the different departments such as production, accounting and sales department must be harmonised. The accuracy of internal material flow and the cost calculation methods within the sales, production and bookkeeping departments must be carefully checked. The figures must be compared to the deliveries of goods. Book numbers have to be checked by different staff members and on a regular basis against the physical numbers and manual records must be checked against booked values. The issuance of bank cheques and the controlling of them also have to be done by different people and the booking of cost has to be done in time. It is also important that the authorisation of payments with particular limitations is fixed and followed up. Bank transactions have to be reconciled against the book values on a regular basis. Physical reconciliation of stock and the raw material flow must be done thoroughly. It is also important that purchase invoices are cross-checked against the goods received notes and the sales invoices against the goods deliveries notes. Such notes must also be acknowledged by the receiver.

Summary/Recommendations

The controlling of the business operation is very important to the management. It is recommended to have a tool to compare the actual with the planned finance and other important operational business data. It is also relevant to have an overview on the potential weaknesses in the organisation. They have to be analysed and evaluated on a regular basis in order to prepare quick reaction and adjustment measurements in time.

9.5. What insurance is required, recommended or not necessary?

The insurance market in China is still dominated by state owned companies. However, international competitors are already represented through their own representative offices and insurance brokers such as Marsh Inc., which are serving their international clients in China as well. The Chinese government is already, step by step opening the insurance market as a consequence of its WTO membership. International investors are interested in insuring the business risks according to the same standards and amounts present in all their other global operations. Such globally operating clients want to standardise, maintain and extend their master liability insurance system all over the world. With such a system the total insurance policy covers larger assets and liabilities with relatively lower rates. The rates to be paid can be further lowered if an insurance company already has experience with a client and the risks of his business.

The most important range of insurance polices for business operation in China

- Property all risk/Property damage: The rate amounts to approximately 0.1–0.2 per cent of the insured value.
- Loss of profits: The rate amounts to approximately 0.14–0.3 per cent of the insured value. This insurance is similar to property all risks/property damage or machinery break down insurance and is not really required in

the loss-making phase. Business interruption is also included in the loss of profits insurance and is sometimes also covered by the headquarters' master policy.

- Employer's liability: The rate amounts to approximately 0.8 per cent of the insured value. The premium is calculated on the employees' annual salary basis. The policy indemnifies the insured against his liability under the labour contract of employment to pay medical expenses and compensation in respect of death or bodily injury by accident or through occupational disease to the employee whilst being engaged in work.
- Product liability: The rate amounts to approximately 0.15–0.3 per cent of the annual turnover, however the major part may be included in the master policy of the headquarters. This insurance will mainly indemnify to the insured such sums, when the insured becomes legally liable to pay in respect of claims made against him. Such cases can arise from bodily injury or death or damage to property of one or more persons using or consuming the insured products or goods. This insurance only covers liabilities excluding the sold product itself. Such cases require detailed observance of legal conventions as described in the Chinese 'product quality law'.
- Public liability: The rate amounts to approximately 0.15–0.3 per cent of the insured value. It may be covered by the headquarters' policy.
- Machinery breakdown: The rate amounts to approximately 0.15–0.25 per cent of the insured value. This insurance (without business interruption) is not normally really required and refers to the operation of the insured equipment.
- Erection all risk: The rate amounts to approximately 0.15–0.25 per cent of the insured value. The insurance is arranged locally and the insurance period lasts from the beginning to the finalisation of the erection, including commissioning and start-up. It is especially recommended for larger or sensitive projects.
- Fidelity guarantee: The rate amounts to approximately 0.15–0.25 per cent of the insured value. The insurance is mainly designed according to the client's requirement and operation, but it is normally not vital.
- Money insurance: The rate amounts to approximately 0.7–1.2 per cent of the insured value. This insurance covers the risks associated with money and cheques in the office.
- Inland transit or marine cargo insurance: Approximately 0.08–0.2 per cent of the insured value.

In China the major local insurance companies are PICC (People's Insurance Company of China), CPIC (China Pacific Insurance Company), which belongs to the Bank of Construction and PAIC (Pingan), which belongs to the Bank of

Commerce. The PICC is the biggest and oldest insurance company in China, with a market share of up to 90 per cent. The insuring firm AIG (American International Insurance Company) is only active in Shanghai to date. The Japanese Tokyo Marine Insuring Company is operating a joint venture with a local partner. The Swiss Wintertur insurance company recently also received a licence for China; there are now around 14 foreign invested insurance companies with these licences. Presently, only Shanghai and Guangzhou are open for a few international insurance companies. In 2000, between two and five more cities followed. With joining the WTO, more cities are now opening to foreign insurance companies, although they are still restricted to joint venture operations. With the WTO, the insurance premium can be expected to remain more or less unchanged. The premium is more related to the investment or property value.

Most of the insurance companies specialise in particular aspects of insurance so it is most convenient to work with a broker. He can help in the composition of insurances that best fit the individual circumstances of the company. The worldwide leading broker companies with presences in China are the Marsh Inc. and AON, both headquarters are in the US. In 1998, the two leading brokers Sedgwik and Marsh & McLennon merged to form Marsh Inc. They have business licences in Shanghai and Beijing, approved by CIRC (China Insurance Regulation Committee). Seven to ten other broker companies run representative offices in China and are still waiting for business licences. The normal commissions for the brokerage amounts to approximately 15 per cent of the total of paid premiums. However, discounts are negotiable in special circumstances.

Chinese joint venture partners normally prefer to minimise both the number of insurance polices and their breadth of cover. The foreign investor usually urges to cover the risks and liabilities according to his usual international level. These contrasting views must be mutually discussed. A compromise may be possible to include some risks in China into the master policy of an international insuring company with the headquarters. For the running of a production facility the minimum requirement covers Property all risk, Business interruption and Employer's liability insurance. The Public liability and Product liability insurance may be covered by the headquarters' master policy. The placed ranges of insurance must be annually checked in order to be sure that they still meet the requirements and cover all existing risks. Adjustments in the composition or covered value may be necessary.

Summary/Recommendations

Foreign investors normally prefer to contact insurance brokers such as Marsh Inc. or AON for the composition of a suitable insurance package. However, in China, the insurance market is not yet developed to international standards. In many cases of damages or losses, they only cover a part of the liabilities. Exceeding risks may be covered by a master policy at the headquarters and their international insurer such as Allianz, Gerling, Dubbs or others. However, the insurance service market is beginning to open for other international firms. Many of them are already represented with their own representative offices in Beijing and Shanghai.

9.6. How can I finance the daily business through RMB loans?

The banking sector is still limited by many restrictions for the operation of local and especially foreign banks. But recently the situation has improved. Meanwhile, the first foreign banks are also allowed to do some business with the local currency (RMB) in Shenzhen and Shanghai. However, the major part of RMB business for financing and daily business transactions still has to be done with local Chinese banks. They rely very much on safe guarantees and good reputation of their clients.

The most important criteria for receiving local RMB loans

- The daily business can be financed through local bank loans or by payment terms and credit limits of major suppliers or the headquarters.
- Bank loans depend very much on granted guarantees, preferably through the international house bank of the foreign investor.
- The loan policy is very restrictive. Chinese banks operate only within limited credit contingents. References and reliable guarantees are important.
- RMB loans can be received more easily in larger cities and through smaller banks.
- Only some international banks in Shanghai or Shenzhen can issue RMB loans so far.

The local Chinese banks are very restrictive with their loan policy for the financing of daily business operations. They suffer with huge levels of bad debts. This especially applies to many of the state owned companies, which are in trouble; in the past, the loans to them were often politically motivated. The businesses of many debtors are doing very badly, so it is difficult for the bank to collect such outstanding money. The legal system for money collection procedures is developing, but it is still difficult and very time-consuming to get money through it. Some banks have recently used 'special forces' for money collection with attractive bonus payments if successful. Financing of the daily business operation is possible through bank loans or by payment terms and credit limits of major suppliers or the headquarters. Bank loans depend very much on guarantees, preferably through foreign banks with good reputations or through the parent organisation. Banks normally do not accept guarantees or securities of joint venture partners with poor financial performance or management. But the foreign investor should only accept loan guarantees according to their own share ratio in the company. Increasing the stake in the company to improvement of working capital may be considered.

The loan policy is in general very restrictive. The headquarters of Chinese banks issue credit contingents to their sub-branches. They check references and fixed assets (machines and buildings etc.) quite properly. The banks don't accept 'letters of comfort'. They insist on securities of the parent company and hedge credits, which sometimes are even higher than the granted loan itself in order to cover possible foreign exchange losses. The interest rates of annual loans are up to 7.5 per cent. RMB loans can be received more easily in larger cities and through smaller banks such as the Bank of Communications, CITIC Bank, Mingsheng Bank or Everbright Bank. Branch offices less able to grant loans are limited to issuing loans of approximately 20 million US dollars. The Shanghai Bank issues loans for foreign equity companies with limitations in amount and time period. Some international banks can only issue RMB loans in Shenzhen and Shanghai. The amount of the loans should be limited to a maximum of RMB 200–300 million. The relationship between the credit and deposit situations also has some influence. Eventually, the loan should be opened with two banks. For the transfer of the RMB loans a 'collection account' has to be opened.

Summary/Recommendations

The financing of daily business operation (loans and other business transactions) have to be planned carefully. The possibilities and restrictions of local and international banks should be understood so that the best financing package can be negotiated. It is also recommended to develop relationships with two banks in order to remain more flexible. The headquarters may also be an interesting alternative for short-term financing. In any case it is advisable to look for professional help to support such finance-related issues.

Further sources

Baker & McKenzie (2001), *Operation China: An Investor's Manual*, HK.
China Finance Manual (1998) HK, Asia Law & Practice.

Table 30 Requirements for obtaining an RMB loan secured by a foreign exchange pledge

---

An RMB loan to an FIE secured by a foreign exchange pledge should be handled in the following way:
- The foreign exchange pledged by the borrower may come from its capital, from a foreign loan or from revenue relating to current account items.
- If the pledge is made using funds from a foreign loan, the maturity date of the RMB loan may not be later than the maturity date of the foreign loan. If the pledge involves revenue from current account items, the sum of the pledged foreign exchange amount and the settlement account balance may not exceed the limit on the settlement account.
- The currency of the foreign exchange pledge is limited to US dollars, euros, Japanese yen, Hong Kong dollars, pounds sterling or Swiss francs.
- If the RMB/foreign currency exchange rates change during the term of the loan an adjustment may be made. If the change means that the principal and interest of the RMB loan is greater than the calculated amount of foreign exchange pledged, the lending bank is entitled to recover the excess RMB or require the borrower to increase the pledged deposit. If the change means that the principal and interest of the RMB loan is less than the calculated amount of foreign exchange pledged, then the borrower is entitled to request that the lending bank increase the amount of the RMB loan or to request a refund of the excess foreign exchange pledged.
- If the borrower defaults, the lending bank will calculate the foreign exchange that is payable on the basis of the outstanding principal, interest and corresponding charges, with reference to the relevant foreign exchange buying rate on the day of default. The borrower must make up any shortfall in the foreign currency pledged. Should the foreign currency pledged be in excess of what is required, the lender must return the excess amount to the FIE borrower.
- After an RMB loan contract has been performed the lending bank must return the foreign exchange pledged back into the original foreign exchange account.

Source: Baker & McKenzie (2001) *Operation China, An Investor's Manual*, HK, pp. 118–19.

9.7. How can I finance the daily business through foreign currency loans?

Many daily business transactions such as imports, exports, royalties or the purchasing of equities frequently require foreign exchange loans. Such types of loans can be granted by an international bank's headquarters or by a local Chinese bank in connection with foreign currency guarantees of international banks. The procedures are quite complicated and the regulations with foreign currency bank transaction change often, depending on the current development of the Chinese economy and foreign currency balances of the central bank. The legal framework has been almost annually adjusted within the last ten years for macro-economic reasons, especially in 1998.

Foreign currency exchange transactions require two types of US dollar account

- Current account (free to come into the PRC currency market) Current account items are defined as transaction items which are recurrent in the course of international receipts and payments and which do not have the transfer of capital as their objective. Examples of current account items include revenue and expenditure from international trade in goods and services, and cross-border aid as well as foreign exchange payment or receipt for/from import and export of goods, services and royalties.
- Capital account (strictly controlled from coming into the PRC currency market) Capital account items are defined as capital and liability credit and debit items arising from the inflow and outflow of capital in the course of international receipts and payments. Examples include direct investments, all kinds of loans, and securities investment as well as foreign exchange received as capital contribution to FIEs or from hard currency loans.

Issuing of loans and guarantees

A foreign investor who requires a local currency (RMB) loan from a Chinese bank must issue guarantees for such loans to the issuing bank. Such guarantees can be given in foreign exchange cash deposits, issued by the shareholder or by an international bank with a good reputation. The problem with cash deposits however, is that the Chinese banks request up to 110 per cent deposit for a 100 per cent, RMB loan in order to cover the risks of exchange rate fluctuations. Further disadvantages are the relatively low interest payments on such deposits. For such reasons, it is better to co-operate with an international bank. Usually they offer more attractive conditions and more flexibility. If an international bank is granting the loan by issuing guarantees to a Chinese bank, it may make sense to negotiate the loans in foreign currency directly with the international bank, if it has a respective business licence in China. Loans are classified as capital account transactions and are subject to control by the State Administration for Foreign Exchange (SAFE). SAFE approval is required for both principal repayment and interest payment on foreign exchange loans. Debt registration must be carried out with SAFE for foreign exchange loans granted by institutions such as 'foreign financial institutions outside China', 'foreign funded banks in China', 'overseas branches of Chinese-owned financial institutions' or 'foreign enterprises and other non-financial institutions outside China'. Foreign exchange loans from the headquarters to the subsidiaries in China also follow some procedures. First, a bank account with a Chinese bank has to be opened. Interest payments are only permitted for such loans if it is mentioned in the contract according to market conditions. Such interest payments have to be included in the loan. Shareholder credits can be granted every two or three years. It can be booked as trade receivable. The granted and pay back time must be fixed including the calculation of interest payments; no overdraft time is possible. There are some new regulations for the issuing of bank loans since the end of 1998. Since then, it is no longer possible to pay back US-dollar bank loans early in order to reduce exchange rate risks. Joint ventures outside Beijing with accounts with foreign banks in Beijing cannot pay invoices through such accounts any more. Now, they have to pay through Chinese local banks. Money transfers of foreign currencies are very slow. SAFE requires legal approval before the acceptance of the issuing of foreign currency loans through international banks. They also insist that working capital loans should be paid back first, then equity loans. Sometimes the issuance of such loans is only accepted in one name, not in both investors' names. For the daily business operation it is important to know that officially it is not permitted for customers to pay their invoices in US dollars. It is also important that long-term (more than one year) loans can only be used to purchase equities, but not for daily operating business. Depending on the specific business transaction, a different kind of bank account should be opened such as a borrowing account (less or more than a year), loan requirement account, capital contribution account or temporary account for the required local currency to cover the start-up costs of a company. The payment of intangible assets or royalties such as copyrights, trade marks or transfer of technology have to follow specific procedures with respective documentation. The same is required in the case of remitting foreign investor's profit shares with the bureaucratic and complicated SAFE inspection procedures. It is highly recommended that you seek professional help if such cases arise.

Royalties

Royalties and assignment fees are classified as current account transactions and are thus subject to verification by designated foreign exchange banks. However, the licensing or assignment contract has to be verified by the bank before permitting foreign exchange royalty or assignment fee remittances.

Taxation

In 1999 tax collection became part of the foreign exchange agenda. Since then withholding tax has to be paid for installation and construction, decoration and repair, transportation and commissioning, consultancy and training as well as for acting as agent, management and contracting out projects. Foreign exchange payments for the import of goods are classified as a current account transaction. The withholding tax for such loans is 20 per cent if the lending international bank has no branch in China. If the lender has a branch inside

China, officially only 10 per cent withholding tax is required. However, in practice only 10 per cent of this tax is collected; international banks have relationship networks for such procedures.

Verification system with influence of company reputation

SAFE has established a verification system for two current account items such as foreign exchange payments for imports and foreign exchange receipts for exports. List A enterprises with a good reputation record don't need to undergo SAFE pre-verification. Such companies can approach the designated foreign banks directly. Enterprises with a poor reputation (list B) have to submit documents via SAFE to a designated foreign exchange bank. Same kind of classification applies to exporters in terms of 'trustworthy' or 'untrustworthy' with corresponding influence on procedures. Enterprises which have not violated foreign exchange regulations during the past two years can receive more than 50,000 US dollars without presenting relevant documents in advance, whereas this is not the case for an untrustworthy company.

Letter of credit

The changes in 1998 also influenced the standard procedures for the opening of 'letters of credit' (L/C). The opening of a L/C now has to be issued in the legal base of the company, but not necessarily by an international bank as in the past. For a year it has been possible to open L/C in two Chinese cities. For the opening of a L/C a cash deposit is required in order to secure the payment and for the coverage of the risk of exchange rate fluctuations. Standby L/C agreements are only accepted sometimes.

Summary/Recommendations

The financing of business in China is relatively complicated. This is particularly true of entities with foreign investment. Many financing procedures require the involvement of foreign currency transactions. Such transactions must apply the current regulations of the foreign exchange authority SAFE. The almost annually changing regulations have to be followed up carefully. The subsidiaries of the foreign banks may help in giving the latest information regarding the situations. In 1998, SAFE was worried about increasing foreign exchange arbitrage activities. To crack down on such activities, SAFE tightened controls on taking out and prepaying loans. In 1999, SAFE adjusted foreign exchange rules regarding loans with the aim of making the environment for foreign investment more attractive. As a consequence, the procedure has become more flexible again in the past few years. Due to the frequent changes in the procedures and regulations, it is highly recommended that you approach a professional for help if a specific case arises.

Further sources

Baker & McKenzie (2001) *Operation China, An Investor is Manual*, HK.
China Finance Manual (1998) HK, Asia Law & Practice.
German Business Association (2000) 'The New Security Law,' *China Contact*, 4, Düssuldorf.
Moser, M. (ed.) (2000) *China Troubleshooter*, HK, Asia Law & Practice, ch. 2.
The Treasurers Handbook (1997) HK, Asia Law & Practice.
Wang, Y. (1996) *Investment in China*, CITIC, NY.

9.8. What are the general rules and standards of bookkeeping in China?

In 1985, the Ministry of Finance of the People's Republic of China promulgated the *Law of the People's Republic of China on Joint Ventures with Chinese and Foreign Investment*. The accounting system described in these regulations is applicable to all joint ventures using Chinese and foreign investment. Presently, the accounting standards are still oriented towards the circumstances of state owned companies. But, the gap with international accounting standards is decreasing rapidly through new developments. Accounting records in China are very detailed and well supported by appropriate documentation. In contrast with most western countries, in China the accounting records are often maintained using manual systems. This is primarily because hardware is expensive and difficult to obtain, whereas labour, by western standards, is inexpensive. However, the situation is changing gradually: modern, multilingual accounting software and training programmes are being introduced to achieve international standards. The maintenance of manual accounting records and insufficient audit trails have significant implications for audit and due diligence purposes.

The accounting systems and records require key standards

- Monthly and quarterly accounting periods and use of the Gregorian calendar.
- Accounting records to be maintained in Renminbi or if maintained in foreign currency, the accounting statements must be converted to Renminbi.
- At least one set of accounting records should be maintained in Chinese while a second set may be maintained in a minority language or a foreign language.
- Accounting records are to be kept current, clear and easy to understand.
- Cash journals and bank deposit journals must be updated daily.
- Fixed asset schedules must be updated or prepared monthly.

Note: The provisions and the principles of the 'Accounting Standards for Enterprises' promulgates uniform rules governing the way in which all PRC enterprises should maintain their books and records.

Bookkeeping system

The system of double bookkeeping has been adopted. Loose-leaf ledgers are usual. Journals have to be set up to itemise cash and bank transactions. They should be recorded in a main journal in chronological order and subsidiary debitors/creditors ledgers. They have to be set up for accounts receivable and accounts payable. For each bookkeeping entry an accounting voucher receipt is required. There is also the obligation to preserve business records. Annual accounts, annual balance sheets, contracts and agreements, decisions of the board have to kept for an unlimited time. The preservation limit for accounts, monthly/quarterly closing of accounts, general entries is 15 years. After the expiration of 15 years a list of receipts to be destroyed should be submitted to the official authority. All the books must be kept with complete records, accurate figures, clear description and prompt registration; no record in the books should be scraped, amended, altered or eliminated; all sales-invoices have to be numbered/pre-numbered. Renminbi has to be adopted as the bookkeeping currency. However, a foreign language may be used for records and in balance sheet and profit/loss statements. In case of foreign investors, the foreign currency is mostly US dollars and the foreign language is English.

Standards of valuation

As standards of valuation, a joint venture shall adopt the 'accrual basis' in its accounting. All revenues realised and expenses incurred during the current period shall be recognised in the current period and not be dislocated, advanced or deferred. The principle of 'lowest cost' may not be used. The standard of valuation according to tax rules demands that the fixed assets of a joint venture shall be recorded at their original cost. For fixed assets contributed as investment, the original cost should be the price of the assets agreed upon by all the participants of the joint venture at the time of investment. For fixed assets purchased, the original cost should be the total of the purchase price plus incidental expenses plus taxes. Depreciation on the fixed assets should be accounted for an average basis under the straight line method. Specific useful lives and depreciation rates are 20 years for buildings and structures, ten years for trains, ships, machinery, equipment and manufacturing plants and five years for electronic equipment and transport facilities. Extraordinary depreciation is not allowed.

Standard of valuation for all operating assets shall be the purchasing or production costs. The accounting for inventory/current assets follows specific rules. For merchandise purchased, the original purchase price should be taken as the actual cost for bookkeeping plus transportation expenses, insurance premium, loss during transport as well as selecting and sorting expenses. The cost of imported goods should also include custom duties and industrial and commercial consolidated tax. The actual cost of self-manufactured goods should include the material and supplies consumed, wages and relevant expenses incurred during the manufacturing process. The joint venture should adopt the 'valuation of stock' by its weighted average costs and it should use the first in first out (FIFO) method. Once the accounting method is adopted, no arbitrary change should be allowed. If a change of accounting method is necessary, it must be submitted to the local tax authority for approval and disclosed in the accounting report (annual report).

Receivables and outstanding

Receivables/outstanding accounts have to proceed according to regulations. If collection is impossible the reasons for it have to be established and responsibilities must be identified. If the board of directors gives permission, outstanding accounts can be written off as irrecoverable loss if within allowed provision. Such writing-off has to be approved by the tax authorities if the value is beyond permitted provisions. If the board of directors has not determined the impossibility of collection, neither general credit risks nor individual risks have to be taken into consideration. Long-term liabilities are bank loans for capital construction during its preparation period or for increasing fixed assets.

Summary

In China, the establishment of authoritative accounting standards lies with the Ministry of Finance (MOF) which is responsible for the formulation, promulgation and administration of accounting regulations. The Accounting Society of China (ASC) and the Chinese Institute of Certified Public Accountants (CICPA) are responsible for regulating, governing and monitoring the reform and development of the accountancy profession in China. The CICPA also has the administrative authority delegated by MOF to serve as a bridge between the government and practising accountants. In most western countries practices or standards are not legal requirements. By contrast, in China, the accounting regulations issued by the government are a matter of law and are mandatory requirements. This structure does not allow much flexibility in application.

Further sources

Cooper & Lybrand (1994) *Guide to Reporting and Accounting in PRC*, HK.
Ernst & *Young (1994) Doing Business in China*, HK.

9.9. What are the major differences between Chinese (PRC GAAP) accounting practices and international standards (IAS GAAP)?

This question summarises key accounting practices and compares them to International Accounting Standards (IAS). The PRC regulations are derived from Accounting Standards for Enterprises (July 1993), General Rules for the Financial Affairs of Enterprises (July 1993), Accounting Regulations for Selected Joint Stock Limited Enterprises (January 1993) and Accounting Regulations for Foreign Investment Enterprises in the PRC (July 1992). The latest published regulations are included in Table 31. The application of these PRC regulations to the various types of enterprises is not always clear. The Accounting Standards for Enterprises and General Rules for the Financial Affairs of Enterprises ('general PRC standards') apply to all enterprises established in the PRC and therefore form the basis for all accounting and disclosure requirements.

The most important differences in PRC and IAS accounting standards

In PRC GAAP the annual write-off rates are limited to 3 per cent for inventory as well as for receivables. Therefore, there must be other methods used within the financial statements policy for the consolidation of figures such as free warranty deliveries to customers etc. However, such methods also cause some tax losses on the respective amounts as no VAT refunds are possible. In IAS there are no limitations to writing off; it can proceed according to the group policy. In PRC GAAP the depreciation and amortisation policy is quite restricted. It always remains at a residual value of 10 per cent, which can't be written off. The length of time of such depreciation and amortisation is also quite long (i.e. machinery, equipment within ten years and software etc. within a period of five years). In international GAAP regulations such articles can be depreciated within much shorter periods such as five years or a one or two years respectively without any required residual values. The PRC GAAP depreciates buildings (20 years), machinery and equipment (ten years), office equipment and vehicles (five years) etc. Pre-operational expenses (before the start-up of production) can only be depreciated for over five years after beginning operation. The IAS allows the depreciation already within the first year.

Losses can be cumulated and forwarded for a maximum period of five years and offset with respective profits of the following years. Then there are two more years tax free and another three years only subject to a 50 per cent tax load. Some special economic zones or regions even grant further tax holiday arrangements over and above normal. The VAT tax of raw material purchases can be offset with the VAT of the sales. In PRC GAAP the VAT tax credits are filed on the liability page of the balance sheet due to the fact that they are not refunded but only offset with later tax payments. The IAS files it on the asset page with the possibility of refunding within the year of operation. Within the

PRC GAAP, the personal costs, social benefits, pension fund, depreciation and amortisation are separated according to the different departments similar to the IAS, but different from the German HGB regulations, which requires them to be calculated as one personal cost block.

Summary/Recommendations

China's economic reform is vitally dependent on foreign investment and the development of its financial markets. Expansion of financial markets will be one of the dominant trends of the near future. China's future depends on the effectiveness of those markets. An essential requirement for the successful operation of the financial markets is the ability to raise foreign capital, which depends on reliable and meaningful accounting and reporting. China is progressing towards its goal of creating modern and complete legal and accounting frameworks for its economy. Unique aspects of China's business environment preclude simple limitations of other countries' rules. China, though, has evidenced a willingness to invoke change. The country is designing new accounting standards and is promulgating new or revised law at a rapid pace.

Further sources

Cooper & Lybrand (1994) *Guide to Reporting and Accounting in PRC*, HK.
Ernst & Young (1994) *Doing Business in China*, HK.

Table 31 Summary of key differences between PRC accounting regulations and IAS

	International Accounting Standards	*PRC accounting standards and general financial regulations*
Valuation of inventory	IAS 2 permits the use of the LIFO valuation method only if the difference between the FIFO or weighted average is disclosed	Valuation on a LIFO basis is not permitted by the general regulations but is allowed for joint stock limited enterprises and foreign investment enterprises
NRV provisions for inventory	IAS 2 stipulates that stock should be carried at the lower cost and the net realisable value	NRV provisions are allowed only by the foreign investment enterprises regulations
Depreciation	Depreciation charges are based on the useful economic lives of assets	Depreciation rates are promulgated by the state
Revaluation	Revaluations of fixed assets are permitted	Revaluations are not permitted unless stipulated by the state

Table 31   (continued)

	International Accounting Standards	PRC accounting standards and general financial regulations
Prior period adjustments	A prior adjustment period should be separately disclosed as either an adjustment to opening retained earnings or in the current year income statement	No guidance is given in the general PRC standards. Joint stock limited enterprises must make such adjustments to opening retained earnings. Foreign investment enterprises must make such adjustments in the relevant current year
Post balance sheet events	Financial statements should be adjusted for events which give a better estimate of conditions which existed at the time of the balance sheet date. Other events should be disclosed	The general financial regulations only address the disclosure of post balance sheet information in the notes of the financial statements
Research and development	Development costs which meet specified criteria may be capitalised and amortised over the life of the product	Research and development costs should be charged to the income statement
Contingencies and commitments	Probable and estimable contingent losses should be accrued while all other such contingencies require disclosure unless deemed remote. Significant commitments such as commitments for future capital expenditures should be disclosed	No guidance is given in the PRC regulations
Deferred taxation	The deferral or liability method should be used for accounting of deferred tax	No guidance is given in the PRC regulations
Segmental reporting	For listed and other economically significant enterprises revenue, profit and assets should be disclosed on a basis of geographical and industry segments	No guidance is given in the PRC regulations
Accounting for leases	An asset held through financial leasing should be capitalised at the fair value of the minimum lease payments	An asset held through a financial leasing should be capitalised, generally, at the cost specified in the lease contract

	International Accounting Standards	PRC accounting standards and general financial regulations
Accounting for government grants	Grant income should be recognised over the period of the related costs. Grants related to assets may be netted off against the assets or treated as deferred income	No guidance is given in the PRC regulations
Related party disclosures	The nature of transactions between related parties as well as the nature of the relationship should be disclosed	Listed companies have to disclose related party transactions
Revenue recognition	Sales returns must be estimated at the time of sale	Sales returns are recognised at the time of the return irrespective of the period of the original sale
Doubtful debts	Provisions for doubtful accounts should be made in accordance with the principle of prudence	Provisions are limited to between 0.3% and 0.5% (3% for foreign investment enterprises) of total receivables
Intangible assets	No specific guidance is given on the capitalisation of intangible assets. Assets should only be recognised if they are expected to have a future economic benefit and should be written down when impaired	A number of intangible assets are specifically identified to be capitalised including land use rights, patent rights, start-up costs. Intangible assets should be amortised over a period of not less than ten years (five years for deferred start-up costs)
Staff welfare expenses	Staff welfare costs should be charged to the income statement of profit before taxation	Transfers should be made from profit after tax to a reserve for staff welfare. The reserve is then utilised when assets are purchased or constructed. Upon capitalisation of the asset an equivalent amount is transferred from the welfare reserve to retained earnings. For foreign investment enterprises the fund is used for payment of bonuses and common welfare construction. Any such FIE welfare assets constructed are not the property of the enterprise

Source: Cooper & Lybrand (1994) *Guide to Reporting and Accounting in PRC*, HK.

9.10. How do I build up a suitable reporting system?

The Finance Bureau, the Tax Bureau, the enterprise's supervisory body and the shareholders require financial statements on a regular basis. The quality of reporting to the headquarters depends very much on the available accounting data. Accounting software packages, which are only designed for the PRC GAAP don't include much of the international GAAP controlling data. If such international data is required, it has to be undertaken by hand and subject to less accuracy. The headquarters should define a clear policy with regards to reporting requirements which best fits the local circumstances. The reports are required on a weekly, monthly, quarterly and annual basis. These reports include relevant financial and sales data as well as the latest management information on the business development.

The most common reporting requirements:

• The profit/loss statement, balance sheet and official statements have to be prepared on a monthly basis.
• The budgeted and actual figures of gains/profits, other income/expenses, expenses account and the short-term income statement of profit/loss have to be followed up on a monthly and a cumulative basis.
• The list of unpaid invoices, turnover by customers and product groups, lists of balances including customers/debtors, suppliers/creditors and ledgers have to be submitted as internal information to the general manager on a monthly basis.
• The weekly report comprises turnover and order income per week and accumulated per month, total backlog of orders and the actual balance of local and foreign currency bank accounts.

All non-listed companies, including state owned enterprises, listed companies, joint stock and foreign investment enterprises, must submit financial statements, in the prescribed format and in accordance with the applicable accounting practices, to the Finance Bureau, the Tax Bureau, the enterprise's supervisory body and to the shareholders. The dates for submission are for quarterly statements (unaudited) within 15 days after the quarter's end, and for annual statements (audited) within 120 days after the financial year end. Listed companies must provide the documents to the CSRC and the relevant securities exchange for interim statements (audited) within 60 days after the end of the first six months of each financial year and for annual statements (audited) within 120 days after the financial year end.

   The interim report and annual report must comply with the accounting standards of the PRC and the relevant regulations of the CSRC and must be signed by a director or manager authorised by the listed company and be under the seal of the listed company. Upon the occurrence of any event designated as a 'major event', a listed company must immediately submit all relevant documents to the applicable securities exchange and the SRC, and issue a public notice setting out the facts of the major event. These events are numerous and include significant new contracts, substantial investments, litigation and changes in ownership. If reported news is considered to be misleading and it affects the market price of the shares of a listed company, the company must immediately issue a public clarification.

Summary/Recommendations

Reporting is a common tool for information exchange and the internal and external control of an enterprise. All stakeholders of an entity require on a daily, weekly, monthly and annual basis important finance, market and management data for keeping an overview of the present state of an invested entity. The set composition of reporting rules depends on the investor's organisational demands as well as on official regulations of the authorities, which have to be followed. The reporting lines also represent a good tool for the management to communicate efficiently with all relevant parties.

Further sources

Brandt, R. (2000) *Auditing and Reporting 2000/2001*, HK, Accountancy Books.
Cooper & Lybrand (1994) *Guide to Reporting and Accounting in PRC*, HK.

9.11. How do I choose a suitable auditor?

An investor wants to be informed of what is going on in his company. He installs controlling and reporting procedures and standards for such reasons. Mostly, local staff carry out data collection and processing under the supervision of a few senior expatriate managers. The accounting, financing and fiscal regulations are quite complicated and are subject to frequent changes. The situation is even more difficult because of intercultural misunderstandings and language difficulties. Therefore, it is quite difficult for the senior management to control and check all accounting and financing data in detail and to optimise the operational business. These circumstances require an auditing firm which is capable and flexible enough to cope with this gap. Both, Chinese and international GAAP regulations must be thoroughly understood and applied during the auditing work with appropriate recommendations for the operational business.

The most important criteria for the selection of a good auditor

- Reputation
- Accuracy of detail and reliability
- Good service packages
- Competitive pricing of services
- Multilingual abilities
- Competence and experience
- Acting as a business partner
- Supply of clearly structured auditing reports
- Recommendation, on how to optimise the fiscal and financial issues of the company
- Recommendations on important controlling issues of the company
- Preparation of the relevant controlling and auditing data
- Checking of the applied accounting regulations

The reputation of the auditor is quite important. The auditing staff must work accurately. A high level of competence and good bilingual abilities to help in satisfying the local customer and the company's foreign headquarters must be present. The auditor must be capable enough to communicate complicated accounting procedures to the responsible management with particular reference to the financial and fiscal regulations. The customer must receive a quick response to questions or problems. The auditing reports have to be clearly structured and must include all the important and relevant data according to the needs of the invested entity and its international headquarters. A competitive pricing level for the auditing work and the related services compared to other premium auditing companies is also of importance.

International and some other well-known auditing firms have a reputation for accurate work and reliability. Some local firms may complete the work within few days and are likely to be receptive to the ideas of the client firm being audited. The competence and the experience of the auditing firm and their representatives should be checked. The foreign headquarters are likely to require international quality levels. It is important that they follow the accounting regulations closely (i.e. FIFO method of stock keeping). The staff and auditing management must be able to give good advice on how to optimise the fiscal and financial issues of the company. They must also make important recommendations on the controlling issues of the company. The preparation of relevant controlling and auditing data should be supported and also the related software.

The writing of a management letter helps a lot in avoiding finance and management control problems. It must be pre-checked so see whether the data collection, cost calculation methods and internal formalities of the accounting department are up-to-date and reconciled within the different departments. In case of mistakes, corrections have to be made. It must also be checked to ensure the international and Chinese accounting regulations are obeyed properly and continue to be correctly obeyed within the current auditing year as well as in years to come.

Summary/Recommendations

A good auditor is an advisor on business issues. He must deliver good and reliable services, including advisory work on the improvement on internal controlling issues. The auditor must act as a kind of business partner. The auditing staff also should be willing to do some clarification work and training for the company's accounting staff if it is needed. A good auditor must help with the definition and correct implementation of the most suitable accounting policy. The applied procedures must meet and correspond with the defined strategic accounting policy of the company. Suitable, tailor-made recommendations and opinions on how to optimise the fiscal and financial implications for the company also should be given.

9.12. How to manage the risks of applied transfer pricing policy?

The transfer price represents the fixed price and the payment for supplies and services between the headquarters and subsidiary company in China. Sometimes, such prices are used to transfer some profits from China to the foreign headquarters, which is not allowed by Chinese laws. There are many reasons for such profit transfers. Higher prices for transferred assets to the foreign investment reduce future profits through higher depreciation and amortisation rates. The tax holidays can be extended by the fact that the longer the phase of loss the later the tax payments begin. The transfer of profits through higher transfer prices also reduce the profits to be shared with the joint venture partner or just reduce the amortisation time for investments. Such potential profit transfers look very suspicious to the authorities, especially if the transactions are made to a tax oasis like Hong Kong or Taiwan. The 'transfer pricing' guidelines of 1998 contain 52 new regulations. These new guidelines switch from the OECD to the American orientation (i.e. 'best method principle' and 'advanced pricing agreements' [APAs], etc.). These new regulations look better to the American than to German tax authorities. In America transfer prices are also compared to general market prices. The Chinese finance authorities are currently updating their transfer pricing policy. They are installing special teams in all provinces to enforce the co-operation within the different authorities.

The most important questions about transfer pricing policy

- What are related companies in the sense of transfer pricing?
- What does 'controlled transactions' mean?
- How does one determine comparable prices?
- What different methods for profit definition exist?
- What is the responsibility of the company regarding documentation?
- What circumstances are suspicious to the authorities?
- How is an official auditing by the authorities enacted?
- Which financial ratios are cross-checked?
- How does one adjust illegal profits?
- What are the advantages of 'advanced pricing agreements' (APAs)?

Transfer pricing *related companies* must meet certain criteria. The shareholder company or a third-party company at least must hold a 25 per cent share of the other company and control the purchasing, sales and other key business. The company must be dependent on the key technology of the shareholding company and 50 per cent of the management, or at least the general manager, must be shareholders. *Controlled transactions* are transferred or leased tangible or intangible assets and financing businesses as well as any kinds of services. *Comparable prices* can be determined by comparing with market prices. The sales prices with special customers such as key account customers or larger wholesalers can be checked. This can be done by evaluating the cost of sales plus fixed and overhead cost calculation methods as well as by the comparison of profit margins, profit sharing methods or by the comparing of net profit margins of transactions. It is up to the auditing authority to proceed with whichever method they prefer. It is advisable to make proposals on the basis of the 'best method'. The *profit comparison*-based methods are not yet properly defined. Therefore, these methods are only applicable for the transaction of tangible and intangible assets. However, such data only exists for state owned companies. The Chinese authorities also have plans to exchange such information and data with foreign finance authorities in the future.

There exist two forms for *documentation* of such transactions. One form is applied for single transactions such as the import of office equipment from the foreign shareholding company to the Chinese company. The other form applies to long-term business relationships. This form must be completed and handed over to the authorities within four months of the end of the business year in March. *Suspicious cases* are characterised by losses after the end of the tax holidays compared to profits during previous years. It also implies huge possibilities for manipulation, if the production materials are imported from the shareholder's company and are sold to foreign related companies. Businesses with companies in Hong Kong and Taiwan are sometimes suspicious, too.

Long-term high-loss-making periods combined with large new investments in the same business may also require explanations.

An officially initiated audit by the *authorities* will begin with a 'desk audit' in the office of the authorities. All relevant documentation has to be handed over to them such as the total amounts and the quantities of past transactions. They cross-check the discrepancies with the average standard ratios. The *applied ratios* are net profit/sales, fixed cost/sales, liabilities/capital, sales/invested capital, net profit/invested capital as well as the quick ratio and the grade of liquidity. However, the availability of such reference data is still quite doubtful. In the case of such an audit the company must prove their innocence. The company has to explain the history of the transfer pricing of their products and services. It is important to co-operate fully with the authority and to submit a full explanation of the company's policy within a period of four to six weeks. It helps to supply good documentation of transfer pricing together with the relevant economical argumentation.

In the case of proved *illegal profit* transfers to the foreign shareholder company, there may arise a taxation problem for dividends related to the soon to be adjusted profits. However, in the case of the existence of a taxation agreement between China and the relevant western country, the taxes do not have to be paid twice. But, in case of already taxed business relationships (i.e. expenses for licences), there remains the risk of double taxation. In addition, the Chinese investment partner may also request compensation for lost profits.

One possibility for avoiding of such external auditing procedures and later profit adjustments are negotiations of preliminary fixed *advanced pricing agreements* (APAs) with the authorities. In such a case, the authority will keep a special eye on the prices to be fixed. Such APAs should be calculated as simply as possible. The calculation method and the data basis should be explained to the authority. First, the provincial authority will check the data. They, inform the state ministry of taxation in Beijing, which is controls and cross-checks the unity and the feasibility of the price level. Detailed regulations for APAs are still to come; currently few regulations have relevance to these due to lack of experience. The approval procedure takes three to six months. The Chinese authorities do not automatically acknowledge APAs of other countries such as the USA. They insist on their own function, risk and efficiency calculations. China also wants to participate in the tax income of the activities of foreign investors.

Summary/Recommendations

Transfer pricing is an important issue for most of the investments in China. A production entity should not wait until the authorities consider initiating an external auditing procedure. A suitable calculation basis with the relevant history of documentation should be prepared, based on internal stringent documentation. The engagement of an external health check may also clarify the possibly existing risks to the company. In the case of latent risks, it is important to check if the negotiation of 'advanced pricing agreements' (APAs) makes sense or not. It may be a good idea to develop a defence strategy and a transfer pricing history in advance. In any case it is always very helpful to keep close contact with the appropriate financial authorities.

9.13. How can I optimise the business policy with regard to strategic, financial and fiscal aspects?

The structure and the design of the balance sheet and profit and loss statement is mainly based on the general accounting regulations of China, but also depends on the general strategic, financial and fiscal policy of the entity and its headquarters. The entity's financial performance is consolidated in the headquarters accounts department according to international IAS GAAP, US GAAP or other national regulations. It is a major objective of the headquarters to optimise the accounting policy of each national company within the limits of the specific legal and fiscal framework. It must be analysed how to best manage the single investments and tax payments with consideration to the whole global business activities of the group of companies. Some costs can be legally shifted within interim business transactions. The depreciation policy can proceed within national legal frameworks. The different tax levels globally with tax reductions and tax holiday arrangements must be included in the strategic investment decisions. The question is how to optimise the total tax payments and business operations.

The most important considerations

- Analysis of the local and national fiscal regulations.
- Definition of when and where taxes have to be paid within the legal framework.
- Minimisation of the global tax load by using tax holiday arrangements.
- Optimal allocation of costs.
- Definition of an appropriate depreciation and finance policy.
- Allocation policy of expatriate costs between headquarters and the local company.
- Bookkeeping of the activities of the board of directors.
- Allocation of payments for rentals, related services and consultation fees.
- Auditing for business start-up operations including legal and auditing services.

- Auditing costs and other costs for required services for the headquarters.
- The national accounting regulations of transfer pricing should be followed.
- The profit and loss and the general business situation of several entities should be analysed and optimised within the major strategic business objectives.
- The limits of the business licence and the foreign exchange regulations should be obeyed in line with the definition of the product and pricing policy.

The allocation of costs and the applied depreciation and finance policies can significantly influence the balance sheet and the profit and loss statement. Many costs can be booked either in the headquarters or in the local investments accounts with noticeable influence on the financial performance of the investment. The mark-up rates of interim supplies and services can also have tremendous influence on the profit and loss statements because of the achieved profits and the potential tax payments. Joint ventures in China enjoy tax exemptions or reductions for the first five profit-making years. Therefore, this is a sensitive issue for the local tax authorities.

Major influences on the operating costs include the salary and benefit packages for foreign expatriates comprising the costs of wages, social benefits, transportation, housing and tuition fees for the children; the costs for commissioning and training of staff within the start-up phase of the company can be high too. The compensation of costs for the activities of the board of directors, rentals for supporting representative offices, professional services and consulting fees are also significantly higher. All these costs can be either paid by the headquarters or by the local invested enterprise. The same applies to the annual auditing consolidation fees and the other costs for the services needed by the headquarters. Therefore, it is important to analyse the profit and loss and the general business situation of the several entities within the major strategic business objectives. The limits of the business licence, the limitations within the foreign exchange regulations and the product policy with consideration to the stage of the product's lifecycle are all vital points in defining the accounting policy. A major strategic objective may be to have a platform for several of the headquarters' products with respective services being offered on a local currency basis. This results in improved customer services and in higher sales volumes and accordingly increased profitability due to lower specific fixed cost levels.

Foreign investors mostly prefer a quicker depreciation policy at the cost of future profit realisations and dividend payments. The development of the company through the re-investment of the realised profits and the gaining of higher market shares in the short term is more important to them. In contrast to the foreign investors, many Chinese joint venture partners are often quite short of liquidity and request a quicker distribution of dividends. Otherwise, they don't see much sense in a joint venture. Therefore, they often make proposals for a later or long-term cost depreciation for buildings, production equipment, technology licences, royalties and land-use rights, etc. according to the actual usage. They may also request leasing agreements for people, buildings and other equipment and services, which are required by the joint venture. In some circumstances the control of such leased people may also play an important role.

Summary/Recommendations

To optimise the business policy with regards to its strategic, financial and fiscal aspects is a major goal for all investors. However, it is a complicated issue. The interests of the headquarters, the local company and the Chinese joint venture partner may be quite different. This especially applies to entities in China. The two investors may have different objectives. It is important to remain within the legal, financial and fiscal framework, even though this is sometimes unclear. This problem can be easily solved by holding companies; they can act more flexibly within the relevant laws and create sources and platforms for professional services.

Further sources

China Finance Manual (1998) HK, Asia Law & Practice.
Deloitte Touche Tomatsu Report (1996) *Avoiding Double Taxation in HK and PRC*, HK, Asia Law & Practice.
Wang, Y. (1996) *Investment in China*, CITIC, NY.

9.14. How is the taxation of FIE's structured?

Taxation is one of the most disliked and complicated issues in running a company. Taxation policy and related laws are different in each country and often quite difficult to understand. Tax rates depend very much on the country's development purposes. Low tax rates and holiday arrangements aim to attract enough foreign and local investment in order to create employment and other public income. Potential investors and their local established management should be well informed about the taxation situation. Such information is required to place the investment on the right location and to optimise other operative business decisions so, the management must be well informed; otherwise, investment funds and working capital might be wasted, if tax holiday arrangements are not utilised or penalties through delayed or improperly made tax payments arise.

The PRC taxation structure for FIEs

- Foreign Enterprise Income Tax (FEIT)
- Value Added Tax (VAT)
- Business Tax (BT)
- Other taxes, e.g. Customs Duty, Consumption Tax, Stamp Duty or Individual Income Tax

Foreign Enterprise Income Tax (FEIT)

The standard tax rates are 33 per cent (30% plus 3 per cent business tax) on net income for foreign invested enterprises or foreign enterprises with permanent establishment in the PRC or 20 per cent (i.e. withholding tax) on gross income basis for FE with passive China-sourced income (e.g. dividends, interest, rental, royalties). The taxable income is calculated by the formula 'taxable income = total income – deductible expenses'. The total income includes production and other operative income, gain on transfer of assets, interest income, rental income and royalty etc. The deductible expenses include production- or business-related costs as well as outgoings and losses incurred in producing the taxable income.

The non-deductible expenses comprise expenditures incurred on the purchase or construction of fixed assets as well as on the acquisition or development of intangible assets. Further non-deductible costs include interest on capital, income tax payments, late payment surcharges and fines in relation to tax payments, fines incurred for unlawful operation and losses sustained through the confiscation of property. Donations other than those used for public welfare or relief purposes inside China, royalties paid to the head office of the enterprise and other expenses unrelated to production or business operation are additional non-deductible expenses. Some losses from natural disasters or accidents are covered by insurance indemnity.

Tax incentives are reduced tax rates, which might be only 15per cent or 24 per cent as compared to 33 per cent. The granted rates depend on location, nature and duration of operations and on the amount of investment or type of tax holidays. The standard exemption is applicable for production-oriented enterprises scheduled for an operating period for more than ten years and comprises full exemption from income tax for the first two profit-making years plus 50 per cent reduction in applicable tax rate for the following three years. Further exemptions are granted for export-oriented enterprises, advanced technology enterprises or special economic zones such as the Guangzhou Municipality Bonded Zones, Shanghai Pudong New Area or the Hainan Special Economic Zone.

Determination of Value Added Taxation

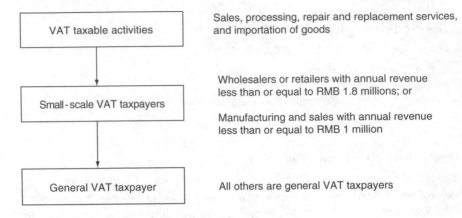

Chart 10   Determination of Value Added Taxation

Tax refund facilities on reinvestment of profits are given under special conditions such as for foreign investors of FIEs, who reinvest its Chinese-sourced profits in the form of capital increase to those FIEs. This tax refund also applies if the profits are reinvested for the set-up of a new FIE with an operating period of more than five years. It is important to note that tax losses can only be carried forward for five years for set-off purposes. Foreign tax paid can be credited against Chinese income tax on the same stream of income. Transfer pricing for related party transactions must be determined on an arm's length basis; otherwise, the tax authorities may challenge and make adjustments.

The VAT-able income in general comprises activities such as sales, processing, repair and replacement services and importation of goods. However, VAT implications could be different for different VAT taxpayers regarding certain activities such as deemed sales activities, mixed sales activities or multiple businesses or concurrent activities. Deemed Sales activities include:

- consignment of goods to others for sale;
- sale of consignment goods;
- transfer of goods for sale between related parties located in different countries and using uniform accounting basis;
- self-manufactured goods or goods processed on a commission basis which are used in non-taxable projects;
- self-manufactured goods, goods processed on a commission basis or purchased goods for investment, distribution in-kind to shareholders or investors, consideration for staff welfare or personal purposes, etc.

Mixed sales activities include transactions, which involve both VAT-able and non-VAT-able activities. Multiple business activities apply, when tax-payers are concurrently engaged in both VAT-able and non-VAT-able activities.

VAT tax rates are usually 17 per cent. For specific items such as cereals and oil, utilities, animal feed, fertiliser, insecticide and other goods as specified by the State Council it is reduced to 13%. Exported goods are not subject to VAT payments.

The VAT calculation for importation of goods is 'VAT payable = taxable value × VAT rate', whereas the 'taxable value = CIF price + custom duty + consumption tax (if applicable)'. Sale of goods or provision of services is calculated 'VAT payable = output VAT − input VAT', whereas 'input VAT = VAT payable on purchases or receipt of taxable services'. It must be noted that non-creditable input VAT means VAT paid on the fixed assets of a business. Collective welfare or personal consumption activities as well as abnormal damages or wastage are considered as non-VAT-able or exempt activities.

The timing of VAT payment is quite sensitive and must be followed properly. In general, except for 'deemed sales', this is determined by reference to the types of the transaction and the mode of settlement. The timing for VAT payment for sale of goods is determined by the individual circumstances of the sales business. VAT payments for provision of services have to be done when the payment for services rendered is received. In the case of importation of goods it has to be done upon customs declaration. The timing for VAT payment for sales is as follows:

- If payment is made to vendor directly: upon receipt of cash or bills for the sales consideration.
- If payment is done by credit/instalment sales: on due date of payment specified under contract.
- If payment is fixed via collection/payment agents (e.g. bank): upon dispatch of goods and completion of the collection procedures with the agent.
- If paid by advance payment: upon delivery of goods.
- If payment is made on consignment sales: upon receipt of sales report from consignee.
- If payment is proceeded according to deemed sales: upon transfer of goods.

The timing of input VAT deduction depends on the nature of business. For manufacturing businesses it has to be done, when the goods become inventory. Wholesale and retail business as well as services such as processing, repair and replacement are due when payments are received. Improper timing in claiming credits of input VAT may render the credit right to be invalid. Such incidents would also be penalised under the rules of tax evasion.

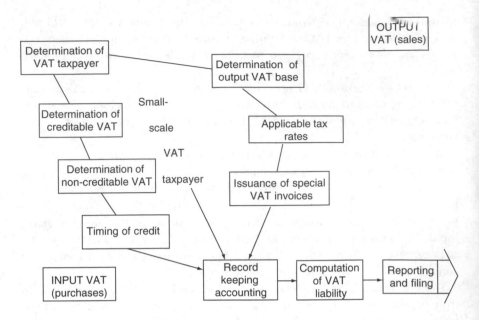

Chart 11   The lifecycle of VAT compliance process
Source: Deloitte Touche Tomatsu (2000)

Business Tax (BT)

Taxpayers are generally units, individuals, lessees or sub-contractors as well as foreign investment enterprises and foreign enterprises. Taxable activities include provisions of taxable labour services, assignments of intangible assets and sales of immovable property. The tax must be conducted within the territory of PRC. The taxable income should include the total amount of consideration and other incidental charges or additional fees. The tax computation is calculated according to the formula 'Business Tax payable = turnover × tax rate'. The turnover comprises the total consideration plus incidental charges and additional fees. However, there are also concurrent activities involving BT and VAT. For instance, a taxpayer may be concurrently engaged in both taxable labour services and VAT-able activities. Then, the turnover generated by the provision of taxable labour services must be accounted for separately from the VAT-able activities. Otherwise, the labour services also may be subject to VAT. The timing of tax liabilities is fixed as the day of receipt of consideration or proof of receipt thereof. Foreign invested enterprises can also enjoy preferential tax treatment under special circumstances. This should be checked more in detail with taxation consultants.

Summary/Recommendations

In China, the taxation of foreign invested enterprises is mainly structured into three major tax classifications, consisting of Foreign Enterprise Income Tax, Value Added Tax and Business Tax. The common rates and regulations are published in relevant official publications of the state and local taxation bureau. Special attention should be paid to the available incentives and refund possibilities, which differ according to location. There should also be a clear understanding about deductible and non-deductible costs for tax calculations. The right timing of tax payments is also sensitive and should be followed properly. Special tax holiday arrangements are especially granted for business tax payments or for VAT refunds in case of export business. Due to the fact that tax issues and regulations are quite complicated and are subject to frequent changes, it is also advisable to consult one of the leading accounting firms. Major changes in the taxation policy are expected since joining the WTO.

Further sources

China Tax and Auditing Manual HK, (1998) *Asia Law & Practice*, 2nd edn.
Deloitte Touche Tomatsu Report (1996) *Avoiding Double Taxation in HK and PRC*, HK, Asia Law & Practice.
Ernst & Young (1994) *Doing Business in China*, HK.
Wang, Y. (1996) *Investment in China*, CITIC, NY, pp. 115–24.

10

How Can I Restructure my Business in China?

Engelbert Boos

10.1. How can I influence external and internal decision-making?

China's highly dynamic business environment requires frequent important strategic and operational decisions by management. Such daily management decisions have implications for the success or failure and profit or loss of the whole business. The daily business decisions also influence the counter-decision-making process of the internal organisation and the investor's head-quarters as well as the competitors on the market. Therefore, the managers depend on a reliable information network. They must also think about how to negotiate with the Chinese joint venture partner and the superior authorities. It is important to think about how to influence decision-making for the achievement of majorities in board resolutions and balancing the different interest groups. Such stakeholder management and lobbying is very important for the success rate in business.

The most important features in how to influence decision-making

Influencing decision-making requires the following steps:

- clear understanding of your partner's situation and objectives;
- SWOT analysis of your own organisation;
- analysis of the internal and external business environment;
- definition of a suitable and feasible strategic concept;
- clear operational implementation of the fixed strategies and objectives.

Supporting tools and behaviour for successful negotiations:

- build up a good and reliable relationship network;
- standardise decision-finding processes and include all parties;

- follow a clear strategy in negotiations and fix limits before the negotiations begin;
- be courteous and avoid causing loss of face;
- include higher decision-makers in critical cases;
- prepare and follow up alternative projects and scenarios.

In order to influence the respective decision-maker or interest group, it is important to understand clearly the individual situation and background with all open or hidden objectives, weaknesses, strengths and the economical and financial situation. It is important to figure out the attitudes and relationships of related key people as well as their functional position and influence on general opinions or decisions. In the case of the relationship with a joint venture partner – i.e. for his required approval to a sensitive board resolution – it is important to understand completely his individual objectives and circumstances. Find out whether he has personal, political, tactical or strategic reasons if disagreements occur. Questions such as 'How far he can decide by himself?' and 'To what extent does he depend on the opinion of his superiors?' may be prerequisites for failure or success. The investment partner's enthusiasm for success in the future must be regularly re-checked. Sometimes it helps to solve smaller individual problems or requests; this can lead to approval for big decisions in the foreign investor's benefit. The present business environment must be analysed within its fast-changing surroundings regarding sales and marketing issues. The decision behaviour of customers, competitors, suppliers, authorities, joint venture partners and other stakeholders must be thoroughly understood. A frequent SWOT analysis of the organisation with its products, markets, financial situation, relationship network and internal hierarchical structures concerning opinions and decision-making behaviour is also very important.

The above mentioned analysis forms the basis for the definition of a suitable and feasible strategic and operational concept. The concept must include all the open and hidden personal objectives of the participants. The implementation of the defined and agreed strategies and objectives, taking special account of the weaknesses and strengths of all the related parties, must be followed up thoroughly. It also helps to build up a good and reliable relationship to the decision-makers and work out feasible solutions with mutual benefits.

Consensus in decision-finding can be supported and improved by the application of some negotiation tools. All related parties should be included in the decision-making and implementation process. The decision-finding and consensus processes should be standardised. Alternatives and limits in the consensus process should be fixed in advance. A large ABC demand catalogue for compensation defined in advance with the other party's support helps to reach an agreed solution more quickly. It is also important to follow up either a consensus or conflicting strategy in order to remain predictable and reliable to the counterpart. Courtesy is important; avoid causing loss of face. This applies both to the Chinese as well as to the western culture. A contract should be negotiated with clear and unified objectives and remain fair and reliable. It also helps to include in the decision-making process higher decision-makers in critical situations and the internal responsible managers, if they are affected by the resolutions. A step by step implementation is better and more cost- and time-efficient. Alternative projects and scenarios should always be well prepared and quickly be followed up if developments are not proceeding satisfactionly or there is too much time wasting and unacceptable pressure from negotiating counterparts.

Summary

External and internal decision-making can be influenced and speeded up by the identification of key decision-makers and by the use of special negotiation skills. A profound analysis of the internal and external environment and the definition of a suitable strategic concept are requisites for the successful achievement of set objectives in influencing the decision-making process.

Further source

Reisach, U., Tauber, T. and Yuan, X. (1997) *China – Wirtschaftspartner zwischen Wunsch und Wirklichkeit*, Vienna, Ueberreuther.

10.2. How can I restructure a joint venture in trouble?

Investments in China often face difficulties for several specific reasons. The western investor enters with his products into a new market (which is not yet developed to western standards) together with a Chinese partner with specific knowledge of Chinese standards. He doesn't know yet what technological standards and service packages are most popular with the customers. In the beginning, it is also quite difficult to acquire reliable data about the real purchasing power of Chinese consumers. The western investor also is not quite sure about the real contribution capabilities of the other investing partners, particularly in view of frequently overestimated market size. A further fundamental reason for trouble and the initiation of a restructuring process may be the stage of the company's lifecycle. Most entities were founded several years ago. They have built up experience with their investment partner and are more familiar with the specialities of the market. They must concentrate now on the improvement of efficiency by reducing costs and increasing production quantities. As an important consequence, the competitiveness on the market can be increased and better profit margins can be realised.

Checklist and analysis of the most important reasons for the initiation of a restructuring process as stable basis for decision-making

- Evaluation of the investor's strong will for success (analysis of the shareholders' and stakeholders' interests).
- Open-minded analysis of existing difficulties and mistakes that have been made by the board and the management of business operation. Difficulties with staff, management and the board. Short- or long-term nature of the difficulties (analysis of leadership and human resources issues).
- Mutual suitability of the investment partners and their strategic objectives (analysis of the strategy, organisational structure and major objectives of business operation).
- Watching products and services related to the market. Realistic estimation of market size and achievable markets shares. Future perspectives of the products and market segments. Competition through other distribution channels of the headquarters (analysis of the key markets and the major products).
- Sufficient funding and liquidity of the entity (analysis of the financial situation).
- Influence of the new management and more control rights or other legal status of the entity (analysis of the legal situation and status).

Some essential questions must be thoroughly and critically analysed, before the implementation of a restructuring process of a troubled investment should begin. A quick and successful restructuring or new start to the joint venture only makes sense, when both parties are open-minded and clear about each other's objectives and interests. A strong desire for success and the balance of each other's interests are required. Otherwise, it may be better to break up the partnership and to start up with a new partner or one's own company. Major external reasons for a crisis may arise from the wrong strategy and an unprepared investment project. The adapted strategy may not be suitable for the Chinese market environment. An unsuitable investment partner as well as a poorly investigated and prepared feasibility study and due diligence analysis of the investment partners may also result in tremendous problems within the operational business. Before a restructuring process can start, a realistic SWOT analysis of the partner, the market and also of the product with special consideration to its influence on success should take place.

Internal sources of potential conflicts can arise from different objectives of the board of directors or management at different levels. The reasons for it must be analysed in detail. The resulting difficulties have to be checked with regard to their short- or long-term nature and according to their impact on further business development. It should be asked whether the existing people in management and on the board are still able to continue with a good co-operation in the long term. They must be still able to continue to work with each other. A high level of mutual trust and reliability is required. A further important question is related to the potential chances and the future of the manufactured product range. The existing product range and technological level are often outdated and not well enough adapted to the Chinese market. This results in the need for a large restructuring process within the production department. In the case of export businesses, questions concerning Asian and possibly also Chinese economic problems with their potential impact on competitiveness may also play an important role. Fierce competition through local and international competitors and possible existing grey imports through Hong Kong or further headquarters' distribution channels may initiate further reasons for conflicts. In many cases, it is not sufficient to rely on the distribution network and business relationships of the investment partner alone. The establishment of an efficient sales and distribution network must be integrated properly into a successful business policy.

The initiation of a restructuring processes may also result from overestimating market size and having too small a market share, too low sales volume or shrinking scopes of supply in case of engineering projects. The decision for restructuring is also greatly influenced by rising risks through piracy on transferred key technology. Existing intercultural and personal problems of management and their employees also play an important role. Competent and loyal employees are desperately required for a successful restructuring process and future development of the company.

Summary/Recommendations

There are several internal and external reasons for difficulties and the initiation of a restructuring process of an entity. The results of a business due diligence analysis may answer the question of whether the business operation of an investment should be continued, restructured or stopped. It is important to analyse whether the situation improves noticeably through higher shares and more control of the company and with eventually some new people on the board and management. Scenarios may be evaluated for a different legal status (wholly foreign owned entity or contractual venture), taking into consideration the respective impacts on solving existing problems. The importance of available business licences may also effect the decision. A new application under present laws may limit the formerly approved scope of supply. The possible combination of an existing distribution and service channel with the headquarters or other market participants channels may also influence the decision for a planned restructuring process. The implementation of new or different strategic alliances or even the sale of shares in the medium to long term are possible alternatives. The company's existing workshop can be also used as service base for other or further products with the convenience of local currency billing. A further alternative may be the use of the workshop as base for tailor-made customer solutions. Finance or fiscal reasons are also important and relevant. All these factors are important, affecting the strategic decisions for the restructuring of the invested entity.

Further sources

Moser, M. (ed.) (2000) *China Troubleshooter*, HK, Asia Law & Practice, ch. 2.
The Life and Death of a Joint Venture in China (2000) 2nd rev. edn, HK, *Asia Business Law Review*.

10.3. Which legal issues are important on exit from a joint venture?

A joint venture in trouble often requires some restructuring measures for an improvement of the performance, greater efficiency or just for the implementation of a new management structure with more strategic and operational control in the company. The need for more funds for an increased production range or for the enlargement of the sales and distribution network also may be a significant reason for the initiation of a major restructuring process.

Possible strategic ways of restructuring and their legal impacts

- Investing, de-investing, withdraw or turnaround strategies
- Merger of several small entities
- Liquidating
- Freezing and/or go-away strategies
- Exit of a joint venture
- Re-entry

Investing, de-investing, withdraw or turnaround strategies

In China, the business development is subject to many internal and external changes. The products, the markets and also the economic situation of the joint venture partner depend on the fast-changing and dynamic business environment. Consequently, the competitive and financial situation of the entity also changes and requires strategic adjustments. The foreign investor may request a reorganisation of the entity, i.e. through additional investments and more operational control in management and on the board. Investments for new product developments or an increase in the distribution network may be required. The foreign investor approaches the Chinese partner in order to negotiate an increase of shares and other adjustments in business strategy. A turnaround strategy may be required. The foreign investor may consider putting more or less money into the equity or decide to leave it just as it is. Such investing or investment withdrawal decisions and strategies confront most joint ventures from time to time. Such strategic changes may also lead to the question whether a new legal form of the company should be introduced. It must be decided whether a joint venture, contractual venture or even wholly foreign owned venture better suits the company's future requirements and strategic perspectives.

The new required investments may only come from one investor (diluting strategy) or from additional or new partners (venture capital funds). New partners without any interest in the operational business may also be the most attractive (i.e. banks or owners of land use rights). An additional partner can move in with fresh capital by a share transfer – that has to be approved separately by the authorities – and a separate subsequent capital increase with the new partner. Part buy-out alternatives may include the joint venture partner keeping minority shares (i.e. 5–25 per cent) in the company including fixed dividend payments at the end of the year in connection with the change of legal structure to a 'contractual venture'. The legal status of a total buy-out option and a change into a WFOE (wholly foreign owned enterprise) is not always possible. Some branches such as telecommunications, automotives or energy supply are still restricted to minority or equal shares of the foreign investor. This alternative option includes the risk of dependence on the former local investor/partner, for example dependence on electricity or other supplies. For such reasons, it is always better to keep a good understanding and cooperation on some mutual interests. A new legal structure of the company may require changes in the articles of association. The superior authorities may also request a higher export quota. Negotiations for changes in share capital are very sensitive and include many potential problems. A new business plan has to be worked out; changes in the upper level of management may be needed. Thus, managers who know the Chinese business environment are an important asset. Organisational processes and functions have to be restructured, especially in the finance and sales department. Costs must be reduced and financing and liquidity planned.

Merger of several small entities

The merger of two or more entities is also a kind of exit strategy and increasingly popular among larger companies with several investments in China. The smaller invested entities particularly must look for greater economies of scale and try to make best use of possible synergies. Such mergers can be done by 'merger of absorption', where the absorbed entity is dissolved and by 'the merger by new establishment'. In the case of a merger with a local Chinese partner, the western shareholder may not be diluted to an interest of less than 25 per cent in the post-merger entity.

Liquidating of an investment

The exit of a joint investment project by using the liquidation option is quite common in western countries, but not in China. A hostile liquidation especially should be avoided. It's always better to go for a solution with the mutual understanding of all investment partners and stakeholders, the preferred objective being to continue with the existing business licence, mainly for fiscal, financial and legal issues. The liquidation option would mean that accumulated losses could not be balanced with future profits from the taxation point of view. The numerous transaction costs and other expenses are huge and especially disadvantageous for the western investor. The sale of assets is subject to various turnover taxes, duties and fees such as import VAT and business tax as well as the payment of import duty for formerly free imported investment goods. Allocated land use rights are also a sensitive issue, which are lost as assets in the balance sheet with the liquidation of a company. Therefore, it is always important to possess granted land use rights. The liquidation of a company also has to be published twice in a national newspaper, an unpopular option with the local investment partner and his relevant superior authorities. It is always better to proceed with other options to liquidation such as a mutually agreed 'part or complete buy-out' of the investment partner or a 'freezing or go away strategy'.

Freezing and/or go-away strategies

Sometimes political, financial, marketing, licence or other important issues influence the decision to avoid the restructuring, buy-out or closing of a joint venture. Freezing or go-away strategies may be applied in such a case, where the operational business will be stopped, all assets withdrawn and the people released. The opening formalities and procedures of a new venture at a different location and in a different form should not be influenced negatively. Tactical and personal reasons as well as keeping the avoiding partner losing face may play an important role. However, 'fictive' board meetings and other minimum activities are still required to proceed. The freezing strategy only postpones the need for a solution to the problem, until both parties realise the senselessness of the venture. The 'just go-away' strategy without any preliminary announcement also bears some risks. There may arise the risk of arbitration in an international court with possible prosecution in the foreign company's home country, when the foreign employees simply leave the company and China.

Such a strategy, is more often used by smaller-sized Taiwanese and Hong Kong companies, who are more interested in short-term profits. The underlying and ancillary contracts must be checked carefully in order to minimise the long-term risks. However, there is always a chance of re-activating the entity in a possibly improved business environment in the future.

Exit of a joint venture

The exit of a joint venture may become quite expensive; there is a danger of being exploited by the Chinese partner. He can require payment of interest on the fixed assets. The land use rights may be highly valued and put under strict restrictions. Allocated land use rights cannot be paid out or calculated into the assets value. These rights are quite often part of the partners' contributed shares. Therefore, it is possible that the contribution of the partner may be of no value. The cost of loans for employees also can be quite expensive. It is possible that arbitrage is required and that the case must be pushed through all instances. Local governments may ignore the case in order to avoid the process of liquidation. At unfriendly liquidations some types of mafia behaviour may arise as well as loss of inventory and pressure for the re-establishment of the enterprise. The reasons for the need to close the joint venture should be explained clearly to the partner; an effort should be made to accept the culture and language of the Chinese. If there are plans to establish a WFOE at a later date, do not underestimate the importance of high-tech status or an export quota of at least 50 per cent in gaining governmental approval.

Re-entry

The local government is in charge of the registration in the case of re-entry into a venture. There may be changes and restrictions within the branch of business; pressure may exist on the business licence or quota system. Nowadays, WFOE seems to be a better way to enter. There is no need to take care of the partner's interests and dependence. Alternatively, the joint venture can be kept and the shares raised to 80 or 95 per cent in which case the management can also take over. The joint venture can be also transferred into a contractual joint venture by taking over the management and the major part of board decision-making as well as a fixed profit arrangement for the partner. Then, the export quota and the problems with the land use rights may not arise. Such status or solution is more easily acceptable for the authorities; a good reputation is an important factor in staying in business.

Summary/Recommendations

The initiation of a major restructuring process should be well prepared. There should be a clear understanding of the reasons for such a process.

The real reasons for basic problems must be analysed in detail. It is not always only the joint venture partner, who is responsible for major difficulties. Based on the analysis, it should be considered how to solve the basic existing problems. 'Is it still possible to continue with the existing partner or not?' 'Which is the best legal and operational structure to overcome former difficulties?' But all possible obstacles which may arise out of the implementation process of a new venture should be considered. It is always better to proceed with a solution of mutual understanding; the restructured venture may then have a real chance to develop better in a bright future.

Further sources

Moser, M. (ed.) (2000) *China Troubleshooter*, HK, Asia Law & Practice, ch.2.
The Life and Death of a Joint Venture in China (2000) 2nd rev. edn, HK, *Asia Business Law Review*.

10.4. When does it make sense to turn an existing joint venture into a wholly foreign owned enterprise or contractual venture?

Each legal form of investment has advantages and disadvantages. Therefore, it is not possible to just recommend one of them. However, recently many investors tend to favour wholly foreign owned enterprises (WFOEs) in order to have independence in decision-making and business operations. The switching of an existing joint venture to a contractual venture connected with capital increase or share transfer procedures has also become more and more popular. This legal structure enables more finance and management control of the invested entity.

The decision for a new legal structure requires answers to crucial questions

- Are there any specific advantages for a WFOE?
- Is any prosperous future development feasible with the existing partner?
- How important and sensitive is the relationship network of the partner?
- Is the marketing of the products easier done alone?
- How important is the need for the former employees?
- How many of them will agree to follow the new entity?
- How high is the cost to lay off staff?
- Is it a friendly or unfriendly implementation?
- What type of reaction from the authorities can be expected?
- Will the WFOE still be under the influence of the district authority or is it in a new location?
- Is the authority interested in the further existence of the venture?

- How important is the political support and back-up?
- To what extent does the joint venture (JV) depend on the location of the partner's company (supply of water, electricity, garbage, etc.)?
- How easy or difficult is it to build up the new relationship network?

Basically, it must be split into two cases. The easiest one is the foundation of a new company without the complicated load of a former joint venture partner. In this case, specific product- and market-related facts and advantages can be decisive. A plan must be worked out relating to the way to build up the required relationships with the superior and local authorities and associations. Key people may be acquired from competitors or recruited on the market in connection with extensive training programmes to be held locally and abroad. Such efforts may take some time, especially in the beginning. However, if well done, it also helps a lot to be in a stable long-term business development. The other and more complicated case is related to the transfer of an existing venture into a WFOE. Such cases are mostly caused by former conflicts and require very sensitive procedures and planning in order to minimise the potential existence of conflicts and delays. Otherwise the whole implementation process risks failure. The foreign investor may have lost confidence in the possibility of a prosperous future development with the former partner.

The separation from a former partner implies a lot of questions about conflicting management. The behaviour of the former employees is very important. The willingness of key people to transfer and to further co-operate with the new entity is necessary. Laid-off workers may cause high costs and other troubles. According to law they can ask for one month's salary for each year spent in the JV and former partner's company, limited to a maximum of 12 months, depending on the region. Huge impact on the business operation and on the total cost of the restructuring process can arise in the case of unfriendly implementations. The crucial situation even worse can get in the case of unpredictable reactions by the authorities, especially when the prospective WFOE is to be under the influence of the same local authority. For such reasons, it is recommended to negotiate with the local partner and the authority an agreement with mutual benefit. This applies especially in cases of products or markets which need political support and back-up. The physical dependence of the factory on the location of the partner's company may also cause negative effects. The supply of water, electricity, heating or garbage disposal etc. may be interrupted. On the other hand it is important to evaluate on how easily the new relationships can be built up. The situation is less complicated for more easily marketed products.

The selection and arrangement of management becomes easier in case of WFOE. It is advantageous that a general manager (GM) and deputy general manager (DGM) not be appointed simultaneously. The transferred new company has the further positive right to appoint the GM and board of directors without the involvement of a partner. With consideration of all the potential difficulties in the case of an unfriendly transfer to a WFOE, it may be better to establish a contractual venture. Under such circumstances, the taking over of the management and control of the company is at the cost of a fixed profit for the former joint venture partner. It is recommended to negotiate a majority share of at least 75–95 per cent of the company.

Summary/Recommendations

Due to unhappy experiences and intercultural misunderstandings, many companies restructure existing joint ventures into contractual ventures or more preferably into WFOE ventures. It is aimed at running the company more easily and more flexibly with more power in management and on the board. A WFOE may be favoured for greater control in keeping the know-how of the transferred key technology and other operational reasons. However, especially in the phase of establishment, the convenient contributions of a potential joint venture partner also have to be taken into consideration. He normally supplies production facilities and buildings and a basic care of employees and workers. The advantages only increase in the medium to long term. Required capital increases in connection with the final transfer into a contractual venture may be also an interesting alternative to the establishment of a WFOE.

Further sources

China Investment Manual (1998) 2nd edn, HK, *Asia Business Law Review.*
Setting Up and Financing WFOE's in the PRC (1997) HK, Asia Law & Practice.

10.5. What kind of outsourcing activities optimise the business?

Outsourcing may make sense for activities within one's own operational functions as well as within the value-added chain of certain products. In special cases, it may even be of interest to outsource the production and after-sales services of a whole product to a related company within the business branch. Outsourcing may be also initiated in relation to a major restructuring process of the entity. The outsourcing process of part of the production is the reverse of a merger and acquisition.

The most important problems in connection with outsourcing decisions

- Outsourcing may reduce fixed costs, but also increases overheads and controlling efforts.

- The advantages of outsourcing must be more than just costs and risk.
- Problems may be the maintaining of quality levels, cost of labour, technology transfer, balance of import/export supply or political issues.

Major reasons for a restructuring process are organisational complexity, reduction of overheads, increased competition, more efficiency pressure from outside or more effective results. The intended reduction of portfolio may also be a major reason for the planned outsourcing. Everything other than core activities can be considered for outsourcing. The liquidation of a production line and transfer to a further entity can also be a special form of outsourcing. The decision for outsourcing of a restructuring process should be oriented on the results of a benchmarking assessment based on the comparison of one's own activities with regards to external competition.

The outsourcing process can be divided into two phases, the decision and implementation phase. Within the decision phase questions arise concerning the importance of outsourcing in relation to the required amount of investments. The core business should be defined with the perspectives for possible developments and required investment. The present existing and future planned supply relationship should be analysed and estimated. Decisions have to be made on whether an activity or product should be cut off or not. These procedures require clearly defined selection criteria. It is important to evaluate potential suppliers who can do the outsourcing task; short- or long-term supplier contracts should be considered. The outsourcing activities must be integrated into existing systems. The organisational integration with the relevant interfaces must be shown. The preparation for the implementation process includes the research and analysis of data for market strategies, the selection of a suitable assessment partner, the definition of sales and marketing issues, the setting up of a controlling system and organisation as well as the final selection of a suitable outsourcing partner.

In China outsourcing decisions of state owned companies are more cost driven. In western countries strategic reasons are more important. Insourcing is sometimes better than outsourcing, especially when production capacities are already too high. Only outsourcing to loss-makers does not work; the outsourcing 'production' company may go bankrupt. The main question is whether the product has a future and a market or not. If prospects for the future are very poor, it may be better to leave it and possibly end production later. Costs influence outsourcing decisions. Sometimes outsourcing is not really outsourcing, but done for political, social and economical environmental reasons. A bypass of two to three manufacturing plants reduces the risks in connection with outsourcing. One potential risk in outsourcing may arise through the fact that although fixed costs may be reduced, there may be increased overheads and controlling efforts. The cut of fixed costs is relevant;

it may be possible to sell assets, but staff may be harder to reduce. The workers, trade unions and the government officials may be aggressive if products without any future are being effected. Always question whether the advantages outweigh the costs and risks.

The outsourcing process must be applicable. The selection of a suitable outsourcing partner is very important. He requires enough time – six to 12 months – to set up the outsourcing project. The successful reduction of portfolio and products requires tight project control. The set time, budget and quality levels must be kept. Especially in the beginning personnel training must be given to support the supplier. Problems may arise over maintaining the set quality level, the cost of labour, procedures for technology transfer, the balance of import/export supply or simply for political reasons.

Summary/Recommendations

Outsourcing can be an important tool for strategic business planning. However, the outsourcing process must be planned, defined and implemented properly. It is important, that potential new suppliers are capable of making the components in a more efficient and profitable way. Otherwise the co-operation will not work. Key competence should be kept in-house to avoid severe dependence on such suppliers and to prevent the creation of new competition. However, the management of a company also has to work with efficient cost and quantity levels to remain competitive on the market.

Further source

Domberger, S. (1998) *The Contracting Organisation – a strategic guide to outsourcing*, Oxford, Oxford University Press.

10.6. What has to be considered during the phase of business establishment?

The real future and long-term success of an investment in China depends very much on the preliminary analysis and the preparation of co-operation. It is important to understand and co-ordinate the strategic and operational objectives of the investment partners based on reliably investigated data. The basics of the major business issues must really work together. Not only are hard facts important such as the evaluation of the fixed assets and financial issues but also soft facts such as the attitudes and capabilities of the partner and his people. The top management must harmonise the business with respect to the inter-cultural environment. The people must be educated in customer-oriented services and obey the defined marketing and sales policy.

The most important considerations during business establishment

- Definition of a long term strategy.
- Fitting of the strategy to one's own portfolio and to the investment partner's strategic objectives.
- Good preparation of the feasibility study, which has to be based on a reliable data basis.
- Definition and implementation of a tailor-made marketing, distribution and sales strategy.
- Suitability and acceptance of the products on the market.
- Management of the profit margin, sales prices and the critical cost factors.
- Finance control and liquidity planning.
- Professional management and organisational structures.
- Efficient management training and personnel development programmes.
- Working attitude and educational background of employees.

Before the final decision for an investment in China is made, it should be thoroughly analysed how to best fit the entity into the overall portfolio of the parent company. It is important to specify clearly the products and key market segments. The target customers must purchase sufficient quantities to make the business profitable within the set cost structure. The customers must accept the offered price and quality level with all the related services. One's own medium- to long-term strategic objectives in China should be set and followed step by step. However, the operational and strategic objectives of the other investors must also be understood. The business will only succeed when the objectives of all parties fit together; otherwise, the business cannot be focused most efficiently on the markets and customer requirements and may finally fail. A good mutual understanding with the people needed for later co-operation is an important requisite for success. The methods of doing business and how to arrive at important decisions in case of different opinions must be understood. The feasibility study must also be well prepared and based on reliable data. Such data from official statistical sources are not very reliable in China. Consequently, they must be proved and cross-checked through reliable third-party sources as basis for the definition of a more reliable business plan.

The suitability and acceptance of the products on the market are essential success factors. The most promising market niches within the competitor's environment must be figured out and proved thoroughly. Preliminary imports of the respective products or test sales on the market may be helpful for the definition and implementation of a successful product, marketing and sales policy with related services. The sales and marketing strategy should adapt the product's specific global strengths to the Chinese market's specific circumstances. The product and service policy must be clearly differentiated from the competitors' and meet the requirements of the marketing rules for premium products. This can be solved through the establishment and definition of sales, marketing, distribution and service strategies. Nowadays, the customer puts an increasing value on short delivery times, flexible payment conditions, co-operation in sales, distribution, product development, tailor-made product solutions, environmental protection, energy efficiency and training packages for product application. Quick and flexible reaction to customers' requirements should be the first priority. The customer visiting frequency and individual service package have to be enlarged and intensified. This especially applies for large OEM (Own Equipment Manufacturers) which is decisive for the achievement of higher production quantities.

The cost structure has to be analysed in detail due to its importance for the attractiveness to larger customers. The controlling of sensitive indicators regarding business operation must be well arranged. Best and worst case scenarios should be prepared in depth with implementation planning. The implementation process must fit the capabilities and attitudes of the existing key staff and management. This should be screened by someone senior and responsible to ensure that careful use of criticism and acknowledgement of achievements helps to create high motivation levels. Accompanying training programmes are also important for good performance. Achievement and the maintaining of high quality levels are necessary for success and competitiveness in the transparent and rapidly changing market environment. This also helps the acceptance of the products and their image on markets. A strict finance control and liquidity planning process supports the creation of a healthy basis of business and reliability on the market.

Summary/Recommendations

During the phase of establishment it is important to have a clear business strategy, which fits the overall business portfolio as well as the strategic interests of the Chinese party. It is also important to market suitable products to clearly defined market segments and to differentiate them from competitors'. The organisation should prepare staff well and efficiently with a strong customer orientation. Together with a strict cost control concept, success on the market should follow.

Further sources

PRC Joint Ventures: Financial Management (1997) HK, Asia Law & Practice.
Wang, Y. (1996) *Investment in China*, NY, CITIC.

10.7. How is the accessing of international equity capital organised?

This question sets out an overview of the two most important ways of accessing international equity capital for Chinese companies. The first, and so far the most common, is through the identification of a foreign investor and the formation of a joint venture. The second is to access equity capital through the equity markets.

The most common ways of attracting international equity capital for Chinese companies

- Direct investment of potential foreign investor.
- Capital through the equity markets.

Joint ventures

When the PRC began encouraging foreign investment in the late 1970s, the concept of Sino-foreign joint ventures was introduced through the *Law on Chinese-Foreign Equity Joint Ventures* of 1979. This allowed Chinese enterprises to access international capital and technology, while providing market entry for foreign enterprises, based on the principle of equality and mutual benefit. Since the 1979 joint venture law there have been many additions to the body of joint venture law in many areas including hiring of personnel and wage requirements. The laws encourage joint ventures in specific fields such as those involving export, import substitution, technology and skills transfer.

Joint ventures are still prohibited in certain sectors, including media and defence, while joint ventures in other sectors, such as public utilities, transportation, wholesaling, property trust, telecommunications, investment and leasing are restricted. In recent years a number of retail joint ventures and joint venture holding companies have been approved. Meanwhile MOFTEC and the Ministry of Information also approved joint ventures in telecommunications and other service industries. The recent acceptance of China into the WTO will have huge effects on traditional ways of funding and possible scopes for business.

Establishment of a joint venture

The first step in the establishment of a joint venture is the identification of a suitable partner and the preparation of a letter of intent signed by all joint venture parties. The letter of intent allows the Chinese party to apply for preliminary governmental approval and begin detailed negotiations with the foreign party. Such 'letters of intent' would, among other things, indicate the legal form of the joint venture proposed (equity or co-operative venture). However, generally they are not considered to be legally binding.

The next step is the preparation of a feasibility study which sets out the detailed economic and technical parameters of the joint venture including the proposed contributions of each party (equity joint ventures must meet certain registered capital requirements). This business plan is relied on by the authorising bodies when deciding whether to approve the joint venture and, particularly, whether to commit state controlled assets to a joint venture.

The final step in the creation of the joint venture is the preparation of the joint venture contract and articles of association for the joint venture company. The approving authority varies, depending on the size and business of the joint venture, and may include several governmental departments, including the People's Bank of China. After approval, the joint venture must register with the local Administration for Industry and Commerce, which will issue the business licence. Although this may be a long and arduous process, the benefits can be far reaching. In China's complicated governmental structure, production and marketing system and regional differences often make a Chinese partner invaluable.

Equity markets

There are presently two official securities exchanges in the PRC: the Shanghai Securities Exchange (since December 1990) and the Shenzhen Stock Exchange (since July 1991). While there has been some pressure, particularly from provincial governments, for additional exchanges to be established, the central authorities have repeatedly indicated that this will not occur until the Shenzhen and Shanghai exchanges are deemed to be 'successful'. The two exchanges no longer have local supervising bodies. They are both under the direct control of the China Securities Regulatory Committee, a committee under the State Council. Further liberalisation is in prospect. Recently these have been some venture capital companies operating on the Chinese market. However, investment volumes are still relatively small due to relatively high risks in business operation and legal obstacles.

Summary/Recommendations

Each new established company in China requires funds for buying fixed assets and for all working capital-related tasks. Such funds can be received from potential foreign investors through the establishment of a joint venture or from the equity market in Shanghai or Shenzhen. The establishment of the joint venture or the movement of funds has to be organised according to special procedures and regulations.

Further sources

Cooper & Lybrand (1994) *Guide to Reporting and Accounting in PRC*, HK.
Wang, Y. (1996) *Investment in China*, NY, CITIC.

10.8. Which international commercial laws are applied to China?

Since opening its doors to foreign investment in the late 1970s, the PRC has made significant progress in putting in place a comprehensive legal framework for the conduct of international business transactions. This has involved not only the promulgation of thousands of new domestic laws, regulations, decrees and administrative rules, but also the ratification of numerous international treaties and bilateral agreements dealing with trade and investment matters. In 1999 a new contract law was introduced.

The most important commercial laws

- PRC law is classified into constitutional law, administrative law, criminal law, civil law, economic law, labour law, law of procedure and international law.
- The Law on Chinese-Foreign Equity Joint Ventures covers areas such as labour management, land use, taxation and contracts.
- Co-operative joint ventures, wholly foreign owned enterprises and representative offices are subject to the laws for technology transfer, environmental protection, and the protection of intellectual property rights, national company law, tax regime, copyright laws, land law and regulations dealing with unfair competition, consumer protection and a host of other matters.
- China is a participant of the Vienna Convention on Contracts for the International Sale of Goods and the New York Convention on the Recognition and Enforcement of Foreign Arbitral Awards.
- China has joined the Brussels-based Customs Co-ordination Council.
- China has joined the World Trade Organisation (WTO).
- China has entered into a number of bilateral trade agreements, agreements for the avoidance of double taxation, investment protection agreements and judicial assistance agreements.
- Legislation expected to be enacted over the next few years includes: laws on negotiable instruments, arbitration and banking; a revamping of the foreign exchange control regime; a law governing the ownership and sale of real property and others. The Foreign Trade Law of PRC came into effect on 1 July 1994 and the Securities Law of PRC came into effect on 1 July 1999.

China has adopted what is essentially a civil law system with similarities to the German and French legal systems. PRC law is classified into constitutional law, administrative law, criminal law, civil law, economic law, labour law, law of procedure and international law. Under China's constitution the power to enact laws and other types of regulations affecting foreign business is vested in a variety of legislative and administrative bodies.

One of China's earliest efforts in foreign investment lawmaking was the *Law on Chinese-Foreign Equity Joint Ventures* of 1979. This was soon followed by a number of related regulations in the areas of labour management, land use, taxation and contracts. As the permissible forms of foreign business activity expanded, new legislation was promulgated to govern co-operative joint ventures, wholly foreign owned enterprises, representative offices, technology transfer, investment in natural resource development projects, environmental protection, and the protection of intellectual property rights. More recent legislation has included a national company law, a major revision of the tax regime, copyright laws, land law and regulations dealing with unfair competition, consumer protection and a host of other matters.

In developing a body of domestic laws and regulations for application to foreign business activity, China has made extensive reference to international customs and practices. In addition, international legal principles and norms have been absorbed directly into the PRC's domestic legal system by China's accession to a growing number of international treaties. For example, China is a participant of the Vienna Convention on Contracts for the International Sale of Goods and the New York Convention on the Recognition and Enforcement of Foreign Arbitral Awards. In addition, in the trade area, China has joined the Brussels-based Customs Co-ordination Council and has joined the World Trade Organisation (WTO). Finally, China has entered into a number of bilateral trade agreements, agreements for the avoidance of double taxation, investment protection agreements and judicial assistance agreements.

China has made significant progress in constructing a legal framework for foreign business transactions. However, that framework and the legal system as a whole is still evolving. Legislation expected to be enacted over the next few years include laws on negotiable instruments, foreign trade, securities, arbitration, and banking; a revamping of the foreign exchange control regime; a law governing the ownership and sale of real property and others. These will further strengthen the legal framework and provide a more secure environment for foreign businesses.

Summary/Recommendations

Since opening to foreign investments in 1979, China has made huge efforts in the development of its legal framework. This was an important prerequisite for success in attracting foreign investment. China has oriented its laws to western legal models in order to meet international standards. This policy promotes the international trade activities of China and attracts foreign investments. The laws are continuously further developing according to the changing business environment and up-to-date experiences from the application of laws. The court system is still influenced by traditional thinking and often executes rather flexibly. Personal relationships some-times also play an important role in definition or application of existing laws. However, more and more foreign investors do not hesitate to go to court in case of copyright violations or unpaid outstanding money to get titles for prosecution.

Further sources

Cooper & Lybrand (1994) *Guide to Reporting and Accounting in PRC*, HK.
Wang, Y. (1996) *Investment in China*, NY, CITIC.

Bibliography

Armstrong, G. and Kotler P. (1997) *Marketing – An Introduction*, NJ.

Austrian Chamber of Commerce Beijing (ed.) (1999/2000) 3/2000, p. 47, 4/1999, pp. 127 ff, and 2/2000, p. 119.

Baker & McKenzie (2001) *Operation China: An Investor's Manual*, HK.

Baker & McKenzie (ed.) (2001) *China and the Internet: Essential Legislation*, HK, Asia Information Associates Limited.

Baker & McKenzie (ed.) (2002) *Guide to China and the WTO*, HK, Asia Information Associates Limited.

Bartlett, C. and Ghoshal, S. (1999) *The Individualized Corporation: A Fundamentally New Approach to Management*, Portland, Diane Publishing Co.

Bassen, A. (1998) *Dezentralisation und Koordination von Entscheidungen in der Holding*, Wiesbaden, DUV.

Beijing You and I Software Development Co. Ltd (ed.) (2001) *2001 Directory – Training Services in China: Company Profiles & Training Capabilities*, Beijing.

Beijing Review (1999) 'China's Reluctant Consumers', June, Beijing, pp. 18–20.

'Benchmarking in China', in (1997) *Fidùcia China Focus Reports – Analysis – Strategies*, HK.

Bendell, T. and Boulter, J. (1993) *Benchmarking for competitive advantage*, London.

Blackman, C. (1998) *Negotiating China: Case Studies & Strategies*, Australia, Allen & Unwin.

Boesken, G. (1999) 'Werbemittel für China – Konzeption, Planung und Praxis der Produktion', in: *China-Contact mit Wirtschaftswelt China*, 7, pp. 10–11.

Brahm, L.J. (1998) *Sun Tzu's Art of Negotiating in China*, NAGA Group.

Brandt, R. (2000) *Auditing and Reporting 2000/2001*, HK, Accountancy Books.

Business China (1997) 'Growing number of MBA providers in China', 23 June, Beijing, pp. 12–16.

Butterfield, L. (1997) 'Developing advertising strategy', in *How to plan advertising*, ed. by Cooper, A., London, pp. 29–47.

Camp, R.C. (1998) *Benchmarking – the search for industry best practices that lead to superior performance*, Milwaukee.

Chang, G.G. (2001) *Coming Collapse of China*, London, Random House.

China Finance Manual (1998) HK, *Asia Law & Practice*.

China Investment Manual (1998) 2nd edn, HK, Asia Business Law Review.

China Media Directory (1999).

China Media Yearbook and Directory (2002), ed. by CMM Intelligence (www.cmmintelligence.com)

China Staff (ed.) (2000) *China Solutions*, HK, Asia Law & Practice.

China Staff (ed.) (1997) *China Staff Case Study Compendium*, HK, Asia Law & Practice.

China Staff (ed.) (2000) *China Staff Training Manual*, HK, Asia Law & Practice.

China Staff Employment Manual (1997) HK, Asia Law & Practice.

China Statistical Yearbook (1999)/www.stats.gov.cn

China Tax and Auditing Manual (1998) 2nd edn, HK, Asia Law & Practice.

Cockman, P. and Evans, B. (1999) *Consulting for real people – A client-centered approach for change agents and leaders*, London.

Cooper & Lybrand (1994) *Guide to Reporting and Accounting in PRC*, HK.

Cooper, R. (1991) *The Design of Cost Management Systems*, NJ, Prentice-Hall.

Coulson, C.-T. (1997) *The Future of the Organisation: Achieving Excellence Through Business Transformation*, NewYork.

Daft, R. (1992) *Organization Theory and Design*, Minnesota.

Deloitte Touche Tomatsu Report (1996) *Avoiding Double Taxation in HK and PRC*, HK, Asia Law & Practice.

Dezahn, Shira & Associates (DSMR) (2001) *China Briefing January 2001: Chinese Consumer Profiles*, Beijing.

Dietz, K. (1998) *Erfahrungen im Chinageschäft, Erfolgsfaktoren, Perspektiven, und Denkanstösse*, Wiesbaden, Gabler.

Domberger, S. (1998) *The Contracting Organisation – a strategic guide to outsourcing*, Oxford, Oxford University Press.

Duckworth, G. (1997) 'Creative Briefing' in: *Excellence in Advertising: The IPA guide to best practice*, ed. by Butterfield, L., Oxford, pp. 147–69.

Ehrlich, W. (1995) *Going China – Mit einer deutschen Marke ins Reich der Mitte*, Hanse.

Eichler, U., Grössl, L. and Neumeyer, C. (1995) *Chancen und Risiken im Zukunftsmarkt China*, Munich.

Einhorn, B. (1999) 'China's Web', in *Business Week*, August, pp. 14–18.

Ernst & Young (1994) *Doing Business in China*, HK.

ESOMAR publication (ed.) (1996) *The Big Brand Challenge*, Amsterdam.

Feng X. (1998) 'The Payment and Reward System in XMPMH', in Lichtenberger, B. (ed.) *Managing in a global world – Case studies in Intercultural Human Resources Management*, Wiesbaden, pp. 35 ff.

German Business Association (2000) 'The New Security Law', *China Contact* 4, Düsseldorf.

German Business Association (2000) *Wirtschaftsforum*, 6, Bonn pp. 6 and 34.

German Business Association, *China Contact*, no 2, p. 49.

German Business Association (2000), *China Contact*, 6, p. 12.

German Business Association (2000), *China Contact*, 10, p. 42.

Gijsen, R. and McLaughlin, B. (1997) *Reaching the Shanghai Consumer*, HK, Asia Information Associates Ltd.

Granet, M. (1985) *Das chinesische Denken – Inhalt, Form, Charakter*, Frankfurt am Main.

Grey China (ed.) (1999) *Building Brand Loyalty in Turbulent Times*, Grey ChinaBase.

Gruenebaum, B. and Janus, H. (eds) (1995) *JV Finanzierungen in der PRC, Marktchance China*, Frankfurt, Campus.

Guo, R. (1999) *How the Chinese Economy Works: A Multiregional Overview* (Studies on the Chinese Economy), Palgrave.

Harrison, R. (1995) *Consultant's Journey – a professional and personal odyssey*, London.

Hax, H. (1999) *Corporate Finance and Corporate Control*, Tuebingen, Mohr Siebeck.

Heilmann, S. and Gottwald, J.-C. (2002) *Der chinesische Aktienmarkt*, Mitteilungen des Instituts für Asienkunde Hamburg.

Helin W. David. (1992) 'When slogans go wrong', *American Demographics*, February.

Ho, S.-C. and Sin, Y.-M. (1986) 'Advertising in China: Looking Back at Looking Forward', in *International Journal of Advertising*, vol. 5, no. 4, pp. 307–16.

Hodge, B., Anthony, W. and Gales, L. (1998) *Organization Theory – A Strategic Approach*, NJ, Prentice-Hall.

Hofstede, G. (1991) *Cultures and Organisations – Software of the Mind: Intercultural Cooperation and its Importance for Survival*, London.

Hofstede, G. (1992) *Culture's Consequences – International Differences in Work-related Values*, Beverly Hills.

Hohenstein, G. (1990) *Cash Flow – Cash Management*, Wiesbader, Gabler.

Holland, L. (2000) 'A Brave New World', in *Far Eastern Economic Review*, 5 October, pp. 46–8.

Huang, G. (1998) *Rechtsfragen der Gründung und des Betriebs von Joint Ventures in PRC*, Amazon.

Huang, M., Wu, A.J. and Yang, T., (1999) *China Employment and Benefits Handbook* HK, Asia Law & Practice.

Huang, Q. (1997) *Business Decision Making in China*, Amazon.

Hutchings, G. (2001) *Modern China: A Guide to a Century of Change*, Harvard University Press.

Jimmerson Peng, J. (2001) 'Advertising and Marketing', in Shaw, A. (ed.) *Operation China: An Investor's Manual*, by Baker & McKenzie, HK, pp. 1–30

Jones, J.P. (1986) *Advertising and the Concepts of Brands*, Macmillan.

Jones, S. (1997) *Managing in China*, HK, B. H. Asia.

Kemenade, W. van, and Webb, D. (Translator) (1998) *China, Hong Kong, Taiwan, Inc.*, Vintage.

Kleimann, L. (1998) *Human Resource Management: A Tool for Competitive Advantage*, Beijing (reprint), pp. 110 ff.

Kotler, P. (1997) *Marketing-Management: Analysis, Planning, Implementation, & Control*, NJ.

Krott, M. (1999) *Marktmacht China, Global Player lernen das Schattenboxen*, Vienna.

Lauffs, A. (2001) 'Human Resources Management', in Shaw, A. (ed.) *Operation China: An Investor's Manual*, by Baker & McKenzie, HK.

Li, G. and Wong, E. (2001) *The Rise of Digital China: Investing in China's New Economy*, China Books and Periodicals.

Lichtenberger, B. (ed.) (1998) *Managing in a Global World – Case studies in Intercultural Human Resources Management*, Wiesbaden.

Ling, N.S. and Wong, J. (2001) *China's Emerging New Economy: The Internet and E-Commerce*, World Scientific Pub. Co.

Localization in China: Best Practice (2000) HK, Asia Law & Practice.

Long, C. (ed.) (2000) *Intellectual Property Rights in Emerging Markets*, AEI Press.

Lu, X. (2000) *Cadres and corruption: The Organizational Involution of the Chinese Communist Party* (Studies of the East Asian Institute), Stanford University Press.

Manager Magazin, DEG, *et al.* (eds) (1999) *Wirtschaftshandbuch China – Praxisnaher Ratgeber für Unternehmen*, Frankfurt.

Martinsons, M. (1996) 'Conquering cultural constraints to cultivate Chinese management creativity and innovation', in *Journal of Management Development*, vol. 15, no. 9, pp. 8–35.

McBeath, G.A. (1998) *Wealth and Freedom: Taiwan's New Political Economy*, Ashgate.

Mediacom/Grey(2000) China: Market Research – An overview of China, December, HK.

Mendenhall, M., Dunbar, E. and Oddou, G. (1987) 'Expatriate Selection, Training and Career Pathing: A Review and Critique', in *Human Resource Management*, vol. 26, no. 3, S. 331–45.

Mendenhall, M. and Oddou, G. (eds) (1991) *International Human Resource Management*, Boston, MA.

Moser, M. (ed.) (2000) *China Troubleshooter*, HK, Asia Law & Practice.

Murphy, D. (1999) 'Expats Feel Pay Squeeze', in *China International Business*, November, Beijing.

Murphy, J.M. (ed.) (1987) *Branding: a key marketing tool*, Basingstoke.

Newstead, S.E. (ed.) (1986) *Cognition and Motivation*, Dordrecht.

Nq, S.-H. and Pang, C. (1997) 'Structuring for Success in China', *Financial Times Newsletter and Management Reports*, HK.

Panitchpakdi, S. and Clifford, M. (2002) *China and the WTO: Changing China, Changing World Trade*, John Wiley & Sons.

Perkins, C. (1999) 'All the world's a big web?', in *Beijing Scene*, June, Beijing, pp. 12–18.

Perry, E.J. and Selden, M. (2000) *Chinese Society: Change, Conflict and Resistance*, Routledge.

Pomeranz, K. (2001) *The Great Divergence: China, Europe, and the Making of the Modern World Economy*, Princeton NJ, Princeton University Press.

PRC Joint Ventures: Financial Management (1997) HK, Asia Law & Practice

Proceedings of The Economist Conference (2000), 3, p. 42.

Pye, L. (1992) *Chinese Negotiating Style. Commercial Approaches and Cultural Principles*, Westport, CT.

Reisach, U. (1997) 'Chinesische Denkstrukturen und Kommunikationsmuster', in *Personal*, 12, pp. 612–19

Reisach, U. (1998) 'Konfliktvermeidung und Konfliktbereinigung', in *Wirtschaftswelt China*, 1, pp. 18–20

Reisach, U., Tauber, T. and Yuan, X. (1997) *China – Wirtschaftspartner zwischen Wunsch und Wirklichkeit*, Vienna Ueberreuther.

Reisch, B. (1995) *Erfolg im China Geschäft – Von Personalauswahl bis Kundenmanagement*, Frankfurt, Campus.

Ricks, David A. (1983) 'Products that crashed into the language barrier', *Business and Society Review*, Spring, pp. 46–50 Illinois.

Rommel, C. (1999) 'Die geheimen Verführer – Die Werbewirtschaft boomt', in *China-Contact*, 7, pp. 6–9.

Ronen, S. (1986) *Comparative and Multinational Management*, New York.

Saatchi & Saatchi (ed.) (1999) *Asia Pacific Market and Media Fact*, HK.

Sacra, E. (1998) *Die Bedeutung des kulturellen Umfelds für die Unternehmenspolitik multinationales Unternehmen*, Munich.

Salisbury, H.E. (1993) *The New Emperors: China in the Era of Mao and Deng*, Avin Books

Salzer, A. (2000) 'Recruiting and Managing a Distribution Workforce', in Moser, M. (ed.) *China Troubleshooter*, Chapter 4, pp. 69ff, HK, Asia Law & Practice.

Saner, R. and Yiu, L. (1994) 'European and Asian resistance to the use of the American case method in management training: possible cultural and systemic incongruence', in *International Journal of Human Resource Management*, vol. 5, no. 4, December.

Schell, O. and Shambaugh, D. (1999) *The China Reader: The Reform Era*, Vintage Books.

Schulte C. (1992) *Hording Strategien*, Wiesbaden, Gabler.

Seligman, S.D. and Trenn, E.J. (1999) *Chinese Business Etiquette: A Guide to Protocol, Manners, and Culture in the People's Republic of China*, Warner Books.

Setting Up and Financing WFOE's in the PRC (1997) HK, Asia Law & Practice.

Shambaugh, D.L. (ed.) (2000) *Is China Unstable? Assessing the Factors* (Studies on Contemporary China) M.E. Sharpe.

Siemens (1999) *Corporate Communications in China*.

Silverman, S. (2000) 'The Dragon online', in *CCN*, May, HK, pp. 32–6.

Solinger, D.J. (1999) *Contesting Citizenship in Urban China: Peasant Migrants, the State, and the Logic of the Market* (Studies of the East Asian Institute), University of California Press.

Solomon, M. and Stuart, E. (1997) *Marketing – Real People, Real Choices – International Edition*, Prentice Hall.

Spence, J.D. (2001) *The Search for Modern China*, W. W. Norton & Company.

Stevenson, W.J. (1999) *Production and Operations Management*, NY.

Studwell, J. (2002) *The China Dream: The Quest for the Last Great Untapped Market on Earth*, Publishers Group West.

Swaine, M.D. and Tellis, A.J. (2000) *Interpreting China's Grand Strategy: Past, Present and Future*, Rand Corporation.

Swiss-Chinese Chamber of Commerce (ed.) (1999) *Bulletin 3*, Beijing.

Tamir, A. (1991) *Technology Transfer in International Business*, NY, Oxford University Press.

Tang, W. and Parish, W.L. (2000) *Chinese Urban Life under Reform: The Changing Social Contract* (Cambridge Modern China Series), Cambridge, MA, Cambridge University Press.

Taube, M. (1997) 'Schutz von Warenzeichen in der VR China', in *Wirtschaftswelt China*, 8.

'The expatriate in China – a dying species?', (1999) in *China Staff*, November, HK, pp. 21–5.

The Life and Death of a Joint Venture in China (2000) 2nd rev. edn, HK, *Asia Business Law Review*.

The Treasurers Handbook (1997) HK, Asia Law & Practice.

Thomas, W.A. (2001) *Western Capitalism in China: A History of the Shanghai Stock Exchange*, Ashgate.

'Training options multiply, but what about the quality?' (1997) *China Staff*, September, pp. 8–11.

'Training the Troops' (1996) *China Business Review*, March–April, Beijing pp. 22–8.

Tsai, I. (2002) *A New Era in Cross-Strait Relations? Taiwan and China in the WTO*, January, Washington, DC, The Heritage Foundation.

Wang, Y. (1996) *Investment in China*, CITIC, NY.

Wang, Y. (2001) *Chinese Legal Reform* (European Institute of Japanese Studies, East Asian Economics and Business), Routledge.

Waterhouse, D. (1987) *Making the Most of Exhibitions*, Aldershot, Ashgate.

Wei-Arthus, H. (2000) *A Study of Authority and Relations in Chinese Governmental Agencies and Institutional Works Units: New-Patrimonialism in Urban Works Units*, Edwin Mellan Press.

Whiting, S.H. (2001) *Power and Wealth in Rural China: The Political Economy of Institutional Change* (Cambridge Modern China Series), Cambridge University Press.

Woods, R. (ed.) (1987) *Printing and Production for Promotional Materials*, NY.

Worcester, R.M. (1986) *Consumer Market Research Handbook*, Amsterdam.

Yao, C. (1998) *Stock Market and Futures Market in the People's Republic of China*, Oxford University Press.

Zhang, X. (1996) *Erfolgreich Verhandeln in China, Risiken minimieren, Verträge optimieren*, Wiesbaden, Gabler.

Zimmerman, J.M. (1999) *China Law Deskbook: A Legal Guide for Foreign-Invested Enterprises*, American Bar Association.

Zweig, D. (2002) *Internationalizing China: Domestic Interests and Global Linkages* (Cornell Studies in Political Economy), Cornell, Cornell University Press.

Index